MORE
DANGEROUS GROUND

MORE
DANGEROUS GROUND

*The Inside Story of Britain's Best Known
Investigative Journalist*

Roger Cook

Book Guild Publishing
Sussex, England

An earlier edition of *Dangerous Ground* was published by
HarperCollins in hardback in 1999 and in paperback in 2000

This revised and extended edition is published in Great Britain in 2007 by
The Book Guild Ltd
Pavilion View
19 New Road
Brighton, BN1 1UF

Typesetting in Times by
SetSystems Ltd, Saffron Walden, Essex

Printed in Great Britain by
CPI Bath

A catalogue record for this book is
available from the British Library

ISBN 981 1 84624 109 3

DEDICATION

*To Frances and Belinda, my long-suffering wife
and daughter, and the hard-working teams without
whom* Checkpoint *and* The Cook Report *would
not have been possible.*

CONTENTS

ACKNOWLEDGEMENTS

I didn't really want to write the first edition of this book. A documentary script is about my endurance limit. That it happened at all was largely due to my friend and former producer, Howard Foster, who did much of the original keyboard pounding – and who also pointed out that there was much more to tell. There wasn't the space in one book to cover more than a small fraction of my radio output and about a third of my television programmes.

Thanks also to Carlton/ITV for the use of video stills from *Cook Report* programmes, to Superior Creative Services for processing the images, to Carlton and the BBC for access to *Cook Report* and *Checkpoint* archives, and to all those whose own recollections helped jog or amend my overloaded memory.

FOREWORD

I have never kept a proper diary. Script notes from time to time, but never a diary. So, although the *Checkpoint* and *Cook Report* stories herein are accurately retold from taped records and programme files, background anecdotes and incidental details are only as reliable as the collective memories of self, family, friends and colleagues will allow. And remember, I have been hit over the head a few times...

PREFACE

I wrote in the acknowledgement to the first edition of this book that "we'd only scratched the surface so far". How right that comment was. So much has changed since it was written. I have therefore been persuaded to take another look, and reminded how often we broke important stories.

Obviously, the historical biographical material remains much the same – though more detailed – but much else is different, and I think, more interesting. Nearly every story in the first edition has been comprehensively updated. Programmes reported on back then have now achieved the results they were designed to. More laws have been changed and criminals sent to prison in Britain and around the world.

Stories not originally included now have current relevance. For example, our 'Terror in the Skies' programme of 1996, now covered on page 320, which chillingly foretold – and warned of – key events and characters involved in the 9/11 disaster.

Much has happened to me too. I have fought and won a major libel battle with a Sunday tabloid, and reversed the unfounded withdrawal of the first edition of this book – a decision which had made it unavailable to many who wanted it. Hardly a day goes by without someone asking when I'll be back on television and what caused my memoirs to be 'banned'.

The answers, and much more, can be found in this new edition. It is largely chronological, but in the interests of narrative, some of the stories are not covered in the order in which they were broadcast.

1

The Making of the Man Behind the Microphone

My first memories of New Zealand are of my father trying to get us out of the country as fast as he possibly could. It was the cold, wet June of 1945 and the Pacific war was still raging. While many of his fellow New Zealanders were away fighting the Japanese, Dad, who was a teacher and therefore in a protected occupation, was growing daily more obsessed with the idea that the enemy was about to launch an invasion in midget submarines.

According to my mother – whose early recollections these mostly are – every evening Dad would draw a dining chair up to the sideboard, switch on our ancient Ekco valve-radio and tune in to the news. Although we had been hearing for some time that the Allies had begun to stem the tide of Japanese advances in the Far East, Dad refused to believe that this was anything other than propaganda to keep the Kiwi population from mass panic.

"We've got to find a flight to Sydney. We'll be safer in Australia because their armed forces are much bigger than ours. But if we try to get there by ship, the damned Japs will certainly sink us with one of their torpedoes," he announced solemnly to my mother as he twisted the radio's big Bakelite switch to the off position.

Mum had long since given up arguing with him. Most of her time was taken up looking after me, rising two, and my sister Jane who was a babe in arms. We had already had two failed airborne escape attempts – one terminated by a mechanical failure and the other by the weather – but she reckoned that we might as well be a poor and struggling family in Australia as in New Zealand. If Dad was happy pestering the civil and military flight schedulers each and every day for seats on a flying boat to Sydney, then that was fine by her.

In view of the previous two failures, Dad apparently insisted it had to be a flying boat. He reasoned that crossing 1,200 miles of

1

enemy infested waters in such a craft doubled your chances, because if you were shot down, a seaplane would still float, which was important since he couldn't swim.

My father had acquired a few friends in the Royal New Zealand Air Force; not what you might expect of a timid, other-worldly artist. However, his skill as a draftsman was then in demand by the military. He was seconded from his day job to produce the exploded technical drawings needed by those assembling de Havilland Mosquito fighter-bombers shipped out in kit form from the UK. They appreciated what he did.

So after weeks of telephone calls and personal visits to his air force friends, Dad came home early one day in a state of high excitement from the art college where he worked. He told my mother to pack only the most essential belongings and be ready with Jane and me for him to collect that evening. With that he strode out of the house, happy for the first time in months.

Full of misgivings – and not a little fear – my mother did as she'd been asked, and crammed clothes, a little food and a few toys, some small prized possessions and important personal papers into a variety of bags and cases. She had just finished when Dad pulled up outside the house in a borrowed utility truck.

He loaded everything in the back, including at the last moment, a large, white bassinet that had been my first bed and was now Jane's. We set off from Auckland's southern suburbs for the harbour. It turned out that one of his air force contacts – probably just to get Dad out of his hair – had arranged a one-way passage for four to Sydney in a Shorts Sunderland flying boat. Mum groaned when it was confirmed what our means of escape was going to be. Jane and I sat happily in the bassinet, unaware of what was about to happen.

The weather was worsening as we left the harbour road for the small quay at Mechanics Bay allocated to air force and naval aircraft. The Sunderland had once been a Tasman Empire Airways civil airliner, but had been pressed into military service – stripped of creature comforts and equipped with a nose-mounted gun turret. It was tied up to a wooden pontoon and was heaving up and down alarmingly, waves foaming over the floats.

My mother later told me that she would have turned round there and then and abandoned our escape bid if she hadn't already handed the keys of our rented house back to the landlord's agent – which meant that we had nowhere to sleep that night.

With the help of the flight engineer and a couple of young aircraftsmen, Mum and Dad stowed our meagre belongings behind a cargo net at the back of the fuselage. Finally, Jane and I were passed by our increasingly-fretful mother across a narrow stretch of choppy water to Dad and the comparative safety of the flying boat cabin.

That journey from Auckland to Sydney has gone down in Cook family history as an adventure of unparalleled foolishness. My sister and I were strapped into the bassinet which Dad wedged in the gangway between the seats. Whenever we started to show signs of distress we were given large, red apples to eat. For a while we were the focus of attention for the dozen or so other passengers, a mixture of servicemen and civilians.

The captain wound up the four engines to a deafening roar and the seaplane bucketed off across the white horses, slowly pulling itself clear of the angry, grey swell. It headed out across the darkening Auckland Bay and then turned westwards for Australia – leaving New Zealand to the mercy of the advancing Japanese hordes, to the eternal, unspoken relief of my father.

But there was still plenty of drama to come en route to the longed-for safety of New South Wales. The bad weather that had been brewing as we left Auckland developed into a full-blown storm with low, black masses of cloud, tearing winds and near horizontal rain.

Eventually, the flight engineer came down from the cockpit above us, looking somewhat nervous. He motioned Dad and some of the other passengers over. He could barely be heard over the din of the engines and the rattling of the rain on the hull. With a series of sharp, pointing motions of the hands upwards and, ominously, downwards, he conveyed the inability of the pilot to maintain the plane's altitude. We were now barely a thousand feet above the waves. He needed a sacrifice, Dad told Mum as he eased himself grimly back into his seat. We were going to have to jettison our cargo – some military supplies and a quantity of luggage, including that belonging to the Cook family.

My parents conferred frantically. Mum had already left behind many treasured belongings. Now she was being asked to sub-divide

3

again what she already considered to be our bare essentials. The flight engineer slid open the side-door of the flying boat and, straining against the icy slipstream, tipped out the official cargo, followed by most of the luggage that had been loaded in front of ours.

Finally, he turned to Dad who, with a resigned nod from Mum, passed through three heavy cases of her clothes. By common consent, he kept the tools of his trade – his paint box and easel. Mum scooped out her few pieces of jewellery from a large, inlaid mahogany box her grandmother had brought from England and handed the empty box to the engineer. The heirloom was whipped away by the wind to join the rest of our lost baggage, scattered over the troubled and fast approaching surface of the Tasman Sea.

Whether the storm chose that moment to abate or whether our sacrifice had actually made a difference, the aircraft's nose slowly started to lift and the wings levelled. We were gaining height and after what seemed an eternity to my parents, but was probably no more than five or six hours, we banked steeply downwards in bright, early morning sunshine to land on the smooth, blue waters of Rose Bay in Sydney Harbour.

We went to stay with Dad's relatives for a few days while we recovered from the journey and he found us a place to live. He had already fixed himself up with a job as a peripatetic teacher of lettering and illustration at Sydney's National Art School. This wasn't going to bring in much money but he planned to supplement his income with commissions for paintings, as he had done back in New Zealand.

Our lack of funds meant we couldn't afford much in the way of accommodation. We moved from run-down place to run-down place with my mother making the most of what was available to us until Dad's aunt found us a quaint, stone-built house to rent in Hunters Hill, a pleasant and leafy suburb on the north shore of Sydney Harbour.

The decor at No. 1 Ambrose Street was uniformly cream over brown, with embossed wallpaper. The linoleum was worn at the joins of the floorboards underneath and the general structural and decorative condition of the house meant that kids could do no lasting damage. The scars of tricycle collisions in the hall merely added to the patina. The slate roof was patched with sheets of zinc, the lights were still powered by gas and down in the basement, gas also fuelled the capacious copper cauldron in which the family washing was done. But whatever the house lacked in amenities, it made up for in character. We children were happy and well-fed for the years that we were there, but conditions were pretty primitive and Dad was always talking about 'moving on to something a bit more modern'. No. 1 had been built in 1842.

Perhaps I inherited some of my father's restless spirit. My mother used to tell tales of my 'escape attempts', of how I was caught half a mile from home towing my billy-cart (a pram-wheeled soapbox) loaded with a boat made of tea chests and orange boxes in which I was going to explore the world. Actually, I saw quite a lot of the road ahead through the holes in the rustic hull, but, aged about four, I was not in the least deterred. God knows what would have happened if I had got as far as the Valentia Street wharf and the harbour beyond. I was apprehended making my escape in this manner more than once.

In later years, I was also caught stowing away on the Woolwich ferry to the city terminus at Circular Quay. The ferries were quite wonderful, and my earliest boyhood dream was to captain one like the *Kanangara*, the *Kameruka* or the *Karingal* – big green and cream double-decked, double-ended vessels powered by steam. From the lower decks you could see down into the engine room and watch the polished steel and brass cranks and rods in action. I found the sights and sounds completely addictive and kept returning to them.

It must have worried mum sick, but I never recall being chastised for my misconceived adventures. Nevertheless, having been foiled in my early attempts to see the world, I'm told I then took to inviting strangers in off the street for a cup of tea so that I could quiz them about what lay over my limited horizon. Mum seemed to take this in good spirit and on selected occasions actually provided the tea. It kept me out of Dad's hair though. He'd never heard of a boy who asked so many questions. To be fair, I still find it difficult to take things at face value.

My father's desire to be left in peace influenced even his most generous acts. For my fifth birthday, he made me a toy soldier's drum and hand painted it royal blue with intricate gold scrolls to decorate the sides. It looked so good I couldn't wait to start beating it. The first tentative tap with a wooden spoon that I'd purloined from the kitchen yielded nothing but a dull thud. I hit it harder –

still nothing of the loud, resonating noise I had so hoped for. Later I discovered that he had stuffed it with the innards of an old cushion so that, although his gift looked good, he would never have to be disturbed by his young son's enthusiastic drumming.

It was my father's love of the quiet life that helped me form my early ambition to become a vet. Before we left Hunters Hill, Jane and I were desperate to have a pet dog – but the prospect of feeding, walking and listening to a puppy was too much for him. When we actually prevailed upon him to let us buy the rather boisterous beagle puppy we had fallen in love with after seeing him in the local pet shop, he surprised us some weeks later by volunteering to take him out for a walk. To our horror, he returned dogless, announcing that he had given him away to a more tolerant home because he was just too badly behaved.

My mother eventually forced a change of heart over the dog issue and brought us home a friendly, short-haired Dachshund which we smothered with love and almost forgave Dad for what he'd done with the other dog. Sadly, the new arrival must have sensed the head of the household's disapproval and tried to escape. Gina snared herself on the wooden palings of our dilapidated and badly-mended back fence, her wound quickly became infected and soon afterwards, despite the ministrations of our local vet, she had to be put down. I resolved then and there never to be helpless in such a situation again. I gave up the idea of being a ship's captain. One day *I* would be a vet.

After the trauma of losing Gina, I had to settle for a box of silkworms. They didn't make any noise and cost nothing to feed as there was an abundant supply of mulberry leaves from the trees in All Saints' rectory garden across the road from our house. So I went over the fence and helped myself. The Reverend Gumbley was a very stern, very Victorian man who viewed the removal of those few leaves as theft preceded by trespass. He said as much in Sunday school. It was for my own good, he added, and I'm sure he believed it, but I was made to feel like a complete outcast.

Some years later, I had another uncomfortable religious experience. My school was a Church of England primary, and liked to see its older pupils confirmed in the faith. When my turn came, the officiating Bishop took a step towards me, tripped on a kneeling cushion and fell over. Then, rising flustered from the floor, he confirmed me in the name of the boy standing in line behind me. I'll never get to heaven now, I thought, because my name's not on the list. It was all very embarrassing, but nobody said a thing.

Nobody said anything either about the paedophile barber of Gladesville Road. If he took a fancy to you while cutting your hair he'd insist that service was followed by another – what he called his 'special massage to help you grow up big and strong', which he would attempt to administer while you were still trapped in his old fashioned tilting chair. He also had an album of 'interesting photographs' which 'you could be in too, if you like'.

I didn't like – and back home was eventually pushed into telling all after I'd refused to have my hair cut for several months. It turned out that other little boys had also fallen victim to this gaunt, wet-lipped man with unnaturally black hair and an egregious manner. It must have been considered far too scandalous to report to the police, because I don't recall that they were ever involved. However, after a visit from a posse of outraged fathers – not including mine – the barber shut up shop and moved away.

In 30 years of investigative reporting, I've been knocked unconscious a dozen times, needed hospital treatment on almost 30 occasions and I've had numerous bones broken because people have objected to my persistence – or simply to the fact that I exist at all. Growing up in Australia in the 1950s seems to have been appropriate preparation for what was to come. It was a young country, scarred by the war – a melting-pot of different nationalities, with an unsophisticated and sometimes brutal education system.

I hadn't really taken much notice of Georgie Kadar until I noticed him cheating in class. We were both about eight years old and under the firm control of Miss Kay, our form mistress at Woolwich Primary School. A tall, stiff spinster in her mid-fifties, she was one of those teachers who seem instinctively to know when a child was doing something they ought not to be. And even if you weren't misbehaving, she made you feel as though you were.

Georgie was a short, stocky boy with sallow skin, dark curly hair and a disconcertingly intense stare that made most of the other kids avoid him at break time.

His Latvian parents, according to my mother and father, had had a terrible time from both the Germans and the Russians who had fought over their homeland during the war. They escaped to the Allies in the immediate aftermath of the fall of Berlin and were given an assisted passage to start a new life in Australia.

Not that any of this would have made any difference to my perception of Georgie as we sat in the peeling-paint austerity of Miss Kay's classroom doing our fortnightly maths test. Though I enjoyed my schooling by and large, being one of those jammy sods who did well on a bare minimum of work, mathematics has never been my strong suit. So when the effort involved in making numbers do what I wanted got too much for me, I looked up from my book and gazed blankly across the room.

He sat two places away with his forehead buried in the palm of his right hand, elbow resting on his paper. On his knees, below the ink-stained oak and wrought iron desk, I saw the cover of our arithmetic course book peeping out. I was staring at Georgie's little deception when Miss Kay's uncanny intuition made her look up.

"It's no use looking at Kadar, Cook, he can't help you." She got to her feet and walked towards Georgie, antennae twitching. She stopped at his side and looked down.

"Get up, Kadar. Let's see what you're hiding down there," she said in her hard little voice. Georgie's game was up and he was led firmly away for six strokes of the thin Malacca cane the headmaster kept behind his study door.

I suppose I should have guessed who Georgie would blame from the hate-filled glare he gave me as Miss Kay led him away. At the time, though, I thought little of it. I hadn't actually told the teacher what I had seen.

Early the following week I walked the half-mile from our house to school as usual. It was a beautiful late-spring day.

I emerged from the shade of the eucalyptus trees that lined the cul-de-sac where the school gates stood open for the steady stream of kids heading for their classrooms.

As I walked past the main hall someone jumped out beside me. It was Georgie Kadar. He'd been hiding behind a water butt and now he was less than two feet away from me, staring intensely into my eyes. Wordlessly, he brought a small metal hammer down on my head several times in rapid succession.

When I woke up I was on a hospital bed, wearing a green gown. It was stained with blood and a doctor was telling me to hold still as he tried to stitch the cuts on my head.

Miraculously, Georgie Kadar wasn't expelled for what he did. Perhaps there was nowhere else for him to go. Maybe his parents persuaded the school that their son would never do it again. When I went back to school after several days under observation in hospital, Georgie was still in my class, staring at me malevolently.

And he hadn't finished with me yet.

A few weeks later Miss Kay asked the class if we had any pets at home. I put up my hand and told her about my box of silkworms. As this seemed out of the usual run of dogs, cats and rabbits, and sounded a lot less trouble, she invited me to bring them to school to show my classmates. I think I heard Georgie laugh when I agreed.

Next day I walked into school – skirting carefully round the water butt by the hall – bearing my box of silkworms which lay replete and dozing after a heavy feed of mulberry leaves.

My demonstration of the process of feeding the silkworms in order to extract the highly-valuable silk threads from their cocoons, accompanied by the occasional prodding of their torpid bodies, went down well with the other children. Even Georgie Kadar seemed grudgingly impressed.

I came back into the classroom after playing footie with my friends at break time to find the box crushed under my desk. While I had been out, heavy boots had squashed the cardboard flat and silkworm body parts writhed and oozed on the floor. Georgie sat at his desk with his arms wrapped around his shoulders. He looked me directly in the eye and smiled cruelly.

I gathered up the remains of the box and the worms and walked past him, out of the school gates and back home. I dumped the crushed cardboard and the worms in the dustbin and vowed not to take on any more pets until I could trust the rest of the world not to take them from me. Not long afterwards, it was the world I knew that was taken from me.

Given Dad's habit of accepting commissions without asking for an advance payment, and his less frequent but more annoying habit of destroying finished paintings because he didn't like them, the Cook family finances were often sorely stretched. Mum even had to pack up and leave him from time to time to find work wherever it was available, in order to boost the family coffers. It may also have been a welcome relief from the trials and frustrations of living with my father.

On one occasion, Dad had promised that in what was to be a two-year absence, he would build us a new house on a plot of land in the then semi-rural suburb of Dundas. Meanwhile, Jane and I were moved to a sprawling sheep station called Gidleigh, just outside the tiny town of Bungendore, some 25 miles from Canberra. Mum had found a job there keeping house and cooking for the owners and a bunch of smelly drovers. The staff accommodation allocated to us was a modern, four-bedroom bungalow with all mod cons. We could expect to have something like it when we got back to Sydney, Mum assured us.

I hated Gidleigh at first; I was ten years old and entirely unused to somewhere so remote. There seemed to be nothing for me to do and I missed my friends. However, it wasn't long before I found new friends and plenty to do – riding, fishing, and above all, exploring. I came to love the wide open spaces – I still do – and I liked those tough, tanned drovers and the rumbustious itinerant shearers who turned up once a year. But I didn't like what some of them did to Horace.

Horace had been given to me as a piglet, having been rejected by his mother. I took her place, and Horace the Landrace grew to be a large and amiable animal who would permit himself to be ridden round the homestead yard. Then, one day on my return from school, I couldn't find Horace anywhere. Nobody would admit to having seen him. To my horror and disgust, I eventually learnt that my pig was now pork. To me he'd been a sentient being, but to those hard-bitten men of the outback he'd just been ham on the hoof. I pined for weeks.

Gidleigh had its own school, serving the children of the station staff and those from surrounding farms. It was a two-roomed, timber-framed, corrugated iron structure perched on slate-topped, concrete piles designed to deter the entry of creepy-crawlies. The front door had a spade standing behind it to deal with unwelcome snakes. The inner door to the teacher's office had a cane hanging behind it to deal with allegedly unruly children. The dozen or so pupils ranged in age from five to 15, and we were all caned with similar vigour, usually for such heinous offences as 'daydreaming', 'laziness' or 'talking out of turn'.

Canings by the headmaster back at Woolwich were relatively infrequent and for much more serious offences. They were administered in a 'this-is-going-to-hurt-me-more-than-it-hurts-you' spirit, whereas at Gidleigh they seemed to be a source of schoolmasterly pleasure. Sometimes, granted, punishment was probably deserved, though you could certainly argue about its harshness. On one occasion, during a Royal Visit, every pupil in the school was marshalled onto the back of a lorry and trucked to Canberra to wave at the Queen.

As my fellow pupils waited patiently, fiddling with their paper flags, I wandered off to do something more interesting and subsequently got lost. Retrieved and returned to school, I then got another six of the best. I must have held the school record for canings before my mother intervened. The crunch came over my reading habits.

I had poured scorn on the school's selection of English literature, a sort of 'one-size-fits-all' collection of juvenilia. I derided it as 'babyish' and refused to read from any of the books in class – or anywhere else for that matter. In retrospect, they were charming little books like 'The Magic Pudding', but they were kid's stuff nonetheless. And the more I resisted them, the more I was beaten. My preferred reading was to be found in the homestead library. It was mostly rousing Victorian stuff from the likes of Rider Haggard, Buchan, Dickens and Conrad.

The only avowedly children's books I would read were Arthur Mee's encyclopaedias. I spent so much time burrowing through those blue and gold bound volumes that Mum eventually bought me a second-hand set of my own. It was cheap because it was incomplete, but I didn't mind too much.

After my mother's intervention I was no longer punished for reading unauthorised books – and as I recall, after an unscheduled visit from the Schools Inspector, the canings virtually came to an end.

The best things about the school were its position – I had come to think that Gidleigh was the best playground in the world – and Dot – who was the best possible companion. Wiry, freckle-faced and tousle-haired, Dot was the ultimate tomboy, an only child who could do anything the boys did, only better. Her father was the station's maintenance engineer, and for a while, I suppose, I was the son he never had.

He helped me build a tiny working steam engine and taught me how gearboxes and internal combustion engines worked. He'd seen me taking my mother and Jane for imaginary rides in the corroded, engineless hulk of an old American car, long abandoned in the station's machinery graveyard. So he taught me to drive for real on a monstrous, rusty-blue, single-cylinder Lanz Bulldog tractor which he had exhumed for me from the same graveyard. I can still hear the sound it made as it accelerated to its top speed of around four miles per hour: 'wak-tak-wak-tak-wak-tak'. Needless to say, Dot could drive already.

We used to look forward to the occasional visits of the travelling picture show, which parked up behind the shearing sheds and projected movies – usually westerns – off the back of an old army ambulance and onto a sheet stretched across a makeshift frame. We sat on the ground or on folding wooden chairs. The chatter of the well-worn projector often threatened to drown out the dialogue, and the station hands' pungent cigarette smoke clouded the evening air.

The bill often included a travelogue too, which transported us to places I wanted to visit one day. The rest of the audience always seemed happy where they were, roaring with laughter at some hapless traveller's attempts at milking a yak or paddling a dugout canoe. And they always cheered for Roy Rogers or the Lone Ranger. Dot and I cheered for the Indians. I wish I knew what became of her.

During the long, languid summer holidays, we could often be found exploring the countryside 'just like Burke and Wills',* we used to think, or propped against the dappled trunk of a eucalyptus, chatting about nothing in particular, watching the parakeets reeling raucously overhead – or even lying head-down on a muddy river bank, silently hoping to catch sight of a platypus. They were halcyon days, and when the time came to leave Gidleigh, I was genuinely sorry to go.

Disappointment awaited us, however. On our return to Sydney, Mum, Jane and I discovered that the promised new house had not been built. It never was.

When my father had been negotiating to buy the plot of land for the mythical new house, he'd spotted one already built, just down

* In 1860, Burke and Wills were the first explorers to traverse Australia from south to north. It was a heroic effort lasting almost a year, but sadly, they starved to death on the return journey and were later accorded almost mythic status – like the more famous, but rather less deserving Ned Kelly.

the road. Buying it ready made, he reasoned, would save him the trouble of getting his hands dirty. What mum wasn't told was that this one had been put up so long ago and had been so neglected in the interim that it was in the process of falling down again. Dad believed he had a gift for spotting houses that 'had potential'. Perhaps he had, but the trouble was, in his hands that potential was never realised.

So our next, and last, family home was extraordinary, even by his standards. On the evening of our return, he took us all out to see it; a property he said had the 'biggest potential' he'd ever seen. In the twilight it certainly looked impressive – much larger than Hunters Hill, built around 1880 in the colonial style with wooden verandas all around it, giving it the air of a miniature plantation owner's spread in America's Deep South. I thought it was very grand because it had a name instead of just a street number.

Daylight brought a more realistic appraisal. 'Glenlyn' certainly had a good position, on a small hill in Emu Street Dundas overlooking half a dozen or so other dwellings and a smallholding. But its condition made Hunters Hill look positively palatial. The roof was corrugated iron and badly rusted, the verandas were collapsing, there was no electricity, no mains drainage and the house hadn't received any maintenance for decades – hence the affordable price.

If the neighbours were looking for the new owners to restore the house to its former dignity, they were in for a big disappointment. The attraction of the Dundas house for my father was probably its very dilapidation. He got as far as having the electricity put on, but apart from a few urgent running repairs and the odd lick of paint, that was about it. End of potential. All he really cared about was his painting; for him, the rest of the world, including his family and the home in which they lived, barely existed.

The house was surrounded on three sides by those crumbling verandas, topped with 'tin' that was so corroded in places that it looked like lace. My sister and I were forbidden to set foot on any of the rotten wooden floorboards, except to reach and leave the front door, where it was still comparatively safe. As children, we didn't give a second thought to the danger. I even thought it was a bit of an adventure having to change bedrooms because part of the ceiling of the one I was in had collapsed in the middle of the night. It took Dad months to get it fixed.

The kitchen was the heart of the place. It was a spacious, homely room with big windows on one side and French doors to a forbidden veranda on the other. Mum had furnished it with an assortment of well-scrubbed pine – chairs, a large rustic table, usually home to a bowl of fruit, and a sideboard on which was displayed what passed for the family's best china.

A square-rigged gas refrigerator with massive chrome hinges and door catches stood in one corner, but pride of place went to the cooker. It was a huge, green and cream enamelled, gas affair, with cabriole legs and several ovens, from which Mum conjured the most wonderful meals. Most mornings we woke to the tantalising aroma of hot bread.

Such ambrosial scents helped break down my resistance to the then current idea that boys should not cook. Mum thought they should, and set about ensuring that I could. I'm still grateful to her for that, though there is some dispute about the subsequent effect on my waistline.

Jane and I loved Glenlyn, but I'm not sure Mum shared our enthusiasm. It was full of interesting nooks and crannies and, though my mother slaved to keep all of them clean, it was a losing battle. She eventually took to disguising what she could not eliminate – for example there was always a flower arrangement in front of the damp patch on the living room chimney breast. There were few of Dad's pictures though, because if he liked them, they were sold.

By contrast to the house, the large garden – which was Mum's sole domain – soon became a showpiece. Somehow she'd found enough time to create it all by herself with little or no constructive help from the family. Occasionally cutting the lawn with an antique Qualcast push mower was about my limit. Mum was the one with the knowledge and over the years had become so well informed about exotic trees and shrubs that she was taken on as a consultant by a leading firm of nurserymen.

To Dad, the family home was also, perversely, a heaven-sent refuge from the family. A week or so after we moved in he laid two planks across the collapsing veranda floor and used them to escape to a room on the side of the house which became his studio. There, out of sight, he set up his easel and carefully laid out his paints. There he would sit, sketching and painting and drifting off into his dream world without being bothered by Mum, Jane or me.

Dad was one of those people you could pass in the street and never notice. He was about five feet nine inches tall with receding, ginger hair and a goatee beard. He was slightly gnome-like and had an absent-minded manner that drove my mother to despair. The result was that she became a *de facto* single parent. In her younger days, Jane needed a lot of attention. The poor girl had been born with twisted intestines and needed several major operations and a lot of nursing. This also meant that Mum had to cope with me competing for her attention.

My mother filled in the many parental gaps my father left. He had but one consuming interest in life, she had many. It was she who stimulated my interest in nature and literature, helped with the homework, shouted encouragement on sports days, and assisted with bicycle repairs. She was tireless and endlessly competent. As a mother, she made a pretty good dad. And through all the years of my youth, though she was clearly working her fingers to the bone, my abiding memory is of a warm and beautiful woman, with rarely a hair out of place. I have no idea how she did it.

We were not poor by European standards – we were well fed and adequately clothed – but there was precious little left over for what my father called 'inessentials' – like holidays. However, there was one notable exception to this rule, from which I benefited. I had come into the world equipped with a pair of large and very prominent ears, which were the object of frequent derision at primary school and eventually earned me the nickname 'Spaniel Ears'. Kids can be pretty cruel and to a seven or eight-year-old their jibes were pure torture.

It took mum more than a year to scrape up the money to have the offending appendages surgically pinned back. The torture then ended overnight, to be replaced by requests from the curious to see my scars. But for the bandages in the first few days after the operation, I don't suppose Dad would have noticed anything. Mum later confessed that she hadn't told him beforehand, on the grounds that Dad would most likely have classified ear retraction as yet another 'inessential'.

Transport, on the other hand, was essential. In order to get about, Dad bought an ancient Austin Seven. With everything he needed in life stowed safely on the back seat, or strapped to the rear-mounted spare tyre – his easels, paints and palette – he would drive off into the Blue Mountains to spend uncounted days painting landscapes, sleeping in a small tent he carried with him and only returning home when he ran out of provisions, or when a new stint at art college was about to begin.

During our school holidays, Dad was once coerced into taking me on a short painting trip. He was attentive enough in a vague sort of way as we drove along, but once his easel was up, he took almost no notice of me during daylight hours, apart from demanding regular cups of seriously strong tea. Our one meal of the day was in the evening. It was a concoction of his own invention, which he called 'scramblage', and it seemed to be all he ate while away from home. I believe the basis of it was a bowl of oatmeal porridge into which he stirred raisins, molasses and a couple of raw eggs. It had the consistency and quite possibly the taste of lumpy wallpaper paste.

I couldn't face it and asked where the 'proper food' was. As a result, I was never asked again. This despite the fact that I'd valiantly pushed the car the last few hundred yards or so home. Dad hadn't 'fed' the little Austin either, and it had run out of petrol.

Dad's absent-minded other-worldliness became well known in the neighbourhood. I now look back on most of his eccentricities with fond amusement, but at the time I found them acutely embarrassing. One day he came home looking rather agitated and announced that 'Silverstar' – as he called the car – had been stolen. He had asked all the neighbours if they'd seen it, but nobody had: "I'm off to the police station to report this. We'll soon catch the beggars," he huffed as he trudged off down the road.

He returned two hours later – at the wheel of Silverstar.

A police patrol had already spotted it before Dad arrived at the station. It was exactly where he had left it – in the art college car park with the driver's door still open. He'd gone in to college to pick up some water-colour paper in preparation for a day's painting in his studio. When he failed to find any he wandered out of the front of the college, his exasperation obliterating the memory of leaving his car round the back.

When I was much older and living in digs nearer town, I called in at home to find Dad sitting alone in his veranda studio. Without looking up he mumbled: "You were home late last night."

I hadn't the heart to point out that I had actually left home more than three months before.

Dad's ability to remain supremely detached from reality didn't stand in the way of his abiding jealousy of his older brother and fellow artist, James Cook. Rivals from their boyhood, the two continued a rather genteel feud through adolescence and into their adult lives. Matters weren't helped by the fact that they both chose the same calling. My father's artistic style was driven by a determination to depict every sheep, cow or tree in minute detail.

Such was his striving for perfection that he would sometimes abandon weeks of work in a fit of artistic pique and start a painting all over again. He could get very emotional over his art, while remaining pretty unemotional about everything else. Nevertheless, it has to be said that he was usually quite an amiable man – just a bit detached from real life.

Uncle James, on the other hand, kept his cool and his grip on reality and prospered. His more interpretative approach to painting was then much in vogue, and he was good at marketing it – so he flourished while Dad struggled. James had also painted his way across Europe more than once, and had successfully exhibited in half a dozen countries. Dad never left Australasia.

But what really peeved my father was that his brother had a better war. After his work on the Mosquito fighter-bomber, Dad had been pressed into producing more minutely-detailed diagrams of military equipment for the benefit of assembly engineers. Useful for them, but pretty tedious for him, I imagine. James, meanwhile, became an official war artist with the rank of Captain, travelling with Australian troops. At home I have one of his water-colour paintings of a ravaged and rubble-strewn Italian town. Next to it hang examples of my father's precise, draughtsman-like down-under landscapes.

In death, both my father's and uncle's work have gained a good deal in popularity and appreciation. I reserve judgement on who was the better artist, but when I stand back and look at Dad's work I remember the man for what he was and I recognise something of myself in that striven-for but rarely-achieved perfection.

In the spring of 1955, not long after the family had moved to Dundas, I turned 12 and my parents finally agreed that I could apply for a place at agricultural college. For the past four or five years I had wanted nothing more than to realise my ambition to become a vet. I had visions of myself striding across the vast acres of the farmsteads of New South Wales to help save the farmers' finest bloodstock from death and disease or the complications of giving birth. Amongst those wishing to show me the deepest gratitude would undoubtedly be the beautiful daughter of the wealthiest landowner in the district. Adolescence had truly arrived.

My mother noticed this first, and much against his will, my father was delegated to instruct me on the facts of life before I left for college. He suggested that we went for a walk together, something we never did, so I knew something was afoot. The poor man walked the walk, but couldn't talk the talk.

My sex instruction began with rather a lot of throat-clearing as my father, eyes averted, walked beside me with his hands behind his back, Prince Philip-style. He did manage to get out a couple of clichéd sentences about the birds and the bees and everything coming from seeds, but he was obviously so embarrassed that I began to fill in his protracted silences myself.

When I had filled in enough of them with relevant information, it dawned on Dad that I already had a grasp of the facts of life and he promptly changed the subject to something more to his liking. With a spring in his step, he turned for home and began to wax lyrical about that evening's cloud formations. Dad collected interesting cloudscapes in his head, with which to embellish future landscapes. As far as he was concerned, I was already a fully-fledged man of the world.

I applied, without visiting, for a place at Yanco Agricultural High School, near Wagga Wagga, some 370 miles south-west of Sydney. It was far enough away for me to board during the week but close enough to make it possible to go home at weekends from time to time. It was only after I had been accepted and turned up there for my first day that doubts about the place crossed my mind.

A hot breeze fanned plumes of dust from the roadside as we approached. What had once been a fine colonial mansion in brick and sandstone was surrounded by a hotchpotch of buildings in brick, timber and corrugated iron. The place looked thoroughly unwelcoming. It felt remote, vaguely threatening and – for a busy school campus – strangely silent. The austere classrooms and dormitories stood out through the heat haze against a distant background of grain silos, stockyards and an assortment of mud-coloured outbuildings. But it wasn't just the aspect of the place that was depressing.

Although only 12 years old, I was six feet tall and weighed over 12 stones, not much of it fat. But my size and fitness granted me no exemption from the initiation rites at Yanco. Like many before me, I was marched round to the back of the college kitchens by a group of senior boys who emptied an industrial refuse bin onto the asphalt quadrangle.

"Pick it up," said one of them to me, gesturing to the rubbish. I hesitated. A fist hit me below the kidneys. I got the message.

I picked up every lump of congealed fat, eggshell, rotting vegetable and God knows what else and scraped it off my hands into the huge galvanised metal bin. When I had finished, they emptied the bin again. The result of an attempt to resist a repetition of events was a monstrous black eye that needed medical attention – no questions asked – by the college nurse.

I did manage, however, to avoid another dangerous humiliation. After lessons, the Sixth Year bullies at Yanco liked to take trembling new arrivals to the college dairy complex where the cow manure, pending use as fertiliser, was stored in concrete clamps, each about the size of a small swimming pool. The sadists would make the younger boys strip to their underpants and stand on one of the concrete walls overlooking the clamps.

"Dive in. It's time for a little swim, turdface," one of the prefects would hiss, and the victim would have to pitch headfirst into five feet of stinking mire. Then it was back to the college shower rooms to wash off the mess, avoiding the masters on pain of death.

In one particularly nasty incident, an unfortunate noviciate lost a foot. We boys were never told exactly what had happened. But the gory story that passed into school lore – to be whispered to chilling effect after lights out – involved school bullies, some pieces of rope and a severed foot, still clad in a brown suede desert boot which was retrieved from the local railway line.

There were several attempted suicides while I was at Yanco. No one much seemed to care. The prevailing atmosphere was tense, and from my lowly viewpoint, the administration appeared to have little interest in the happiness or wellbeing of its charges.

Whether the college principal or his deputies felt life would be easier if they let the bullies be, or whether they suppressed complaints on the grounds that the education department might investigate the running of the college and find them seriously wanting, I just don't know. Of course, it could be that the bullies' routine threats of reprisals against anyone reporting their attacks meant much that went on was undisclosed. In any case, the few incidents that *were* reported drew a response of the 'stop-whinge-ing-and-pull-yourself-together-boy-it'll-make-a-man-of-you' sort.

After my first year, the bullies left me more or less alone, but others were more or less permanent targets. One sorry image still haunts me from that God-forsaken place: the face of a timid, stick-thin boy of 12 or 13 who had the misfortune to have been born with facial features that gave him the appearance of a cat. He had huge, mournful eyes and a wide, flat face that tapered grotesquely to an almost imperceptible mouth and tiny chin. He was known to us all as 'Pussy'.

Universally reviled by the older boys and staff, this poor creature slunk from lesson to lesson, never saying a word – always creeping in at the last moment to sit at the back of the class. Out of the classroom he endured a constant barrage of verbal and physical bullying, but was never heard to complain – or if he did, nobody took any notice. I couldn't help feeling sorry for him, but my occasional, desultory attempts to befriend him were greeted with suspicion and rebuffed. To my lasting shame, I gave up on him and I can't even remember his real name.

If I analyse where I got the motivation to do the kind of job I went on to do, my thoughts often lead back to Yanco and its injus-tice and cruelty. Then, I was helpless. Years later, I could occasion-ally help put a stop to something which shouldn't have happened.

I longed to leave Yanco, but couldn't bring myself to ask the parents I'd pestered to send me there. I had survived my initiation and so I gritted my teeth and threw myself into my studies. I also became the college's self-appointed practical joker. One night I dumped into the swimming pool several hundredweight of orange flavour jelly crystals that I and a couple of helpers had liberated from the kitchen stores. It never set quite like my mother's desserts back in Dundas used to, but it certainly stopped the college caretaker in his tracks when he unlocked the pool house at six o'clock the following morning to check the chlorine levels. I am pleased to report that the culprits were never caught.

My elementary but competent understanding of the physical

sciences led to the small-scale manufacture of a minor explosive called, to the best of my recollection, nitrogen triiodide.

With the aid of a tatty old chemistry manual, out of hours at the back of the chemistry lab, I began to produce glass phials full of a brownish liquid. While my concoction was wet it posed no threat at all, but once it had dried to a thin film of crystals it was full of surprises. My speciality was to paint the class blackboards with it. A minute or two after the mixture had dried, the merest pressure of chalk or blackboard rubber on the surface was enough to cause a minor explosion accompanied by a puff of purple smoke.

It also produced a quite spectacular effect when applied experimentally to a toilet seat, leaving the shocked victim with a virtually indelible purple stain on his behind. Luckily for everyone else, an informant gave me away before I was able to instigate a school-wide toilet seat campaign. I was given 'six of the best', then made to write out my chemistry manual, in longhand – twice – and denied the privilege of telephoning home for a month.

The social highlight of the year was supposed to be the annual school dance, when the girls of our 'sister' school were bussed in the 50 or so miles from their establishment to ours. The event took place in the assembly hall, a barn of a place that doubled as the school gym. Music came from 78s played on an old gramophone amplified by the PA system. Even then we thought it was bloody awful, but also by then we were so desperate for female contact, or perhaps an illicit glimpse of a soft thigh, that we fought for position in the queue to get in.

Without wishing to appear rude, it was fair to say that for the most part, the girls were hardly the pick of the crop, hence the desire to get in early. This particular evening I had my eye on a small strawberry blonde with a trim figure and baby blue eyes. Hers and mine met, but as I approached her, wearing what I imagined to be my Mr Cool look, I was descended upon by something out of The Ride of the Valkyries. She was large, lumpen, slightly malodorous and generously endowed with underarm hair. Giggling inanely, she grasped my arm and dragged me away. She clasped me to her ample bosom. I struggled free, but as she was actually bigger and stronger than me, I was soon in her mantis-like grip again.

Then someone put Bill Haley on the record player and she became a thing possessed. Shortly afterwards, in mid-jive, she cracked me like a whip and sent me skittering across the polished dance floor on my backside, to end up in an ungainly heap under a pile of stacking chairs. Manfully, I struggled to my feet – and fled. Brunhilde was still pursuing me, fortunately only by post, months later.

These isolated distractions weren't enough to dispel the unhappiness I was feeling at Yanco and, although it took me many months to get through to him, my father eventually accepted that his son was desperately keen to get away from the place. I ended my secondary education much closer to home as a day-boy at a sports-mad agricultural college called Hurlstone, on the outskirts of Sydney.

Despite my new school's lack of academic emphasis – the headmaster's first question to me was to enquire in which position I played Rugby Union – I kept my resolve to be a true country veterinarian. And I did play Rugby actually. Not brilliantly, but what I lacked in tactical and ball handling skills, I made up in speed. As something of a star sprinter, I got away with quite a lot out on the wing, and, injuries aside, thoroughly enjoyed myself. The school team did pretty well in state-wide competition – as, surprisingly, did the debating team of which I was also a member. I did devote some time to study however, and having passed my matriculation exams with flying colours, I was accepted by Sydney University to study veterinary medicine.

Looking back, and with the exception of Yanco, my school days were mostly enjoyable. My trouble always seems to have been with cheats, bullies and those in authority who either abused that authority or, in my view, didn't deserve to wield it. After school, out in the real world, my difficulties were financial.

The snag was that I couldn't afford to embark on such a protracted and difficult course as veterinary medicine without financial help, and Dad was not in a position to offer any. Members of the so-called 'squatocracy' – families who had grown rich from land their ancestors had simply occupied in the nineteenth century – had the money to go it alone, but chaps like me needed a scholarship. These were usually funded by – and tied to – veterinary pharmaceutical companies, and I didn't like the idea of that.

The alternative was to do as I did. Take any job during the day that you could find to pay for your tuition, which, in those days you could elect to receive principally at night. It was the day job that caused my passion for my chosen profession to wane and it wasn't long before my career ambitions began to move in an entirely different direction. I had discovered the attractions of journalism. Mind you, I've never lost my love for animals, as evidenced by the number of my journalistic endeavours in their defence.

While finishing my exams at Hurlstone, I had found myself a job as a copy boy on the *Sydney Daily Telegraph*. The atmosphere inside the news building captivated me. Every evening, along with half a dozen or so full-time copy boys, I would sit in a little office waiting for the reporters in the adjoining newsroom to tear the paper from their typewriters and wave it in the air. That was the signal for one of us to rush in and bear a few more paragraphs of the next day's story via the sub-editors to the typesetters.

I liked the whole system and I liked the reporters for their lively, sometimes half-drunken sociability and the power that they wielded in our everyday lives. Having barely started studying veterinary science, I switched to an English course – I was going to be a journalist instead.

I did not enjoy the lectures much – this being the time when you were supposed to learn the lecturer's thoughts and repeat them by rote. But I did very much enjoy the tutorials and the written exercises in which you could advance your own ideas and challenge the accepted view of things. However, my academic career didn't last, which was a pity, since I was apparently doing rather well.

Several things happened. Firstly, the practical joker in me resurfaced. I had already received warnings from the university authorities for my sometimes drink-fuelled, often juvenile antics during Rag Week. These had included attacking innocent passers-by with water pistols filled with coloured dye and the reappearance of the annoying effects of home-made nitrogen triiodide.

I had also been rapped over the knuckles for the unauthorised use of the stacks at the Fisher Library. I was caught there one night in company with a young lady, but my protestations that we were only there for research purposes wouldn't wash, because reading books does not usually necessitate taking any clothes off.

They were heady days, partly I suppose, because many of my friends and fellow students had discovered the joys of smoking cannabis. I tried to discover them too – determinedly and on numerous occasions. Whilst President Clinton famously denied inhaling, I almost gave myself a hernia trying. Much to my chagrin, though most of my contemporaries got nicely high, for some physiological reason, I remained firmly earthbound, if a little dizzy sometimes. Some of my friends still 'skin up' on a regular basis, but fortunately I've had plenty of enjoyment of life without the help of chemical stimulants – well, other than those provided by the grape and the grain.

They played a major part in my final departure from university when, not so fresh from an all night party, I rode unsteadily into the main lecture theatre on my Rabbit Rolamatic motor scooter. Then, having stalled it a few feet from the podium, I apparently spent several minutes noisily, but fruitlessly, trying to kick-start it, almost entirely drowning out an appeal being delivered by the vice-chancellor.

I don't recall the subject of this appeal, though I'm told it was a plea for more restrained behaviour on the next Rag Day, due the following week. I don't recall much of what happened after I fell off the motor scooter, but I do remember receiving a note from the vice-chancellor's office the following day advising me to stay at home to 'consider my position' at the university. I considered very carefully. My time there had given me a lot: intellectual stimulation, academic discipline (believe it or not) and my lifelong best friend – a fellow broadcaster called Barry Eaton. But in the self-inflicted circumstances, I clearly wasn't going to get a degree.

Secondly, in search of more money to pay for my education, I had answered an advert for a job as a cadet announcer at a Sydney commercial radio station called '2GB'. The early sixties saw a blossoming of independent broadcasting enterprise, fuelled by a boom in advertising as Australia's economy moved out of the post-war doldrums.

On the strength of my letter, *2GB* had called me in to the studios and asked me to read a few news stories. To my surprise, they offered me a part-time job which, at that stage, fitted in with my study requirements.

The prospect of a career in broadcasting appealed to me far more than the idea of treating some blue-rinsed dowager's yapping toy poodle. So, long before the motor-scooter incident, I had begun spending less time than I should at my studies and far more time than I should hanging around the studios. The inevitable eventually happened. I'd have jumped even if I hadn't been about to be pushed. To my mother's intense disappointment, I abandoned university and started full-time work at *2GB*.

It took about two weeks for the scales to fall from my eyes about the glamour commercial radio liked to sell its listeners – and of which I now thought I was a part. *2GB*, which was owned by a large commercial broadcaster called the MacQuarie Network, ran a very popular quiz programme called *The Ampol Show* – sponsored by a well-known Aussie petrol brand. As a young boy I had tuned into *The Ampol Show* and marvelled at the huge wealth of prizes the successful contestants could pull in.

A simple question and answer session narrowed the competition down to two finalists. Then listeners would hear the lucky winner being handed a golden telephone in the studio and, upon hearing the words 'Ampol Treasure House, number please?' would recite the prize number he or she had selected. The winner could choose any number from one to a thousand.

These prize numbers, therefore, could run into four digits, giving the impression that the range of goodies on offer was substantial. It was only after joining the station that I realised the warehouse-size Ampol Treasure House didn't exist. There was just a middle-aged woman who answered the winner on a battered old telephone and, whatever combination of numbers was quoted, there were only ever half a dozen or so prizes on offer.

A few weeks later, the station held more auditions – this time for a permanent on-air newsreader/announcer. Beginner's luck got me the job. Suddenly, I was earning the princely sum of 500 Australian dollars a year.

Sadly, the euphoria didn't last.

The reality of the job I was so thrilled to have landed was working atrociously long night-time hours in a cramped studio, operating every piece of equipment myself and broadcasting to a tiny audience of insomniac Sydney residents. At first it was a tremendous thrill to see the studio console light up when I threw the switches and, at times, when I slipped on the headphones and spoke into the microphone, I could barely keep the excitement from my voice. I listened to the radio professionals on both the presentational and technical side and soaked up their advice like a sponge.

Control and delivery are not easy skills to learn, however good the 'raw material' of your voice. Sounding authoritative and natural at the same time isn't easy either, which is maybe why so many of today's news reporters don't seem to have bothered.

But for me, once the novelty of radio broadcasting and the mastering of the sheer mechanics of it were over, boredom and disillusionment began to set in. The hunger for content to go with the presentation took hold. I felt I wasn't getting anywhere; it wasn't the kind of journalism that I wanted to be involved with. Youthful arrogance had me thinking about some of the news items I was handed: 'I shouldn't just be reading this, I should be changing it.' And practical action might be even more satisfying than practical jokes. But as yet, I was in no position to change anything, even if I'd been allowed to try.

Also, I was finding it almost impossible to meet girls with my permanently nocturnal working schedule. You couldn't go to parties or drive-in movies if you worked, as I did, a 9pm to 3am or a midnight to 6am shift. And in the Australia of the sixties, drive-in movies were where the action was. A willing partner away from the parental gaze, fogged up windows, and if you struck lucky, what the lads then saw as a badge of honour – stiletto heel holes in the headlining of your car.

And then, at 19, I fell in love; head over heels in love. I'd been used to calling the tune, but with Liza it was different. I became a misty-eyed romantic who wouldn't have dreamed of mauling her during a movie. Liza worked for one of our advertisers – and I thought she was just perfect – bright, petite and beautiful, with short black hair framing an elfin face and luminous green eyes. I couldn't take mine off her. I saw her whenever my nocturnal schedule allowed, but I thought of her constantly. I neglected my work and I muffed my news bulletins. It is almost impossible to describe your first love without resorting to clichés. So I won't, but they're all true.

I still remember the *frisson* brought on by the sound of her voice. I will never forget how it all ended either.

We'd arranged to meet at a New Year's Eve party in Rushcutters Bay. We'd even talked of announcing our engagement there. Liza was coming with friends and I was to turn up later, from work. But Liza and friends never arrived. At about two o'clock in the morning, there was a phone call from the police. The celebrations stopped instantly. We were told that there had been an accident some hours earlier on the Pacific Highway. Liza's friend's car had left the road on a bend and hit a telegraph pole.

Of the four people in the car, only one had been seriously injured. She was the one in the front passenger seat – which had taken the full force of the collision. My heart stopped. It was Liza – and as we learned in a subsequent call – she wasn't seriously injured, she was dead. Dead. I've never felt so empty in my life, before or since.

At the time, in what I then regarded as a cruel twist of fate, rather than just an unfortunate coincidence, a Harry Belafonte calypso hit was getting a lot of airplay on local radio. The chorus went something like: 'Every time I remember Liza, water come to me eye. Come back Liza, come back girl, water come to me eye.' Every time I heard the damned song, it invariably came to mine.

I was inconsolable, and went into a sort of purdah. I couldn't even bring myself to attend her funeral, something I still regret. Eventually, when I felt I was able to think straight, I decided that I had to get away; from my job, my flat, everything. It had been a promising job and it was a great flat, full of fond memories. But now nothing was as it had been, and the only way to break out of my cycle of self-pitying lethargy was to strike out anew.

In the end, perversely, I kept the flat and changed the job. I answered the lure of the Oxberry Aerial Image Animation Camera. This state of the art gizmo belonged to a marvellous man called Eric Porter who used it to make cartoons. It had a room of its own at his production studios, which it almost filled. Until I saw Eric's advert for a film assistant I hadn't really considered getting involved in movies – however tenuous the link he was offering was to 'proper' film-making. But Eric persuaded me.

He was a small, pipe-smoking, bespectacled figure in his late fifties who put me at my ease during the interview by spending most of it talking with schoolboy-like enthusiasm about the sophisticated animation camera he had just bought in America. What distinguished it from other cameras used to film drawings for animation was its ability to give great depth to the pictures. In the right hands, it could give a cartoon a three-dimensional quality that the animations of the 1960s usually lacked.

Eric was everything my father wasn't. Where my father withdrew into his shell, refusing to communicate with his family, Eric bowled you over with his desire to make you understand how everything in his world worked and interrelated. Within weeks of my joining his company, his enthusiasm had totally drawn me in. He became like a favourite uncle to me – interested, considerate and apparently concerned to make me good at every aspect of animation.

Eric had come onto the animation scene at around the same time as Walt Disney and used to claim that he'd managed to get the first fully-animated cartoon film on screen some months ahead of Disney. But while everyone remembers Mickey Mouse, who remembers Willie the Wombat?

Unfortunately for him, Australia lacked the distribution network and the financial clout to back Eric's innovation and he got left behind by his American rivals. Typically, he shrugged off his disappointment and kept on developing new animation techniques, paying his way by making numerous commercials and some short cinema films of the kind that used to precede the main feature. He went on to produce several internationally successful animated television series – including Superman and Charlie Chan – and eventually fulfilled his ambition to produce Australia's first full-length animated feature film.

Once I had mastered the Oxberry, Eric encouraged me to develop my script-writing abilities on some of those short cinema documentaries and sent me on location to film them as an assistant director. From long hours spent solo in a darkened animation studio, I had graduated to going out with a real film crew. Hollywood it was not, though it was enormous fun, despite the initial spate of practical in-jokes at the new boy's expense. We worked with tiny budgets and on subjects which were hardly earth-shattering, but the experience was as valuable as it was enjoyable – and left me with a pretty good working knowledge of the technicalities of film-making which subsequently eased my career on both sides of the camera.

I spent two very happy years working for Eric. Towards the end, with the emphasis more on the creative than the technical, I was allowed to take charge of several documentaries – from conception, through filming and editing, to completion. I found it a completely addictive process and was hungry for more. So when a reporting job came up at the Radio Talks Department of the Australian Broadcasting Commission – which offered the prospect of taking my emerging skills further than Eric's small company ever could – he persuaded me to apply for it.

2

From ABC to BBC

*Broadcasting beginnings, making waves with
authority, a broken marriage and making my
way in British broadcasting*

Landing the job at the ABC felt like the culmination of everything
I had been working for. The ABC is Australia's version of the
BBC – there really was no better platform for someone like me, or
so I thought. I was 21, ambitious and keen to show Australia's
biggest broadcasting organisation what a journalistic trailblazer
they had hired.

During my time with Eric Porter Productions I had been my
own boss in many respects. I researched my subject, I wrote an
outline of what I proposed to film, got approval from Eric, then
went out filming, and also wrote the accompanying script. I had
developed my own ideas on how to keep an audience's attention.
Sadly, they differed mightily from those of my bosses at the ABC.

Like the BBC, the ABC then regarded itself as the standard-
bearer of the nation's broadcasting values. In my view, however, it
sometimes talked down to its audience, not crediting it with the
common sense to make up its own mind about the merits of an
issue. This nannying attitude was backed by a vast, unwieldy
bureaucracy which had long since learned to stifle the new or
unorthodox by doing what all such organisations do best – as little
as possible as slowly as possible.

At times, I felt like I was back at Yanco. The overwhelming
sense that you had no one to turn to if you needed help or wanted
a fair hearing was exactly the same.

In the 1960s, the ABC documentary style was that of an illustrated talk, using a narrator to explain the issues, and seldom

29

allowing the listener to hear the story via interviews with the people directly involved. I thought this approach was often boring, and also gave the impression that the ABC was, in some way, filtering the facts and deciding how it should present them.

I started writing scripts for a magazine programme called 'Scope' and occasionally reporting for a weekly show called 'News Review'. In both these cases, I tried to include more interviews with the individuals concerned in the story and cut down on the waffling commentary from the reporter – who was, in most cases, myself.

I ran into trouble straight away. As a new recruit unversed in ABC culture, my scripts were monitored closely. When my section head saw what I was doing, he immediately passed the script to the news editor, who smartly passed it on to the head of the Talks Department. Broadcasting was for broadcasters and I had given over far too much of the programme to interviewees. There was rewrite upon rewrite. My scripts would be handed back to me having passed through three or four different hands – each individual imposing house-style more and more strictly until what was finally broadcast bore absolutely no resemblance to my original, nor, in some cases, to the facts.

I got some support from middle-management colleagues, but it was more in the nature of restraint. Some of my wilder ideas – though not without merit, they said – were tantamount to professional suicide. Better to work from within, they said. Outside meant no outlet. Why didn't I take the odd regional posting to reflect and perhaps to cool down?

I took their advice and accepted a couple of temporary jobs out in the sticks, but they only served to increase my sense of professional isolation. On the up-side, however, it certainly gave me a knowledge of broadcasting from the ground up. One outpost was so small I had to do everything, including turning off the transmitter at night and on again in the morning.

To have a new radio station was a big thing for a small Australian town in the 1960s. The mayor of this particular place had made it plain how pleased he was to have me there and that he would go to any lengths to show it. Unfortunately, these lengths included installing his daughter in my hotel bed just before I got back from work one night. I made my excuses – as they used to say in the Sunday tabloids – and left.

On my return to Sydney I was greeted with a pleasant surprise.

I was to be tried out on television. My first assignment was as a co-presenter on a documentary about new baby animals at Sydney's renowned Taronga Park Zoo. The two star attractions were a baby gorilla and a tiger cub. The tiger was cuddly and the gorilla was seriously cute – despite the fact that his father was called King Kong. Little John would make a sort of giggling noise when tickled and would get quite upset when eventually returned to his cage.

All went well until we had to abandon filming for the long summer school holidays. Hordes of excited young visitors had made filming impossible. When we resumed filming our young stars had grown up somewhat – and now conformed to type. First to discover this was my co-presenter, Bob Sanders. He strode into the cage and gathered up the young tiger in his arms. There was a brief struggle and Bob turned to face the camera with his immaculate suit jacket in tatters. I shouldn't have laughed really, because my turn was to come.

Little John was no longer so little or so compliant. He leaned back in my arms and after a brief pause for thought, hauled off and hit me in the eye. The result was a colossal shiner that lasted for a month. There was one slight benefit however – the pleasure of being able to honestly say to those who asked how I'd acquired such a spectacular black eye: "Simple – a gorilla hit me."

The programme was counted a success and I was given another one to present, this time on my own. As I recall, it was meant to be an innocuous news feature about the introduction of pre-packed school lunches on a trial basis in selected primary schools. The crew and I were dispatched to a location in what was then regarded as a deprived area. Filming in the playground, I noticed several pupils chucking the relatively nutritious meals provided straight into the bin in favour of bags of crisps, fizzy sherbet or sticky sweets.

Camera rolling, we approached one of the pupils concerned, a stocky little chap with ginger hair and freckles. "Don't you ever stop to think that there are millions of starving people in Asia who would be grateful for what you're throwing away?" I asked. "Yeah?" came the cocky reply, "Name two!"

This cheeky put-down got me going. Much to the bemusement of my colleagues, the rest of the feature turned into a bit of a diatribe about waste and isolationism. It wasn't what management wanted and it actually wasn't very good, so the item was scrapped.

Back in radio, nothing had changed. I still thought most pro-grammes were too accepting of the status quo and lacked chal-lenge. I tried appealing to my section head, to the news editor, the deputy and head of the talks department – all to no avail. This was how things were done at the ABC. I tried insubordination. I recorded my own items as I had originally written them and tried to sneak them through, but they were spotted before broadcast and critical reports began to appear on my employment record.

Things came to a head when I confronted the Head of Talks in his office. Refusing to listen to his secretary's protestations that he was in a meeting, I barged in to find him closeted with a member of the ABC board of governors. I said my piece, mindful that with every word I was talking myself closer to unemployment. I left them sitting in stunned silence and went back to my desk to await the inevitable summons and retribution.

One redeeming feature of a large, civil service-like body like the ABC was that it was almost impossible to be sacked. It would have been an admission of failure on their part, so it was considered far better to make disapproval plain and invite resignation rather than cause a stink. Two days later, therefore, I was called in to see the Head of Talks.

"Cook, we have a short-term vacancy in Western Australia which we should like you to fill – just a few months until we can find someone permanent over there."

In other words: 'Take the hint and resign now, or go to Perth and annoy someone else for a while. Meanwhile we'll quietly forget all about you here in Sydney.'

I have a stubborn streak and I decided these bastards weren't going to force me to resign. Rightly or wrongly, I believed the listener was entitled to hear what the reporter had discovered was the truth about a story – first hand, from the people most closely involved in it – and I was determined to carry on until they were forced to recognise I was right, or until they sacked me.

Perth, though a very attractive place to live, was the end of the professional world as far as I was concerned. This was years before the huge commercial expansion of the city and the acquisition of the glitzy image it now enjoys as an international yachting centre and a playground of the rich and beautiful. I felt like a latter-day convict, sentenced to transportation to what was then – and still is – the most remote city on the planet.

Nevertheless, propelled by youthful self-confidence, I said good-bye to a worried Mum and a disinterested Dad, who were still living in semi-dereliction in Dundas, and caught the plane westwards with a surprisingly light heart. I had nothing to lose.

The boss of the ABC in Perth was a grey, company man called Arthur Povah – a charmless time-server who had obviously been forewarned about me.

"This is Perth, not Sydney, and we won't be wanting any of your big city tricks here," was his message.

It was advice I didn't heed, and it wasn't long before I landed myself in trouble with the management. In a weekly news magazine programme which I presented, I had decided to substitute one item I considered fairly pointless for another, totally unauthorised piece about proposals to ship Nyoongar aborigines out of East Perth to a reserve several hundred miles away.

It was obvious that the authorities had become exasperated by constant complaints from some shopkeepers and local residents that the aborigines were causing a nuisance. Their main 'crime' was to get drunk and sit about the streets, which they said they did mainly because no one would give them proper jobs. The locals claimed they were unemployable because they were indolent drunks.

I felt it was inappropriate and inhumane to herd these people out to some shacks in the arid hinterlands. They were overwhelmingly fourth and fifth-generation city dwellers to whom the ancient aboriginal way of life meant very little. Far better, I argued, to address the problem where it lay, in the city, and to try to do something about it.

My opinion was not popular with Arthur Povah and the city fathers. Another black mark was splashed across my annual report – but it was worth it.

In the days following the programme, which included interviews with aborigines and white townspeople alike, a campaign against the proposed move began and eventually the plan was quietly dropped.

I still get a charge out of a result like that. Before the broadcast friends who knew what I had in mind had counselled me against 'treading on dangerous ground'. After the broadcast I realised I'd enjoyed being there. I'd risen to a worthwhile challenge – and personal repercussions aside – had prompted a positive outcome.

But it was another of my unapproved activities that caused the most trouble with the ABC in Perth.

My response to the new libertarianism of the Age of Aquarius had been to co-found a satirical magazine which gloried in the title 'Grot'. My 'partners in crime' were a commercial radio producer and an advertising executive. It was first published about the time that Richard Neville and his friends started *Oz* in Sydney. Unlike *Oz*, an underground magazine that was eventually published and prosecuted for alleged obscenity in the UK; we never offended anyone enough to end up in court.

Even when we *tried* to offend, we were thwarted. In an effort to challenge the stultifying status quo in local publishing, we arranged to reproduce recent excerpts from the first periodical in Australia to use the word 'fuck' in print. That is, we attempted to use them, but when we collected the latest issue from our printer we found that he had taken it upon himself to censor not only the offending word, but also the context in which it appeared. So our article, under the headline 'The Boundaries of Obscenity' and intended as a wry but reasoned plea for *less* censorship, was rendered both pointless and meaningless.

None the less, everyone had a pretty good idea of what we had tried to do and the ABC was not amused.

I had also managed to persuade the local commercial television station to run a short weekly insert entitled 'The Grot Spot' on one of its shows. With hindsight, it was an unwise move, since I derived my main income from Australia's public broadcasting body. That's how Arthur Povah saw it, too, as something of a conflict of interests.

Official disapproval reached its height after *The Grot Spot* revealed that the coast of Western Australia was patrolled by a single naval vessel whose duties included the defence of a huge local ammunition store. We had discovered that the one thing this ammo dump didn't have in stock was any shells of the right calibre for the ship that was supposed to defend it. In other words, after the first few salvos, our bit of the Royal Australian Navy would have been powerless to prevent an enemy attack.

The magazine soon ran out of printers who were prepared to work with us and *Grot* bit the dust, but not before I received a terse memo from Mr Povah which read something like: 'From next week you will be moved to newsreading duties until further notice. You will never be allowed to read one of your subversive scripts again.'

Reading the local news wasn't my idea of cutting-edge journalism, but I wasn't in any position to object. And I even managed to get myself into trouble doing that.

One of my first newsreading shifts was on television. The ABC television service in Perth was on a split, two-level site. The newsroom and editing suites were on the upper level and the studios themselves were 50 yards away down a narrow access road. The form was that you'd be given your script and the roll of 16mm film to go with it and you'd stroll down to the studios.

On one of my first shifts though, the film editor was running late and I was going to have to sprint down the hill. That was the theory. In practice, I stumbled out the door and dropped the film, which, to my horror, set off down the hill on its own, unwinding as it went. It rolled straight past the studios, across the road and into the park opposite. There was no chance of recovering it.

Channel Two viewers, having been told we had 'technical problems', were treated to a sort of elongated radio bulletin that night, with the missing film clips hurriedly summarized in script by the news producer and solemnly intoned by me. Much of this had to be done on the fly, and in those pre-autocue days, that meant my colleague working on his hands and knees, handing edited pages up to me from beneath the desk. In the circumstances, I thought we managed it pretty well. Management thought it was a bugger's muddle.

Ill fortune struck again that very weekend. I was then sharing a flat in South Perth with a TV producer called Jim Stafford, a man so laid back he was virtually horizontal. He thought it was a leg-pull when a hollow voice rang him at work asking to be rescued. I had been repairing my Renault Gordini on the drive. The car was up on ramps with the sump half off when the phone rang. The call disrupted my train of thought and I forgot that I'd not drained out all the oil. So when the last bolts came out, the weight of the oil in the asymmetrical sump pan flipped it over – and on to my head.

"You look like a giant pelican rescued from an oil slick," said Jim, calmly mopping me down. He was probably right. I now have some idea how a sludge-covered seabird must feel, and it isn't pleasant. The sump was very reluctant to come unstuck. We did eventually remove the thing, but somehow managed to tear my earlobes in the process. They were stitched back by a casualty doctor at the local hospital, who did a pretty neat job considering how much he was laughing.

You can't read TV news with a bandage round your head, so that – along with my last performance I suppose – meant that it was back to radio for a while. It was more fun anyway, thanks largely to the activities of one of the senior announcers.

Peter Harrison looked every inch the consummate professional. Tall and serious, casually but impeccably dressed, everything about him said he was a company man. What our bosses at the ABC rarely saw was his other side – his immense capacity for disruption and mischief-making.

Peter's favourite targets were young announcers fresh out of training. Waiting until they had just gone on the air, he would ignore the red 'On Air' light outside the soundproofed studio and wander in, putting a reassuring finger to his lips to imply he was there purely in a monitoring capacity. The nervous reader would plough on, glancing up at Peter from time to time.

The next thing the victim would see was the station's most senior newscaster dropping his twills and underpants and lowering his buttocks down onto the grey metal wastepaper basket. He would stare fixedly at the now panic-stricken newsreader who would stutter, lose his place and generally wish for his mother to come and take him away.

Peter would then up the ante, and start to strain and grimace, producing barely-audible grunts. Nothing that the listener would ever hear, but loud enough for those in the studio to pick up.

The end result was usually near-hysteria and a newsreading performance that left the listener confused and often concerned for the health of the young broadcaster. The broadcaster, having gratefully handed over to the continuity announcer, would watch, slack-jawed, as Harrison pulled up his pants, did himself up and strode out of the room as if nothing had happened. Sometimes his victims would try to persuade themselves that nothing *had* happened, particularly when Peter greeted them later and nonchalantly gave them some small piece of advice about their performance.

One of his many victims was a talented young man called Peter

Holland, who went on to become Perth's best-loved TV news anchor. In those days, Peter's abilities did not include getting up in the morning. This had often meant that I had to do the first few minutes of his shift and mine – opening two stations at once. This was a nerve-wracking and potentially very confusing procedure, and Peter's early absences left him wide open for ambush attempts by the amiable but undeniably predatory Harro.

I was lucky enough to avoid such treatment because Harro probably considered me a comparatively old hand at broadcasting after my experience at *2GB* and the ABC in Sydney. He had another, more technical prank in mind for me.

My new duties included evening stints as a continuity announcer, informing the listener about what was coming up next. On this occasion I was about to read out details of a live concert when I sensed someone standing behind the sound console a few feet in front of me. Seconds before I was due to read the script to introduce the concert, I glanced up to see Peter, smiling evilly and holding two unplugged microphone leads – one in each hand. If what I was about to say was going to be broadcast, those wires would have to be plugged together again, and fast.

"You stupid bastard, what the hell do you think you're doing," I hissed.

I turned at the sound of an urgent tapping from the engineer in the glass sound booth behind me.

He stabbed his finger repeatedly at Peter, so I turned back to see Peter drop the two leads he had previously been holding and reach solemnly down behind the console to produce the real microphone cable, still safely connected.

I had remained live and on air throughout, and as far as the ABC's local audience was concerned, it sounded as if I'd accused them of idiocy and illegitimacy in the one breath.

Mind you, the audience should have been used to rudery on the radio if they'd listened to the live relays of proceedings in parliament from Canberra. The chamber was then equipped with omnidirectional microphones which gave equal emphasis to speakers and hecklers alike. To sit in the studio as the duty announcer during a parliamentary broadcast was to be amused as often as one was bored. "Say that again," bellowed one backbencher who'd not got the message being delivered by the MP on his feet. "If the honourable member spent less time sitting around and whipping his twig, he'd have understood what I was saying," came the not so witty rejoinder.

During another broadcast, a much-disliked member of the Country Party interrupted a devolution debate by exclaiming: "But I'm a country member!" A number of MPs could distinctly be heard responding: "Yeah mate, we remember!" And *I* remember that sometimes such crude pronouncements were what passed for the voice of democracy in Australia all those years ago.

Peter Harrison's victims eventually decided that it was payback time and we hatched our own plot to crack his imperturbable façade. Several of us waited until Peter was well into his stride with the main evening radio news bulletin and then slipped into his studio. I carried a fire bucket, emptied of sand and filled with ice.

Peter scarcely looked up, though he realised we were close to him. We waited silently until a tape insert was being played. Then, two of us held his arms while his trousers were swiftly undone and the contents of the bucket shovelled down the front. Tape over, we stood back to await results. Nothing. Old Harro was already so cool that he just went on reading the bulletin as if glacial interference with his nether regions was part of his daily routine.

Another spectacular revenge attempt was staged by Big George, a local sports reporter, who had arguably been Harro's most regular victim.

Big George was, by all accounts, monumentally endowed. One afternoon, when Harrison was live on air, Big George treated him to his party trick. He backed slowly into the studio, obviously carrying something. As he approached the announcer's desk, he turned to reveal, laid out on a tray and garnished with salad, his enormous appendage.

Without blinking an eye, or fluffing a word, Harrison flicked off his microphone, and smote big George's mighty organ with a steel ruler. He then turned his microphone back on and continued to read as if nothing had happened, leaving Big George hopping round the studio in the background, trying to stifle howls of agony. Harro was absolutely bombproof, and everyone thereafter more or less gave up trying to prove him otherwise.

Mind you, there were some memorable, frontier-style characters to be met outside the ABC too. Most memorable of the lot was a lanky, lantern-jawed pilot called Jimmy Woods. He ran Jimmy

Woods Airlines, the world's smallest airline with, he claimed, the world's shortest scheduled service.

He flew his ancient Avro Anson from Perth to the tourist island of Rottnest, 20 miles off the coast. He sometimes did it with one or both of the engines switched off halfway, nonchalantly asking his passengers to move from one side of the aircraft to the other in order to change trim as he glided towards his destination. This practice saved him fuel, but did little to boost the confidence of his clients.

Jimmy was a fund of stories of derring-do in the early days of outback aviation. Perhaps he should never have tried to modernise, because some years later, not long after he'd bought himself a new-fangled helicopter, he managed to fly it into a mountain – with fatal consequences.

I first met Jimmy when I was sent to interview him at the downtown motel where he was staying. "He's expecting you," I was told as I was directed to his room. The door was open and I could hear the sound of a shower running, so I sat on a chair and waited. Eventually, Jimmy appeared, dripping wet and wrapped in a towel. On his head was an equally wet bush hat. I couldn't help asking the reason for this unusual bathroom attire. "Well son," he said patiently, as if addressing a curious toddler: "Obvious isn't it? Without the hat, the bloody cigarette won't stay lit." A genuine, original, independent spirit was Jimmy.

Those few diversions aside, life working for the ABC was, though useful experience, fairly depressing at the same time. My documentary output in Perth had been halted and there was little indication that the station would ever move into the second half of the twentieth century and start treating its audience – which included the likes of Jimmy – as if it had a mind of its own.

I kept being reminded of what a self-censoring, toe-the-party-line organisation the ABC had become. I often found myself thinking of the brave departure of two journalists I much admired, Michael Charlton and Bob Raymond – the presenter and editor, respectively, of *Four Corners* – the Australian equivalent of *Panorama*.

They had resigned over the ABC's craven capitulation to the right-wing government of Sir Robert Menzies after the broadcast of a programme on his administration's failing public housing policy. It was a well-researched exposé revealing serious flaws, and, naturally, required an official response. None was forthcoming and the government's presumption seemed to be that if the Housing Minister, one Senator Spooner, did not wish to appear, then the programme could not be transmitted.

The view of the ABC seemed to be that it was there to repeat the views of the government, not to challenge them. So when Bob Raymond managed to get the programme broadcast more or less intact, it caused quite a stir. Then came the political backlash. Menzies himself got involved, the ABC was reminded where its funding came from and the back-pedalling began.

The government demanded, and got, total access to the next edition of *Four Corners* and the minister took almost the entire programme to air his views unchallenged. Bob Raymond thought it made Spooner look the pompous prat he was, but such direct political interference and organisational toadying could not be tolerated. Having failed to get any assurance that the same thing would never be allowed to happen again, the editor and presenter resigned. Michael Charlton came to Britain to report – without undue interference – for *Panorama*. Should I follow his lead?

What had happened to those very senior journalists was, on a much smaller scale, happening to me too. This was not the way honest journalistic enquiry should be treated and, if I stayed – or remained silent – I was acquiescing in the whole sordid process. I'd had enough of Perth politics and was professionally disillusioned. I imagine my employers were pretty disillusioned with me too. I was clearly not going to make progress in an organisation where I was regarded – perhaps with some justification – as something of a loose cannon.

Besides, I had fallen in love again and a master plan had formed in my fevered mind which was going to take me away, but which would also take time to bring to fruition.

I had met Madeline while working on a story for the ABC on overseas students. My research took me to the library of the University of Western Australia where I came across a beautiful, slim Oriental girl with long, black hair, reading at a desk. We fell into conversation and, having discovered that she was the President of the Students' Union, I ended up making her a major part of the programme.

Her family were well-to-do Singaporean Chinese who had sent their very bright daughter to Australia to study law. She had two years to go in Perth and had set her sights on joining a solicitors' practice in London. Her vision had set me thinking.

For many people of my generation, growing up after the war in Australia or New Zealand, Britain was still 'back home'. The Cook family had only emigrated to New Zealand via Australia in 1891 when my great-grandfather left Lincolnshire with an open berth one-way passage from Liverpool on the SS *Orient* – price £17–17–0. I still treasure the ticket.

The Cooks had connections in Whitby and a belief – totally unproven – that the family tree links us to the famous explorer, Captain James Cook. So I, like many of the male members of the family, have James amongst our forenames. My mother's family, although from Wellington, were only recent immigrants from England. After Dad died in September 1970, Mum moved back to the UK until her own death in 1994.

Madeline and I started to make plans together. My options in Australia were restricted. I was partly responsible for that myself, of course, having fallen out with the biggest and most powerful broadcaster in the country. However, I still had enough callow self-confidence to believe that I had something significant to contribute to broadcasting; I knew a fair bit about film-making, documentaries, investigations and radio. Britain felt like the place where I could put my talents to best use.

Madeline wasn't free to go to England for two years and I was going to need substantial financial backing if I was to survive the early times before I got established there.

My decision to start afresh lifted a weight from my shoulders. With a light heart, I wrote my resignation letter to Arthur Povah and stuck it on his office door.

I landed on my feet almost immediately.

Bill Warnock ran one of the most successful advertising agencies in the country from its Perth headquarters. We met, got on well, and he offered me a job running the radio and television arm of the business. Red-bearded, energetic and filled with creative enthusiasm, Bill was a dream to work for, and so the work he got out of everyone was top quality, prize-winning stuff.

The office often echoed with laughter, in stark contrast to the sombre official mood at the ABC. I stayed at Warnock Sandford for two years, saving hard for the move to England. I bought camera equipment for freelance documentary work and squirrelled away as much cash as possible for accommodation and living expenses while we were both looking for work.

Madeline graduated with one of the best firsts Perth had awarded in years. We spent a blissful year in our own flat. We went to parties, we soaked up the increasingly liberal atmosphere of the Flower Power era and kept saving. It was an exciting and enjoyable period in my life. Unfortunately, the very process of enjoying yourself encourages you to overdo it and to take your eye off the ball.

I had long been bitten by the motor racing bug and was now tempted to blow a chunk of our travel fund on a Fiat Abarth 850 TC. I had been driving since I was about ten, having initially learnt on that old Lanz tractor at Gidleigh, and by this time I'd had a competition licence for several years. But I'd never had the proper competition car to go with it – so I selfishly succumbed to temptation and bought the Abarth, though I didn't keep it for long.

I was soon reminded of the true cost of competing on a regular basis – buying spares, rebuilding engines, finding race fees and paying for fuel and tyres. Common sense prevailed, and I raced rarely, though quite successfully, until I sold the car to another petrolhead – luckily for pretty much what I'd paid for it.

However, I remain a petrolhead to this day. I love watching motor racing and I have an interest in a small sports car manufacturing company. As a devotee of British performance cars, I cherish a much-modified Costello MGB V8, and have owned a number of Jaguars. Over the years, I have bought and sold a succession of exotic, cash-guzzling vehicles from Alfa Romeo to Zagato. If only I'd kept a few. Some of them would be worth a small fortune now.

The oldest car in the list, was an 1898 single-cylinder, three and a half horsepower de Dion Bouton. I half-owned it with a friend called Michael Grigsby, and we used to take her on the London to Brighton run. We were both substantial lads and the poor little car couldn't really cope. On hills, one of us would have to get out and walk alongside. On the notoriously steep Pyecombe Hill, both of us had to walk, controlling the progress of the vehicle with the hand throttle. Two overweight chaps and one elderly motor car, wheezing up the hill together. But I digress.

Madeline and I decided to get married before we left for

England. It was a simple ceremony conducted in a neighbour's home by John Hudson, the ABC's local head of religious broadcasting. John had become a friend and was notoriously un-vicarlike. He arrived for the ceremony wearing a long, black cape and announcing himself as 'Batman'.

Mum was the only parent present. Neither of our families was there. The whole thing was so low-key that it hardly seemed worth asking Madeline's family to come all that way. I had seen little of Dad since I'd moved out West, and I honestly felt that to involve someone as vague and other-worldly as my father in the wedding of his son to someone as exotic as Madeline might have embarrassing consequences.

Happily, in later years Dad began to mellow a little. He had given up teaching to spend more time painting, and – surprisingly – with his wife. He took on some interesting projects, like designing some of the notes for Australia's new decimal currency. He began to communicate with other artists instead of ignoring them. He argued technique with William Dobell and Russell Drysdale and compared technique with William Dargie, who, like my father was an art teacher. Also like my father, he had been commissioned to paint an official portrait of the great aboriginal artist Albert Namatjira.

Dad had been amazed and appalled when he met Namatjira at his tribal home. Amazed at the depth of the man's talent and appalled at the way it was being exploited. He told me how Albert had been persuaded to barter a valuable batch of paintings for a second-hand refrigerator when there was no electricity available for hundreds of miles. I'd like to be able to say that this incident gave Dad an insight into what motivated me – but it didn't.

A traditionalist through and through, he hated modern art, though Australia in the fifties and sixties produced some wonderful modern artists. Dad agreed with William Dargie that 'modern art is anti-democratic and the last refuge of the snob and the reactionary'. He did have some respect for Sydney Nolan though, because he said that unlike most modernists, the man could draw.

My father is remembered mostly as a water-colourist, though his friends spent a lot of time trying to persuade him to work more in oils. Oil paintings were thought to be more permanent and more profitable, but Dad thought they were too easy. He got more of a kick trying to get a watercolour wash right in weather so hot the paint was virtually dry as it left the brush.

During this period he finally got round to building the house he'd promised my mother so many years before. It was in Moss Vale in his beloved Southern Highlands – and the couple who'd bumped rather than rubbed along for so long almost became second honeymooners. He even bought her a washing machine. Not very romantic, I know, but she'd never had one.

Sadly, this state of bliss wasn't to last. By this time, having established a toehold in England, Madeline and I were on holiday in France in the autumn of 1970, when one of those BBC long wave SOS messages was relayed to us: "Would Roger Cook, believed to be travelling on the Continent, please contact his mother as a matter of urgency as his father is seriously ill."

By the time we got the message, some two weeks after it was broadcast, Dad was dead and buried. He'd been admitted to Bowral Hospital with a suspected ruptured appendix and had instead died overnight of a massive heart attack.

But all that was still to come.

Back in Western Australia, having got hitched, Madeline and I wanted to get moving. Perth had begun to pall, and outside the groves of academe, Madeline had begun to experience racial prejudice. I'm not a violent man, but one particularly obscene racist slur did bring down the red mist. It happened as we were walking along one of Perth's main streets, St. George's Terrace, early one evening. A couple of thugs began shouting abuse, but the more we tried to ignore them, the closer and louder they got. Eventually, one of them was so close we were being flecked with his spittle with every taunt.

I could take it no longer, and despite Madeline's protestations, I planted my fist firmly on his jaw. Then, as he began to wobble, I upended him and rammed him head first into a nearby open-topped litter bin. I told the police our story and they told me I'd broken both the man's collar bones. I was ashamed of my actions and, mindful of the physical and legal results, I have never hit anyone again.

These days you'd probably be prosecuted for what I did and be forced to pay compensation to the foul-mouthed racist. But then, the police reaction was that I'd taught him a well-deserved lesson. Nevertheless, it now really was time to explore new horizons – hopefully, more tolerant and less hidebound horizons.

For quite a few Australians and New Zealanders of my generation, the UK – 'the old country' – was home. A place to look up to, and as many had, defend. It was a bit disconcerting to discover that I seemed to be rather more patriotic than the average Brit. I remember going to the cinema not long after we arrived. We had front row seats in the circle. In those days, they still played the national anthem at the end of the performance and the audience was expected to stand. We did so, but by the time the last strains of *God Save the Queen* had faded away, we were the only ones left in the theatre.

The day I walked through the doors of Broadcasting House in London – 14th May 1968 – I had no idea what the future held. I had arrived in England knowing nobody apart from Madeline. I had no appointments arranged, but I did have a name – Andrew Boyle, the editor of *The World At One*, the lunchtime news programme known to insiders as 'WATO'.

Although I didn't know it at the time, I was in good company as I approached the cluttered, cream-painted *World At One* office to see Andrew; Nick Ross, Jonathan Dimbleby and David Jessel all started work there at about the same time and we remain on good terms even now. Already on contract then were two more imports from down-under, Sue McGregor and Nancy Wise – 'The Colonial Contingent', as we three later became known.

Andrew Boyle agreed to see me straightaway and I decided to take the bull by the horns. "I like what you do here and I know I can do it too, but with a rather different approach which I think you'll approve of," I began. It was a bit over the top, but I meant it. Boyle invited Bill Hardcastle, the programme's legendary anchorman, to join us.

I told them what I had been doing in Australia and that I could work almost any equipment they cared to throw at me. They heard me out, and then put me to the test. I was given the best kind of audition by being handed a BBC standard-issue *Uher* tape recorder and sent straight out of the office to cover a breaking story.

Just around the corner from Broadcasting House stood the Sierra Leone High Commission. Dozens of African students were milling around, doing what many students did in 1968 – occupying and protesting.

I found the ringleaders, helped release the Deputy High Commissioner from the broom cupboard, and did my interviews. I taped an attempt to telephone the Prime Minister in Freetown, during which the call somehow got diverted to the local animal shelter. Meanwhile, outside in Portland Place, union workers led by a brass band were staging a protest march of their own. So all my recordings were accompanied by the strains of *Colonel Bogie*. The report I put together was therefore fairly surreal, but it made that day's programme and, two days later, Andrew Boyle offered me a contract.

I loved the brisk, challenging style of *The World At One*, or 'The World at Sixes and Sevens', as some wags dubbed it. You never knew what you would be doing until you arrived in the busy office around eight in the morning and Andrew Boyle or Bill Hardcastle approved your story for the day. Bill would sit as if enthroned at the editorial table – six smaller tables pushed together, if I remember correctly – and he completely dominated it. He was an imposing, bejowelled and balding figure with a cigarette always on the go, his shirt sleeves hitched up with flexible metal bands and his eyebrows protruding over his heavy-rimmed spectacles like an ill-trimmed privet hedge.

Andrew would sit beside him, ruddy of complexion and with an unruly banner of silver hair perpetually flying across his face. Andrew, who was also a respected biographer – the man whose book *Climate of Treason* exposed Anthony Blunt as the mysterious fourth man alongside the infamous spies Philby, Burgess and Maclean – was the brains behind the programme. Bill, you might say, was the brawn, though there was nothing wrong with his brains either. A former editor of the *Daily Mail*, he had a finely tuned nose for a news story.

But whoever found the stories – and the unspoken rule was that you never followed the newspapers – Andrew would come up with a way of taking those stories further or doing them differently. His difficulty was in explaining what he wanted – his briefings could be extremely obtuse. It amused him to be an irritant to the establishment, which at times included BBC management, and each success was greeted with his odd, schoolboy giggle of a laugh.

Every morning we reporters would sit round that big, untidy editorial table, which was usually covered in a layer of newspapers, scripts, coffee cups and overflowing Bakelite ashtrays. We would tentatively offer our own story ideas or compete for those already decided upon if what we proposed wasn't considered interesting enough. If the latter was the verdict, Bill would usually announce it by muttering 'WGAS'.

I later learnt that WGAS was an acronym regularly appended to stories from a particular correspondent in America. It was short for 'Who gives a shit?' Someone later replaced the neatly typed sign on the office door for one that read, not 'W.A.T.O', but 'W.G.A.S.'; it stayed there for months.

The World At One was based in a string of interconnected offices on the third floor of Broadcasting House, the last and largest of these being given over to the reporters. It was there that we crouched over our editing machines, headphones clamped to our ears, cutting tape with razor blades – as was then the practice. It was a fiddly job, not helped by the pressure of deadlines, and many is the time I found myself on my hands and knees looking for a small piece of tape I had dropped, or spooling through the unused material looking for another version of the missing word to use instead.

The closer it got to transmission, the more hectic it got, with reporters, producers and secretaries rushing about as the running order was changed, items were rejigged, or worse if it was one of yours – dropped altogether.

I really thrived on the adrenalin, knowing that when you left that office, armed with your tape recorder, you had to bring a story home. Then there was the editing to make it as succinct and immediate as you could and, finally, the satisfaction of hearing it go out to as many as three million listeners.

It was that enormous listenership that drew the interviewees in, politicians in particular. That the programme was also hugely influential was largely due to the fact that the newspapers usually followed us, rather than the other way round. *The World At One* had changed the face of factual programming on radio and it was the place to be heard. One leading politician at the time said that five minutes on *The World At One* was worth ten minutes on any television channel – and he was probably right.

However, the programme did not always take politicians as seriously as they took themselves. On one occasion, Andrew Boyle was taken to task by a very self-important Tory MP called Sir Gerald Nabarro, who I believe had objected to the amount of airtime allocated to his golden words. Eventually tiring of his insistent phone calls, Andrew sent him a short telegram. It read "Stuff you for a start, abusive letter follows."

The missive worked, the phone calls stopped, and the letter wasn't necessary. However, none of this stopped Sir Gerald from appearing on the programme again. In fact, he was one of those MPs flagged on the WATO Roladex contacts index with the letters 'HRS'. This denoted a contributor willing to come into the studio at the drop of a hat and stood for 'has roller skates'.

For three years I was totally immersed in day-to-day news. It gave me the chance to do all the things I had yearned to achieve in Australia. Instead of some sober-suited announcer filtering the facts to the audience, we gave it to people right from the shoulder. It was liberating. But there was still the odd culture shock in store for me.

For example: I remember parcelling up some scripts for postage and asking one of the secretaries for some sticky tape. Unaware of its British significance, I used the trade name of what was then Australia's equivalent of Sellotape: "Could I borrow your Durex please?" The virginal Mary, a Reithian creature to whom a request for a condom would have been as unwelcome as it was unexpected, looked rather flustered.

I mistook this reaction for concern that I might permanently abscond with her tape dispenser. "It's OK," I added reassuringly, "I'll bring it back when I've finished." Blushing furiously, the poor thing fled. I was later taken aside and cautioned about crude colonial behaviour, but I'm not sure my explanation about unwittingly embarrassing trade names was considered entirely convincing.

Eventually, my work pattern and preference metamorphosed. I began to present *The World At One* and the *PM* programme when Bill Hardcastle was on his day off; the latter programme as a co-presenter with a bright, bald-headed Welshman called Bob Williams. Working with Bob was enormous fun, but involved the use of a certain amount of sign language.

I'm partially deaf in the left ear and Bob was totally deaf in the right. So working in the studio required us to devote our limited faculties, via our headphones, to following the programme and receiving updates and other instructions from the producer on the other side of the glass. This meant that direct communication between us was almost impossible, even though we were sitting opposite each other. Hence the sometimes frantic sign language and a plague of post-it notes.

It must have been a very odd spectacle, but it went unseen by the audience and ours became a very successful partnership – which we regularly celebrated. At the end of every shift together, it was our habit to decamp to a wine bar in the Marylebone Road where we would share a proper conversation and a bottle of champagne. Laurent Perrier, it was, at one pound nineteen shillings and sixpence the bottle – according to an old receipt I unearthed recently.

The *PM* programme ran to an hour and had more time to devote to softer topics such as the arts and the latest books. But such was the pressure we all operated under to fill that time that preparation for interviews often left something to be desired. On one occasion I was faced with a log jam of prerecorded studio interviews to do. One of them concerned a plan to open toy libraries for children, the other a plan to legalise brothels. It was fortunate for me that the interviews *were* taped, because the toy library lady did not react too well to questions about the sex industry.

However, it was amazing what you could get away with on almost zero preparation if you were a good listener. When the distinguished economist Professor J.K. Galbraith came in to discuss his latest book, *Economics, Peace and Laughter*, my briefing – not for the first time – was 'Here's the book, he's in the lift.' I just managed to read the dust jacket and the chapter headings before the professor was ushered into studio 3B. I listened very carefully and reacted to what he had to say.

He had obviously enjoyed the process and I had successfully bluffed him into believing that I had read and digested his prose, because before he left, he insisted on signing the book. On the flyleaf he wrote: "Many thanks for a very pleasant and stimulating talk." Still, as Bill Hardcastle later remarked: "You should be able to hold your own with Albert Einstein in a well-edited two minutes and 45 seconds."

Editing might have improved Bill's presentation too. His breathless, urgent style often led to the message getting scrambled. He once even managed to introduce himself as William *Whitelaw*, then the Home Secretary. But he was compulsive listening and a great puncturer of the pompous. And despite his gruff exterior, if he took a shine to you, he was inclined towards trying to manage your life. Once, in an effort to encourage the marriage of one of our number to a girl of whom he wholeheartedly approved, he actually bought them a double bed.

Latterly, his concern for me was life insurance. He insisted that I should have adequate cover and even enlisted the help of his former City Editor at the *Daily Mail* in order to pull a few strings. Unfortunately, the more risky the assignments I came to tackle, the less insurable I became. Eventually no insurance company would touch me – at least at a premium I could afford.

As time went by, more of my reporting was done for WATO's sister programme, *The World This Weekend*, which was broadcast between one and two every Sunday afternoon. At an hour in length, and an airing only once a week, it could accommodate longer, more in-depth reports that were prepared in days rather than hours. In 1971, one of these stories set me on the uninsurable path I am still following today.

For a few weeks, we had been receiving letters about the activities of a loan-sharking company calling itself the Turret Mortgage Company in Bristol. The letters seemed genuine and came from individuals unconnected with each other but all making the same complaint, that Turret was charging extortionately high interest rates and that when its customers had difficulty repaying the loan, threats soon followed.

I called on some of the complainants, checked their paperwork and recorded their stories.

More than one interviewee told harrowingly of home visits from Turret employees accompanied by a pair of fierce Alsatian dogs.

I did my homework on the company and decided to challenge its boss to discover why he was so aggressively rapacious towards his clients. I found him at his office a couple of days later and, armed only with my trusty *Uher* tape recorder and microphone, asked him, amongst other things, what his qualifications were for running a finance company, apart from being a former professional heavyweight wrestler. Silly question.

By way of reply he grabbed me in a bear hug and threw me down the stairs. The entire encounter was safely recorded on the now crushed *Uher* and I made it back to the studio and put together the story. But not before retrieving the tape spool, which had bounced off down the road, unreeling the tape as it went. I remembered the same thing happening with a reel of news film back in Perth.

This time, I sat on the kerb with a pencil pushed through the middle of the spool and carefully wound all the tape back. Happily, the Turret Mortgage Company went out of business shortly after the programme, but – sadly – long before the authorities got round to regulating the activities of those offering financial services.

The public response to what we broadcast was amazing.

Letters started arriving addressed to me personally, starting with phrases like: 'It takes a brave man to do what you do, you should have a look at this company . . .' We had unwittingly tapped into a huge well-spring of public concern. Complaints about finance companies, crooked businesses and even large institutions and government departments flooded in. Some of them ended up on air as the genesis of *World At One* items, which gave Andrew Boyle and me an idea.

On the basis of what the public was telling us, there looked to be scope for a series of radio programmes founded on investigations. And it was clear that the remit should be to examine injustice, criminality and bureaucratic bungling.

To anyone reading this now, that sounds pretty obvious. But in the late sixties and early seventies, there was no such thing as investigative broadcast journalism as we've come to know it. Sure, there was *The Braden Beat* on television, but it treated matters humorously, ending with a virtual nudge in the ribs, and a sly wink – as if to say: 'Please don't take us so seriously as to take us to task.' There was also *You and Yours* on Radio Four – but that was all about consumer affairs and value for money. It was worth doing, but it could hardly be described as hard-hitting.

Although Andrew Boyle became a firm believer in the validity of an investigative radio programme, persuading the powers that be to get on board was another matter. The Controller of Radio Four was a man called Tony Whitby. He was familiar with my work at *The World At One*, but though he quite liked some of the pieces I was doing, he didn't accept that there was scope for a whole series of exposés. He also thought that I would open a Pandora's Box of further complaints and repercussions.

He had nicknamed me 'The Colonial Pirate', coupling my membership of WATO's Colonial Contingent with my alleged reputation as a bit of a swashbuckler. He declined several invitations to listen to the pilot programme that Andrew and I had put together outside office hours. I heard on the grapevine that he thought I was too brash and determined for my own good and he was not about to let me loose with my own series.

For the next 18 months I plugged away at *The World This Weekend* and *The World At One*. The letters kept on coming in from the public, and were filed away for future reference in case the series ever came to pass. Some actually made it to air on WATO. They ranged hugely in subject matter from large-scale, high-pressure, door-to-door sales rip-offs to the press treatment suffered by Jess Yates, who presented a Yorkshire Television religious programme, *Stars On Sunday*.

The tabloids had pilloried him for his private love-life and effectively hounded him off the screen, dubbing him 'The Bishop'. They accused him of having an affair with a much younger woman, but neglected to mention that he had been legally separated from his wife for ten years. They raised his age and lowered hers to make the relationship look more inappropriate.

The couple had done nothing wrong, but they couldn't go anywhere without a long lens focusing on them or another piece of speculative tittle-tattle being published. (Who knows what Jess would have made of the 1990s disclosure that Paula, the daughter he doted on, was actually fathered by Hughie Green?

We took up this unwarranted invasion of Jess's privacy and decided to give the newspapers involved a dose of their own medicine.

Two senior reporters found themselves the subject of the same kind of impromptu interview to which they had subjected the hapless Mr Yates. One paper even threatened to issue a writ without realising that one of its own executives had given us an interview largely confirming what we had said in our report. The writ was never served.

I might have pursued press injustice even harder if I had known then what I do now, having had my own private life examined closely – and inaccurately – in recent years.

The intransigence of the BBC was making me impatient. The sense of iniquity I used to feel back in Australia about the college authorities who condoned the bullying at Yanco and the management at the ABC with its head-in-the-sand attitude was fast bringing me to a new confrontation at Broadcasting House.

I decided to storm the bastion of power. I grabbed Andrew Boyle from his office one evening and dragged him down the corridor to Tony Whitby's offices. I told his secretary that Andrew and I would wait outside his door until he agreed to listen to our pilot programme. Poor Andrew just nodded helplessly in agreement.

The tape was duly passed through to Whitby by his secretary and, after sitting for an hour wondering whether I'd done the right thing, she came out and told us we could have an audience in the inner sanctum.

Whitby sat hunched over a large sheet of paper covered in small, inked squares each filled with cramped, indecipherable lettering. He was hard at work on a corner of his sheet with a huge eraser.

He ignored us for a full minute and then looked up: "In case you're wondering what I'm doing, I'm putting your series into the programme schedules. It's going to work, gentlemen," he said, as if he'd known it all along.

Sadly, a few weeks later Bill Hardcastle died. He and Andrew Boyle had been incredibly close and Bill's death seemed to knock the dynamism out of Andrew. I needed him to help fight my corner as we geared up to make the new series, but he just didn't have the heart to commit himself to it and plainly felt that he had to channel his remaining energy into *The World At One*.

I then made the mistake of going away on holiday. When I came back I found that the new programme had been transferred to another department. Instead being part of News, it would now be produced by CAMP – Current Affairs Magazine Programmes – the same people who ran *You and Yours*.

They were pleasant enough people, but they seemed to have no real idea of how this newly commissioned series had been conceived – what ground it was to cover and in what style. What was more, they had chosen the name of the new show in my absence – it was to be called 'Checkpoint' and it was to be another consumer programme. I wasn't even given an office, just the corner of someone else's desk. There was no researcher or secretary and we were expected to function on an almost non-existent budget.

All the same, if the new series was to go ahead at all, I had to keep quiet and bide my time – and I had to keep working a full rota at *The World At One*. Indeed, even after *Checkpoint* was up and running, I continued to do so for five years.

As we got underway, it became obvious that producing a programme like *Checkpoint* was going to involve something of a culture change at the BBC. Some within the hierarchy were horrified by what I was beginning to do. It was almost unheard of, for example, to mention the names of firms and advertisers on the air – critically or otherwise. Nobody had ever gone so far as to carry out research into suspect companies or individuals without their full knowledge of the investigation, let alone broadcast the results, but that's exactly what we did.

The previous form had been to go, more or less cap in hand, to the subject of your 'investigation' to ask for co-operation. If that wasn't forthcoming, that was probably the end of the programme.

Our very first programme proved, in the words of the series producer, Walter Wallich, to be a 'baptism of fire'. We decided to investigate the monopoly that opticians then enjoyed in the supply of spectacles – and the resultant over-pricing and over-prescribing. In what was then an original approach, we sent the same undercover 'patients', first to eye hospitals and then to opticians. We were not surprised to discover that profit-motivated opticians were many times more likely to recommend glasses than were the eye hospitals.

The opticians' professional body complained direct to the BBC's Director General, disputing our figures and saying its spokesman had been interviewed too aggressively and hadn't been given enough air time to put their case. Apparently, they thought he should have been given half the programme.

The fuss over that broadcast and others that followed unnerved some in senior management. They decided that a way had to be found to rein the programme in – to turn it back into a relatively inoffensive consumer programme. That avenue opened when the target of a subsequent programme wrote to complain about my lack of deference and my allegedly iniquitous treatment of him.

After he had refused a formal interview, I'd had the temerity to attempt an interview in the street. He was sent a letter from BBC middle management inviting him to complain again, more forcefully, in a form suggested in the letter. They apparently also put forward other complaints he might care to make against me.

There were plenty of people around who wanted me to fail and I imagine they rubbed their hands with glee when I was temporarily suspended without pay.

However, the complainant, who despite his commercial failings must have been a fair-minded man, eventually responded in a way my masters did not expect. He wrote back to say he did not wish to be manipulated into becoming a rod to beat me with. And he didn't wish to pursue the matter further because, on reflection – though he didn't much like what I'd done or how I'd done it – I was only trying to do my job after all.

The 'internal investigation' dragged on for a few months more. One of the department's senior producers, who felt she too had been manipulated into voting for my suspension, resigned in protest. I was back on air, but without backpay. Mind you, I didn't starve in the interim, because I was still working 40 hours a week at *The World At One*. And when I was given my baby back, that meant working 80 to 100 hours a week, 44 weeks a year.

Despite the faltering start, it's only fair to record that those executives who took the trouble to find out at first hand how *Checkpoint* operated were very supportive – and that something as radical as the programme then was would probably not have got going at all outside the BBC.

Surprisingly, the most supportive group of all turned out to be our BBC lawyers. Once they'd got the hang of how the programme was made and the standards to which we worked, they ceased to be part of the 'Programme Prevention Department'. I have fond memories of the late Tony Jennings, then the BBC's Senior Legal Adviser. After listening to a preview tape of an early *Checkpoint* and having considered the accompanying file of evidence, he asked a few questions of me and the producer and then fell silent. This, and his furrowed brow, made us worry that he was about to pull the programme.

After what seemed like an eternity he said: "The question is not whether you'll get a writ, but how many and when. But I think the programme is justified, responsible and defensible – and you should go ahead and broadcast it." He was right. There were several writs, real or threatened, but after a robust response from Tony, not one of them was pursued.

Ten years on he still held us in high regard. In a contemporary press interview, he had this to say: "Because the programme has broken new ground and continues to do so, it constantly challenges accepted ideas, and has changed the way we think about investigative journalism. And what I find particularly interesting is that after so many years of intense operation, the programme is still stimulating. It hasn't become 'show biz'. More importantly, it still goes after real targets, not soft options." I couldn't have put it better myself, Tony.

Legal eagles like Tony Jennings, Rhory Robertson, Glen del Medico, Ron Bennett and Roger Law were actually our security blanket. But they never smothered us, and without them, there were some in management, and some others in the Legal Department, who might have done just that. However, once we were safely established, I could rely on support from one of Tony Whitby's successors, Monica Sims, and also from the Head of Radio 4, Richard Wade.

I loved radio – and still do. It is more immediate, more direct and less cumbersome than television. Somehow you feel you're addressing the audience directly, as individuals. And without the necessity for a phalanx of supporting technicians, it's as much of a hands-on business as you want it to be. In my case, I did all my own tape editing and scripting, and was able to choose, or at least approve, the subjects we covered.

In our first series we tackled a huge variety of subjects, 90 per cent of which were prompted by listeners who got in touch with us. We examined exploited au pair girls, cowboy estate agents, the movement and dumping of toxic waste, fairground safety, pyramid selling and computer crime. It's both sad and surprising that most of these subjects are still giving cause for concern more than a quarter of a century later.

During the course of our early work, we upset the National Housebuilders Registration Council by allowing our contributors to question the worth of the NHBC guarantee scheme and the undue influence this flawed system exerted on the granting of mortgages. The Council protested to the Director General, then to the Chairman of the BBC Board of Governors. The NHBC's complaints were rejected, but in 1974 the BBC felt it wise to introduce a formal code of practice to guide us. We were then given a series of guidelines that were, by and large, sensible – covering subjects like secret tape recording of interviews and where possible attempting to balance the arguments of both sides in a disputatious programme.

I found it rather amusing that most of these guidelines were remarkably similar to the *Checkpoint* in-house code of practice that I had penned nearly two years previously. It was later expanded and refined in collaboration with senior researcher David Perrin, and I have followed that code throughout my career. I won't go into detail, but here's a flavour of the controls we imposed upon ourselves:

Except where we knew we were dealing with a hardened criminal, or someone we had good reason to believe would 'do a runner' rather than answer the questions, we would give the subject at least a week's notice of any proposed interview and a clear outline of the areas we wished to discuss.

Where possible, we would attempt to minimise collateral damage to innocent colleagues and family by arranging to interview our target alone, at or near his business premises and away from his home. We also kept the uncut original of the interview to prove that our editing had been fair.

We would not secretly record anyone who did not already have a proven record for the particular type of dubious activity we were investigating. We would act as *agents provocateur*, but only to offer our targets the opportunity to demonstrate what they habitually did for a living.

Meanwhile, our reputation was growing. Around 400 letters a week were arriving from members of the public. We were given more staff – ending up with a producer, a co-producer/senior researcher and three researchers. We even got a suite of three small offices on the seventh floor of Broadcasting House, overlooking Parliament Hill.

At the height of *Checkpoint*'s 12-year run, around 1985, we had over two million listeners, and were second only to the *Today* programme in popularity. We started to win awards, we helped get laws changed and criminals gaoled – and, rightly or wrongly, I earned the sobriquet of 'The Most Beaten Up Journalist in Britain'. Unfortunately, it was pretty much inevitable that violence occurred. So often we pursued criminals and demanded explanations from them in programmes that could easily – and sometimes did – result in prosecution and imprisonment.

In all, I was assaulted 16 times at *Checkpoint*. I suffered broken ribs, concussion, fractures, lacerations and bruises. But there is one incident that people still remind me about to this day – astonishing when you consider it happened over 25 years ago and injured no more than my pride.

We were investigating two families – the Sumners and the Randals – who had been systematically ripping off the British public on a grand scale through adverts offering useless or non-existent goods or services in exchange for money sent by post – money which was not returned when the goods or services inevitably failed to materialise.

When we were about to catch up with them they tried to pretend they had packed up and emigrated to Australia, but we found them living just outside Penrith in Cumbria, still running their web of fraudulent companies. I don't like confrontations, but the purpose of *Checkpoint* was to report first-hand where possible, and so I waded in.

The Sumners and the Randals swore so much – even during the edited version of the interview – that we had to get special permission from the Managing Director of Radio to broadcast it, even with bleeps inserted where necessary.

For the record, this is how the BBC preserves the edited text of that encounter:

> (Sound of Cook knocking on the Sumners' door.)
> COOK: Mr Randal?
> RANDAL: Yeah?
> COOK: Could I speak to you and Mr Sumner, please, about your business activities and about firms like Interlink and Randal Travel Publications?
> RANDAL: No.
> COOK: My name is Roger Cook from the BBC *Checkpoint* programme and I've come to interview you now. . . . There are many things you ought to talk to us about. . . . Would you like to call Mr Sumner, please? . . . We know he's in. . . . There

are many, many dissatisfied customers of the business ventures you tried to mount all over the world. . . . Have you nothing to say? (A woman appears.) Ah, you are Mrs Sumner?

MRS SUMNER: Who are you?

COOK: My name is Cook, from the BBC *Checkpoint* programme.

MRS SUMNER: Fuck off, or you'll get swilled.

COOK: I beg your pardon? . . . An explanation is due . . .

(A chamber pot is emptied over Cook from an upstairs window.)

MRS SUMNER: Fuck off!

The slightly bizarre thing about that confrontation – and many others – was that because radio is a non-visual medium, I had to give a running commentary about what was happening as well as attempting to ask the key questions: 'that was the sound of a chamber pot being emptied over me' or words to that effect had to be uttered at the appropriate point. On other occasions, the question and the commentary might be combined, as in: 'What do you think you're doing with that baseball bat?'

After Mrs Sumner had 'swilled' me, Messrs Randal and Sumner charged into the road after me, knocked me down and ripped open the tape recorder in an attempt to get at the tape. Their unsuccessful efforts were broadcast to the nation and the subsequent police investigation led to the arrest of both families. Randal went free, but his wife got 18 months and Gordon and Barbara Sumner were gaoled for five and three years respectively.

What I remember most vividly though, was what happened immediately after the event. The stakeout had taken a couple of hours. It was 11 o'clock at night, I smelt revolting and I was a long way from my hotel. I was so keen to clean and deodorise myself that I stuck some money in a local all-night car wash and walked through it fully clothed. I didn't mind the second soaking, because this time it was only soapy water.

I have sustained accidental damage to myself at work, even when villains weren't involved. When *The World This Weekend* sent me to interview the then Lord Chancellor, Quentin Hogg, at his home on Putney Common, he had warned me to beware of 'strange men' on the Common, but hadn't thought it necessary to warn me about his neighbour's maniacal Alsatian dog. As I left after the interview, the snarling animal hurdled the fence and sank its fangs into my right thigh. I was taken to hospital pouring with blood, needing 14 stitches in my leg and a whole lot more in my trousers, but the interview still made it onto the programme.

Not that I always need to put myself in harm's way to sustain personal damage. I am rumoured to be one of the most accident prone people on the planet.

During the early *World At One* days and before *Checkpoint* got going, there was never any firm guarantee that my employment would last. I was on a rolling short-term contract that meant the BBC could kiss me goodbye at any time, so I decided to keep my private freelance work going. When the chance came to make a short promotional film for The Reliant Motor Company, I jumped at it. I also bought one of their four-wheeled vehicles, a handsome Scimitar sports estate.

The film was to be about a manufacturing project in Turkey and it was to be a memorable trip. Reliant had realised that amongst the things that an emerging nation wants most are an airline and a car plant. They had made themselves expert in setting up the latter at an affordable price, supplying the designs, the tooling and the know-how. On this occasion they were helping to realise the dreams of a local multi-millionaire called Vebi Koch, who had built a suitable factory at Scutari, near the site of Florence Nightingale's hospital during the Crimean War.

He arranged to have me and my cameraman, Hugh Davey, met at Yesilkoy Airport. The solid, taciturn man he sent turned out to be Kemal Ataturk's former bodyguard. Obviously still a man of influence, he had us waved through Customs and Immigration without any of the usual formalities. We discovered that he still drove the founding President's car, an enormous American luxo-barge, complete with a couple of bullet holes in the windscreen which had been neatly sealed with chewing gum.

As our ferry crossed the Bosphorus from the European to the Asian side of Istanbul, the water suddenly became unaccountably choppy. "Earthquake," remarked our driver tersely. He was right. When we eventually got to the site of our intended hotel, a site was what we saw. Much of the building was being taken away in wheelbarrows. "Better find another one then," said Hugh – a laid-back expatriate Brit who had been my first cameraman in Western Australia.

Turkey's new car was to be called the Anadol, which sounds like something you'd take for a headache – and filming it certainly was. To a man, all the drivers seconded to filming duties seemed to be would-be rally pilots, determined to impress. Hugh miraculously escaped injury when during our final shoot, the car he was filming *and* the one he was filming from both rolled over.

Back at our substitute hotel, we thought we'd earned a relaxing last night. Unfortunately, Hugh overdid it on a particularly potent, Pernod-like liqueur called Raki – which, we were to discover, had a delayed action kick.

In the morning, with a sore head and a dry mouth, Hugh seems to have thought a swim would sort him out. But first he swilled down a couple of pints of water – with the result that he was drunk all over again. He leapt through the French doors of his room and straight into the swimming pool – which had been drained overnight for repairs.

Fortunately his room was not adjacent to the deep end. "I suppose it's heartening to see this sort of thing happening to someone else for a change," he wheezed as I helped him to his feet. Somehow he'd escaped serious injury and we got home safely to complete the film. I was on my way to show it to Reliant's bosses when my turn came round again.

I set off from London in the Scimitar on an early spring morning. I had patted the bonnet as I left home and told the car it was going home to its birthplace for the day. I zoomed up the A5 towards Reliant HQ in Tamworth with my expensive camera equipment stowed carefully behind the back seat.

Princess Anne had just been caught by the police for speeding in her Scimitar and, as a long stretch of road opened up ahead of me, I thought, 'Well, what are the chances of two relatively rare cars like ours being stopped in the same week?' I glanced around, checked my mirrors and put my foot to the floor. But the adrenalin rush that followed had an entirely different cause.

From the front of the car came the acrid smell of burning wiring. This was followed by the unwelcome sight of flames beginning to lick from beneath the bonnet, and because there was then no fire retardant in a Scimitar's fibreglass body, those flames soon threatened to engulf the whole car. I pulled into an approaching lay-by and jumped out, sprinting across the A5 to avoid incineration. A police patrol car, alerted by the thick pall of smoke hanging over the road, screeched to a halt beside me. The driver coned off the lay-by and radioed for a fire engine.

That was when I remembered that the insurance on my camera equipment had expired just before the weekend. I had been too busy to renew it.

The fire engine arrived and soon put out what was left of the fire. The police and I recrossed the road and stood surveying the smouldering and blackened remains of the car.

At this point, a 32-tonne articulated lorry approached the scene. The driver, who I later discovered had gone well over his regulation hours, chose that moment to fall asleep at the wheel. His truck ploughed through the middle of us. Blue uniforms and yellow fire helmets scattered everywhere. A lorry tyre scrunched over a policeman's foot and the front wing of the truck hit me full on, sending me flying 20 feet through the air. I landed on a grit bin at the far end of the lay-by and rolled into a ditch full of stinging nettles. I think that's what they call adding insult to injury.

I was taken to the Hospital of St. Cross in Rugby where, after emergency treatment, I was trolleyed to the only available bed. It was in the geriatric ward. I had two fractured vertebrae and was trussed up like a chicken. The smell from the longer-term occupants of the ward with their relentless diet of over-cooked cabbage and root vegetables was unspeakable. I tried to have sympathy, but I was in too much pain.

Then the ward sister discovered that I worked for the BBC and brought me a sheaf of comedy scripts she had written and insisted that I should pass them to the Light Entertainment Department. Add to this that Madeline and I had been having a rough time recently. She had also found it very hard to come and visit me as we no longer owned a car, and I hadn't seen her for over a week. I was anxious to get home and sort things out. Against medical advice, I decided to discharge myself.

It would have been impossible for me to catch a train or sit in a taxi for any length of time, so I called Chris Drake, a friend in the BBC radio newsroom in London, and begged him to come and take me away. As soon as he had agreed and put the phone down I realised my mistake. Chris and I shared a passion for powerful sports cars and he was bound to turn up in something barely big enough to carry a pair of double-jointed midgets.

I was right. Some hours later, Chris pulled into the 'Ambulances Only' parking space at the front of Casualty in a bright red E-Type Jaguar coupé. I tottered out to meet him in a surgical collar and pyjamas topped with a tweed sports jacket.

The hospital insisted that I be strapped to something to help keep my spine stable and the Jaguar's tiny bucket seat clearly wasn't that something. It was removed and stowed behind the driver. Then a junior houseman had a bright idea and spoke to some workmen repairing a wall outside.

Minutes later the young doctor had laid a short length of scaffolding plank down the passenger side of the car and applied some padding in the form of a sleeping bag that Chris happened to have on board. I was carefully lowered onto it by three disbelieving porters and secured to the plank with crepe bandages. I lay at a shallow angle with my head just short of the rear window and my feet tucked under the dashboard. In this awkward, slightly comical position I was ready to make my escape.

Five weeks lying in a hospital ward largely populated by senile old men had left me depressed. I had had ample time to reflect on the uninsured loss of my camera equipment and whether my injuries – which would take some time to heal, if they healed at all – would mean that my British broadcasting career would never get off the ground again.

I put these morbid thoughts to one side as we arrived at the flat Madeline and I shared in Highgate. The makeshift padding turned out to be next to useless, so the journey had been pretty uncomfortable. I had felt every bump and pothole on the way as my back jarred against the unyielding plank. I thanked Chris profusely as he undid the fastenings and stood me upright on the pavement.

"Come up for a drink, mate, you deserve it," I suggested.

"I'd like to see you make it up the stairs without me," he grinned.

With a lot of grunting and grimacing I shuffled and limped my way up three flights of stairs to the door of the flat, Chris solicitously holding my elbow and pushing when required. I fumbled for the keys and let us in. Madeline wasn't in; she was probably at work at Crawley de Reya – forerunners of Mishcon de Reya, then the Queen's solicitors – where she was blazing a trail as a media law specialist.

I hobbled slowly across to the drinks cabinet in the corner of the kitchen. I noticed a small, white envelope on the table, but left it until Chris and I had downed a stiff Macallan and he had gone on his way.

I returned to the kitchen, sat down gingerly at the table and picked up the envelope. It was addressed to me in Madeline's neat handwriting. I opened it and read the short note. She had left me. She was sorry, we had tried everything, but we were fundamentally unsuited and our relationship was over. She was going to stay with some friends for the time being and she had already taken her personal possessions. I could keep the rest.

At first I was stunned, then rang every friend I could think of, without result. Were they lying or was she? I wasn't to know that she had actually gone to live in France.

While success was beginning to come for me, I still had no job security. I had been lurching from one short-term contract to another at the BBC, but Madeline had already put her foot firmly on the bottom rung of the legal ladder and started to climb. Her rise was inexorable. Although a newcomer, she impressed the partners with her grasp of her chosen branch of the law. She was spoken of as a future star, and, while my meagre income dribbled inadequately into the household, her regular and increasingly-fat pay packet kept us going and even paid for a few luxuries – like the now defunct Scimitar.

In my unreconstructed chauvinist state in the early 1970s I suppose I resented the fact that Madeline had become the main breadwinner. To some extent it was a surprising attitude for someone whose own father had stood idly by while his wife gathered the children up and decamped to the outback to skivvy for sheep shearers just to keep a roof over their heads and food in their mouths.

It was a source of tension, but Madeline never argued, she just fell inscrutably silent, which I found even more difficult to deal with. To my great shame, I sometimes resorted to shouting at her. With hindsight, I was still pretty immature. I had driven her away I suppose, and I had no right to miss her – but I did.

I was nothing without her, I thought. And I hurt, physically and emotionally. I might not be able to work again either. I began to think it was not worth carrying on. I eyed the almost full bottle of Macallan on the sideboard, and the bottle of powerful dihydrocodeine pain killers that I'd been given at the hospital.

I poured out another dram and emptied the pain killers into a saucer. Was now the time to call it a life? I sat and stared into the glass for what seemed like hours. Then the phone rang. It was Andrew Boyle, bless him, asking how I was and when I might be able to come back to work. I downed the dram – and slowly put the pills back in the bottle.

Fortunately, the spectre of being alone, jobless and, to cap that, physically impaired, soon began to fade. Andrew Boyle arranged for me to be fetched and propped up in the corner of the studio conducting interviews and editing my material, and I eased myself back into my work. Between us we kept the preparation of *Checkpoint* going and eventually, with the help of the physiotherapists of the Whittington and North Middlesex Hospitals, I got independently mobile again. I also got some compensation from the lorry driver's employers, but I was left with a permanent bad back and, as I've mentioned already, a partially deaf left ear.

As a present to myself and as a respite before *Checkpoint* was officially unveiled, I took a week's holiday in Ibiza. I have never been a beach bum type, so I chose to stay in a small hotel in Ibiza town, close to the old bullring.

I spent the first two days asleep in my room, grateful not to have to get up and get on the Tube to the Beeb. Then I started to explore and discover the delights of the harbour and its wonderful restaurants. Over the next couple of days, I sampled the *zarzuela* – the Iberian equivalent of bouillabaisse – and some wonderful *riojas*.

Batteries recharged, I decided to hire a small car and head off to the beaches on the south coast. I left the harbour in search of a car hire office. Halfway down the street, my world suddenly imploded. I felt a terrific blow to my neck and shoulders and collapsed onto the pavement. Something heavy was pinning me to the ground. There was a lot of shouting and I heard footsteps running towards me. The wind had been completely knocked out of me and I didn't have the breath to shout for help. Then I lost consciousness.

When I came round I was lying in a hospital bed in the firm grip of a surgical collar. My first thought was that I had been mysteriously transported back to the geriatric ward in Rugby. I looked around – even small movements were very painful – and remembered Ibiza, leaving the restaurant and the terrific crash. But what had happened?

A few hours later, a Spanish doctor and an interpreter from the British consulate came to my bedside to explain that I had unwittingly been responsible for saving the life of one of Ibiza's foreign residents. The interpreter told me that the man, a German hippie in his early forties, had a history of depression and of taking hallucinogenic drugs. The two elements had unhappily combined just before I chose to stroll underneath his third-floor balcony. I had innocently interceded between suicidal hippie and pavement, leaving me with severe concussion and two broken collar bones. Was this fate paying me back for causing the same injuries to that racist thug back in Perth?

As for the hippie, he wandered aimlessly away from the scene, apparently unhurt, and survives to this day for all I know.

I was determined to take a relaxing break at some stage in the immediate future. After the first, successful run of 44 *Checkpoints*, and once we had been assured by our masters at the BBC that we would have another series, I telephoned an old chum from Sydney who had recently been appointed the manager of one of the best hotels on the beautiful Caribbean island of St Lucia. His euphoria over the promotion prompted an offer of a heavily-discounted stay at the hotel. All I had to do was pay for my flights. Just what I needed.

The holiday season hadn't quite started when I arrived, but there was to be a lavish welcoming party in the newly-refurbished ballroom for the few dozen guests who were already in residence, me included. I had even brought my tuxedo with me – not bad for someone who only wears a tie about twice a decade.

I was just easing myself into a second Martini and was about to walk, Bond-like, over to a small group of attractive young ladies when I heard a loud metallic snapping noise above my head. Then came the blackness to which I had by now become accustomed.

The main chandelier, which had been taken down and put into storage during refurbishment, apparently hadn't been anchored properly when it was replaced. All its weight had been trusted to one, inadequate cable. When the inevitable happened, guess who was standing directly underneath.

Miraculously, considering the weight of the chandelier, no bones were broken, but I did have to spend the remaining ten days of my dream holiday lying concussed in a darkened room listening enviously to the squeals and shouts of my fellow guests enjoying themselves in the swimming pool below my window.

In the late 1970s, *Checkpoint* regularly worked on co-productions with the BBC1 early evening magazine show *Nationwide*. One of these concerned an expensive supposed cure for blindness in which sufferers had to submit to being stung by bees – and were later stung financially by a strange Middle European lady.

I took one of her victims for a walk along the shores of Lake Windermere, which he loved to visit. Sadly, he wouldn't be able to see it for much longer and we were filming what was a very poignant interview when he stumbled on some rocks. I managed to dive forward and make a grab for him before he fell into the lake. In fact, he stayed dry and I flew straight past him into the water, dislocating my shoulder en route in an effort to halt my headlong progress by grabbing at a another rock.

The local doctor who levered my arm back into place suggested that my injury might have been aggravated by my weight. He was not the first, nor will he be the last to have commented on my size. Usually, it's the tabloids. Sadly, I've had a weight problem since knackered knees forced me to give up playing Rugby when I was in my mid-twenties. I love good food and wine, and friends have unkindly suggested I should have given *them* up instead of Rugby. From long experience, I say diets make you fat and television screens make you look even fatter, even when you're not wearing a bulletproof vest under your shirt.

My uncanny ability to attract personal injury from positions of complete safety became legendary in BBC Radio. At my leaving party from *The World At One*, they presented me with a T-shirt that bore the simple legend: 'Stand clear. I'm an accident waiting to happen.' The engineers, responsible for repairing many items of recording equipment damaged by my reluctant interviewees, gave me a *Uher* microphone bent in half and beautifully mounted on a mahogany presentation plinth.

Of course, not all my work on *The World At One* put me at personal risk. A good deal of it involved producing the radio equivalent of newspaper features and interviewing politicians. This too could be interesting – and entertaining – stuff. You often got to learn more about politicians in *The World At One*'s cramped, cream-painted hospitality room than you did by reading the cuttings on them. One lunch-time in that very hospitality room, George Brown, the infamously inebriated Labour MP for Belper, both confirmed his reputation and allowed a small insight into his real character.

He arrived, pre-refreshed as it were, complaining that interviews were a chore he could well do without. He could also probably have done without his public face, which in the tabloids at least, had more than once been seen upturned in the gutter as he fell over the kerb or out of a taxi.

However, the interview had to be done, and it should be said he performed very well. Perhaps that's because I adhered to George Brown's rules for interviewing George Brown. "Listen, lad," he'd confided earlier, an over-generous gin and tonic in hand, "this is the first time you've had the pleasure, so always remember, before the third G&T I'm not worth interviewing, and after the fifth I'm not capable of being interviewed!"

Maurice Macmillan liked a drink, too, perhaps because he found the job of Secretary of State for Employment at the time of the miners' strike too much for him. His grandfather, Harold, had often played the duffer, but plainly wasn't. Maurice, sad to say, wasn't playing. I arrived at his Sussex estate on Sunday morning to prerecord the big interview for *The World This Weekend*. I was shown into the drawing room where tea for two was immaculately laid out, and just being poured.

The butler explained that Mr Macmillan would be down very shortly and indicated that I should take tea while I waited. He handed me a cup, having added the milk requested. I'm glad it was only he in the firing line and not my prospective interviewee. The 'tea' tasted suspiciously like gin and as it hit the back of my unsuspecting throat, it brought on a coughing fit that had the 'tea' all over the butler's waistcoat.

It was only 9:30, but when Mr Macmillan arrived and sat down, it became obvious that he'd already had some tea. I did my best with the interview, solemnly thanked my interviewee and he ushered me outside to the spot where I'd parked the car. It wouldn't start, and the amiable Mr Macmillan offered to help push-start it. I didn't think this was a good idea, but he insisted. My last sight of

Her Majesty's Secretary of State was of his upended legs as he turned turtle on his perfectly groomed drive.

Back at the studio, it was quickly decided that the interview would barely survive as a sound-bite. Andrew Boyle was sympathetic. Despite the difficulties, he remarked wryly, I'd come back with one of the most sensible answers anyone had ever got out of Maurice Macmillan: "I'm sorry; I didn't understand your question."

I got an even shorter performance out of Reginald Maudling, one sunny Sunday morning in his Hertfordshire garden. The first question, again following (this time unadulterated) tea, involved reading out an extract from Hansard. The warmth of the morning, the buzz of the bees, perhaps the drone of my voice, had an unfortunate result. Mr Maudling fell asleep. My recorded attempts to rouse the somnolent and latterly snoring Home Secretary so embarrassed him that he decided to postpone the interview to another, less relaxed occasion.

By contrast, Lord Carrington was very much on the ball when I interviewed him at his elegant Buckinghamshire manor house. This was the time of the first oil crisis, and he was Minister for Energy. I had arrived slightly early, and was pacing aimlessly about on the front steps when, to my surprise, His Lordship rolled up in a seven-litre Jensen Interceptor. I was welcomed inside, and the interview turned out to be a fair example of civilised cut and thrust, the results of which I imagine pleased us both.

After the recording we chatted about politics and politicians in general, and I eventually summoned up the courage to draw his attention to his current mode of transport in particular. Was a seven-litre, gas-guzzling behemoth, however stylish, an appropriate vehicle for the man in charge of energy in an oil crisis? The atmosphere, still civilised, seemed to cool somewhat, and I departed fearing that I may have overstepped the mark.

The following week, my fears seemed to have been realised when I got a call from Broadcasting House reception. Could I come down immediately please as Lord Carrington wished to see me? The lift doors eased open and His Lordship, standing in the marble foyer, beckoned me outside. There, at the kerb sat a gleaming 1.3 litre Radford Mini Cooper. "The Jensen's in moth-balls now," he said, "I'm driving this instead." His face cracked into a smile. "Satisfied?" With that, and a mock genuflection, he drove off down Regent Street, waving regally as he went.

Politicians can, of course, be over-confident – as was Stanley Clinton-Davis during an interview he gave me when he was a Labour Trade Minister in the early seventies. The subject was the new regulations he wished to impose on Britain's inshore fishing fleet. All the vessels in the fleet would have to pass a stability test, which was, said the trawler men, completely inappropriate for the type of boat involved. Most would fail, and this in turn would result in widespread bankruptcies.

I'd originally heard of this problem on a local radio programme while on location in Devon, and had sought out the most vocal complainant, one Stan French. He was to become a lifelong friend and was pivotal in the making of the television film that followed. Stan was a big man in every sense of the word, with silver-grey hair, a mahogany complexion and a Devon accent so broad that the editor suggested subtitles.

With his help, and that of a few of his friends and sympathisers, we tested the Fisheries Protection vessel involved in administering the stability test. During the interview, Mr Clinton-Davis would not hear of the new EU-driven regulations being inappropriate. "These fishing boats are dangerous," he insisted. 'Better bankrupt than dead' was the thrust of his argument. With a little encouragement, he made it crystal clear that he thought anyone who went out in a potentially unstable boat or permitted the use of one was grossly irresponsible.

The look on his face when we presented him with the proof of failure of his own Fisheries Protection vessel was something to behold. The inshore fishing fleet kept on fishing, and Stan French's beloved boat *Our Adriatic* – which had also failed the stability test – won the next annual Brixham trawler race and went on trawling safely until she, and Stan, retired.

Long after Enoch Powell had retired, he was still in demand as an interviewee. On the publication of one of his many books, *No Easy Answers*, I went round to his Eaton Place home to talk to him. The interview was entirely consistent with the title of the book and amounted to his usual compilation of carefully considered, but not necessarily direct replies.

Afterwards, he asked me if I'd read the book. I had to admit that I'd only had the chance to skim through a review copy, so he asked me if I'd like one of my own. What could I say? Mr Powell retreated into his inner sanctum and returned with a book, which he handed to me. "That will be £10, please", he said. What could I do? Luckily, I had enough cash on me to avoid further embarrassment.

It was always interesting to look at the Duty Officer's Log after a Powell interview, so powerfully did he polarise the audience. But soon afterwards in that same log, following a feature I had done on union militants, came a neat example of how you can't please all of the audience all of the time. There were two listener comments, listed one immediately after the other. The first described my feature as the work of 'a fascist reactionary', while the second thought I must be 'a dipso pinko'. However, since one viewpoint obviously cancelled out the other, I suppose you could argue that the piece must have been perfectly balanced.

On another occasion, shortly after I had finished presenting that day's *PM* programme – and following, it should be said, a couple of well-executed telephone wind-ups from mischievous colleagues – I received a further dubious sounding call. The caller wished to challenge a point made by a Labour MP whom I had just interviewed. "May I ask who's calling?" I enquired. "It's the Bishop of Borneo here," he replied. Suspecting yet another prank, I answered, quick as you like: "And I'm bloody King Canute!" Unfortunately, it really *was* the Bishop of Borneo.

If you think these anecdotes have a slightly vintage feel, that's partly because I haven't done overtly political stories or met politicians on a regular basis for some time now – and partly because they really don't make MPs like they used to. They don't make them like the former Tory Home Secretary, Robert Carr, for example. I remember the occasion when he was unable to answer a particular question in a live, off-the-cuff interview on the *PM* programme. "I don't know about that," he said frankly, "but I should and I'll find out and let you know." This he duly did, less than an hour later, in a personal phone call.

Quite a contrast to Frank Dobson, many years later, when I interviewed him in his capacity as Health Secretary. He was responding to a disturbing *Cook Report Special* on errant and incompetent doctors. He'd insisted on having all the questions in advance, but didn't rule out relevant supplementary questions. On the day, he would answer just one of the agreed questions and threatened to walk out if asked anything else. Times – and attitudes – have changed.

The one thing Mr Dobson did say, however, was that the government would legislate to make it possible for the General Medical Council to strike rogue doctors off the register for life. While our research told us the general public believed that striking off was permanent, the facts were that a lifelong ban was not legally possible, and that many errant doctors were back in practice less than a year later. And that was if they were brought to book at all. But more of this later.

Back in my radio days, the more general features I made for *The World At One* covered a huge range of subjects from the deadly serious to the plain eccentric. My colleagues tell me that one particular item in the latter category is worthy of recall because, they say, it speaks to my character. They may not be entirely serious, but here goes:

We had heard rumours from darkest Wales about an extraordinary man called H. Arnall Bloxham. He had acquired a reputation as a pioneering hypnotherapist who could regress people to previous lives. He obviously had good connections, with a claimed roll-call of famous subjects, from Napoleon to Good Queen Bess. Intrigued, I phoned him and he agreed to be interviewed, but insisted that would be all. So I appealed to his ego and eventually he agreed to be put to the test on tape. I did not know at this stage that Mr Bloxham was, apparently, Sir Walter Raleigh.

In the darkened front room of his gloomy Victorian house in a quiet Cardiff suburb, Mr B. attempted to hypnotise me. He tried various methods, none of which seemed to work. Eventually, according to the observer I brought with me, I succumbed to the cliché of a swinging pocket watch.

I began to ramble on about life on the run and told tales of eighteenth-century derring-do. The whole process took the best part of a day. I described my childhood in the alehouse that my father ran, my long-suffering mother, my apprenticeship to a butcher, my first robbery, and my beautiful black horse – all in great detail. I even described, with some difficulty, my hanging at York in 1739 for the heinous crimes I had committed. You've probably guessed it: I was Dick Turpin, highwayman.

Mr Bloxham later explained that my preoccupation with 'righting wrongs' in this life was a way of making amends for the sins of a past existence. Too good to be true, eh? I think so too. However, having checked my tape with the known facts, what I still can't explain is how I apparently came to know so much accurate detail about a man and a period of English history that I don't recall ever having read about, let alone studied. My colonial education had given preference to an equally bold, but rather more recent 'bush-ranger' called Ned Kelly. It might have been easier to turn me into him. But back to *Checkpoint*.

'Legal' stealing from the public – by companies and individuals manipulating the laws of limited liability became a *Checkpoint* preoccupation. Many a programme exposed those who took your money for goods and services one day and 'went bankrupt' the next, with malice aforethought. They were playing what we came to call the 'change-the-name-and-do-the-same game'. The most successful such player we came across was an egregious Yorkshire-man called Harry Hepworth.

He specialised in home improvements. Wall coatings, roof treat-ments, cavity wall insulation, double-glazing – you name it, some-where in Britain Hepworth had a company doing it – or at least promising to. He was the subject of several *Checkpoint* pro-grammes, including one we titled 'Harry Hepworth, This Is Your Life – of Crime'.

We calculated that he'd had it away with £20 million in cus-tomers' and suppliers' money. He disputed the figure, but boasted that he'd 'turned over more companies than I'd had hot dinners'. And back then, he could do just that – and there was little the law could do about it. We lobbied for change on air and our pleas were heard by the late Sir Kenneth Cork, who chaired the newly formed Insolvency Law Review Committee.

I saw a lot of Sir Ken and we provided him with a great deal of anecdotal and other evidence which he later said had informed his recommendations. These included disqualifying people like Hep-worth from being company directors – and, on the other side of the coin – making the law on personal bankruptcies less draconian.

We showed Sir Ken a number of cases where people were bankrupted – as a result of their own incompetence or carelessness rather than dishonesty – when they had the assets to more than cover their debts. Then all those assets were swallowed up in cumbersome and expensive bankruptcy procedures. Their debts still didn't get paid and people who weren't technically bankrupt were made so by the system. Fortunately, things are different now. Not perfect, but better.

The fraudster with the greatest staying power we unearthed had also been an MP. Dennis Kendall was MP for Mrs Thatcher's home town of Grantham. During the Second World War, he also ran a company making 20mm cannon for Spitfire fighters. Eager for a quick profit from the war effort, he held up deliveries until he got the terms he wanted and was later found to have overcharged the MOD by £1.7 million – the equivalent of around £67 million today.

After the war, his next venture was a £100 'people's car'. He claimed that he would employ 20,000 people, making 100,000 cars a year. Investors were recruited, brochures issued and orders taken, but only two rough prototypes were ever produced and the company went bust in 1946 owing more than half a million pounds – £19 million at current values.

Undeterred, Kendall decamped to California and turned to quack medicine. Then in his seventies, he began a global marketing campaign for a miracle arthritis cure which he said was '80 per cent successful'. He set up clinics in North America and the UK where patients paid £350 for a course of injections.

What they were given was DMSO, or dimethyl sulfoxide, a powerful industrial solvent. Audrey Webb from Leicester, who had suffered from arthritis for 13 years, took the treatment in 1980, with appalling, but sadly typical results. She passed blood in her urine, was virtually paralysed for two months and spent the following six in a wheelchair. Frances Bagley's treatment was followed by a stroke, partial kidney failure and a complete blood transfusion – without which she would have died.

After the programme, the Department of Health issued a warning against the use of DMSO, pointing out that it was untested, unlicensed and unsafe. Kendall's business dried up, but by then, after more than 40 years of fraudulent activity, he had more than enough money to retire in luxury. He spent his final years in a Californian mansion with a kidney shaped swimming pool and an electric organ that would not have disgraced Blackpool Pier. Who says crime doesn't pay?

Kendall was not the only unprincipled ex-MP we targeted, and far from the only quack. As for the latter, none was more bizarre than David and Helen Elizaldes, so-called 'psychic surgeons' based in Australia. They claimed to be able to open a person's body with their bare hands and remove whatever malignancy they had determined was ailing the patient. They had managed to impress the Spiritualists' National Union and its leader, Gordon Higginson, who had sponsored them on a tour of Britain. We were allowed to film them at work, and it certainly *looked* impressive.

The operation site was always the stomach. The soft flesh was kneaded vigorously by Helen Elizaldes, while her husband began pushing wet swabs between her fingers. Bits of matter appeared to have been removed from the bloody stomach area, and it was all over, without any sign of scarring. However, patients promised a cure for their various ailments began to complain within days. For example, the kidney stones said to have been removed from Phillip Towner, were still painful and still showed on X-rays.

We called in American illusionist James Randi, de-bunker extraordinaire, who examined our film closely and dismissed the Elizaldes as mere conjurers. To prove it, we filmed him 'operating' on me. On film his technique appeared identical to that of the 'psychic surgeons' – the heavy massage, the introduction of swabs and the removal of bits of bloody tissue.

Apparently, the trick was to palm onto the massage site a condom filled with pig's blood and pieces of chicken giblets. The condom was then burst and lost in the mess it contained. Randi called this whole process 'digging for gold', since desperate patients had been persuaded to part with a good deal of money.

Gordon Higginson also allowed us to film an 'operation' on him for leg ulcers. This took place at the Spiritualists' National Union headquarters, Stansted Hall, in Essex. Once again, the procedure was performed through the stomach. Unbeknown to Mr Higginson, members of our team took away samples of the blood clots which the Elizaldes had pretended to remove from him, and had them forensically analysed. The results allowed me to ask one of my favourite ever questions: "Mr Higginson, either the Elizaldes are charlatans or you're a pig. Which is it – because you don't appear to be the latter?"

Mr Higginson was clearly shocked, but continued to proclaim his faith in psychic surgery for the rest of the interview. However, shortly after the broadcast, the Elizaldes tour was cancelled and the police told us that they'd be prosecuted if they ever set foot in Britain again.

Another constant theme running through the *Checkpoint* years was property. Where there are substantial sums of money involved, there will always be someone plotting to relieve you of it, and in the area of timeshare and homes in the sun there were some real experts. Paul Prew-Smith was a prime example.

Through his company, Sun Developments, he managed to sell people holiday and retirement homes in Spain which simply didn't exist. You might ask how buyers could be so gullible, but they were flown to Spain for a site visit, met the architect and signed 'official' documents in a lawyer's office. They were even taken to a warehouse to choose their kitchen and bathroom tiles.

Unfortunately, only the tile warehouse was real. The sites didn't belong to Prew-Smith, the architect seems to have been an out of work actor, and the lawyer had long been disbarred. But if you didn't know that, the impression given was that of a well organised and professional business. The man was so plausible that his victims included a main board director of one of Britain's largest public companies and a QC.

Given that Prew-Smith was very good at his nefarious job, he was not so good at answering pertinent questions about it. When I approached him in London's Hanover Square, he jumped into a passing taxi and slammed the door on my hand. As the taxi drove off, and until the driver realised what had happened, I was dragged along beside the vehicle.

When we stopped and I disengaged my hand, I found that the tendon of my index finger had been severed. In the meantime, Prew-Smith had bolted out of the other side of the taxi and disappeared. After the broadcast blew his cover, he gave up selling Spanish property, and after he'd run off down Oxford Street, the taxi driver ran me to hospital – 'no charge Guv'.

Prew-Smith, obviously a dyed-in-the-wool serial fraudster, later became involved in a number of other notorious scams, including The Ostrich Farming Corporation – which cost investors £21 million – and Fisher Prew-Smith, which ran an equity release scheme targeting elderly homeowners. Between them, the homeowners lost £12.5 million.

Prew-Smith had also conned the West Bromwich Building Society into becoming financially involved in Fisher Prew-Smith. When his company failed to pay the compensation the industry regulator had ordered, the High Court disqualified Prew-Smith from acting as a company director, and the West Brom was left to compensate his victims – which they duly did.

Almost in the same league, but specialising more in timeshare, was Graham Maynard. He had timeshares for sale at *El Capistrano* in Spain and in Danny la Rue's former country house hotel, Walton Hall, in Warwickshire. He'd made millions – he claimed £50 million – by either selling property he didn't have title to, or by selling the same timeshare periods in property he did own to several unsuspecting buyers at once. He wasn't keen to answer questions either when approached at a beach side restaurant in Nerja.

He chose three weapons to defend himself – a bowl of boiling hot *moules marinière* which he hurled over me, his Alsatian dog, and a large piece of timber. Fortunately the dog was more interested in licking off the *moules* than biting me, and little damage was done with the piece of four by two. The ensuing programme, however, put paid to his business and he was eventually convicted in the UK on a number of counts, but not sent to prison because of the considerable time he'd already spent in Spanish gaols awaiting extradition.

Robert Miller was another nasty property shark whose territory was closer to home. As the M4 motorway corridor opened up to the west of London, houses along its route became more valuable, because a daily commute into the capital now became feasible. Armed with this knowledge, a glib tongue, several aliases and a range of faked local authority paperwork, this despicable man targeted elderly homeowners in soon-to-be-sought-after areas.

He found many of his targets by researching electoral registers to find voters who had been resident in the one place for a very long time – and were therefore likely to be elderly. He then persuaded them that they would have to move because the County Council was about to compulsorily purchase their homes in order to improve access to the motorway – and he had made the scam difficult to detect by pre-empting the system.

Miller's basic method was to show his victims a false Compulsory Purchase Order and an 'official valuation', and once he'd got them really worried, offer to buy the property for a slightly better price. He claimed that he could afford to do so because he had the contract for the improvement works and a ready market for salvaged building materials. It came as no surprise to learn that he would even arrange the conveyancing at his own expense.

You *would* be surprised how many people fell for this pitch, without checking his credentials or contacting the council. But fall for it they did, and when the dust had settled, Miller was able to sell on the houses he'd fraudulently acquired for three or four times what he had paid for them. The few vulnerable people who found out they had been taken in didn't complain, following threats of violence.

I tracked Miller down to Frome in Somerset, where he led me a merry dance. I had numerous sightings, but no contact. Then came a contact I could have done without. I was walking down a side street when a car mounted the pavement at speed and knocked me down. I woke up in the Royal Victoria Hospital in Frome, aching all over and unable to move my neck. Then, in a scene reminiscent of a B-movie, a face swam into focus above my bed. The face belonged to a ginger-haired Australian doctor, and I asked him how I was. "Jeez, mate," he said, "put it this way, if you weren't built like a brick privy, you'd probably be dead."

No one saw the incident happen, and no one, not even the police, were able to find Miller again after that. It was believed that he'd fled to South America with his ill-gotten gains. Unfortunately, the programme was never completed. I was in hospital for several weeks, and after it became known what had happened to me, none of Miller's victims would go on tape.

The only other *Checkpoint* not to be finished was also scrapped as a result of the witnesses' reluctance to talk. It was a story about an East End fraud involving rival gangs and it gave me a pretty good idea of how it feels to be hunted. On the ground for the first morning of research, a trusted, long-term contact had introduced me to a couple of people with interesting stories to tell. It was arranged that we would meet to record them that afternoon in the Blind Beggar pub on the Mile End Road.

Bells should have rung – since this was the pub where the notorious Kray twins had murdered fellow gangster George Cornell – but they didn't. I was led out the back 'for a bit of privacy' – and given a thorough going over by three thugs. 'Two to hold and one to work', as they used to say. Nothing that showed above my shirt mind you, just three broken ribs and a badly bruised chest. The beating was followed by a warning that worse was to follow if I didn't desist. They could destroy me and my reputation.

Back home a few days later, my next door neighbour noticed

someone going through my rubbish bin one night, and offered to provide a deterrent. They'd just had a baby, and from then on, all their disposable nappies went in my bin. Later that week, my car had paint stripper poured all over it, and the following week, this time while parked at work, it had an incendiary device fitted to it.

I was halfway home when it went off. There was loud bang followed by a sheet of flame which removed my fringe and my eyebrows before I was able to bail out. The car was completely gutted and the fire brigade found the remains of a detonator and a large can of lighter fuel under the dashboard.

By this time I was getting a little nervous, but all was calm for a week or two and I began to relax. Then, returning home one evening, I was greeted by a man you could only describe as looking like an East End villain – scarred face, broken nose and all. I must have flinched, because he told me not to worry and, flashing a semi-automatic pistol at me from under his coat, said he was there to offer me protection.

Apparently, the rogues we had targeted had been ripping off unsuspecting elderly East End locals, some of whom were members of well-known gangland families. "Where I come from, you don't piss on the old folk and you don't crap in your own nest, my son," he said, "so you go ahead and do 'em over and we'll keep 'em off you." I did wonder why he hadn't taken direct action himself, but decided it was better not to ask.

I politely declined his offer, explaining that I couldn't now get anyone to talk to me anyway, and the last thing I wanted was to escalate a small radio programme into a major fire-fight. He mumbled his assent and trudged off into the night. I guess he and his friends must have taken their own disciplinary measures, because no more was heard from either side, and the sum total of *Checkpoints* fell by two.

There were nearly 700 *Checkpoint* programmes in all, and you couldn't fit a fraction of them in one book. All I can do is give a flavour of what we did. And looking at the list, it's amazing how many stories we covered first and how many of the same stories and the same personalities keep coming back.

Sometimes it takes years to get laws changed and villains put away. Take Nicholas van Hoogstraten, for example. In the early seventies we did the first of several exposés of his Rachman-like activities as a landlord. His specialty was buying run-down property with sitting tenants at knock-down prices, and then getting vacant possession by any means he deemed necessary. We met two elderly spinsters he had failed to evict from their basement flat. As a result, they told us, their exterior doors and windows were bricked up.

We discovered that he had a string of convictions and had served a four-year gaol sentence for the firebombing of the home of a rabbi – who fortunately survived the attack. At his trial in 1968, the judge described van Hoogstraten as 'an emissary of the devil'. Van Hoogstraten later said his only regret was that he hadn't gone round himself and 'cut the rabbi's bollocks off'.

He referred to his tenants as 'scum' and 'filth' and subjected them to a reign of terror, cutting off water and electricity, tearing out staircases, removing roofs and walls from their dwellings and organising 'nasty accidents' for those who would not do his bidding. He thrived on, indeed cultivated, his appalling reputation – it made his job easier, he said. His total lack of humanity and morals helped make him a fortune estimated at £200 million, and although regularly in trouble with the law, he avoided imprisonment again until 2003.

Even then, it was not for the brutal way he dealt with his legions of long-suffering tenants, but for ordering a revenge attack on a former business associate, as a result of which the man died. The hit-men got life for murder, but van Hoogstraten was freed on appeal one year into a ten-year sentence for manslaughter, because the judge at his trial had apparently given 'flawed' directions to the jury. This legal farce cost the public purse some £10 million. Sadly, there'll always be a job for good investigative journalists to do – if the prevailing commercial and political climate allows.

As *Checkpoint* consumed more and more of my time and energies, I found it increasingly difficult to work a full rota at *The World At One*, and so made the reluctant decision to leave. That, and the complementary decision to cut the number of *Checkpoint* programmes to 30 per year, would leave me with some time for other projects.

Checkpoint was a remarkably close-knit operation, but as with all success stories, I suppose, jealousies occasionally surfaced. They certainly did as the programme neared its tenth anniversary. My old friend John Wilson had been commissioned to write a book to celebrate the occasion. He had resisted the attempts from some within the BBC to turn it into a kind of school report, filled with laudatory comments about people who had damn all to do with the programme. As a result, and unbeknown to me at the time, John wasn't invited to the tenth anniversary/book launch party. It was a shameful and small minded act.

The party itself, at the Rugby Club of London, just round the corner from Broadcasting House, began well enough. About half-way through the proceedings however, one of our then researchers, Andrew Jennings, burst into the room, gleefully waving a copy of the latest *Private Eye* in which he had managed to plant a string of malicious falsehoods about the programme and its 'incompetent' presenter. Needless to say, the event rather fell flat after that, but happily, the next edition of Lord Gnome's organ carried a letter signed by a dozen of my closest colleagues, setting the record firmly straight. Jennings' contract was not renewed.

My *World At One* years behind me, I embarked upon the making of two well regarded series of hour-long radio documentaries. One, called 'Time For Action', I co-presented with Nick Ross. The other, named with an intentional pun, 'Reel Evidence' won a couple of awards.

Both were largely produced by a slight, bearded, Irish perfection-ist called Ritchie Cogan. They were heady days, some of the most enjoyable of my working life. One of my abiding memories is of Ritchie, in thoughtful mode in the early hours, as we struggled with a script or editing schedule, sitting as he often did, cross-legged and leprechaun-like on top of a large loudspeaker.

In *Time For Action*, Nick and I would champion opposite sides of an issue on behalf of those involved – and then combine forces to take that issue to the organisation responsible. Typical was the edition we made about what then amounted to a feud between fishermen and oilmen in Peterhead.

It was a stimulating format, and I'm surprised no one else took it up and did it with pictures. After all, radio has spawned a number of popular television programmes. *Reel Evidence* was much more straightforward and covered such subjects as the dumping of outdated and outmoded pharmaceutical drugs in what was then called the Third World. It was my first large-scale international foray, and it won one of those awards.

Another in the series won an altogether unique distinction – a transcript of the programme was reprinted in *New Musical Express*, and the broadcast itself was repeated on Radio 1. *Rock Bottom*, as its title implied, was an early exposé of exploitation in the world of pop music.

The biggest shark in the sea at that time was a notorious manager called Don Arden, who seemed to relish his reputation for violence and financial impropriety. He boasted of having suspended one of his own artists by his ankles from a window until the terrified man signed a new contract on Arden's terms. Small Faces guitarist Steve Marriott was said to have had his hand crushed in a vice until he succumbed, and Lynsey de Paul told how Arden drove her to the point of suicide.

Arden knew I was coming, and rather than face the music in person, decamped to Los Angeles. As transcribed, his response when I telephoned him was as bizarre as it was aggressive:

"Roger Cook, you can go fuck yourself, you're already guilty of slander and you'll be served with a writ shortly. If you want to dig up dirt about me, I'll take your last five pounds for [doing] it. I know you've got a tail on me and if I find him I'll break his neck." This wasn't true, so I asked Arden if he'd like to break my neck instead. Arden refused to give a straight answer but said he could thrash me "with one hand shoved up his arse" and invited me to "rot in hell".

He then added a typical Arden challenge: "Mr Cook, you have chosen to destroy me, but if you want to fight me, then fight me, but remember one thing. If you fight the champ then you've got to be prepared to go the whole way. If you think that's the end of it after your programme then you're mistaken."

I was considering my response to this extraordinary outburst when Arden opened up a new line of attack. "You're not a man, you're a creep. I've been making enquiries about you and your homosexuality."

"You've been listening to the wrong people then, but we've been listening to clients of yours," I replied. "Don't you want to answer for what you did to them?" Arden slammed the phone down after this ringing but unhelpful riposte: "Why don't you get off my back you stupid fucking homo!"

This was pretty strong stuff for Radio 4 at the time. By way of contrast, the programme was followed by *Listen With Mother*. It was also followed by a steep decline in Arden's career, but not the promised writ.

Other musicians told stories of exploitation at the hands of other sharks. The legendary Bo Diddly couldn't trace those who had taken the money due to him for dozens of the classic songs he had penned, though he'd searched for 30 years. The recollection of this reduced him to tears.

Noel Redding, bass player with the Jimi Hendrix Experience, had made almost nothing out of any of the group's multi-million selling albums. By his reckoning, band members had been conned into signing away a minimum of £8 million each. He was reduced to living in a tumbledown farmhouse at Clonakilty in the west of Ireland, and playing pub gigs for a tenner a night, still wearing his frayed sixties flares.

As we sat around his kitchen table he eventually produced enough documents to cover it several inches deep. The money that was rightly his appeared to have been siphoned off to places like the Cayman Islands and the Netherlands Antilles via a succession of impenetrable offshore companies.

Noel, scarecrow thin, but with big hair and NHS wire-rimmed glasses had a look of perpetual puzzlement as he leafed through page after closely-typed page. "I'm just a muso, man. I was never going to work this lot out. While the Experience was on the road or in the studio, we didn't have time to be businessmen, even if we'd been up to it. We were turned over, man, by a bunch of faceless bastards." Mind you, he did ruefully admit that the group's conspicuous cannabis consumption hadn't done much for their business acumen.

By the time I met him, part of the farmhouse roof was falling in and he couldn't afford to have it fixed. I suggested that the Fender jazz bass that he'd played with Hendrix was probably a very valuable collector's item and that now might be the time to sell it. Noel shook his head vigorously: "I could never do that," he said dolefully, "It's part of me, man."

We stayed in touch and the next time we met, he was smartly

turned out and altogether more chipper. He'd had the roof fixed and bought a newer car – but how? "Remember that jazz bass I wouldn't sell?" he asked with an impish grin, "Well I've sold four of 'em now!"

Alfred Cook.

Lin Cook.

Jolly Roger, aged nine months.

Going nowhere, with mother and sister Jane.

Going racing, in a FIAT-Abarth 850.

Broacasting on ABC Radio in Sydney.

In Perth, on ABC Television.

Editing a 'Checkpoint' tape at Radio 4, 1980.

On the Costa del Crime: Fraudster John Corsecadden and wife put their umbrellas to a novel use.

A unique vantage point for the filming of Ronnie Knight's Spanish hideaway.

Clifford Saxe takes aim...

... and fires.

A Dutch child pornographer dismantles a video cassette to make smuggling easier...

... and attempts to avoid the inevitable questions.

In Northern Ireland, UDA men approach my car with extortion in mind.

Baby Bruna - stolen and sold to Israel - on her way home to Brazil.

3

Nemesis in a Leisure Shirt

From the BBC to ITV and the birth of
The Cook Report

*British fugitives on the Costa del Crime, paramilitary
extortionists in Northern Ireland, child pornographers
and Britain's richest criminal*

After my marriage to Madeline had broken up and as soon as I
was fit enough to work more or less normally, I sold our little flat
in Highgate and traded up to a small Georgian house round the
corner. For the next ten years I concentrated on my career. I had
a series of fairly short-term relationships – once or twice attractive
young women actually moved in with me – but nothing had any
real permanence. I was afraid of getting hurt again and I wasn't
really much of a proposition as a hands-on partner.

I would head off to Broadcasting House on Monday morning
and show up back at Highgate when the *Checkpoint* investigation
of that week was over. When I wasn't away on location, I might
well be 'back at base', working through the night in a tangle of
tape and a pile of research notes. Nevertheless, there came a time
when friends and family thought it was high time I settled down
again.

In 1982 I had introduced my sister Jane to her future husband,
then one of the legal team at *Checkpoint*. Jane, a highly-qualified
speech therapist, had followed me to England from Sydney in the
seventies. She and I had never been particularly close, but she
clearly felt the need for a bit of sibling *quid pro quo*, and following
my efforts at playing Cupid for her, I was often invited round to
her Fulham flat to be introduced to women who she thought were
my type. Unfortunately, they never were.

I was just gearing myself up to tell Jane that I really didn't see any merit in carrying on with these pleasant but pointless gatherings, when she persuaded me to go round once again 'just to meet a good friend'. And that's when I met Frances.

Physically, we couldn't have been more different. Frances was petite, pretty, bright, blonde and Irish. I was an overweight workaholic from down under, pushing 40 and fast becoming reconciled to permanent bachelorhood. She was working as the senior PA at a large architectural practice and was the life and soul of the evening. She lifted my mood instantly – I was charmed by her personality and, for some reason, she seemed to get on well with me. It got better and better the more we saw of each other.

Within six months we were married and she moved out of her tiny house in Notting Hill. It was what's quaintly called a 'flying freehold' – rooms built over an archway – and at barely eight feet wide, I found it almost impossible to fit into.

So now I had someone to share my Highgate pad with again – but this time for keeps. And, before long, there would be three of us, with the birth of Belinda at the end of April, 1985.

It had been arranged that Frances would be induced – as it turned out, at a time to suit the consultant's golf commitments and not my work schedule. When I politely but firmly pointed out that as I'd been present at the conception, I'd quite like to be there at the birth, a compromise was amicably agreed.

Belinda's arrival was a heart-stopping moment. She was simply gorgeous; blonde-haired and blue-eyed, just like her mum. Workaholic though I am, I was much prouder then than I've ever been of any programme. Unfortunately, that didn't stop me going straight off on location again. It wasn't until I rang in from several hundred miles away that I learned Belinda was now very ill and in the Special Care Unit. I rushed back to discover that the poor mite had a serious infection and was in an incubator festooned with tubes and wires. She made a full, but painfully slow recovery from what we now know was a potentially fatal *Streptococcus B* infection.

Checkpoint had now been on the air for 12 years. The programme had become an institution and, although not exactly sharing Groucho Marx's sentiments about not wanting to live in one, I was ready for a change.

The programme had achieved a substantial number of modest successes. Fly-by-night businesses, fraudsters and con men were exposed and effectively shut down. The public were warned and hopefully didn't fall for their tricks again. Sometimes, laws and regulations were changed or tightened up because we had demonstrated that there were loopholes in them. But our mailbag was telling us that we had also whetted the public's appetite for bigger-budget investigations on a broader canvas. 'Why isn't the programme on television?' was a frequently asked question. So perhaps the audience was ready for change too.

For about a year I had been wooed by television companies wanting to put a version of *Checkpoint* on the screen. Mike Townson, then the editor of Thames Television's weekly *TV Eye* programme had suggested I present a regular investigative edition; David Elstein, then at Brook Productions proposed a series of half-hour programmes, as did my old friend Bob Southgate at TVS.

Bob had interviewed me for a job as a reporter at ITN soon after I arrived in London from Australia in 1968. Although he'd confessed to me over a post-audition drink that there weren't actually any vacancies at the time, we kept in touch with each other as he climbed the television executive ladder from one independent station to another.

Bob and I had talked about my joining him at TVS in Southampton in 1982, but he warned me that he was involved in serious political in-fighting and he didn't know how long he would be around in order to get any new series off the ground. His instincts were proved right and he eventually moved on to Central Television in Birmingham, where he became Controller of Factual Programmes.

Checkpoint, or at least the *Checkpoint* style of journalism, did make it onto BBC TV in the early seventies. For nearly five years, almost every run of the *Nationwide* series featured a fortnightly investigation researched largely by the radio team and presented by me. Sometimes they were even television versions of the latest *Checkpoint*.

They were popular to the point that some talented *Nationwide* staffers began to mutter that they were being consigned to the filming of skateboarding ducks while these radio 'upstarts' were getting to do the more important stuff.

Then, without any consultation or warning, researcher Mike Robinson and I found our television efforts transferred to the newly-created *Newsnight* programme on BBC2. At first the *Newsnight* editorial team didn't want Mike; they said he'd be better off back at Radio 4, but I insisted we came as a set. They were wrong to doubt Mike's abilities and right to change their minds. He went on to become the editor of *Panorama*.

We were at *Newsnight* for a year and, towards the end of the run, we filmed an investigation into a national swindle involving fake *Netsuke* ivory carvings. The villain of the piece had targeted elderly people with stories of the 'guaranteed investment potential' of what were actually pieces of plastic. When confronted, the man took to me with an iron bar. Then, realising that the evidence of this unprovoked attack had been captured on film, he went for the cameraman instead.

I managed to head him off and was rewarded with another beating and three broken ribs. This made me a bit of a hero in the camera pool. That aside, our *Newsnight* film was considered good enough to warrant a separate airing as a programme in its own right. I had always wanted a solo spot on television and now, with a recent television example fresh in management's minds, by chance I was presented with the opportunity to lobby for one.

I found myself at Heathrow, bound for the Edinburgh Radio and Television Festival. I joined the queue at the check-in desk and did what most people do when they are in a slow-moving line at an airport – stare at the person at the head of the queue and marvel at how long it takes to process one individual's ticket. I focused on the overcoated figure a few places ahead of me. He looked familiar. With a start, I realised who it was – Alasdair Milne, then the Director General of the BBC.

My brain went into overdrive – perhaps I could repeat the success of my *Checkpoint* lobbying of more than a decade before. It was worth a try.

After what seemed an eternity, but was probably only ten minutes or so, I reached the British Airways desk. Using my softest, and, I hoped, most persuasive interview technique, I explained quietly who I was and that it was *very* important that I had a seat next to Mr Milne, who had checked in a few minutes earlier.

The check-in clerk consulted her screen. I held my breath. She started to rattle the keys, then looked up and told me that she'd been able to move another passenger, yet to check in, and that would be fine. "Have a good flight." I scooped up the boarding pass, thanked her sincerely and walked through to departures. Now it was down to me.

I avoided the DG in the lounge and waited until he had boarded the plane and found his seat before I stepped into the cabin. His head was down, reading some papers, and I recognised his thick, dark head of hair a few rows in. The seat next to him was empty.

I feigned surprise at being in the seat next to Mr Milne and was relieved that he seemed to know who I was. We slipped quite easily into conversation about Edinburgh and the festival. I waited until the air stewardesses had done their safety stuff and the captain had assured us of his and the rest of the staff's devoted attention before taking the plunge.

I had steered the chat towards television and radio crossovers – then, as now, fairly uncommon.

"I really think *Checkpoint* should be given a chance on television," I said, watching the Director General's face for a reaction.

He sipped his coffee and gave a barely-perceptible nod, appearing to mull over the notion. He turned his head slightly towards me and I took this as the cue to proceed with my argument for translating *Checkpoint* from the airwaves to the small screen. I gave it my best shot for a full five minutes, glancing at him anxiously whenever I felt I could.

"It's a possibility," he conceded after a silence that had me wondering if he had dropped off to sleep. Then he added, with a smile: "You've certainly made the most of your luck in getting a seat next to me."

I smiled back at him. "In this case I'd say I made my own luck. If I see a worthwhile opportunity, I generally try to grab it with both hands."

He told me to speak to Brian Wenham, the Controller of BBC Television, when we got back to London. He assured me that he would 'have a word' with Mr Wenham first. I could do no more. I couldn't help wondering whether he meant what he had said or whether he was trying to fob off this burly, insistent fellow who he had heard was always barging up to people, demanding interviews.

Our conversation turned to other, more general, matters and we parted with a handshake at Edinburgh Airport – he to climb into his chauffeur-driven car and I to seek a taxi. When we bumped into one another at the festival, we simply exchanged a cordial nod.

A few anxious days later I made the call to Brian Wenham's office, half-expecting to be greeted with incomprehension. But my call had been anticipated. *Checkpoint* for TV was being examined – I just had to be patient for a while and they'd be in touch. A few weeks later, they were.

Checkpoint was given a six-week trial run on BBC1, albeit on little more than radio budgets and, apart from the camera crews, with radio staff. In presentational terms, it showed, but the quality of the journalism appealed to the audience. The average viewership was something over eight million. Management pronounced the exercise a success, but the trial run remained just that. There were never any official explanations.

One insider suggested that the demise of the BBC's attempt at a British *Sixty Minutes* – a very successful American TV current affairs show – had left the Corporation with a number of highly-paid staff with nothing to do. Some of these people could be employed to develop one of the elements of the failed *Sixty Minutes* format as a solo programme. As today, *Watchdog* already had an investigative, although consumerist, bent and the perception may have been that a TV *Checkpoint* was surplus to requirements.

Alternatively, perhaps we had been pigeon-holed as a radio show. The Corporation had accepted our investigative style but seemed happier keeping it where it was, literally, out of sight. A move to television was just going to cause more high-profile ructions because of the subjects we would tackle, and maybe the powers that be weren't prepared to fight any battles they saw as unnecessary.

Checkpoint team members were then moved out of their new offices and offered their old jobs back at Broadcasting House. In the short term, I had no option but to go with them.

I wear disappointment badly sometimes, and it became openly known that although Auntie was always high in my affections, the time had probably come to undo the apron strings. An opportunity to do so was not long in coming.

*

The telephone rang in our house in Highgate one winter evening in 1985. It was Bob Southgate with a proposition. Now securely ensconced at Central TV, he was convinced that he could persuade the company to take my kind of investigative programme to television on a permanent basis at last. We met to talk it over. Times and our waistlines had changed since we first met in 1968, but Bob's handsome face, sharp mind and penetrating gaze were pretty much as were. I agreed, in principle, to jump ship.

I discussed the offer with my agent, Jon Roseman, another chap with a sharp brain, in his case complemented with a huge dose of chutzpah and an anarchic sense of humour. We concurred that I should go ahead and jump. Jon then went into negotiating over-drive and a few days later I handed in my notice at the BBC. It was greeted with an almost deafening silence. General relief at my going was tempered only when Michael Grade, then the Controller of BBC1, subsequently told the press that the Corporation should not have let me go.

After 17 years with the BBC, I cleared my desk and went home. I felt a mixture of sadness, anger, mystification – and a strong sense of anticipation.

Independent television worked very differently from the BBC in the 1970s and 1980s. Where the latter retained complete control of its programme output, each department providing the requisite number of dramas, comedies, news and current affairs shows to fill the schedules, ITV was much more competitive. Every independent station – in those days the likes of Central, TVS, HTV, Thames, LWT, Granada, Tyne Tees and Yorkshire – fought its rivals for programme slots.

There was a beauty contest of contenders to fill, for example, the eight o'clock slot on Friday evenings – or to be the sole providers of a particular kind of factual programme. Back then, the larger companies had an absolute right to a certain amount of airtime into which they could pitch programmes they particularly wanted to make. Central prepared to wheel and deal what they decided to call 'The Cook Report' onto the air.

These days, the arrangement is different; the judge and jury in these regularly-held beauty contests are now the senior officers of the ITV Network Centre. The Centre was originally established at the behest of the Office of Fair Trading to 'hold the ring' between

15 rival TV contractors, and to make sure that the smaller ones got their fair share of network air time.

Since then, there have been a series of mergers and takeovers, and there are those who say that with the merger of the two remaining major companies – Carlton and Granada – to form ITV plc, the Network centre will have become redundant. But at the time of writing, its executives are still amongst the most powerful and widely-courted figures in television.

Bob confessed that Central had missed the boat to get me on air for the 1986 season, but with his political skills, learned over years of intriguing in the corridors of ITN and TVS, he was confident he could land me a series for 1987.

First, he needed to recruit me to Central so we could start to plan the new series and find the right personnel. For a year, I would work on a major new regional programme – 'Central Weekend' – a live, Friday night studio discussion programme in front of an invited audience. The programme would usually tackle one major issue a week, often beginning with a pre-recorded investigation, on, say, medical negligence. Then, using that film as a starting point, we would open up the debate to the studio audience afterwards. I was to work on the investigations and co-host the debates with two consummate professionals, Sue Jay and Andy Craig.

One of the producers, who would double as a cameraman for the pre-recorded parts was Peter Salkeld, who was to become a good friend and international travelling companion in the *Cook Report* years.

'Salk' was one of the most unusual people I had ever met. Wiry and incredibly energetic, he had a large, bushy grey beard, several missing front teeth and a high-pitched, cackling laugh that was soon mimicked throughout the office. Though he looked rather like a Muslim Mullah, he was actually a lapsed former Baptist lay preacher. As such, he retained an absolutely rigid sense of right and wrong which, though often endearing, could also make him incredibly awkward. Indeed, his unbending attitude almost cost him his job on several occasions. After our first few meetings I could tell we would get on well, and this heartened me for the future.

*

Had we not been highly motivated, the embryo *Cook Report* team's new accommodation in Birmingham might have put something of a damper on creativity. Deep in the basement of Central's headquarters in the city centre – a former engineer's exhibition hall converted *circa* 1980 – the new team was totally isolated from the outside world. The walls and the furniture came in two colours – grey or a drab pinky-beige – and the whole ensemble was illuminated by strip-lighting set into low, oppressive ceilings. For reasons which escape me, the place had been nicknamed 'Fraggle Rock'.

We used to say that the atmosphere there was such that even the plastic pot plants died. We had to rely on the most recent visitor to let us know what the weather was like outside, so that we could dress appropriately before the long walk through corridors and gangways that led, eventually, to the security desk and out into the fresh air.

Belinda had not long been born, and the three of us moved up from London and took a flat in Edgbaston, not far from the studios, so that we could be together as much as possible. Sometimes, I think that if I had known what pressure this change in my career was going to put all three of us under in the years to come, I wouldn't have done it. But, at first, the workload was gladly borne.

Two of the senior researchers, Paul Calverley and Tim Tate, had come with me from *Checkpoint*. They'd both learnt their trade at the *Yorkshire Post*. Paul was a solid, quietly determined lad from Manchester, with an impassive face and a receding hairline. Tim was, by contrast, generously thatched with sandy hair, voluble and full of interesting ideas. He also boasted a pronounced Yorkshire accent, even though he'd been born in India and brought up in Surrey. He'd married a Yorkshire lass and enthusiastically taken up the accent and the robust outlook of his adopted county.

Although neither of them had much experience of television, both were talented investigators to whom the smallest snippet of news, however much buried in the columns of a heavy newspaper or trade magazine, could represent a programme idea. They were used to sifting through several hundred letters a week from the public. They had contacts in most of the police forces and Customs offices in Britain.

Several times a week, sometimes two or three times a day, we would all troop into the smoke-filled office of the new *Cook Report* editor, Mike Townson, and engage in head-banging sessions to thrash out programme ideas. Townson had been hired on his reputation as a hard-working and inspired editor at Thames Television where, for ten years, he had run the successful current affairs series *TV Eye*. I had first met him in the early-eighties when he tried, unsuccessfully, to recruit me to his programme. Now he had joined mine.

Quite by chance and soon after I joined Central, I had come across Townson in Regent's Park. I was looking for my car, abandoned the night before in anticipation of a boozy party in Primrose Hill. Mike was sitting on a bench looking for all the world as if he was waiting for the hangman. He told me he was about to be fired. It was a familiar story in independent television. The man he'd sacked several years previously had just been appointed his new boss. Retribution was imminent.

I was carrying a Vodaphone mobile with me – a monstrous thing, the size of a car battery in those early days. I dialled Bob Southgate and told him I was with someone he should talk to. I handed the phone to Mike.

Bob had worked for Townson as a reporter on *TV Eye*, and there was a mutual respect between the two men, although Bob knew that Townson could be tough on his staff. With a wry smile, Bob later told me that on occasion, Townson would put two teams of reporters and researchers to work on the same story without letting either side know. Whoever, in his judgement, had made the most progress in a week got to make the film. Now, the same pattern of role reversal that was ousting Townson from Thames Television was about to ease him into a new career with Central.

After ten minutes on the phone, he had been offered the job of editor of *Central Weekend* with the tacit understanding that he would also edit *The Cook Report*. I went on to search for my car and Mike went back to Thames Television to enjoy the luxury of resigning before he could be fired.

The *Cook Report* office was a puzzling as well as a slightly depressing place. Where were the staff, visitors to this largely empty but untidy open-plan space would sometimes ask? Where was the frenzied activity that must surely accompany the pursuit of the action-packed programmes that became the hallmark of the series?

Pat Harris, our utterly unflappable programme manager, would usually be at her desk in the middle of the floor. Next to her would be Gaynor Scattergood, Tracey Bagley or Kay Haden – one or other of the programme's hard-pressed secretaries. An accountant would be hard at work, poring over programme costs and occasionally querying expenses. Along one side of the open space in which they sat were three partitioned-off offices.

In the largest of these, wreathed in smoke, would sit Mike Townson, consigning information to his desk-top computer, puffing at his Benson and Hedges. Townson's dress sense made my casual style look positively *haute couture*. He would plod into the office, a cigarette on the go despite Central's strict 'No Smoking' policy. He'd likely be wearing shabby trainers, sagging tracksuit bottoms and a gaudy T-shirt stretched tightly over his pot-belly.

I once encountered him in the Terminal Three check-in hall at Heathrow. He was dressed in his usual tramp's cast-offs and was holding a Tesco carrier bag. I was surprised to see him, as I thought he was supposed to be in the office.

"Hi, Mike, where are you off to?"

"South Africa," said Townson. "Just for a few days."

"Where's your luggage?"

He waggled his half-empty Tesco bag. "This is it. No point in going to too much trouble." He grinned, exposing a substantial set of nicotine-stained teeth and pushing his enormous black-framed glasses back up the bridge of his nose. He loved to shock, but behind the jocularity a shrewd and ruthless brain was at work.

A few feet from Townson's office door sat his long-suffering secretary, Desna Markham, who had long ago learned not to get overfussed by Townson's abrupt demands, which she habitually greeted with a smile and a small, dismissive wave.

Next to Townson's office was mine, and next to that was another shared by Peter Salkeld and Clive Entwistle. A Lancastrian former *Sunday People* reporter, Clive was our first outside recruit, brought in by Townson from Thames. Newer arrivals, producers and researchers alike, usually shared desks in the open-plan hinterland, behind an assortment of hessian-covered screens.

But where were they all?

More than likely, producers and researchers would be 'on the road', trying to convert raw information into television programmes. This meant long stints of 'phone-bashing' at the early planning stage of a new series, but that would probably be the last time anyone would see the office other than to drop videotapes in *en route* to somewhere else.

My office would normally be empty and locked, its occupant engaged in long-haul travel. Roger Cook and his inconvenient insistence on influencing the course of investigations were thousands of miles away. Producers were expected to telephone Townson every day to report on progress – and during the course of these calls, the editor usually issued new orders, which were then added to or amended throughout the day and night by phone or fax.

Mike Townson loved the office's 'ghost town' atmosphere. It meant that all his staff were out information-gathering or filming something for him. 'Townson's Train Set', we used to call ourselves. Not that Townson always got his own way. We quickly learned to use his control techniques against him and only fed in the information we wanted him to get – so sometimes stories we favoured – and he didn't – actually made it to the screen. Oftentimes a programme owed its success to his influence; sometimes it did well despite him. And, because of his background in daily current affairs, few programmes ever got finished until minutes before transmission.

It was all a game at times. We would take perverse pleasure in being on assignment in some far-flung location where there was no way of telephoning the office – or of the office telephoning us. Townson was forced to concede that the person on the ground probably had a better grasp of what was happening than the one sitting in a smoke-filled office thousands of miles away. It was a situation I manipulated in my own – and I hope the programme's – interest quite frequently.

Mind you, there have been occasions where I have desperately wanted to communicate but haven't been able to. I remember getting a message to phone home while I was in one particularly remote West African location. I made countless failed attempts, then, with the help of a pre-booked call, several helpful international operators and a military radio telephone, I finally got through.

Belinda answered. "Hi, Dad. Sorry, but *Neighbours* has just started, can you please ring back in half an hour? Bye." The little so-and-so hung up on me.

The question that visitors to the office most frequently asked was: "Where do you get your programme ideas from?"

It was a good question. If I'd been asked that while working at *Checkpoint*, I would undoubtedly have replied: "From you, the listener. We get 400 letters a week and there are always stories to be found amongst them."

But things had changed. Typically, in those far-off days, one programme would spawn the next. Mind you, with 36 programmes a year to fill, that was often a blessing. If we broadcast an exposé of a rogue garage chain, for example, the next week we would receive dozens of letters about another, similar scam. New names and companies with other, equally nefarious ways of conning the public, would be unearthed by the researchers and off we would go.

But in my view, a dozen letters of complaint about a company's high-pressure sales techniques and shoddy workmanship didn't add up to a half-hour television show. With six slots a year, we could afford to be much choosier. We had moved on in both subject breadth and the public's expectations. I used to check myself when I responded to a programme idea by asking: "Is it taking a sledgehammer to crack a nut?" And if it was, the idea was discarded or filed for future reference.

Every member of the new team knew that a lot was expected of us, and we each felt honour-bound to deliver a series full of strong, visual stories which would expose the crimes, unmask the criminals and, with luck, get justice for the victims. We also planned to make our programmes as involving and, yes, entertaining as we reasonably could – on the purely pragmatic basis that your message won't get through if you're so boring that people switch off.

Organised crime, drug-smuggling, child-pornography, animal cruelty, the IRA – we sat in Townson's office and talked through the latest developments on all of these subjects. Somewhere there was a programme to kick off *The Cook Report* in fine style.

However, while I was pretty confident we could deliver on the ideas we had discussed, dealing with production logistics was another matter altogether. Culturally and financially, ITV was very different from the BBC and light years away from radio. In radio, you could go quite a long way on a modest budget. I was the complete crew – reporter, scriptwriter and technician. In ITV, the first crew I was allocated consisted of: a cameraman and his assistant, a sound recordist and his assistant, a producer/director, a production assistant, two electricians and a make-up girl. It was obvious that significant chunks of our seemingly generous budgets would disappear before we'd even left the building. On location, and particularly in our line of work, the result of this largesse often turned out to be counter-productive, unwieldy and, thanks to the unions, pretty inflexible. I've nothing against unions and I'm a member of two, but in those days in commercial television, the union tail frequently wagged the company dog.

You didn't need nine people to film a man from behind a tree, as I tried to explain to one especially stroppy shop steward. His response was to accuse me of trying to do his co-workers out of a job. He wasn't interested in the fact that being saddled with so many unnecessary bodies might make my job impossible. Then, to my surprise and puzzlement, he began to argue against himself. Donning a Health and Safety hat, he claimed that because what we were doing was potentially dangerous, many of his members would refuse to work on the programme and that the union would support their refusal. I was clearly getting nowhere, so I abandoned the debate and referred the problem upstairs.

By tradition, the electricians – who operated the lighting – were the stroppiest technicians of the lot. On one occasion a 'sparks' cost us a key doorstep with a man who had made a fortune retailing counterfeit university degrees around the world. His best-seller was apparently in medicine, mainly in Asia and Africa. On the day, instead of turning up at the agreed rendezvous, the unthinking electrician went straight to our target's office, intro-duced himself and asked if he might have a cup of tea while he waited for the rest of us. Predictably, he was denied his tea and we never got near the target again. My requests to have the sparks brought to book over this were politely ignored, I imagine because his union brothers had the power to take the station off the air.

Nevertheless, the incident did serve as a sort of reality check and *The Cook Report* was eventually allowed to operate with a 'stripped down' crew – minus the make-up, the assistants and one of the electricians – but all of them volunteers. In later years that number was reduced to just two, the cameraman and the recordist.

*

The first programme was due to be aired on 22nd July 1987. It was now April and we needed to decide soon which subject to go with. One programme was almost complete, but Townson wasn't convinced that it was right to open with. Producer Clive Entwistle, researcher Tim Tate and I had just got back from Brazil where we had investigated the horrifyingly active trade in stolen babies. Ruthless gangs of thieves were snatching up to 400 carefully-selected babies a month – often from poor families – to sell them on to childless couples in the USA, Europe and Israel for upwards of £10,000 each.

Tate had found one young mother – Rosilda Goncalves – who was scouring the country looking for her ten-month-old daughter Bruna. The little girl had been stolen by her babysitter from Rosilda's house in the remote interior city of Curatiba. Luckily for her – and the *Cook Report* team – the local police decided to help us and told Tim Tate which gang they suspected was behind Bruna's disappearance. One senior member of the gang was in the process of informing on his colleagues in the hope of a reduced sentence, and Tate discovered from him that Bruna had been sold on, via Paraguay, to an Israeli couple who lived near the airport in Tel Aviv.

Rosilda and I flew to Israel to see if baby Bruna really had been taken there. Acting on local research, we staked out a flat in a stark, modern block and waited. A few hours later a woman in her late thirties appeared, manoeuvring a pushchair down the steps at the front of the building.

From our vantage point across a busy road, Rosilda peered anxiously at the child. She gripped my arm and whispered urgently, "*Sim, sim ... e ela.*" Yes, it was Bruna. We told the Brazilian embassy in Tel Aviv what had happened and their advice was to seek legal assistance. The search was on to find a lawyer willing to act to get Bruna back to her mother. Eventually, we found one motivated more by principle than by potential profit.

But first Rosilda needed to get a closer view of the child she believed was her own. Almost 18 months had passed since Bruna had been taken and we were now dealing with a toddler who looked significantly different from the baby who had been snatched from her cot.

The camera crew, hired locally to overcome the language barrier and Israeli red tape on filming permission, operated from the back of an unmarked van as Rosilda approached the woman with the pushchair. Once the approach had been filmed, we joined Rosilda with the crew and an interpreter.

The adoptive mother was horrified – doing her best to steer the pushchair and its tiny occupant away from us as we explained what we believed had happened. It was extremely awkward. The Israeli woman admitted quite readily that she and her husband had bought the child and adopted her. She believed that she had done nothing wrong and invited us round to her flat later that day. The adoptive mother was plainly sympathetic to Rosilda, but the father was not, repeating over and over again "It's mine, I paid good money for it."

I double-checked with the interpreter. Had he really said 'it', not 'she'?

He had.

For the time being, at least, Bruna – or Carolina as she had been renamed – would remain with her adoptive parents as the legal process got underway. Rosilda was in with a good chance of having her child restored to her, once DNA tests had proved beyond doubt that she was Bruna's mother. It was, inevitably, going to be several months before the whole process would be over. In the meantime, we had a very strong story, to which we could return later in the series with what we hoped would be a happy ending.

Clive Entwistle had a burning ambition to be in Rio for Carnival. Mike Townson had got wind of Entwistle's intentions to stay on for it, and had absolutely forbidden any of us to remain in Brazil for longer than necessary. Carnival was six weeks off when we arrived in the country. Our investigation moved slowly, however, complicated by the reorganisation of the baby-snatching gang we had targeted, and its move across the border to Paraguay. Three weeks in and my money was definitely on Entwistle. Problems with the Brazilian crew we were working with and the apparent disappearance of some of our film delayed things even further. Entwistle was almost home and dry.

Victory was his when Townson had to concede that the Brazilian police had made us an offer we couldn't refuse. They could lay on an interview with an imprisoned American paedophile who had been caught with a couple of stolen toddlers, and also an armed guard for a trip into the bandit-infested slums of Rio, in search of the suspected ringleader of one of the gangs.

Rio de Janeiro is truly spectacular. There is no finer site for a city – and there could be no greater contrast than that between the lifestyles of the super-rich, whose marble-halled apartments border on Ipanema or Copacabana beaches – and those of the million plus Rio residents forced by circumstance to live in the *favelas* – the hundreds of sprawling shanty towns that overlook the city's wealthy enclaves from the surrounding hills.

We filmed in Pavaozinho, home to some 20,000 *favelados* – if you can call home a haphazard accretion of squalid, mud-brick, reclaimed timber and corrugated iron shacks, usually without even the most basic amenities. For most of the time Pavaozinho was a no-go area for the police, and so had become a refuge for some of Rio's many gangsters.

As we approached, flanked by machine gun toting officers, a brightly-coloured kite spiralled up into the air ahead of us – and then another, and another – the local signal to watch out because the law had arrived.

Eventually, and by then without our increasingly-nervous police escort – which had fearfully abandoned us – we found and interviewed a self-confessed baby snatcher, whose main line of business was actually drugs. He told us that his successful sideline was not simply a matter of snatching street urchins. They had little value. The market preference was for fair-skinned, blue-eyed babies – and these could be more easily found in the southern province of Curitiba, where many of the early settlers had been of German descent.

Indeed, so bold had the baby snatchers become that maternity hospitals in the region had been forced to hire armed guards. It was an oddly disconcerting sight. Maternity wards with rows of babies – swaddled, local fashion, like so many pink pupae – and patrolled by swarthy men with automatic weapons.

Back in Sao Paulo, as promised, we were taken inside the grim, Aids-ridden Carandiru prison to film a recently arrested paedophile. The authorities, without telling him what he faced, led him before our cameras in an interview room. Off-guard, he confessed that he had been buying and importing little boys into the United States for years. What he and his friends did with them doesn't bear thinking about.

Our excitement about getting this key interview soon turned to depression and, ultimately, to anger. The camera may have been rolling, but the Brazilian cameraman hadn't loaded the film properly – and it had all been fogged. The interview was irreplaceable, but the cameraman was not. He was fired on the spot.

A couple of weeks later, this time with a competent cameraman, we were taken into the Curitiba women's prison to speak to a notorious baby snatcher called Arlette Hilu. She had once been an accountant in a lawyer's office and had seen the demand for babies for adoption. She cut out the middleman and the ethics, and according to the Federal Police, had arranged the kidnapping and export of around 1500 babies which had netted her gang in excess of £15 million.

Glaring at us from behind the bars of her cell, Hilu was clearly unrepentant: "As a professional, I am entitled to charge a certain rate, but it is not true that I became a millionaire, as some people are claiming." She would not be drawn on the provenance of the children she dealt with and waved us away, but our prison visit was made especially memorable by our meeting with the prison governor.

We had expected Rosa Klebb – and got a Cindy Crawford look-alike, albeit a brunette one with a degree in criminology. She was straight off the cover of *Vogue*, and we reckoned her outfit and her jewellery probably cost more than our camera gear. We were so stunned by this incongruous vision of loveliness that we quite forgot to ask what a nice girl like her was doing in a place like that.

Getting to the carnival wasn't as easy as we'd thought either, for two reasons. The first involved an incident on the Puente de la Amistad Bridge over the Parana River, where it forms the border between Brazil and Paraguay. It was through Paraguay that researcher Tim Tate had traced Bruna's route to Israel, and we wanted some local footage.

Filming in Paraguay with or without permission was impossible, so it was agreed that we would film clandestinely out of the back of a van. Space was at a premium, so Entwistle would wait for us on the bridge. It was around nine o'clock in the morning, but the outside temperature was already nudging 32 degrees centigrade, and the interior of the van was swelteringly hot. We left the rear doors slightly ajar in order to improve the ventilation. Unfortunately, as we approached the border post, the doors swung open, revealing all.

The cameraman, the interpreter and I were dragged out at

gunpoint and arrested. Our lives now turned into something out of a low-budget action movie. We were lined up against a wall and searched. Our camera gear was painstakingly inspected – turned every which way, as if the guards had never seen anything like it – and they probably hadn't. There were shouted conversations over a two-way radio. We were bundled into ancient Jeeps and driven to the military barracks at Cuidad del Este, from which the province was governed.

The colonel in charge ran the administration of the area in the mornings and the official cocaine concession in the afternoons, we were told. We were herded into his office. He was a short, podgy figure in camouflage trousers, a grey *Playboy* sweatshirt and Gucci shoes, the soles of which faced us across his cluttered desk.

He would have none of our explanations and apologies, and to emphasise the points he was making in rapid and incomprehensible Spanish, randomly fired his pearl-handled pistol at a row of soft drink cans nailed to a plank in the courtyard outside the window.

When he had finished we were taken to a windowless, almost airless room and left, literally, to sweat it out. Our terrified interpreter told us she'd tried to explain that we'd been making a travelogue, and had got lost. "Lost for good," had been the reply.

In what then amounted to a police state, our isolation was total. I now understood the increasingly paranoid tone of the phone calls we'd been getting from Tim Tate as he'd followed the baby trading trail undercover, across Paraguay to the handover point in the capital, Asunción.

Eventually, without further explanation and minus some of our camera gear, we were loaded into the Jeeps again. It was seven hours since we had been arrested. What now? To our immense relief, we were driven back to the bridge and dumped. As a parting gesture, one of the guards helped himself to my watch. It was a nice watch, but in the circumstances he was welcome to it.

The next problem to overcome was a lightning strike by the staff of Brazil's internal airlines. We had flown down from the Paraguayan border to Sao Paulo, but from there, no one was going anywhere. At the airport, massive queues had attached themselves to every ticket desk. In Rio, carnival was due to start in just 36 hours' time.

The ever-enterprising Entwistle disappeared. Half an hour later, he returned wearing a smug grin. Using the substantial cash float that he, as producer, used to carry, he had hired a light aircraft. It had been the only one available, it had ten seats, and it had cost an arm and a leg. Entwistle then scurried up and down the ticket lines until he had sold the six surplus seats, covered the cost of the charter and maybe even turned a profit. Against the odds, we were heading back to Rio.

We had a day to kill before the big event, the morning of which we spent on Ipanema beach, and in the nearby Veloso Café, where they say Antonio Carlos Jobim composed *'The Girl From Ipanema'*. Some of those beach girls were unavoidably eye-catching, clothed in bikinis so skimpy they were known in the local slang as 'dental floss'. Despite our unfashionable pallor and even more unfashionable swimwear, both Entwistle and I were approached by several very attractive young ladies who asked us outright whether we were American or English, what our business was back home, and if we were married. They were clearly looking for a ticket out.

That evening we retired to our favorite charcoal grill, or *Churrascaria*. Sadly, the Brazilians seem to like their meat chewy and their wine sweet. But if you ignored the wine and carefully selected what was carved for you from the huge skewers of meat that were paraded amongst the tables, then you could dine quite well. The real appeal of this place was the beer waiter. On a chain round his neck he wore a large thermometer, which he plunged into customer's mugs as he did his rounds. If this ritual revealed that your unconsumed beer was now tepid, he fetched you a cold one instead. Outside, the locals, the *Cariocas*, were already warming up for *Carnaval*.

Next day, Carnaval began in earnest and did not disappoint. Four hectic days and nights of the biggest, noisiest and most colourful pageant any of us had ever seen. A seemingly endless stream of fantastical floats, surrounded by a swirling sea of exotically costumed singers and dancers and accompanied by marching bands thumping out an infectious samba beat. The event dwarfs that in Notting Hill – just as I was (fortunately) dwarfed by the Carnaval's 'King Momo', traditionally a man of ample proportions, on this occasion weighing in at 38 stone. Pity the winner of the most beautiful girl in Brazil competition turned out to be a bloke too.

*

Back in Birmingham, Townson's instinct was still that the Brazilian baby story, although strong, wasn't right to open the first series. We needed something more relevant to a British audience. We were told to find something else – and quick.

Paul Calverley had brought with him to a meeting a cutting from that day's *Telegraph*. It listed the names of half a dozen British criminals who had taken advantage of a loophole in extradition law to evade capture in Britain and flee to Spain. They were living the life of Riley on their ill-gotten gains.

Calverley, who had cut his broadcasting teeth on *Checkpoint*, had a reputation for working long and hard on the most unpromising material if he 'felt there was a sniff' of a transmittable story to be gleaned from it. He had already read every article in the Central cuttings library on the politics of the Anglo-Spanish extradition problem and had just returned from London where he had sounded out a senior Scotland Yard contact on the strength of feeling in the police force about these fugitives and how many we might be talking about.

A year before, a gang of east London villains had pulled off one of the most spectacular robberies in recent history – relieving a security company of £6 million in cash during a raid on one of its vans. The police knew exactly who was behind the robbery, but the principals had got clean away to the Costa del Sol, now nicknamed the Costa del Crime.

"The Security Express squad is jumping up and down because the government won't go to the Spanish and get them to kick these guys out," said Calverley. "My man is willing to give us six more names that haven't even hit the newspapers yet. They're all there on the Costas and he'll give us their previous and their addresses in Spain. The cops really want us to go and stir this thing up to make Thatcher do something about getting the buggers back."

The Costa del Crime had been written about before, but had never been subjected to close scrutiny by television. The criminals had certainly never before had a large man with a microphone and a couple of camera crews confronting them.

To judge by the frenetic beating of his computer keys, Townson's interest had been aroused. He listened to a few more ideas from the rest of us and then concluded the meeting. A few minutes later his door flew open and he bellowed to his secretary to get Clive Entwistle back into his office.

Townson and Entwistle went back a long way – to Thames Television days – when Entwistle had been Townson's trusted confidant. Small, bespectacled and given to wearing sharkskin suits and an air of confident superiority, Entwistle delighted in 'putting one over' on the other fellow – including his colleagues from time to time. He had the flamboyant approach Townson wanted for this first programme and, like his boss, he had a reputation as a 'deliverer'. Unfortunately, also like Townson, this was sometimes at other people's expense, and he could be seriously bloody-minded when he didn't get his own way.

Entwistle had been in with Townson for half an hour when the latter's secretary was loudly instructed to summon Paul Calverley and me into the office. Townson looked up from his desk and smiled at me. "Well, Roger, looks like you're off on a nice working holiday in the sun. Don't forget your swimming trunks."

He turned to Calverley and told him to go back to his friend at Scotland Yard and get that promised list of names, background details and addresses on the Costas.

At the top of that list was Ronnie Knight. More famous for having once been married to Barbara Windsor, Knight was also a prominent East End gangster. He had slipped away to the Costa del Sol before the police could arrest him for his part in the Security Express robbery – then Britain's biggest ever cash heist. His disappearance and subsequent re-emergence in a luxury Marbella villa with his glamorous girlfriend Sue Haylock had caused a sensation in the British tabloid press. Public opinion demanded to know how Ronnie Knight was being allowed to get away with it.

Then we heard a whisper that Ronnie and his girlfriend were about to get married, and it was Clive Entwistle's idea that I gatecrash the wedding party strapped to the outside of a helicopter.

Entwistle had somehow managed to find the oldest helicopter and the oldest pilot in Spain to fly us. The aircraft was an ancient Allouette Mk I, with its doors held on with baling wire, and the pilot actually held Spanish helicopter licence Number One, as he proudly showed us – mercifully after the flight was over. Unfortunately, the old bird had broken down on the day of the wedding and we had to film what we could from the ground.

The next idea was to overfly Ronnie's villa, *El Limonar*, which was perched on a steep hillside between the mountains and the sea just to the north of Marbella. With luck, we might film the man enjoying his luxury lifestyle – perhaps in the company of some of his fellow villains.

We imagined them scattering spectacularly as we descended, circled and hovered above them. I could also be filmed from the ground, clinging to the helicopter, a sort of *deus ex machina* come to spoil one of Ronnie and Sue's regular barbecue parties. But it wasn't going to be easy.

As our chopper was small as well as elderly, it was limited in terms of carrying capacity. We planned to make two sorties; first with me, filmed from the ground – and second with the camera crew, filming from the air.

The pilot had landed on a rocky outcrop overlooking *El Limonar* and we joined him there. He pointed out, through our interpreter – local freelance journalist, Nigel Bowden, who later became our eyes and ears on the Costas – that there would be a strong up-draught around the house because it was built on an escarpment, and that the helicopter would be difficult enough to control even without exterior cargo. I heard this and felt a twinge of unease. Neither the pilot nor I were keen to have my ample frame hanging outside the cockpit, but Entwistle was having none of it. I'd be letting the side down if I didn't go up, and that was that.

He passed me a safety harness with which I was to be supported. I tucked it under my shirt, clicked the catches shut, and passed the ends back to Clive beside the helicopter. Seconds later he stepped back and gave the pilot a brisk thumbs-up. I clung on to the door frame and we juddered slowly skywards.

We approached the villa from the north and dropped down-wards. As yet, there were no visible guests. Ronnie and Sue abandoned their barbecue preparations and fled indoors. God knows what they made of me. Smoke from burning sausages swirled under the rotor blades. Through my headphones I could hear the pilot's increasingly agitated commentary, translated for me by Nigel Bowden, who sat in the passenger seat.

"He says his helicopter is handling like a pregnant pig – whatever that feels like," Bowden reported nervously.

This assignment was a little out of the ordinary for Bowden, who had been a marine biologist in a previous existence before marrying a Spanish girl and settling down to a life of eventful uncertainty as a freelance journalist in Marbella.

By now, the shots of me from below were safely in the can – and we were wasting valuable flying time which could be put to better use by our cameraman, Gerry Pinches.

We landed back on the flat-topped rock and everyone climbed out. I tried to open my fingers but they were locked shut round the door frame and remained that way for what seemed like several minutes.

Eventually, I was able to prise those frozen fingers free and leaned back on the harness to ease my aching back. The result was not far short of a somersault as I fell over backwards. I pulled at the webbing of the harness. It was slack. As I hauled it towards me, I heard the clunk-clunk-clunk of the metal clasps scraping along the cockpit floor. The safety harness had never been attached to the anchor-points inside.

The cold sweat that then came over me was a classic illustration of my usual reaction to some of the bizarre and dangerous things the programme has called upon me to do. 'Fear in arrears', I call it. We always try to plan what we do very carefully indeed, but no plan and no participant is perfect. If you analysed the risks too closely, you wouldn't do the job at all.

I retired to my hotel room for a stiff drink, while the crew got on with the aerial filming of the villains' villas.

A couple of days later, we targeted one of Ronnie Knight's partners in crime, Clifford Saxe. He was also wanted for his part in the Security Express robbery. Back in London, Saxe had run the pub where Knight and his gang had planned the job. He, too, had taken advantage of the extradition loophole and fled to the Costas.

We spent some time tracking him from his home to the variety of bars he frequented and planned to confront him as he drank in his favourite – *Wyn's Bar* – an expat watering-hole in the hills above Marbella.

At *The Cook Report* we called such an engineered confrontation a 'doorstep'. That's actually a misnomer, because long experience has taught us that the last place you should beard your target is at his or her front door. It's only common sense, because all they have to do when your unwanted presence is made known to them is step back and slam the door in your face. You don't get your interview and you probably don't get a second chance either.

Far better to choose a location where the inquisitor can control what happens. Until British villains had watched enough *Cook Reports* to realise that cameras and recording equipment can be hidden very easily in cupboards, bathrooms and behind curtains, the hotel room was a favourite.

I have lost count of the times when the villain of the programme has got his comeuppance after I have posed as the room-service waiter. It is difficult to escape through a narrow door frame blocked by someone of my size, and there was generally ample time to fire off some telling questions. As the villains got more wary, we could usually find an appropriate venue for the *denouement* of every story, but the bait to get them in front of the cameras remained pretty constant – more often than not, a carefully tailored proposition that would appeal to their egos or their greed – or both.

If we couldn't get our target to a suitable location by prior arrangement, then we'd plot his movements and choose somewhere public. Somewhere with plenty of space to manoeuvre the two crews we generally took on such occasions. A second cameraman was always useful in a potentially volatile situation. Here too, the element of surprise usually worked in our favour, because it gave me just enough time to do what the audience expected of me before the subject recovered his or her composure and headed for the nearest exit.

We'd thought we had all these factors under control when – while waiting for Saxe to appear – I challenged a fugitive Blackpool drug dealer called Alan Brookes as he emerged from his Ferrari Testarossa on the quayside at Puerto Banus. He'd once escaped the Moroccan authorities by skimming across the Gibraltar Strait on a jet-ski, but now he was blocked in with nowhere to go.

It was an awkward situation and we'd had to rely solely on radio microphones. Unfortunately, the unsuppressed ignition of a motor scooter idling nearby completely obliterated the signal from the mikes, so the doorstep was unusable. This meant we had no choice but to do it all over again while we still had the opportunity, provocative though that might have seemed. Brookes must have thought we were mad – but he played it cool and we got our encore.

Nigel Bowden had warned us that, by contrast, Clifford Saxe was likely to react unpredictably when approached. In the few months Saxe had been resident in Marbella he had been involved in several alcohol-fuelled fights, turning on friends and strangers alike when the mood took him.

We decided to risk it. Clive Entwistle was being bombarded with calls from Mike Townson demanding to know when I would be free to join Paul Calverley in Amsterdam, where Paul had found and secretly filmed a gang supplying child pornography – complete with instructions on how to smuggle it past Customs. My presence was also required in Northern Ireland where our undercover team was attempting to expose Protestant paramilitaries who were demanding protection money from large construction companies – with dire consequences if they didn't pay up.

Saxe hadn't been seen for a day or two, so Bowden stationed himself outside his house at ten one morning and waited. The film crew and I were a mile away in our hotel, keeping out of sight until we heard whether or not Saxe had appeared and if he had, where he was heading. Ninety minutes later, Bowden rang us to say that we were in luck; Saxe was out of his house and installed safely at Wyn's. We set off for the 'doorstep'.

Saxe's first reaction when he saw the camera and me was to pick up a heavy glass ashtray and hurl it at my head. I ducked just in time and it bounced off my shoulder instead. "Shouldn't you be returning to Britain to face trial for the Security Express job?" I suggested. Pandemonium broke out in the bar. Saxe's drinking pals crowded round him, pulling him back as he tried to follow me outside but, suddenly, he broke free and lunged forward at me, raining blows down on my head and back.

There's no point in retaliating; it makes you look as bad as the person you are trying to question. I retreated a few paces and asked Saxe once again for the chance to conduct an orderly interview. He swore and spat at me before being led back inside the bar, successfully this time, by his friends.

It was useless to carry on. We'd tried our best and had got unique footage of one of the 180 most wanted Brits successfully evading justice in the sun. And we'd shown him up for what he was.

For my pains, I had an absolutely glorious black eye and assorted other bruises to my back and neck.

Loud shouts and scuffles from inside Wyn's Bar indicated that an attempt to snatch our film was probably imminent. It was time to climb into our getaway car. But it wasn't where we had left it. At the first hint of trouble, the driver, who had clearly never seen anything like this before, had taken fright and driven off down the road, leaving us stranded. The cameraman spotted the car parked at a junction a few hundred yards away and we headed away from Mr Saxe and his friends at a brisk, but I hope decorous trot.

In a subsequent programme, we asked how several of the Costa del Crime fugitives survived, indeed prospered, after their original ill-gotten gains had been spent. The answer, in many cases, was drug dealing. We decided to show the British public what these wanted men were up to now.

This led us to a memorable trip across the narrow stretch of Mediterranean between Spain and Morocco. The trip was arranged by a former drug dealer turned police informant. With the protection and backing – we were assured – of Moroccan Police and Customs officers, we trekked into the remote Rif Mountains, where the rule of law hadn't been in force for years. There, we were to meet the men who farmed the hashish. Our story was that we wanted to export it to Britain in considerable quantities.

Some miles short of our destination, our escorts got nervous and turned back, but we pushed on. When we got to the meeting point – a rundown mountain town – we were put up for the night in an abandoned holiday hotel, built but never occupied because the area had become too dangerous for tourists. It was staffed by a one-eyed bandit whose culinary skills ran only as far as a seemingly-endless supply of boiled eggs. There was no bedding or electricity and the only water available – apart from the bottled variety – lay in a mixture of green sludge at the bottom of the swimming pool.

Eventually we met and secretly filmed the main grower and negotiated our theoretical deal under the watchful eyes of his armed escort.

"How will we take delivery of our shipment?" I asked the grower.

"You may pick it up at sea, beyond the twelve-mile limit," he replied.

"And what about the police and Customs?" I wanted to know.

"No problem," he concluded with just a flicker of a smile. "They will deliver it to you."

Never has an answer given me such a *frisson*.

There we were, deep in enemy territory, with our promised protection clearly working for the other side. Luckily, we were able

111

to talk our way to relative safety back in Tangiers, saying that we needed to consult our bosses before going ahead with the deal.

At this point, we didn't know who we could trust anymore and decided – not for the last time in a *Cook Report* – to leave a country by the back door as it were, in order to avoid unwelcome attention. Some of us took a nondescript boat to Gibraltar, and the remainder of the crew, including me, slipped away via Ceuta, a tiny Spanish enclave on the north Moroccan coast. Nevertheless, it had all been worth it. The Rif Mountain filming became part of a very successful programme.

There was just time for one more 'doorstep' in Spain before catching the plane for Amsterdam. John Corsecadden looked a lot more respectable than Clifford Saxe, but, then, he was a much more accomplished crook. Dozens of creditors knew to their cost what a skilled fraudster he was. Over the past few years he had embezzled more than £3 million from a series of companies he he'd supposedly been trying to rescue from bankruptcy. He, too, had availed himself of the Spanish extradition loophole and had fled with his wife to a substantial, detached villa overlooking the bright blue Mediterranean of the Costa del Sol.

With Nigel Bowden's help, we tracked the Corsecaddens down and, when they went for a stroll into Marbella after a heavy, early summer downpour, Gerry Pinches, sound recordist Steve Phillips and I walked up to them.

I had hardly got the first question out when both Corsecaddens, who must have been in their sixties, set about all three of us with their umbrellas. Steve Phillips was so incensed he grabbed John Corsecadden's umbrella from his grasp. For one awful moment I thought he was going to whack the couple with it in retaliation, so I told him to drop it. Unfortunately, he handed it back instead. Corsecadden, umbrella reclaimed, then rained down another half-dozen blows on my head, ably assisted by his wife.

Once again, I wondered why I was going through this, especially since my attempt at an interview wasn't eliciting any relevant replies. And yet I already knew the answer to my unspoken question; once again, we were here to show Corsecadden for what he was – cowardly, greedy, unprincipled and selfish. His victims would appreciate it.

John Corsecadden eventually outstayed his welcome in Spain

and returned to Britain, where he received a three-year prison sentence for fraud. He was released early due to ill-health and died shortly afterwards.

I was glad to board my flight at Malaga and relax for a couple of hours before landing at Schiphol.

Four hours and a visit to Amsterdam's Red Light District later, I had concussion and burns to add to my black eye and bruises.

Paul Calverley had met us at the airport and taken us down-town to confront a loathsome creature called Justin, who had been selling him child pornography from under the counter of his sex shop for the past few weeks.

Justin had been secretly filmed by Calverley as he showed how paedophiles smuggled the material through British Customs con-trols by repackaging the videotape on typewriter-ribbon spools. He'd claimed that his organisation did substantial mail order business with Britain. Revealing footage of Justin's demonstration was already safely back at Central studios.

Calverley, accepted as a regular customer, went into the sex shop first to establish if Justin was at the counter. He wore a radio mike so that we could also hear whether or not Justin was on duty. As soon as our sound recordist picked up Paul's conversation with our target on his headphones, I walked in with the camera crew at my shoulder and confronted him. Justin had uttered a few pseudo-shocked denials when the lights went out and a sharp, painful blow was delivered to the back of my head.

Only when I looked carefully at the footage back in Birmingham did I see what had happened in the gloom of the shop. The burly proprietor had returned – and he wasn't happy. He could see the camera crew and obviously decided to make filming as hard as he could by plunging us all into darkness. Then he picked up what appeared to be a billiard cue and ran towards me. He started to belabour me while we were still inside the shop – that was when I felt the pain in my head – and he was still hard at it as the crew and I beat a retreat outside.

Next he turned his attention to the microphone I was holding. Everything he and I were saying was actually being recorded by a tiny radio microphone out of sight under the collar of my jacket.

The hand-held mike was a legacy from my *Checkpoint* days when we wanted it made obvious to the interviewee that he or she was being recorded. It wasn't really needed, except as a back-up.

My assailant tried to pull the hand mike away from me. The struggle took us away from the shop and we lurched dangerously close to the edge of the canal. Suddenly, he reached for the short, fat cigar he'd had clenched between his teeth and stubbed it hard into the back of my hand. The pain was instant. I let go and, with some satisfaction, he hurled the microphone into the water.

Then, quite without warning, the cigar-wielding shop owner was himself set upon by several fit young men and pushed roughly back inside his own premises. Surprisingly, our rescuers turned out to be performers from the 'live sex show theatre' a few doors away. They had heard the scuffle and, when they found out that their neighbour was peddling child pornography, angrily rounded on him. Selling pornography was OK by them, they said, but the films should only involve consenting adults. Child pornography was completely beyond the pale.

The shop – and others in the same chain – were shut down by the Amsterdam police a month later.

Back in Blighty, while doing one of the last interviews for the pornography programme, I came the closest I've ever come to losing my temper with an interviewee. The man was a convicted paedophile who had defiled scores of little girls and filmed himself doing it. He then sold copies.

For this he'd served time in Albany Prison on the Isle of Wight, where he did little else but fantasise about what he'd do when he got out. He wanted to make his own so-called 'snuff movie' and regularly prowled through amusement arcades on the south coast looking for potential victims. He openly admitted having great difficulty resisting the temptation to make his fantasy real. But there was nothing the law could do about it unless and until he did – and nothing I could do either, though as a relatively new father then, I seriously wanted to strangle him.

After that, all I wanted to do was go home. Happily, I was able to snatch a couple of days at the Birmingham flat with Frances and Belinda who, thank goodness, was rapidly taking after her mother in looks. But, after my 48 hours' respite, Mike Townson was on the telephone once again.

"The UDA's taken our bait. They're expecting Mr Rogers over from London to discuss the protection money tomorrow. On your way, Mr Rogers."

I don't think there's any way you can tell your wife that you're about to confront a gang of Ulster paramilitaries and expect her to rest easy about it. I played down the risk element and told her I'd ring as soon as it was safely over. Frances put on a brave face – particularly commendable for a girl steeped in Irish history.

Of all the places *The Cook Report* has gone for its material, Northern Ireland is one of the toughest in which to carry out an undercover investigation. In 12 years of programme-making we embarked on six deep-cover projects there. Five have gone to air. The sixth remained unfinished, because several key witnesses changed their minds about the risks involved in going public.

Our contacts with the Royal Ulster Constabulary had always been good, going back to *Checkpoint* days. Paul Calverley, in particular, had close contacts within C13, the specialist anti-terrorist squad which had its headquarters in a rundown manor house on the Bangor Road a few miles east of Belfast city centre.

C13 officers are convivial to a man. When you work under the pressure they do, the odd glass of whiskey is always welcome – and it was in such an atmosphere in the bar of the Culloden Hotel, on the outskirts of the Protestant suburb of Holywood, that one of the squad's senior officers offered Paul the way into a story which might do the RUC and *The Cook Report* some good.

In 1987, the British government was pumping £475 million a year into an intensive building programme in Ulster, replacing the appalling tenements that had blighted the province's inner cities for decades. Yet the project was going nowhere. Contracts weren't being fulfilled, the overspend was massive and, for no obvious reason, builders were going out of business every week.

The reasons for the shambles, the RUC man explained, were the all-pervasive protection rackets being run by paramilitaries on both sides of the religious divide. A contractor would be approached in his site hut by a small group of hard cases offering their services as security men. It would be explained that for a down payment of a few thousand pounds and a weekly payment of a few hundred pounds, the security men would ensure that no harm befell the builder and his men, that there would be no sabotage, and that no materials would disappear off-site in the middle of the night.

Those who expressed reluctance were taken to one of Belfast's many drinking clubs and shown the barrel of a gun. Few refused to pay up. Those who still didn't pay like as not ended up in a ditch in Omagh or Fermanagh with a bullet in the back of the head.

The political issue – and this was something Westminster was not keen to have pointed out in public – was that vast sums of money were being poured into Ulster only to be stolen by the terrorists. British troops were being murdered with bombs and bullets paid for unwittingly by the British taxpayer.

The man from C13 knew who was behind most of the building-site rackets. They were fast becoming wealthy men, and so were the organisations that they represented. For all their good inside information, the RUC was having only limited success with its network of informers. Now, if somebody from the mainland with a credible background was to come along and ask these bogus security men for protection for their new Ulster building project . . .

This was to be the genesis of our first *Cook Report* sting. Ten years earlier, back in radio days, we'd quickly come to the conclusion that the best way to nail a villain involved a two pronged approach, which I believe we pioneered. We would not only rely on documentary and anecdotal evidence from his victims, but would also construct a scenario in which we could record or film him 'at work', as it were.

It was a very successful technique, and where a confrontation had to follow secret filming, because otherwise you'd not get another crack at the target, it might also give us a degree of control over what happened when the target turned up. Of necessity, and for safety reasons, a variation on this theme was the kind of sting required here.

Journalistic experience, tempered with streetwise police advice, built a cover story for Paul Calverley. He flew to Belfast as John Daley, the representative of a London-based property company planning to tender for the contract to extend the new shopping centre in the town of Craigavon.

He needed to find the biggest fish in the building-site protection business and arrange for him to meet Mr Rogers, the chief executive of the London property company.

116

The story would be that Mr Rogers wanted the multi-million pound contract very badly – but he also knew that to get the building done, he was going to have to pay serious protection money.

C13 had their suspicions that one of the main gangsters involved was a man called Eddie Sayers, who ran the aptly-named Borderline Security from a farmhouse on the North/South Irish Border in Armagh. Sayers was also an active senior member of the Ulster Defence Association – legal in the late 1980s, but subsequently proscribed for being a front for Protestant paramilitaries. He was a canny individual, we were told, and we were unlikely to meet him in person.

Calverley contacted Borderline Security by telephone and explained the position. He suggested the firm call his office in London and ask for Mr Rogers. A *Cook Report* researcher manning a telephone with an untraceable number sat in a small office in Central's London offices in Portman Square and waited for the call.

He didn't have long to wait.

"Is Mr Rogers there?" asked a male voice with a thick Ulster accent.

"He isn't at the moment, but I can get him to ring you back. Who shall I say called?"

There was a pause before the message was delivered. "Tell him it's Mr Davies and that if he knows what's good for him and his firm he'll come and see us in Belfast tomorrow." He left a number and hung up. I returned the call an hour later and arranged the meeting.

We couldn't be sure that news of our subterfuge hadn't somehow leaked out. The paramilitaries on both sides had pretty good intelligence systems. It was a harrowing time for Calverley, our man on the ground. Not for the first – or last – time in Northern Ireland, he found himself having to change hotels and hire cars several times a week.

The next day, I flew into Belfast Aldergrove airport, picked up a rented Ford Granada and drove it to the much-bombed Europa Hotel in the middle of the city where two *Cook Report* technicians were waiting for me in the car park. Making it look as though they were mechanics repairing an electrical fault, they carefully fitted hidden microphones covering both the front and back seats.

117

Back in the early eighties, reliable mini-cameras small enough to conceal in situations like this were not available. The pictures would have to come from a full-sized professional camera with a telephoto lens, concealed in a van.

As soon as we'd tested the Granada's mikes and found they were working, camera crew, producer and researcher set off for the rendezvous in a *Cook Report* surveillance van. The team arrived at the sprawling car park in Craigavon two hours before my meeting. The driver got out and went off for a cup of tea, leaving behind what appeared to be just an empty, blue Ford Transit, parked up for the day.

I set off alone for the same destination. The adrenalin was flowing, but I concentrated on the brief that Paul Calverley had given me. I needed the men who came to meet me to make the running. They were the ones who had to make the demand for money – it wasn't incriminating enough if I just offered cash for my building workers to be left alone.

I also needed to establish, if I could, who I was dealing with. Would it be the notorious Mr Sayers? Was the outwardly respectable Ulster Defence Association really behind the protection racket? I tried not to think about what would happen if they were suspicious and wanted to search the car.

In no time, it seemed, I was at the rendezvous. I saw the surveillance van and parked so the cameraman could get a clear, unobstructed view of whatever happened. I also noticed that they were too far away to help if needed. I sat and waited.

Half an hour went by. Two figures made their way towards the Granada. Both wore ill-fitting, dark suits that flapped in the wind. A gust blew the taller man's jacket open as he reached for the front passenger door handle. I saw the distinctive, black, cross-hatched butt of a semi-automatic pistol sticking out of his trouser belt. The big man opened the door and sat down heavily next to me. His partner, a small, sandy-haired man, slipped into the back of the car. I felt his breath on the back of my neck.

Why do I do it?

There's the challenge of beating the odds – of bringing back the impossible story. There's the chance that what you do may change things, may do some good – and then, when things get really dangerous, something rather peculiar happens: it isn't me at all. I am just an onlooker.

It's difficult to explain. The best illustration of the phenomenon is the shocking footage from a cameraman at work during a South American revolution, as he calmly frames up and focuses on the man who shoots and kills him. The presence of a camera, the idea in the back of your mind that this is only television, somehow removes you from real life. You wouldn't behave like this in real life, would you?

I applied the lion-taming principle – show no fear and no harm will come to you. My heart was thumping nevertheless.

"So, gentlemen, you know I'm pitching for this business in Craigavon. Mr Daley says I need to speak to you first – what can you do for me?"

The smaller man in the back answered first. "We'll make sure you get no hassle. That's very important round here. Things can get very heavy if that sort of thing starts."

"And how much is that likely to cost me?" I asked.

The big man next to me lifted his back from the seat and reached towards his trouser pocket. Here we go, I thought.

He pulled out a pocket calculator and looked at me. "Tell me how much this contract is worth to you if you get it," he growled.

I looked at his cold, lined face. "And would you mind telling me your name?"

"Sayers. Eddie Sayers is my name," he replied. "That's my real name, by the way, so don't tell the police."

The hairs on the back of my neck prickled. I tried to keep as poker-faced as possible. We had hooked a really big fish. In fact, rather bigger than we'd been led to expect. Now it was a matter of reeling him in as carefully as I could. I told him that the contract would be worth £3 million. His sausage-like fingers battered the tiny keys of the calculator. Twenty seconds later he looked up: "The amount we would be looking to get from you is £9,000 per million pounds."

In circumstances like these, it really is a case of 'in for a penny, in for a pound'. You can't take your bat and go home – that could get you killed. The alternative is to play the game for all it's worth.

I knew from Calverley's briefing that I was to expect a demand for at least ten per cent of the contract value – £100,000 per million. "So, you're giving me a discount, are you?" I said.

He nodded and said gruffly: "Because you came to me direct

that's exactly right. Ten per cent off – you pay £9,000 per million." According to my briefing, he'd got his sums wrong by a factor of ten, but in the circumstances I wasn't going to query his maths or his mastery of the pocket calculator.

The pair of them went on to tell me that they were backed by an armed organisation that would 'settle' any problems I might have on the site. I chanced my luck again and asked which particular group that was. I got the answer I had been hoping for: "The fuckin' UDA," said Sayers with a self-satisfied smirk.

I had one more question. "And if I don't agree to pay you?"

Sayers turned in his seat to face me, his watery eyes six inches from mine, and said quietly: "When you and my colleague here were talking on the telephone today, there was a man being buried by his family in Belfast. He was in the same business as you. Read the newspapers."

The man in the back chipped in. "We wouldn't like to say what would happen exactly, but use your imagination. You'd never work again."

I told them I would get back to them after talking to my partners. With that, they got out and walked back to their own car, passing our surveillance van without giving it a second glance, and drove away.

I leant back into the seat, exhaled slowly and relaxed my shoulders. A minute later I switched on the ignition and drove ten miles to the prearranged rendezvous to meet the rest of the team. I knew we'd have the pictures, but I prayed that the microphones had relayed our conversation back to the surveillance van.

I needn't have worried; everything had been filmed and recorded perfectly. A jubilant Paul Calverley called his contact in C13. There was an impromptu premiere of our material for him in Paul's room in the Europa hotel and something of a celebration downstairs in the bar afterwards.

By the time I was back in Birmingham, the RUC had decided to arrest Sayers and two others immediately after our programme. They were to be charged with racketeering offences and our filmed evidence in the Craigavon car park was to be the main plank of the prosecution's evidence. As with the IRA, the UDA's funding came largely from extortion, robbery and the like – and with 20 years previous experience of covering stories in Northern Ireland, it seemed to me that paramilitary activities on both sides usually had little to do with deeply-held religious or political beliefs and much to do with the carving up of territory to be exploited for purely criminal ends.

A couple of hours later, Mike Townson's laid-back secretary stuck her head into my office to say there was a telephone call for me from a man in Belfast who wouldn't give his name. I asked what he wanted.

"To kill you, I think," she said simply.

The telephone rang. I picked it up. The caller was a fairly agitated man who told me that the consequences of what I had done would indeed be dire. He must have been calling from a public telephone box because, in mid-threat, the pips went and we were cut off.

Five minutes later, Townson's secretary popped back "It's that man again."

I picked up the call. It was indeed the same fellow. He started by apologising profusely; he had run out of money, he said. He'd had to go to the corner shop to get some change in order to finish the death threat – which he duly did before hanging up. How's that for an Irish story?

The RUC recommended that, although the Protestant paramilitaries didn't have a network of active members established on mainland Britain – unlike the IRA – I should change my routine and hotel frequently.

"And when you come to give evidence at Belfast Crown Court, we'll be there to look after you," our C13 man assured me confidently. I sincerely hoped so.

Meanwhile, I had other things on my mind. *The Cook Report* was about to go to air and we had to choose which story to show first. Mike Townson had already decided to hold on to the Brazilian baby story and go with something he felt was more directly relevant to our audience. By then he had choices.

The Ulster terrorist racketeering story had a lot going for it – the exposure of crime with the tension of secret filming of the crime being committed. The child pornography programme was powerful but harrowing. On the one hand, it was going to be watchable not least because of the violence which I had encountered in Amsterdam. The downside was that the subject matter –

without any pictorial illustration, of course – was likely to be a switch off for the average viewer, particularly with younger family members in the living room.

There were a couple of other options too, including the sad victims of Britain's hopeless 'Care in the Community' policy for the recovering mentally ill, and the strange tale of several West Country families whose homes were inexplicably catching fire all the time. Secret radar-system testing by the Ministry of Defence was thought to be to blame.

In the end, Townson decided to go with the Costa del Crime programme. He knew our audience would be outraged that the expatriate Costa crooks were 'getting away with it' and would be delighted to see them confronted. We would also be raising important questions about extradition procedures from Spain. That said, progress on this subject has been frustratingly slow. I have made in all, five programmes involving criminals living beyond the reach of British justice in Spain, and until recently, the extradition process was unduly cumbersome and all too often biased in favour of the fugitives.

I can vividly remember the atmosphere in the Birmingham office as we waited for the transmission of that first programme in July 1987. There was a real sense of excitement. We knew that we had a good story to tell. One or two television critics had expressed doubts as to whether the Roger Cook style could make the transition from radio to television.

One leading newspaper critic even said that he would eat his hat if we were able to deliver a good programme and a decent-sized audience. He believed that what I did was much more effective when the action was left to the imagination on radio than it would be when shown on TV. We secretly hoped for five or six million viewers.

Frances brought Belinda down into the Fraggle Rock bunker. Everyone tried to remain calm and have a few glasses of champagne. After the transmission, the party carried on in a bar around the corner from the office.

The next morning there were a few aching heads as we gathered to read the papers and – most importantly of all – wait for the audience researchers to telephone with the viewing figures.

The newspaper reviews were amazing. One critic described me as 'Nemesis in a leisure shirt'. Another as 'Meatloaf meets the

Equalizer'. 'Powerful and purposeful' seemed to be the consensus. However, 'We're all eating our hats now' was, for me, the most satisfying comment of all. I had a gut instinct that we would surprise people with the size of the audience. We were new, different and, if you have a good story to tell, people will usually sit back and listen.

At 11 o'clock, the production manager, Pat Harris, decided she could wait no longer for word on the figures and dialled the audience research department. I watched her as she jotted something down and replaced the receiver.

"We got ten million viewers," she shouted across the office. The news was beyond anything we could possibly have hoped for. The place erupted. Even the normally taciturn Townson allowed himself a smile of satisfaction before drawing deeply on his cigarette and continuing to pummel the keys of his computer, pounding out a draft script for show number two. Frighteningly late, when you thought it was going to be on air in less than a week's time.

Herograms from senior management at Central flew in all directions. Bob Southgate was ecstatic. He'd risked his credibility by bringing me to Central from the BBC and, albeit at this early stage, it looked as if he had been justified. Frances rang from the flat to say that an enormous bouquet had just arrived for her from Central management.

The rest of that series didn't quite reach the heights of that first show in terms of audience levels, but we weren't disheartened. We were then broadcasting to a nation on holiday. The sun shone, people sat in pub gardens and drank, or lit a barbecue and stayed outdoors. No other current affairs programme was reaching anything like our figures. We were down a million or so occasionally but our overall share of the viewing audience remained high, almost touching 50 per cent at times.

In other words, of those people still bothering to watch television in August, almost half of them were watching us. And that's the kind of rating that independent television companies – and their advertisers – like to see.

Our initial flurry of good reviews brought to an end a 15-year unbroken run of honourable mentions. I can't remember a bad review for *Checkpoint*. The first radio review, oddly, was from *The Evening Standard*'s film critic, Alexander Walker. However, *The Cook Report* was to be another kettle of fish entirely. The programme's profile attracted a lot of attention, some of it rather unpleasant.

Never having had to deal with this sort of thing before, at first I found it rather difficult to cope with. Put it down to inexperience – with a touch of naïvety, perhaps – but I very soon learned of the peculiar relationship between the British press, particularly the tabloids, and television.

They don't actually like TV much, but they live off stories from and about it – though it should be said that some of these stories have been promoted by television producers in search of publicity. The papers also love to build you up in order to knock you down again, and as *The Cook Report* began to make news as well as reviews, this became ever more obvious.

The reviews seemed to fall broadly into two categories. The first was highly personal, usually involving the denigration of 'this fat, self-appointed vigilante', as one critic put it; the second was unstinting in its praise of our 'ability to make public service broadcasting not just informative, but gripping too', and our 'physical, moral and journalistic bravery'.

"Well, you can't please everybody, but at least you're getting noticed," Townson used to say – but then he wasn't directly in the firing line. Still, good reviews outnumbered bad by about two to one. There were often highly polarised critiques of the same programme – and our very worst and very best review were written by one man – Craig Brown of *The Daily Telegraph*. Since they both still make me wince, I shan't trouble you with either of them here.

The last programme of the series was an update of everything that had gone before, a practice we followed from then on. We were able to report that the police had arrested the group of paedophiles we had discovered trading in child pornography. The head of Scotland Yard's Obscene Publications Squad, Superintendent Ian 'Moose' Donaldson said we had highlighted a legal loophole which allowed paedophiles to possess or to exchange child pornography without breaking the law. As long as they didn't sell it, they were safe. He thanked us for our work, and called upon the government to do something. It took a little time, but the law was eventually changed to make the possession of child pornography a criminal offence. The Moose gave us credit for making that change possible – and after a subsequent programme, his successor,

Michael Hames, credited us with prompting further legal changes which then made it much easier to deal with computer pornography.

Gangster Freddie Foreman was expelled from Spain. The Spanish extradition procedures were improved and Ronnie Knight decided to come back to Britain of his own accord. Both went to prison – at last – for their part in the Security Express robbery. Knight got seven years and Foreman got nine.

The most spectacular result from the first series was not to come for two years. But when it finally did, it proved worth the wait.

The trial of Edward John Sayers and his UDA associates opened at Belfast Crown Court in October 1989, two years after the programme was first broadcast. I was called to give evidence for the prosecution against Sayers. Court ushers had placed television monitors in front of the judge, Lord Justice Turlough O'Donnell, and counsel for both sides. Our tapes were played to a hushed court room. Then I was called to the stand. Sayers glared at me from the dock.

His counsel, a flamboyant figure much given to dramatic posturing, began in a vein I have heard in almost all the court cases in which *The Cook Report* has been involved.

"Mr Cook, you set my client up, didn't you?" he asked, drawing himself up to his full height.

"Yes we did," I replied. There was an awkward silence. A ready admission had not been expected and from the outset the defence was not going as planned.

Counsel cleared his throat. "Such tactics are surely unethical," he ventured.

I disagreed. "They would be if we had encouraged an innocent person to do something illegal and out of character, but we never do that. What we did in Mr Sayers' case was give him the opportunity to demonstrate on film what he routinely does – extort money from people. And that film proves he needed little or no encouragement."

The defence changed tack. Throwing back his shoulders and contriving to pull his gown tight across his chest, his thumbs behind his lapels, Counsel intoned: "Mr Cook, I suggest that you were solely motivated by a desire to impress your audience and that you were involved in nothing more than an exercise in blatant theatricality."

I couldn't resist. Backchat is frowned upon in court, but hoping I'd read the judge correctly, I ventured: "You should know."

Lord Justice O'Donnell raised an eyebrow and intervened. "Quite so, Mr Cook, quite so," he murmured, with a faint but knowing smile.

My evidence took two days to complete. At the end of day one, I was escorted to the police yard at the back of the heavily-fortified court and driven to a 'safe house' – a small hotel in Donaghadee on the pretty coastline of County Down, 30 miles to the east of Belfast.

My two RUC minders took great care of me. They had been issued with automatic weapons and powerful walkie-talkies and we sped through the countryside in our unmarked car. This was a little unnerving, since they both seemed to spend more time looking behind them than at the winding road in front.

We had dinner at the hotel and then adjourned to the bar to partake of the landlord's selection of whiskeys. My minders tried to involve me but, although I love good malt whiskey – and there was plenty on offer – I knew I had to keep a clear head for giving evidence the following morning. As one, the minders nodded in agreement. "Sure and we'll get you to bed early and you get your head down," they told me. They were very good company.

By one o'clock they were also a little the worse for wear, but reluctantly eased themselves from their barstools, picked up their weapons and slowly climbed the stairs.

"Get a good night's sleep, Roger. We'll be here if you need us," said one as they ambled back to their rooms.

We were to sleep in three bedrooms at the back of the hotel. They had put a walkie-talkie in each, leaving them switched on so that we could alert each other in an emergency. Within five minutes of climbing into bed, the pair of them were fast asleep and I was forced to listen to their prodigious snoring until I finally dozed off at 4am. In the morning, they were as bright as buttons, and it was I who had trouble getting up.

Three weeks later, Eddie Sayers was sentenced to ten years in gaol. His accomplices got ten, seven and four years each. In court, Lord Justice O'Donnell praised the courage of those who had appeared in the programme, which itself he described as brave, skilfully made and compelling – "all in all, an exceptional example of public service broadcasting."

After the programme, a number of building contractors – some ruined by the extortion racket and others on the brink of bankruptcy because of it – made formal complaints to the police about what was happening and more prosecutions of UDA and IRA men followed. One of the contractors told me that it was the bravery of the victims of terrorism who had contributed to our programme that prompted him to speak out.

Even today, when I go to Northern Ireland, I have to be circumspect. Since the first programme on Mr Sayers and the UDA, *The Cook Report* had also investigated IRA racketeering and had twice revealed the terrorist past of Sinn Fein's Martin McGuinness. So I remained very much unforgiven by the bad boys on both sides in Ulster.

A year after the Sayers trial, I was invited to take part in a late night chat show on Ulster Television. My fellow guests were the singer and humanitarian Midge Ure and my old friend Trevor McDonald. The show's host had hardly had time to introduce me to the studio audience when the phone rang in reception. The brief conversation that followed apparently went like this:

"Tell Mr Cook he's not welcome here," said a man's voice. "In fact, he'll be leaving in a box."

The RUC were waiting at the end of the show. I had to forget the convivial drink I had planned with Trevor and spend another night in another safe house, miles from Belfast.

On his eventual release, Sayers went to work for solicitors Taylor & Co of Donnegal Pass, having studied to be a legal clerk during his sentence. The firm had a number of violent Protestant paramilitaries amongst its clients, including the notorious Johnny 'Mad Dog' Adair. With this in mind, it was rather foolhardy to misappropriate clients' funds, but that's what Taylor & Co did, and the practice was subsequently closed down by the Law Society.

Sayers went on to run a hotel which failed spectacularly, and in December 2006, HM Revenue & Customs successfully petitioned to have him made bankrupt for non payment of tax.

*

127

After the end of the first series, though exhilarated by its success, I went through one of my occasional bouts of self-doubt. Had we really found the best and most effective way of presenting our chosen stories – and was I the right man for the job? In particular, I had really come to dread the confrontations that the programme required, yet I could see no viable alternative.

Those confrontations were seized upon by an advertising agency called Gold Greenlees Trott, which had been hired by ITV to promote their flagship programmes.

The story board they came up with for *The Cook Report* had a punch bag with my face on it being pummelled by a disembodied boxing glove. I vetoed the idea immediately. Not only was it crass and belittling of the programme, but it was also not in line with our audience research. This had found that viewers didn't actually want to see me hit, but did like sitting on the edge of their seats to see how far we would go. I rang the agency's chairman and told him so; he told me that he was the expert in advertising and that I didn't know what I was talking about.

I protested to Central's management, but despite this, the ad was screened – and it took a threat of resignation to have it withdrawn.

However, the first series having achieved such critical acclaim and such colossal audiences, there was now nothing to stop *The Cook Report* – and there was obviously so much criminality to uncover, it looked as if it was going to be a long time before we worked ourselves out of a job.

We were told that our initial commission to make six pro-grammes per year was to be extended to 26 half-hours. It was a totally unrealistic target, and I said so. Nevertheless, Frances and I felt financially reassured by the network's commitment to us, and decided it was time to find somewhere permanent to settle down with little Belinda.

One thing had become clear in my short experience of Mike Townson – my life was going to be lived constantly out of a suitcase. Two factors brought this about. One was the nature of the job. As many as six programmes were being worked on at any one time. As each one developed, it required my presence and I found myself boarding planes from one African country to another, over to Europe, across the USA and then back to inner-city Glasgow or London in the order in which producers and researchers needed me. Factor two was that my initial concerns about the way Townson worked had turned out to be justified. He had revealed himself to be a dyed-in-the-wool control freak whose game plan seemed to be to keep all of us moving while he conjured up the bones of each programme in his head – then rattled them, unfettered, onto his computer keyboard.

This sometimes meant that one or other of us would return to base to discover that Townson's initial computerised creation bore only a passing resemblance to the story we were supposed to be pursuing. Fortunately, the facts always won out in the end.

Life with Mike Townson could never be described as dull. I veered sharply from revering him as a near-genius with a true populist touch in modern programme-making, to regarding him as a near-despot for whom almost any means justified the programme. There were times when the personal cost to others simply didn't enter the equation.

The end result was that it didn't matter where the Cook family decided to settle because I would be away travelling so often. So, when Frances and I paid a visit to friends in the West Country – an area we knew well – and I remarked to her as we drove back to Birmingham that where we had been 'felt like home', we quickly agreed we'd go back there and find ourselves somewhere to live.

Over the next few weeks we embarked on an intensive house-hunt, mindful that the next series was looming, and that soon Townson would be barking down the telephone and firing me off to faraway places.

In those early days, security wasn't such a priority with us or I don't think we would have chosen somewhere so close to a main road. At least we chose a house surrounded on three sides by thick woodland and a steep escarpment, so access isn't easy and that has been a comfort, particularly to Frances, when the death threats have been made.

I won't disclose the location. It's not a matter of being melodramatic or precious. Over the past few years our personal security became a real concern – particularly to my local Regional Crime Squad or Special Branch, whose officers have had occasion to arrive armed at the house.

Belinda has still not forgiven the officers who had to carry out a search of the house when she was about six. Our burglar alarm had gone off in our absence. They came in with a sniffer dog which ran up to her bedroom and so terrified her hamster that the poor thing immediately keeled over in its cage and died of fright. Try telling a six-year-old that it's a small price to pay for peace of mind! To this day that incident is known in our household as 'the night the police murdered our hamster'.

The worst times have been when I was working away from home and the call has come through to me – either from the office, the police, or Frances herself to say that we were on red alert.

On one occasion, I was filming up in Glasgow when Pat Harris, our always unruffled programme manager, rang me on my mobile. Could I, she asked, please telephone a particular Detective Superintendent at the South West Regional Crime Squad? They had just arrested a man who claimed he'd been contracted to ambush and 'terminate' me at my home. Before I could make the call, someone got hold of the story and leaked it to the press.

The following morning's tabloid headlines announced that the police had foiled an attempt to assassinate me, but some of the stories beneath those headlines struck an unnecessarily cynical note. Surely this was a bit of pre-broadcast hype to increase the *Cook Report* audience? Nothing could have been further from the truth.

Frances and Belinda had returned to the house to find it surrounded by armed policemen. A police helicopter hovered above, and my wife and daughter were quickly corralled down the drive while a close search was made of our house and gardens.

I flew to the South West from Scotland as quickly as possible and, after hugs of reassurance with Frances and Belinda, I had a briefing which chilled me to the marrow.

A few months earlier, *The Cook Report* had exposed the international money-laundering activities of John Palmer, a self-professed, near-illiterate who had nevertheless become Britain's richest criminal. *The Sunday Times* Rich List claimed that he was wealthier than the Queen. Nearly a decade before, a jury had acquitted him of melting down the £26 million worth of gold ingots stolen in the 1984 armed robbery of a Brinks Mat bullion van at Heathrow Airport. At the time it had attracted enormous press attention, because it was the world's biggest ever robbery.

However, Palmer somehow managed to convince the jury that he was unaware of the origins of the industrial quantities of gold he had smelted in a makeshift furnace in his back garden. It earned him the sobriquet 'Goldfinger'. Since then, he had made a fortune estimated at between £300 and £400 million from his timeshare operations in the Canary Islands. His methods were fraudulent or violent or both, and he bragged that many senior government and police officials in Tenerife were 'in his pocket'.

We had recently recruited Sylvia Jones, Fleet Street's first female crime correspondent, who provided a welcome leavening of our all-male research team and a number of new contacts. She and Clive Entwistle had heard from police sources that Palmer was also 'laundering' illegally-obtained funds for the criminal fraternity and making a hefty profit in the process. This was of much more interest to us than timeshare, a subject we had visited several times previously. So we designed a sophisticated sting to encourage Palmer to demonstrate his money laundering skills in the drugs trade – the obvious source of large quantities of dirty money. Using as bait two representatives from a Burmese heroin cartel – a link surviving from a programme in which I had trekked through the steaming jungles of the Golden Triangle on the back of a mule to meet the cartel's boss – *The Cook Report* lured Palmer in.

Because they were the real thing, Palmer couldn't fault our Burmese friends – though he subsequently tried to claim that they were actors and that he'd seen through them from day one. He greedily agreed that twice a year, he would launder around $60 million worth of post-harvest opium profits for them, and boasted that his rates were the best in the business.

In return, Palmer asked if they could supply him with untraceable 'soldiers' to act as enforcers for him. Every meeting was secretly filmed until we had Mr Palmer well and truly 'bang to rights'. It was a peach of a sting, probably our best, though it was one which the police had initially advised us against. Palmer was just too sharp, they said, and 'pretty nearly untouchable'.

He tried to deny all the evidence when I confronted him in the tea rooms of The Ritz in London. The perfect location, I thought, because that's where the Brinks Mat robbery had allegedly been planned. We had done a little planning too. My arrival in the tea rooms had been coordinated with police raids on all Palmer's UK addresses.

As he bolted out through the revolving doors and into a taxi, I was able to fire off the relevant questions – backed of course, by his own claims on film. He tried to stay cool and uncommunicative as the taxi moved off – only to stop a few yards further on when the traffic lights turned red. I opened the taxi door and repeated the questions – at which point Palmer obviously saw red. He was so angry that the startled taxi driver rang *The Cook Report* office to tell us about it afterwards. When the lights changed, Palmer had hurriedly rung all his homes and offices – only to have the calls answered by the police. Shaking with fury, he then hurled his phone through the taxi window. By the time he saw the programme when it was broadcast a few days later, he must have been beside himself.

We pieced together the events of the succeeding weeks from underworld contacts and the police. The belief was that one of Palmer's lieutenants had apparently enlisted the services of a British-based criminal who, for £20,000, had agreed to kill me. He was picked up by the police in an entirely different connection and, in the course of trying to do a deal with the arresting officers, spilled the beans about what he claimed he had been contracted to do.

The briefing officer, having told me that the tariff on my life was £20,000, and having assured me that this particular potential assassin was now temporarily out of circulation, asked dryly if I wasn't a bit miffed that the sum on offer was so low!

Palmer later denied any connection with this particular plot and issued a writ for libel – which was never pursued. Nevertheless, the advice from the police at the time was that I should take extra precautions. I stepped up our home security, but it still took us all a long time before we could relax as we came up the drive or keep our eyes from scanning every corner of the garden or every stranger walking past the gates.

The Palmer programme had been produced with the full knowledge of the Metropolitan Police Special Operations Department. We had agreed to steer clear of his timeshare activities, concentrating instead on the much sexier subject of money laundering, and they had used the upcoming broadcast as a reason to raid all Palmer's UK premises. They took away van loads of evidence of systematic timeshare fraud.

The rationale for the division of interest was that the police wanted Palmer exposed, but didn't want anything broadcast on the matters they wished to prosecute, so nobody could claim we'd prejudiced a fair trial. And so nobody could make the further claim that we had colluded with them, we only passed on our evidence on the eve of transmission.

By the time Palmer got to court, five years later, the first edition of this book had just been published. It contained a brief reference to the money laundering programme which was then drawn to the attention of the judge. Unaware of our working agreement with Special Operations, because nobody had bothered to tell him, the judge reported me and my publisher to the Attorney General's Department for contempt of court.

This meant that the book had to be withdrawn and pulped. It then had to be reprinted, with all reference to Palmer deleted and a new ISBN identifying number. Withdrawals are thankfully rare, and perhaps as a result, there was some confusion in the book trade as to which printing was which and what could or could not be sold. Some bookshops sold the original edition and returned the reprints in error; others thought the book had been 'banned' for good. Most, however, reported heartening initial sales for what was then the authorised version. Not that this got us onto the bestseller list, where the sales figures indicated we should have been. The organisation which compiles the list had apparently been tracking the wrong edition.

And then, after all that palaver, the Attorney General's Department wrote to us to say that no action for contempt of court was called for. Presumably they'd checked our working arrangement with Scotland Yard. So the book needn't have been withdrawn at all. But by then it was too late, the impetus had been lost, Amazon.com, Waterstone's and other leading booksellers listed it as out of print, and a promising, well-reviewed book was dead in the water. Pity.

When his trial ended, 52-year-old Palmer was found guilty and sentenced to eight years in prison. His fraudulent activities had claimed 17,000 victims and legal moves are still afoot in an attempt to reclaim as much as possible of the £80 million estimated to have been involved.

Unfortunately, these moves will now probably have to rely on civil rather than criminal procedures. In April 2002, after Palmer's conviction, he was served with a confiscation order for £33,243,812.46, but the order was subsequently overturned because the Crown Prosecution Service had apparently used incorrect paperwork – though nobody had any doubts as to the validity of the claim on Palmer's criminal assets.

A year on, the Court of Appeal ruled that the confiscation order should never have been quashed, but that it was now procedurally impossible to reinstate it. Sadly, this is yet another of the many examples I have come across where, by applying strict rules rather than common sense, the law has made an ass of itself.

4

Takes Two, Three and Four

*The Brazilian baby trade, the African ivory trade,
the shocking failures of the World Wide Fund for
Nature and the real Martin McGuinness*

It was to be eight months before *The Cook Report* went back on air. During that time, the team continued to work hard developing new ideas, but the good luck that had helped us in the first series seemed suddenly to have vanished into thin air. For one reason or another, stories fell over like ninepins, and our 'leading-edge' camera technology sometimes defeated, rather than aided us.

We were particularly keen to develop further our methods of catching out the bad boys on screen, and secret filming was the obvious way to go. We'd started experimenting when we set about trapping the child pornography dealers in Amsterdam and, despite the unwieldy nature of our hidden camera, had succeeded.

Nowadays, everybody's doing secret filming – in programmes ranging from current affairs to light entertainment – using ultra-reliable colour cameras half the size of a matchbox. We pioneers didn't have it so easy. Our earliest 'box of tricks' was a briefcase containing two bulky and rather primitive cameras aiming out of each end. One recorded in colour for shooting in good conditions, the other in black and white, which picked up far better images in low-light or night time situations.

Of course, you had to remember which end of the briefcase had which camera pointing out of it – then aim and switch on the right one in the right conditions without making it obvious. It wasn't that simple, and I remember one occasion when Tim Tate managed to film an hour of his own out-of-focus knees as he sat pointing the 'dead' end of the case at an unwitting pornographer. Blurred pictures of knees in jeans are not very useful evidence.

And if you didn't have operator problems, then the equipment, or the weather, or even your target could ruin your efforts and leave you looking pretty silly. Early radio microphones were notoriously unreliable, so you might end up with silent pictures.

On other occasions you might get the sound, but no useable pictures – as, for example, when we leapt from our steamy surveillance van one cold winter morning and the camera lens misted over almost instantaneously. The only images we got were of the cameraman's fingers, furiously fumbling to clean it off. And on one particularly memorable occasion, we were seen off by the technical knowledge of the target, a dodgy antiques wholesaler who had once been in television himself.

At this stage and where possible, we had ceased relying on radio microphones and had reverted to old fashioned cables connecting the cameraman and the sound recordist. As we approached our target in his warehouse, and before we could get filming in earnest, he produced an evil looking oriental knife.

There was a quick corporate intake of breath. Fortunately, he didn't go for any of us, but for that vital umbilical cable, which he severed with a single stroke. He finished us off, in television terms, by turning off the lights. It was all over in a few, heart-stopping seconds and produced no useable material. After that, we doubled up on every connection, using both cable *and* radio.

For Series Two, we had adopted a new means of filming secretly, based on the very first Pulnix high-resolution mini-camera. For us, this was a giant step forward in technology – it produced good pictures and was generally reliable. We installed this then very expensive device in several housings, including a briefcase, a portable television, a wall clock and a rather fetching flower arrangement. It was in this last guise that the camera was first used. The camera sat inside a lily and the bulky recorder that went with it, in the vase below.

In 1988, the British tabloid papers were involved in another of their regular circulation wars. *The Sun* had gained the upper-hand, not least because it was offering huge prizes in its Bingo competition. We got wind of a fiddle being worked by a small group of printers who helped produce the official cards for the *Sun* Bingo game. They were supplying winning cards in advance of publication to their friends, who were duly raking in many thousands of pounds. This buckshee booty was later distributed amongst the gang.

Our informant, posing as another printer, persuaded one of the gang to come to a meeting to explain how the scam was working. It had been suggested that our man might produce and distribute yet more cards in another part of the country, so as to reduce suspicion and increase the take.

The pirate printer stipulated that the meeting take place in a quiet corner of the foyer of the Hilton National Hotel at Manchester Airport. We arrived early and placed our own, impressive flower display on a convenient table, the Pulnix safely hidden inside, its lens pointing at the seat opposite where we planned that the target would sit.

He arrived and sat down exactly where we wanted him.

Then, as he started to tell us how to make an unauthorised fortune out of *Sun* Bingo, an elderly Hilton maintenance man ambled slowly towards the table, carrying a small watering-can. He reached us just as the printer was starting to name names. There was a faint fizz and a brief, barely audible crackle as the water hit the flowers. Hilton man moved slowly on, oblivious to what he had just done.

The rest of the conversation was pointless. It's risky to ask a criminal to go back over what they've just told you, 'What was that again? I've forgotten the detail, I'm afraid', because he may well smell a rat if you do.

As soon as our villain had gone, we bore the sodden display and its £7,000 worth of short-circuited electronics back to Birmingham to view the film in Townson's office. Everything had worked perfectly at first – you could even make out the maintenance man as he hove into sight behind our target. Then the sound spluttered out and the picture on the TV screen turned to a flickering snowstorm.

The following week, before we could arrange another meeting, the gang disintegrated in a dispute over the sharing of the spoils. There being no honour amongst thieves, jealous gang members betrayed each other to the police, leaving us without the planned programme.

The lead-in to the second series was also a time in which my fears about Mike Townson's controlling tendencies were reconfirmed. The team would spend weeks on complete wild-goose chases as he chopped and changed his plans. In theory, the selection of stories was a fairly democratic process. In practice it was often rather less so.

The distribution of *Cook Report* staff around the world grew wider as Townson piled on the workload. He telephoned us all constantly, demanding updates on what we had done, who we had seen and when we expected to film something important.

In the end, we started the second series with the Brazilian baby trade programme that we had almost finished the previous year, and followed it with programmes on the dangers of prescribed medicines, loan-sharking in Scotland and, more spectacularly, badger-baiting. Peter Salkeld and I had hunted the badger-baiters together in all weathers, ending up leaping from a helicopter to confront a group of these brutal men in the rugged hinterlands of West Wales. We interrupted their preparations to stage a fight to the death between their dogs and a badger that they were in the process of digging from his sett.

They stood their ground rather than flee without their dogs, which were still underground. That gave me the time to fire a few questions at them. At first they claimed that the sett was deserted, and then when the RSPCA inspector who had accompanied us produced evidence that badgers were still in occupation, they changed tack and insisted that they were engaged in a legitimate sport. Nevertheless, as soon as they'd retrieved their dogs, they were off into the gathering dusk. One badger saved, six men shamed. Don't ask how much hiring the helicopter cost.

The jaded *Cook Report* team convened for the transmission of the first show in Townson's office. Memories of Rosilda, Bruna and the atmosphere of Rio at Carnival came flooding back as I sat crammed onto a sofa in the corner of the room. I looked around and thought how tired everyone looked. No surprise really, when you consider that 100-hour working weeks were not uncommon – *and* there was still a long way to go before we completed every programme in the series.

The second programme we made about Bruna and Rosilda gave us enormous satisfaction. I'll never forget the emotions we felt when an Israeli judge found in Rosilda's favour, or when, at the end of our return journey from a successful mission in Tel Aviv, the aircraft door opened at Curitiba Airport to reveal a welcoming party of more than 100,000 people. We were almost as elated as Rosilda.

Bruna's story had become a *cause célèbre* in Brazil. It had also become one in Israel, but for very different reasons. The Israeli media attacked us for interfering in their country's internal affairs, quite forgetting that it was not Roger Cook who had authorised Bruna's return to Brazil with her natural mother, but an Israeli judge, following a conclusive DNA test.

A child psychologist and a specialist social worker who had assessed both mother and daughter decided that Rosilda was an exceptional mother and that despite their protracted separation, Bruna's best interests would be served by sending her home.

Ignoring all this, the Israeli media line was taken up in the UK by *The Mail on Sunday*, which despatched a reporter to Brazil to interview Rosilda. Rosilda didn't believe that the reporter wanted to do the kind of sympathetic story she claimed she would write, and sent her away with a flea in her ear. Despite this, *The Mail* persevered with the story.

To it were added the claims of an Israeli cameraman that we had falsified some of the footage of Rosilda's first sighting of Bruna in Tel Aviv. The facts are that, despite instructions to the contrary, he had filmed the event in such a way that it couldn't be properly edited, and from such a distance that Rosilda's reactions on seeing her child couldn't be clearly discerned.

At the chastened cameraman's suggestion, close-up shots of Rosilda were taken the next day – with her full co-operation and understanding – to try to reproduce what had happened 24 hours earlier. One of those brief supplementary shots – misguidedly – involved the use of eye drops to replace the previous day's genuine tears of emotion.

Misguided, yes. Dishonest, no. But the end result was a disproportionate amount of fuss over two seconds of air time. Mind you, there was no fuss at all when the programme was broadcast.

The cameraman only complained months after the initial filming when he realised that he wasn't going to be re-engaged to shoot the second Bruna programme. By then, we had been given the services of a top-notch Brazilian crew free of charge. After pressure from *Cook Report* lawyers, *The Mail on Sunday* eventually published a full apology.

Years later, we were given a further drubbing in the national press following another programme on the baby trade, this time from Guatemala. Newspapers had swallowed whole and apparently unchecked, the wholly false assertions made by a London-based organisation called the Guatemalan Support Group (GSG). They had suggested that we had sent a pair of actors to Guatemala to mock up the adoption of a child which they then presumed would be abandoned after filming. In fact, the couple concerned were perfectly genuine, and had come to us because they had found the adoption process to be beset with unscrupulous middlemen and corrupt lawyers. They were particularly dubious about the Support Group, members of which had been advising them – and had volunteered to allow us to follow their adoption efforts on film. Avoiding the pitfalls and doing the adoption scrupulously by the book took rather a long time, but the couple were ultimately successful and their little boy (who can't be named for legal reasons) settled happily in the UK.

Once the lad was legally able to leave Guatemala, we had re-visited the story with a view to including it in one of our regular update programmes. What we then found was a whole new market-place in which children were no more than commodities and those who dealt in them grew extremely rich. Guatemala's most famous adoption lawyer, Juan Varela, who was initially involved in the adoption we were following, was reputed to earn up to 50 times as much as his country's President and 400 times the salary of a judge. This was an update that deserved a complete programme on its own.

In fact, it was the way the GSG operated that was the real story – which the papers either missed or chose to ignore. Caught on secret film, those advising our couple were at best extremely naïve or at worst totally irresponsible. They recommended ways of 'getting round' UK immigration law, the obtaining of private Home Study Reports from a since disbarred social worker who barely bothered to interview prospective parents and didn't bother at all with the requisite background checks, and the professional services of Lya Sorano, who turned out to be a notorious 'baby broker' who had been banned from working with children in the United States. However, she continued to operate in Europe, charging up to $20,000 per child adopted.

Amongst her many disgraceful transactions, Sorano had 'sold' children who had been kidnapped, children who didn't exist, and 'healthy children' who actually had severe disabilities, including one so ill with a congenital heart defect that the poor mite died within weeks of being delivered to her horrified adoptive parents. Sorano was not pleased to see us when we tracked her down in Atlanta – and Juan Varela, her unscrupulous Guatemalan legal associate wouldn't see us at all, preferring to stay surrounded by armed guards in his luxury compound in the hills overlooking Guatemala City.

The newspaper coverage was completely uncritical of the morally bankrupt money-grubbers Sorano and Varela, while we were portrayed as cavalier, self-appointed meddlers who had condoned the adoption of a stolen child. The truth was that his natural mother had voluntarily given him up for adoption in exchange for money from Varela. When we broke the story, the Guatemalan authorities took him into state care and he was placed in a private orphanage – paid for by his prospective parents – until the legal adoption process was complete, nearly a year later. Actually this was a *Cook Report*, like many others, which we were asked to make by the victims of the rogues they wanted us to expose. If we were appointed at all, it was by our viewers.

Bad press notwithstanding, the programme was also followed by an official investigation into the activities of Juan Varela – who, like Sorano was forced out of the baby business – the introduction of compulsory DNA testing to determine the true parentage of children up for adoption to the UK – where adoption laws were also strengthened in 1999 and again in 2002 – and action by the UN, which sent a Special Rapporteur to Guatemala to investigate what had become the country's largest 'non-traditional' export. The GSG no longer exists.

Sadly, though the overall situation has improved somewhat, Guatemala has yet to meet the standards required for accession to the Hague Convention on Intercountry Adoption – something that would give both children and adoptive parents a measure of protection. It is still a very impoverished country, plagued by bouts of civil unrest and not long recovered from the ravages of civil war. When we were filming, even the Coca-Cola delivery trucks carried guards riding shotgun. The rule of law still doesn't run very far, and Guatemalan children continue to be exploited – arguably in an even more callously commercial way than we had previously found when we investigated the baby trade in relatively prosperous

141

Brazil. Prospective overseas adopters need to be very careful indeed.

The day after our Brazilian programme was broadcast, the viewing figures confirmed the way I felt: down to just over six million, compared to ten million for our first ever outing. It looked as if the undeserved negative publicity had done us some damage. Though the figures soon improved, they did not fully recover for the rest of the series. Even the badger programme, which had involved six weekends of very exciting, and very expensive, helicopter pursuit of the Welsh badger-baiters, failed to dig us out of the doldrums. Self-doubt began to creep back. Had we lost our touch?

No, said the audience researchers, blame the good summer weather which is keeping potential viewers outdoors, and perhaps the fact that the initial novelty value of Cook-style journalism might be wearing off. Fortunately, in terms of the size of our viewing audience, we never had another series like it, although our figures were still streets ahead of any of our rivals. A third series was commissioned without hesitation.

Everyone took a much-needed break after the second series ended. I went to the West Country to try to get to know my little family again, especially five-year-old Belinda. I had been alarmed by reports from her primary school about how much she was being affected by my prolonged absences.

On one occasion, she and her classmates had been asked by their teacher to take part in a short public-speaking exercise – 'My father's job'.

"My father," said one youngster, "is a doctor and he makes sick people better."

"My father," said another, "is a farmer and he grows food for us all."

"Mine's a train driver," chimed in another, "He can take you to London."

And so on, until it was Belinda's turn.

"My father," said Belinda firmly, "is a telephone."

"He's a telephone. My Dad's a telephone," explained Belinda under interrogation. The teacher gave Frances a call.

For the previous four months, while the second series was being made, nearly all the contact I had with my daughter was brief, tender moments on the line from whichever hotel I was staying in. No wonder the poor child was confused. We took a long holiday together, and this time there were no telephones.

My prolonged absences were accepted – but never welcomed. Frances had learned that a call from me in Birmingham often heralded a trip away of anything up to three or four weeks. Very sensibly, she took up a mature degree course – studying day and night, in between looking after Belinda and the house. Frances came out with a 2:1 and one of her tutors came out with an unintended and unforgettable put-down at the degree ceremony: "Mr Cook, you must be so proud of your daughter!" I was mortified.

When Belinda was very small, I would sneak away at the end of shoots wherever we were in the world and head for the nearest and most expensive-looking children's clothes shop. I would emerge with several beautifully-made but arguably over-priced and over-fussy outfits which I would proudly produce out of my suitcase back at home under the quizzical gaze of Frances. Some outfits she allowed Belinda to be dressed in. Others I never saw again.

Nobody really tells you how to be a father. I certainly hadn't had much of a role model in my own Dad. We were never close and I always had the feeling that yes, of course, my sister Jane and I were his children but we were rather a lot of trouble. He was an artist first and foremost and there isn't much room for impromptu fun and frolics when all your energy is going into paint and canvas. So, without much of a memory of how it should be done, and a whole lot of guilt that my job made me such an absentee parent, I often got it wrong. The real solution, of course, would have been to control my rampant workaholism and to spend more time at home. But it was easier said than done.

The all-consuming job had other unfortunate side-effects too. I love good music – usually classical, and good books – preferably biographical, but I got precious little of either. I found it difficult to relax for very long and the amount of paperwork I had to plough through professionally meant that when I did get home, I was suffering from print fatigue. I never did the domestic paper-work either – poor Frances got landed with that.

I went to the theatre with friends when I could, but my social life always involved more last-minute cancellations than events attended. I gave up going to the cinema because I was forever being buttonholed by people with problems, and for years the only movies I saw were those available on long-haul flights. Four out of ten, Cook. Should have tried harder.

Belinda soon realised what a soft touch my shortcomings made me. As she grew a little older, she realised the true strength of her bargaining position when she wanted something. One day I'd be confronting a multiple murderer or one of the world's biggest drug barons to demand an explanation for their heinous crimes. The next, I would be promising almost anything to a little blue-eyed girl who would finally win her argument by looking up at me and asking – at least on one occasion: "Okay, Dad, how cute do I have to be?"

Home was a million miles from the punishing schedule of *The Cook Report* and was heaven to return to. But there is a balance to be struck. Anyone who has ever seen me during one of my rare enforced lay-offs from work – usually caused by injury – can tell you that I just want to get involved with the job again.

As one of my several orthopaedic surgeons once remarked: "I see a lot of patients with relatively minor injuries who don't ever want to go back to work, and here you are with a broken neck and all you want to do is get back to work immediately. This time you'll have to be patient." Patient? There has never been a more impatient patient.

It's in situations like that when I can become a little Townson-esque myself. Colleagues can expect a telephone call at work or home as I demand to know the latest development on some story – and the gossip too. The *Cook Report* office was full of very talented journalists and programme-makers with contacts absol-utely everywhere. To tap into it was to learn the most extraordinary things.

At any one time, the inside-track knowledge in the office would include details of secret police investigations, imminent arrests of high-profile public figures, and ongoing international criminal activ-ity as well as scandals brewing in the political world.

More than once, we've all sat down to weigh up whether it really was in the public interest to investigate the private sexual activity of a member of the government. On occasion, we've been actively encouraged by one section of law enforcement to look at someone's aberrant behaviour – only to be taken aside by another department which asks, or demands, that we lay off.

In the early 1990s, we were getting monthly reports of a secret squad of police officers moving to arrest a leading Conservative politician with bizarre sexual proclivities. The reports then ceased abruptly, and we were later told that the squad had been heavily rebuked by an even more 'secret' police team with orders to hush things up and curtail any investigation.

It is both extraordinary and exciting to be privy to such information, but in this case we would not have used it. Personally, I believe sexual activity between consenting adults is, and should remain, their own business. Likewise, stories about the recreational drug-taking habits of D-list celebrities, so beloved of the tabloid newspapers. There is a line to be drawn between genuine public interest and mere prurience.

Mind you, you shouldn't get the idea that everything we do is exciting. Much of it is distinctly unexciting routine. Waiting for research to be completed, waiting for witnesses to respond or targets to turn up. I couldn't calculate how many hours I've spent in the back of a surveillance van for example – days and nights in company with colleagues including the aptly nicknamed 'Mr Methane', a man so potentially noxious he had to be banned from eating curries.

Long hours locked up in a van brought with it other alimentary problems. For example, how to relieve ourselves when nature called. Well, thanks to one of our original production assistants, we had a system. Her consideration followed an incident in which a sound recordist, who had to leap from a van into a frozen winter evening after eight hours in a van, actually wet himself.

Professional to the last, he kept on recording, and our fraudster target was brought to book – but the soundman's embarrassing plight required a solution. The PA disappeared round the corner to a nearby hardware store, to return half an hour later with a large plastic jerry can and a set of colour-coded funnels. That became The System.

Far from chasing swindlers in the snow, Salk was keen to produce more programmes on the plight of endangered wildlife. He firmly believed that the British public's love of animals would broaden

145

our audience appeal. He loved filming the natural world and the two of us agreed that we would support each other at *Cook Report* meetings if Townson resisted research into the general subject.

In early September, the telephone rang in the Cook household. Frances passed the receiver to me. It was an excited Salk. Once he'd calmed down a little, he told me he'd found an important and appealing wildlife story and he also thought he'd found a way to convince Townson to make the programme.

Intensive scouring of wildlife magazines had yielded a cutting from a correspondent in Hong Kong who had implicated a company there in large-scale illegal ivory dealing. Salk had also amassed a wealth of material on the impending disaster facing the African elephant. In 1988, the world was only just waking up to the fact that the trade in tusks was threatening one of the best-loved creatures on earth with total extinction.

"What's more," cackled Salk, "you'll have to go to the Far East and at least three African countries. Townson will love it – you'll be out of his hair for weeks."

He was right. Townson saw the attractions of the story straight away. If *The Cook Report* could be the first to present filmed proof of the desperate plight of the African elephant and at the same time expose those who were making big money out of it, the programme could win back the viewers it had lost in the second series – *and* it meant I would be out on the road while he was left to his own devices.

For a week, Salk hit the telephones in the Birmingham office to find a starting point in Africa. A call to one of the wildlife charities put him on to a white hunter turned conservationist operating in Zambia. For months, Alistair Gellatly had been sending in reports of the wholesale slaughter of the elephants in Luangwa, in the east of Zambia, where he now ran his photo safaris. Salk eventually tracked down a number for Gellatly and, on a crackling line, discovered that the killings were happening almost every week. Gellatly told him he was welcome to join him – while there were still some elephants left to film.

Salk and his sound recordist, Bill Dodkin, arrived in Zambia two days later to find heavy flooding throughout the Luangwa Valley. They made it by safari truck to Gellatly's camp, but were warned that it would be foolhardy to venture out until the crocodile-infested waters receded.

The following day, they woke to the sound of voices outside Gellatly's house. A black African game warden was talking excitedly to the ex-hunter. Gellatly shouted across to Salk and Dodkin and pointed down a mud track behind the encampment.

Six African rangers were ambling slowly into the camp in single-file. Each had an ancient rifle strapped across his back and a stick resting on his shoulder. From each stick dangled a thin, grey, tufted tail two or three feet long. Despite the storms and floods, here was proof of the continuing massacre of the elephants.

The rangers told Gellatly that they had found the bodies of five elephants lying in a small group a few miles away in dense bushland. They had been machine gunned down. The sixth, a tuskless female, had managed to run off. But the loss of blood from her wounds had brought her crashing down in a clearing half a mile from the other members of the herd. All the magnificent ivory tusks had been hacked off with chainsaws and carried away by the poachers within an hour, leaving their prey to the bush scavengers and the flies.

Salk started the lengthy process of dialling Townson on Gellatly's decrepit old telephone. Eventually, Salk heard his editor's brusque voice bellowing down the receiver to him to speak up. Salk explained the situation in equally stentorian manner.

"Right," yelled Townson. "Roger's on his way – aren't you Roger?"

I guessed I was. I had rushed into Townson's office to catch the last part of the high-volume conversation. It had been impossible to miss it. Everyone was staring through Townson's open door wondering what the hell was going on.

I called Frances to tell her I was flying to Zambia that evening. In anticipation of this, I'd already had the necessary jabs and was well underway with my anti-malaria tablets.

"Take good care of yourself and don't get shot by poachers," she said.

Or deafened by mad editors on the telephone, I thought.

I had been booked to fly to Lusaka on a now, happily, defunct African airline which consisted at the time of one ageing DC10. This one plane, however, had been taken out of service when I arrived at Heathrow and we were to travel in a hired-in replacement.

I knew it was going to be 'one of those flights' when a fight

147

broke out during boarding. The cabin crew were trying to seat us according to a DC10 seating plan, which simply did not work, because the replacement was a rather smaller DC9.

No one got the seats they paid for. You took what you got, or you got off. I ended up right at the back, crammed between a very large, chocoholic German lady and a very tall African gentleman who constantly hummed an out-of-tune dirge and rattled through his worry beads.

The plane pressed into service had obviously come from the aeronautical equivalent of rent-a-wreck. It didn't have the range of the DC10, so our direct flight now included a stopover in Cyprus. Unfortunately, the air crew seemed to have great difficulty in finding Cyprus, and then in finding the right airport. They also had trouble raising the wherewithal to pay for the fuel, landing-fees and on-board catering. After a delay of several hours, the pilot reluctantly agreed to pay for the fuel and landing fees on his personal credit card. Food, we had to forego.

It was a rough onward flight to Zambia. The ancient plane creaked and groaned. A lady up front, soaked by a regular trickle of condensation, hysterically proclaimed that there was a 'petrol leak'. You can imagine the reaction of her fellow passengers.

During a particularly unpleasant spell of turbulence, the over-head clamshell lockers all opened as if choreographed, disgorging their contents over cowering passengers and into the aisles. My immediate travelling companions took this latest incident particularly badly. The worry beads clicked like high-speed maracas and the large lady, who had been scoffing chocolates as if they were the last supper, announced that she was going to be sick – which she duly was, all over me and the worry beads.

In the interests of personal hygiene, I headed for the lavatories. Of the two nearest to my seat, one had been – literally – boarded up, and in the other the bowl was clogged up with what appeared to be a straw hat. The tap over the hand basin produced no water, and there was no sign of soap.

On my way to the alternative facilities, I was almost bowled over by one of the rent-a-wreck hostesses as she charged past me carrying a mask and an oxygen cylinder. My confidence in the chances of surviving this bizarre flight, already pretty near rock-bottom, plunged to uncharted depths when I realised that her destination was the cockpit.

Somehow, we limped into Zambian airspace and made the descent, landing at Lusaka without further mishap. The fact that the first airport taxi I engaged somehow caught fire with me in it didn't faze me one bit. After all, it had happened twice before.

I seem to have been on some of the world's worst flights. Later, during the same shoot, flying with Salk up to Dar es Salaam in Tanzania, our post-lunch reverie was rudely interrupted by a loud bang and a violent juddering. Salk pointed out of the window towards what appeared, to me, to be a large chunk of engine spiralling earthwards.

The captain's eventual attempt at reassurance didn't really wash in the face of the visual evidence, let alone its basic implausibility. "Not to worry, ladies and gentlemen," he said in an almost impenetrable African accent. "The vibrations you have felt were perfectly normal. Because we were going very very fast and may have overshot our destination, I have just had to put on some reverse thrust."

At 32,000 feet?

Fortunately, the other three engines stayed in one piece and we made our descent into Dar, where they put screens around the affected wing before they would let us off the aircraft. They told the passengers travelling onward to stay aboard. Sensible people didn't stay long, and the plane was still there when we left the country two weeks later.

I firmly believe that bad things, particularly those of a similar sort, happen in threes. Later on the elephant shoot, Salk and I had to leave the game reserve by light aircraft. The aviation fuel, hand-pumped from a stack of 44-gallon drums beside the bush airstrip, had been filtered through a pair of nylon tights, but the pilot still wasn't sure it was entirely clean. He also thought it might have contained some water, but there was nothing more we could do about it. In any case, the engines eventually cranked into life, so we thought the fuel couldn't have been too contaminated after all.

It was. At 14,000 feet over the Luangwa Valley, both engines spluttered briefly and cut out. In the awful silence that followed, I was transfixed by the needle on the altimeter. We fell nearly eight thousand feet before the pilot managed – with commendable coolness – to restart first one engine, then the other.

Stories about your life flashing before your eyes at moments like

149

this *are* true. But nothing flashed before Salk's eyes. He'd managed to sleep through the lot.

After that first rent-a-wreck adventure, I finally found a taxi that wasn't about to spontaneously combust and got to a hotel for a much-needed sleep. Several hours later, suitably refreshed, I was joined by *Cook Report* researcher Kevin Dowling for the onward flight from Lusaka to Luangwa. A serious, schoolmasterly man of about 45 who had covered the world as a newspaperman, Kevin had joined *The Cook Report* a few months earlier and this was the first time he had been abroad for months. He was clearly relishing the experience. I wondered whether he'd feel the same after a week or two in the bush.

Salk and Bill Dodkin came to meet us at the Luangwa airstrip. The sound man was wearing baggy, khaki shorts and a green safari shirt. His exposed skin was covered in mosquito bites and he was clearly suffering, to judge from his inflamed legs and the time he was devoting to scratching himself. Salk was wearing what he usually wore wherever he travelled in the world – a two-piece grey suit, a white shirt and a tie. He'd even gone skiing on an assignment in Colorado wearing the same outfit.

But Salk's eccentric dress-sense was paying dividends in the Zambian bush. "Bill's even got mosquito bites on his mosquito bites," cackled Salk, "The mozzies can't find anywhere to get me."

I too was glad that I had on my usual khaki field 'uniform' of long-sleeved shirt and long cotton twill trousers. Nevertheless, as rumour had it that the mosquito-borne malaria parasites here-abouts had now developed a resistance to the particular anti-malarial tablets we were taking, I crossed my fingers that they'd work.

Before my arrival, Salk had been hoping to get some preliminary filming done by boat, but Alistair Gellatly had said no. Hippos had followed the crocodiles into the floodlands and he was fearful that the boat would be capsized. The hippopotamus may look like a smiling, benign cartoon character but, in reality, they kill more people than lions and crocodiles put together. It's apparently not uncommon for a human to be bitten in half by an enraged hippo, despite the fact that they're vegetarians. Salk had taken Gellatly's warning on board, and agreed to wait for me to arrive and for the floodwaters to abate.

By the time we all got back to Alistair Gellatly at his camp, the waters had receded enough for us to make an attempt to reach the scene of the elephant massacre by four-wheel-drive vehicle.

We set off in Gellatly's truck at daybreak. Our team comprised Gellatly himself, three Bantu African rangers, Salk, Dodkin, Dowling and me. There was talk that the poachers were still in the area, scouring around for more prey, armed with Kalashnikov automatic rifles. Our rangers carried World War II Lee Enfield rifles but, we were dismayed to learn, only two bullets each.

All the dirt roads had been washed away by the rains. The flood waters might have receded, but there were still vast, deep lakes where the scrub would usually have been. Gellatly had anticipated this and, whenever the waters started to lap over the hubs of the truck, and the wheels began to spin on the underlying mud, he would hand one of the rangers the looped end of a long roll of cable. The other end was secured firmly to a winch on the front bumper of the truck.

The ranger would then wade ahead until he found a tree some 30 yards ahead. The cable would be tied round the trunk and, after a wave of approval from the ranger, Gellatly would switch the winch mechanism on and, foot by foot, we would move forward, the cable stretched taut in front of us. It was a slow, tortuous process.

We had only gone about a mile and a half before we realised that our task was impossible. The turbid water was getting deeper and suitable trees to which we could attach the winch rope were becoming fewer and farther between. Gellatly turned to me from the front passenger seat. "The rangers say we're still a couple of miles away. We can go back and try again another day but the longer we leave it, the less there will be left to see, if you catch my meaning. Or we can get out, carry your gear and wade."

I looked across to Salk. We weighed it up. There were crocodiles and hippos out there – not to mention the possibility of trigger-happy poachers toting Kalashnikovs. The pictures, though, would be the most eloquent, though disturbing evidence of the wholesale slaughter we were trying to show the world. In two days' time the ravages of heat and scavengers might render that evidence unrecognisable.

"Sod it, let's get out and walk," said Salk. He hefted his tripod onto his shoulder and climbed gingerly over the side of the truck. His long, suit-clad leg sank knee-deep into the mud-coloured water.

Everyone but the third ranger would press on to find the scene of the massacre. He would drive the truck back to the camp and we would make the entire journey to and from the scene on foot.

The going was difficult. The ground under the water was slippery, deceptively uneven and strewn with rock and fallen branches. Sometimes we left the water behind altogether, thankfully squishing through deep mud or even finding stretches of almost dry land. We walked in single-file, the ranger who had first discovered the elephants taking the lead.

Everyone helped carry the camera and sound equipment, while keeping a constant vigil for crocodiles and hippos. Several times one of us would stumble and almost plunge headfirst into the water, inches away from ducking the camera, batteries or tapes and making the hazardous trip a complete waste of time.

Four hours later, the leading ranger turned to Gellatly and pointed. "Not far now. A few hundred yards more of this and we'll see what you've come all this way for," Gellatly told our sodden, mud-streaked and panting group.

There was the sound of faint, ragged cheering from the middle-aged and unfit *Cook Report* personnel.

We could smell it before we saw it. Kevin Dowling pulled a handkerchief from his pocket and clapped it round his nose and mouth. The stench was overpowering. The flies swarmed about us in clouds. Dowling turned away and vomited violently. It was all I could do to avoid doing the same.

Ahead of us, on a raised, dry mound of bleached earth lay the bodies of the elephants. Each face had been, literally, hacked off with a chainsaw to make the removal of the precious tusks easier.

Salk and Dodkin set up the camera and sound rig while Dowling and I joined Gellatly and his men as they searched for the injured female which had struggled off to die alone.

Half a mile away across the marshy bush-bog, there she was, lying on her side, riddled with bullets and smelling hideously of decay. Slaughtered even though she'd never had the tusks the poachers' paymasters in the Far East coveted so much.

Today, the world knows all about the illegal ivory trade and how it nearly wiped out the African elephant. There has been a ban on the culling of elephants – about to be lifted in some countries – for years. But as I stood surveying the grisly scene in the African bush in 1988, the general public knew little of the animal's plight – and

152

no one had ever sought to expose those responsible. The anger welled up in me. But at least I had it within my power to do something about it.

For the next few hours, we filmed everything. I rehearsed and recorded a number of pieces to camera for Salk until we realised that it had become too dark to film anymore.

"Shit," said Dodkin, "we've got to walk back in the dark. What do you think will get us, the crocs, the hippos, the poachers or the lions?"

He had a point. Four or five miles of bush-trekking and flood-wading in blazing sunshine was one thing but how the hell were we going to find our way home safely on a moonless Zambian night?

Gellatly didn't seem at all fazed. "It's not a problem. My guys will find the way for us. They know every part of this reserve, day or night. It'll be like an evening stroll."

Some stroll. The rangers walked slowly in front, their World War Two rifles – complete with two bullets – slung over their shoulders. They sometimes stopped to confer but, as Gellatly assured us, this was only to best pick a route that avoided the worst of the flood water.

Bill Dodkin was the first to hear a noise off to our left.

"It's a bloody lion," he whispered hoarsely to Salk, who was just in front of him. Salk passed on Dodkin's fears to Gellatly who murmured quietly to the two rangers at the head of our group.

"No, it's not," said Gellatly after he'd heard the Africans' reply.

"Well, what is it then?" returned Dodkin, who was growing more uneasy by the minute.

"It's not a lion, that's all they'll say," replied Gellatly.

"How the hell do they know?" Dodkin was getting beside himself.

"Because if it was a lion, you wouldn't hear anything until it was too late," said Gellatly with a finality that made further comment pointless.

The noises continued. Totally un-reassured, we trudged on.

Suddenly, I felt my legs sliding away from me. I hit the ground. I tried to get up but found I couldn't. Something was gripping my legs. Strangely, there was no pain, just downward pressure. I called for help.

Gellatly swung his torch around and shone it down on me.

"You've fallen into something. Let's have a look at you." The beam of the torch flicked briefly back and forth and it soon became clear that our white hunter was not taking my predicament entirely seriously: "Well old boy," he said with barely concealed mirth, "now you really are in the shit."

And I was. We had wandered across an elephant latrine and I had fallen into a pit full of elephant droppings and stinking mud left by the receding floodwater. The suction gripped my lower legs. I didn't know whether to laugh or cry as I slowly sank up to my armpits. I consoled myself that at least nothing had bitten my legs off.

I was hauled out by the arms until, with a satisfying slurp, my legs came free. My boots and socks had remained behind, however, in the stinking gloop of the pit. I finished the homeward trek barefooted. We joked warily that it was the overpowering smell of rotting elephant dung that kept the stealthy lions away from our exhausted band that night.

The next day we all slept in. After a leisurely breakfast of fruit, rice-cakes and mugs of strong tea Salk retired to his tent to change out of his pyjamas. He probably thought it would have been improper to sleep in his underwear like the rest of us. When he emerged I thought he'd suddenly come down with rabies. He was foaming at the mouth, his beard flecked white. Fortunately, the reason for this turned out not to be a tropical disease, but the fact that Salk didn't trust the water and had been cleaning his teeth with beer. Reassured, I decided we had better call Townson and let him know what we had managed to film.

"It's been great not having him on the phone every half hour," Salk muttered as we walked over to Gellatly's office. "There are compensations for falling up to your armpits in elephant shit," I replied.

One thing we weren't going to tell Townson was the state of Bill Dodkin's health. He had woken up with such back pain that he was actually crying. There was no way he could keep on working but he'd begged us to keep quiet about it. Rumours were rife that Central Television was about to make substantial staff cuts. He feared that if the company got to hear of it, he'd be the first to lose his job. *The Cook Report* team decided to let him rest.

Townson was delighted with what we'd filmed in the bush but, as usual, wanted more. A spectacular visual image that viewers would find memorable – but which would also put his colleagues in mortal danger.

"Go out into the bush with this Gellatly character and get me a shot of the biggest bloody elephant you can find. I want it rearing up at the camera as if it is about to charge," he demanded – and hung up.

"He doesn't want much, does he?" Salk mused as we went to find Gellatly.

Luckily, Alistair knew exactly how to achieve what our demon editor wanted, without getting us killed. The next day Salk and I left an agonised Bill Dodkin lying in bed. Kevin Dowling was preparing to fly out of Zambia to arrange interviews in Burundi, the small Central African country given as the source of hundreds of tons of illegal ivory on the forged paperwork which usually went with it.

We knew the ivory couldn't be coming from Burundi, as we had established that they only had one elephant left – and that was in Bujumbura zoo. We also suspected that if so much dubious documentation originated in Burundi, the likelihood was that those behind the trade could be found there too. We were right, as it turned out.

We dropped Dowling off at the airport and joined Gellatly in his truck and headed out in search of the biggest male elephant in the whole reserve. By now, the flooded bush had all but dried out in the intense heat of the sun and travelling was relatively easy. A couple of hours into the bush, Gellatly picked up his binoculars and searched the tree clumps in front of us.

"What do you make of that?" he asked me as he passed the binoculars over.

About 300 yards ahead of us, moving slowly through the trees, was a truly enormous bull elephant. We were down wind of him and he hadn't yet noticed us. There was a hillock behind us and we retreated there to plan our approach. We decided to leave Salk to set up his camera and tripod on the back of the truck. Gellatly and I would walk through the waist-high grass towards the elephant and, as he sensed our presence, hope to get him to issue a vocal warning, which Salk would film.

Gellatly and I moved off the high ground and waited for Salk to give us the signal that he was ready to roll the camera. We walked slowly forward. Gellatly, who was holding his rifle over one shoulder, suddenly touched my arm with his free hand.

"He knows we're here now. Just stick close to me," he whispered.

Sure enough, a hundred or so yards ahead, the magnificent male was staring suspiciously out of the undergrowth, a large, leafy branch hanging motionless from his mouth. We'd got his attention all right, but how, I asked Gellatly, do we get him to give us Townson's 'angry' shot?

Gellatly produced two stones the size of small paperweights from his pocket. "I'm going to crack these two together. Elephants have piss-poor eyesight, but fantastic hearing. When he hears an unfamiliar noise, he'll probably think he's under attack. It's my bet this big bugger will basically stand his ground, but he might just decide to charge us."

I looked back at the truck and Salk, both several hundred yards behind us. It seemed a long way away.

"What do we do if he does actually charge us?" I enquired as nonchalantly as I could.

"Run like fuck," said Gellatly – and he struck the stones together.

The effect was instantaneous, and terrifying. The huge creature swung round and faced us. His enormous ears rose up around his head and his trunk shot vertically skywards. He let out a deafening and outraged trumpet and started to shift his front legs from side to side as if preparing to charge.

"Hold still," said my companion. "Do you think Salk got his shot?"

"If he didn't, I'm not bloody well going to do this again for anybody," I whispered.

We stood, statue-like in the grass as the elephant continued his menacing posturing. Then, after a minute or so, he must have felt he'd been imagining things, because he slowly turned his back on us and returned to stripping the nearest tree of its leaves with his trunk.

We moved cautiously back to the hillock. Salk was very happy with what he'd got. It was an image that Townson was to use at the beginning of the programme to such effect that viewers remembered it for years to come – just as he wanted them to.

Two days later Salk, the still-crippled Dodkin and I left Gellatly and headed for Dar es Salaam to interview Tanzanian Government officials on the threat to their elephants. After a couple of weeks roughing it in the Zambian bush, we decided we wanted the home comforts of a good hotel. Our travel department back in Birmingham had chosen the Hotel Kilimanjaro, which was registered in the travel books as of five-star standard.

The building was in darkness as the airport taxi dropped us and our luggage by the entrance. We staggered in with the countless bags, suitcases and metal boxes that all television crews are destined to travel the world with. A candle flickered at the back of the foyer and, through the gloom, we made out the check-in desk and two or three members of the hotel staff standing idly behind it.

With much fumbling and holding up of registration cards to the candlelight, we became guests of the Hotel from Hell.

The entire establishment had been without electricity for several weeks. Not only was there a major fault at the city's main power station but the local back-up generators had also failed. The three of us had been allocated rooms on the eighth floor. We grumbled, but were told they were the only rooms they had left and were directed to the lifts. We were halfway there before we remembered what was needed to power them.

If Bill Dodkin had been in pain before, his suffering reached new heights as we helped him lug his baggage up eight floors. At the top of each landing stood a guttering candle stuffed into the neck of a beer bottle. After an eternity, our bags were safely stowed. Despite his back, Dodkin decided to join me for a meal. Salk, who isn't a big eater at the best of times, declined and stayed in his room.

Dodkin and I can't remember to this day what they served us in that restaurant; it was too dark to see properly. I just recall the after effects – the worst vomiting and diarrhoea I'd ever had. It didn't help that during the night, the hotel's water supply also failed.

Two days later, I felt well enough to want a bath. I turned the tap – still no water. I managed to summon room service and asked for water to be sent up so I could, at least, have a body wash. Ten minutes later a bucket was handed to me. It was full of what appeared to be liquid mud.

We moved out – to a one-star motel behind a petrol station

157

where, despite the fact that the rates were a fraction of those charged by the Hotel Kilimanjaro, the plumbing and the air conditioning worked, and the food was usually edible.

Poor old Dodkin was now in a very sorry state, so we decided to send him home. The plan was that he would leave some basic sound recording gear with us and we would say nothing to the office that he had returned to the UK. The rest of us embarked on an intensive schedule of filming in Tanzania, Kenya and back in Zambia. We weren't too bothered that we now had no sound recordist – Salk had been one in a previous incarnation and I had mostly been my own technician in radio days. No problem.

In Dar es Salaam we had been given permission by the Government to film in a large warehouse full of illegal ivory. It contained thousands upon thousands of tusks – the last relics of herd upon herd of dead elephants. Under the corrugated iron roof, the temperature soared to nearly 50 degrees centigrade. We had worked out a complicated piece to camera which involved us weaving our way through the rows of musky tusks – from the baby ones on shelves at the back to the monster-sizes formed into arches at the front of the building.

Sweat dripped from my every pore. Salk had to take his own shirt off to mop me down between takes. There were 14 of them before we were satisfied that the words and the choreography were just right and we had what we wanted. By this time, changes in TV technology meant we no longer used the traditional 16mm film, but Beta videotape. Though the picture quality was not quite up to that achieved on film, tape was a fraction of the cost and had the added advantage of instant playback. So Salk clamped the headphones over his ears to check that the tape was okay. He looked up at me, puzzlement and then profound embarrassment spreading over his face.

"We've got an air gap here," he said. "Two so-called pros forgot to plug in the sound lead between the camera and the mixer. We've just made a silent movie!"

These mishaps occur in television from time to time and it's no big deal. But it was bloody hot, the equipment was in danger of overheating and neither of us felt like doing much except having a beer and a lie down somewhere cool. Fortunately, the hours of silent rehearsals produced a perfect 15th take.

There was one key witness we wanted to interview in Burundi –

a secretive middleman we believed to be the link between the African elephant poachers and the ivory traders in the Far East. It was a circle we badly needed to square. We joined up with Kevin Dowling in Nairobi and tried to get into Burundi. However, there was a small civil war going on and we had to think again.

To add to our problems, other *Cook Report* programmes being shot in Britain and America were in an advanced stage of readiness and my presence was required. Also, Salk had found out that ITN were planning to broadcast a programme on elephant poaching on 16th May 1989. Our first show was scheduled for 15th May. We desperately wanted to go out before the competition.

Townson suggested that we should fly the ivory middleman Dowling had unearthed down from Burundi into Kenya and do an interview there. Zuli Rahmentullah refused, politely but firmly, saying that his business affairs were private and that he was about to attend a religious festival with his family. I asked him what his religion was. Ismaili, he replied.

Later, I tried a long shot.

The head of the Ismaili religion is the Aga Khan. His word is his followers' command. Years before, I had met his cousin, Sadruddin Aga Khan, who was a keen conservationist and founder of an influential environmental organisation called the Bellerive Foundation. I telephoned him at his home on the shores of Lake Geneva and explained the problem. Could he, perhaps, arrange to have a little pressure applied?

"Leave it to me," he said and took down my contact details.

We were staying at the Norfolk, a grand old colonial hotel in Nairobi, and I was semi-submerged in a huge iron bath with polished brass taps that wouldn't have disgraced a steam engine, when the response arrived.

There was a knock at my door and a message was pushed under it. Dripping wet, I opened the envelope. Inside was a cryptic note from Sadruddin, which read simply: "Pressure on. Regards. S."

Within three days, our previously unwilling interviewee had arrived in Kenya. Relaxed and urbane, he explained that he and his father before him had many business interests in East Africa, and that ivory was just one of them. He had not really given it much prior thought, but now he had concluded that the trade was completely unacceptable, and said so on camera. He also described in detail how the poachers and smugglers worked, named names –

159

and invited us to lunch. I'd guessed right. When a blood relative of the man you revere as your supreme religious leader tells you to do something, I suppose you just get on and do it.

Ivory is particularly prized in the Far East, usually in the form of intricately carved ornaments. The trade revolved around Hong Kong, and at the very centre of it sat the Poon brothers, Tat Hing and George. As the owners of the ivory trading company whose reported activities had set Salk on the trail in the first place – and as we now knew, the buyers of most of the poached ivory from Burundi – they were our next targets.

It turned out that the Poons were the biggest illegal ivory traders by far. The extinction of the elephant would have been good news for them, since, by their own admission, it would have vastly increased the value of their colossal secret stockpile of illicit ivory.

I rang home from Jomo Kenyatta Airport. Frances had long since given up being surprised about my unpredictable travels around the world. At least, she said, the long-haul trips for this series were almost over. I reassured her and Belinda that I would be home in a few days' time. I didn't mention the trip that would probably follow almost immediately – to the USA to confront a British taxi driver suspected of multiple murder.

Salk and I flew into Hong Kong and headed straight for the Poon brothers' headquarters, an innocuous looking shop in downtown Tsim Sha Tsui. These greedy men were the major players in a cruel and despicable trade and I was anxious to put them on the spot. They had made millions from the carnage they had commissioned in Africa and now owned whole streets of valuable residential property. We tried to get into the shop but they saw us coming and retreated to the back office, bringing down the steel security grilles behind them.

A couple of hours later, the grilles were up and the glass front door opened a couple of feet. T. H. Poon himself stood at the entrance. This time we had him by surprise. I fired off a couple of questions. His response was to run inside and throw a hefty bronze statuette at Salk. It smashed into the lens of his camera and bounced off his shoulder. The lens was completely shattered and further filming was impossible.

As we walked back to our hotel Salk turned to me and said: "For the first time, I know what it's like to be in your position, mate. When I saw what he had in his hand I wanted to get the hell

160

out of there but I knew I had to stand my ground, take whatever was coming, and get what we came for."

His steadfastness had got us what we wanted.

We made it back to Birmingham, exhausted but with concrete evidence of the vital link between the African poachers and the ivory traders of the Far East. ITN brought their programme forward in order to beat us to the punch, but, in fact, their efforts served as a trailer for ours. Nine million people chose to watch us. More importantly, the film gained international recognition and Sadruddin Aga Khan was kind enough to say we had 'played a pivotal role' in achieving the worldwide ban on ivory trading which followed the transmission of the programme.

The Hong Kong Government introduced much stricter controls on the import and export of ivory in any form and the Poon brothers told the *Hong Kong Standard* newspaper that they were closing their business down. The reputation of *The Cook Report* was enhanced and the team felt it was well and truly back on track.

Viewers clearly liked the mixture of wildlife, scenery, detective story and confrontation that the ivory programme had contained. Townson decided to tap into this rich vein of audience-captivation and mine it for all it was worth – so it wasn't long before we were off on another story that had me and the trusty Salk digging out our sunblock and insect repellent for the long haul to the plains of Africa. It was also a trip that ended with a regrettable but unavoidable incident that could have seriously dented *The Cook Report*'s recently refurbished reputation.

Soon after the ivory programme was broadcast, I received a letter from Charles de Haes, Director General of the Worldwide Fund for Nature – formerly the World Wildlife Fund – congratulating us for our exposure of the illegal trade in tusks. It was, he said, 'a model of conservation journalism'. A few weeks after that, we were contacted by a senior member of the WWF who wanted to convey a different message altogether.

He told us that the WWF had commissioned an Oxford academic, Professor John Phillipson, to report on the fund's internal workings and to evaluate its performance since it was founded in 1961. The report's findings, he said, had shocked the organisation so badly that it had suppressed them immediately.

Amongst other bombshells, Phillipson had said that each of the WWF's key projects – to save the elephant, the panda and the black rhino – had failed miserably.

Much money was being wasted and the WWF was getting itself involved in grand conservation schemes best left to the international aid agencies. African elephant numbers were down – 150,000 had been killed since the fund took up their cause. Black rhino numbers had dwindled from uncounted abundance to just 3,000. Most embarrassing of all, the WWF had pumped £1 million into a project to protect the panda in China but, instead of using the money to set up a panda breeding project, the Chinese had devoted a large proportion of it to building a dam that had actually flooded part of the panda's natural habitat.

Our early investigations also discovered the existence of a secret report exposing the late Jomo Kenyatta, President of Kenya, as the chief organiser of his country's illegal ivory trade while he was in power. Senior WWF figures had read the report and quietly kept it a secret for 17 years. Meanwhile, the Fund had awarded Kenyatta the Golden Ark – the highest possible accolade for wildlife protection.

Secret WWF documents were leaked to us – including a fax from Prince Philip, the organisation's International President, in which he voiced his great concern about the Phillipson Report. He pointed out that the WWF was damned whatever it did. If it hushed the report up, someone would find out and accuse the fund of a cover-up. To go public willingly would subject the organisation to the full blast of criticism contained in the report.

But what shocked me most was the discovery that the WWF was actually involved in a scheme in Zimbabwe to provide white hunters with prey. The charity gave out leaflets telling you which Zimbabwean game ranches to visit to join the hunt. For 500 dollars you could shoot several species of antelope. For a few thousand dollars, you could kill one of the WWF's cherished elephants, provided you were prepared to join the three-year waiting list for the pleasure.

This was part of an experiment in 'sustainable use', a controversial policy which decreed, amongst other things, that the best way to preserve a species was to give it an economic value, not only to the hunter but to the local population as well. Now while a policy of sustainable use might have a point in some circumstances, you might find it extraordinary, as we did, that an endangered species like the elephant should be made available to hunt in any circumstances – and by a wildlife protection charity to boot.

Salk and I booked ourselves into the Humani Ranch in the middle of Zimbabwe. We decided to apply for permission to the government to film officially. The Zimbabweans agreed and said that they would inform the WWF of what we planned. We caught the plane to Harare from Heathrow, into which I had flown only three hours before from another assignment in Islamabad.

We arrived to find a message from the *Cook Report* programme manager, Pat Harris, waiting for us at our hotel. The Zimbabweans had decided that it was too sensitive for us to film the shooting of animals in their country.

"Bollocks to that," said Salk in his usual, succinct way.

I agreed with his sentiment. We'd already made the journey. There was no way we were going home empty-handed, leaving the wildlife undefended. A little subterfuge was all that was required.

We had brought with us a small Hi-8 camera for use on those occasions on which it was advisable not to appear as a TV crew. We ditched most of our equipment and half our baggage at the Meikles Hotel in Harare and telephoned the Humani Ranch on spec. Two tourists wanted to book a few days' hunting – did they have room for us? They did? Good. We'd be on the next light aircraft.

On the flight out, we discussed the dilemma we had created for ourselves. Yes, we stood a good chance of filming the shooting of all manner of animals, which was what we had originally come for. But what would happen when we had one of them in our sights? We'd soon be rumbled if we refused to pull the trigger.

"But think of the newspaper headlines back home if it ever came out that *The Cook Report* had actually shot the animals it says it's out to protect?" insisted Salk.

It was undeniable. It would be no use trying to explain to the tabloid reporters that we had to do it to expose the practice in the first place. I'd already had experience of the treatment meted out to people like me if Fleet Street thought they detected the slightest whiff of scandal, real or imagined. We'd be crucified. The animal welfare lobby, with which all my natural instincts lay, would be mobilised by the popular press and Central would have no alternative other than to apologise publicly and quietly pull the plug on the programme.

Our worst fears were realised as soon as we met the white hunter who was to be our guide. He could have stepped straight out of the pages of a *Boy's Own* comic: young, enthusiastic, festooned with ammunition belts and never without his hunting knife in his belt and his hunting rifle slung across his back. He was determined that we would be bagging everything from warthogs to antelope from dawn till dusk.

"We're going to have a job avoiding killing anything with him around," murmured Salk after the first encounter with our guide, who we quickly nicknamed 'Blashers'.

We set off at five the following morning. Experience had taught Salk that lounge suits weren't really suitable for safaris and he had now kitted himself out like Indiana Jones. He looked most impressive, perched atop our open 4x4 wagon, the headwind ruffling his beard and lifting the brim of his bush hat. From this lofty vantage point, he was able to film the real hunters when they went in for the kill. Then I would alight and stand near the scene while Salk focused on me, as I pretended to be sending a jolly message to the folks back home.

The first part of my speech would go something like: "Hi, kids, here's Dad out on safari. Bet the weather's not as good as this back home ..."

Then, when no one was paying us any attention, I would slip into *Cook Report* mode and deliver, *sotto voce*, a pre-prepared piece to the camera about the WWF sponsorship of these commercial hunts. I then finished off with another set of witless observations for the family, and so raised no suspicions from our fellow hunters. It would be a simple job for Graham Puntis, our film editor back in Birmingham to cut out the dross and use the central part of my message in the programme. The out-takes would probably find their way into our Christmas compilation of cock-ups to be guffawed at by the *Cook Report* staff after a few festive drinks.

But the fundamental problem still remained. Blashers would direct the African driver across the bush and then order him to halt. "Look, over there," he would whisper to us. Through the trees we would see a warthog, or an antelope – well within shooting range. By now we had decided that under no circumstances would I actually pull the trigger to kill an animal. If anyone was going to do it, it would be Salk. So Salk was now seated next to our gung-ho companion with the rifle across his knees.

He bought time by going on the offensive. "Listen, all I'm interested in is shooting a kudu," he declared. "It's no use you showing us warthogs and that type of thing. We want a kudu – I've set my heart on one."

Salk was taking this aggressive line because no one had seen a single kudu in the two days the hunting party had been in the bush and he was banking on things staying that way. For another two days, our luck held. Then, on day four, disaster struck.

Our safari wagon was bucketing along one of the few dirt tracks near the Humani's tented, central camp when Blashers gave a shout and signalled the driver to stop. He jammed the binoculars to his eyes and stared across a grassy clearing to a clump of thorn trees about a hundred yards away. Something was moving under the low canopy of the trees. I made out a shape about the size of a Jersey cow grazing slowly through the dappled shade. The huge antelope was russet and black – I was almost certain what we were looking at. Then the head lifted and we all saw the magnificent, curlicued horns of a fully-grown male kudu.

Our white hunter ordered the driver to move us slowly off the track and onto the edge of the clearing. He waved Salk off the wagon. "You aim below the shoulder and fire. If you miss or wound it, I'll finish it off," he whispered urgently as the pair of them crept towards the kudu, which was munching leaves amongst the trees, still blissfully unaware of our presence. I made a bet with myself that even if Salk shot the animal clean through the heart, the over-eager Blashers wouldn't be able to resist squeezing off a shot of his own.

Salk and I hadn't had time to confer but we both knew that there was no avoiding killing the kudu. We'd painted ourselves into a corner by specifying the species. The tactic had been useful, though. The delay meant that our 'tourist video' tapes now contained copious scenes of hunting on a ranch recommended and actively encouraged by the WWF. I knew that the British public would probably never be able to view the charity in the same way ever again.

I saw Salk bring the rifle up to his shoulder and rest his cheek on the butt. The young white hunter did the same a few feet behind him.

"Come on," whispered Blashers excitedly. "You'll miss your chance." Salk continued to squint down the barrel, following the animal's movements. I watched as he began to squeeze the trigger. Then from behind us, a shot rang out, with Salk's subsequent effort adding to the echo of the first. Blashers, who had been promised the trophy for himself, had, literally, jumped the gun – as I suspected he would. The kudu slumped to the ground. After a few reflex kicks, it was still. My God, I thought, I wish we hadn't had to do that.

Blashers was ecstatic. He virtually dragged Salk by the elbow to where the kudu lay. I followed, picking up the video camera as I left the wagon.

I filmed as Salk and the hunter examined the carcass of the kudu. For an inexperienced shot, the cameraman had done well. The professional's bullet had entered a few inches in front of Salk's. Both bullets had penetrated the animal's side and ripped through the area of the heart. At least it wouldn't have suffered.

A few minutes later, Salk took the camera from me and I knelt by the kudu and delivered one of my disguised pieces to camera – starting and ending with an excited message to the folks back home and again sandwiching serious words for the programme in the middle. I was holding Salk's rifle for him as I crouched next to the carcass.

I looked up during our filming to see Blashers holding his own stills camera. Before I could do anything, he'd snapped at least half a dozen pictures of Roger Cook kneeling, gun in hand, by a magnificent creature which he had, apparently, just bagged as a trophy. The effect of those pictures appearing in any newspaper right after I'd broadcast a programme supposedly exposing the Worldwide Fund for Nature's game hunting activities couldn't be anything but devastating. The *real* story would be lost in a rush to judgement against us.

"Bad news," I murmured to Salk when we'd finished filming. "He's taken a load of pictures of me next to the kudu."

"Mmmm," Salk mused. "Let's get back to the camp and work out how to get that film off him."

Before we could leave, the kudu had to be lifted onto the back of a truck. The quality of such animals is measured by the length of its horns – and this one had attracted the attention of one of our fellow hunters. Bob was not only keen on game hunting himself, but he had a professional interest in the activity too.

"I'm a taxidermist back in the USA," he drawled as he pulled a tape measure from his trouser pocket and held the extended tape against one of the kudu's dark, shiny horns. "Yup, I wouldn't mind betting that's the best one killed in this area for a year or two," he said. "Congratulations."

This news only made us feel worse about what had happened.

Back at camp, the two of us sat in our tent and discussed what we were going to do about the pictures. No obvious plan came immediately to mind but we decided to talk to the young hunter and find out how many pictures he had taken and whether he would consider giving – or even selling – them to us as souvenirs.

No dice. Blashers obviously took his photography seriously. He had taken eight and he wanted them for a new brochure he was putting together for his own soon-to-open game business. He didn't mind getting copies for us, however, and asked for Salk's address back in the UK.

Thwarted, we retreated and tried to think of something else. We were getting desperate. There was the added problem that the longer we stayed on the Humani Ranch, the more animals we were likely to have to shoot. Time was running out.

Then came our chance. The hunter came over to our tent later in the evening. He apologised, but said that we wouldn't be able to go out hunting at dawn tomorrow because he had to go into the nearest town to collect some supplies – but we could be out on safari after lunch. We made our plan for the next day over a glass of whisky before bed. As soon as the hunter had left, Salk would keep guard outside his tent while I went in to see if he'd left the camera behind.

He'd left by truck at nine the following morning. Salk and I crept out and headed across the compound to Blashers' one-man tent. Feeling like a pair of sneak-thieves, we glanced nervously around us for passers-by. All was quiet. Salk undid the tapes of the tent door and I slipped inside.

As I rummaged guiltily for the camera, the sound of luggage zips and buckles being undone seemed almost deafening. Salk hovered anxiously outside, resisting the temptation to ask if I'd found anything yet. After what felt like an age, I did find the camera –

not packed away at all, but hanging by its strap from the frame of the camp bed. I backed cautiously out of the tent and turned to face my co-conspirator.

"You've got it," said Salk triumphantly. "Now let's get back to our tent and see what we can do."

Blashers had taken 24 pictures. Eight of those – the last eight – were of me and the slain kudu. Salk retrieved his coat from under his camp bed and put it over his knees. Then he pushed the camera under the closely woven fabric and opened the back of it.

"I'm getting the film out without exposing it," he explained. "I'm going to rewind it to the beginning and put it back in the camera."

A couple of minutes later, the film was back in the camera and back to frame one, and Salk had pressed the shutter 16 times with the camera still under the coat. Then he walked out of the tent and, pointing the lens directly at the fierce sun directly above his head, pressed the shutter another eight times.

"They'll be well and truly over-exposed," he cackled. "He'll think there's a problem with the camera but I don't think he'll ever find out he's been sabotaged and be able to make a stink about it."

The camera was slipped back into Blashers' tent and, with a lighter heart than in many days, we downed a couple of cans of lukewarm beer and began to address our remaining problems – how to avoid shooting any more defenceless animals and how to get our film back to Townson, who, as usual, had been leaving us telephone messages several times a day.

After some hours of contemplation, we came up with an idea. Salk would tell the ranch managers that he had just called home to hear that his daughter was dangerously ill. He had to get back to Britain as quickly as possible to see her in hospital. I, as his old friend, would obviously have to go with him for support on the way home.

"I don't like saying it – it's tempting fate," said Salk. "But it is the only thing I can think of that will get us out right away – and it'll shut Townson up for a bit, at least."

We made a telephone call to Townson in Birmingham and told him about the kudu, the camera and our plan to escape. "Okay, do it," he barked down the line. "And, so far as the rest of the world is concerned, the bloody kudu thing *never* happened, got it?"

We got it, though by the time the programme was broadcast

some weeks later, what we'd done and why we'd done it were included – and there were no complaints.

The programme was also involved in revealing the massive mess that was then the WWF-funded Rain Forest Project at Korup in the northern Cameroons. The planned commercial exploitation of a vast swathe of the forest appeared to have got out of hand. For one thing, little or no account was taken of collateral damage – the damage caused by building a network of access roads, and the fact that for every tree felled and removed for its timber, dozens more were damaged or destroyed. The big international logging companies seemed to be doing pretty much whatever they wanted.

Having left Yaounde, the tiny capital, far behind, one of our first tasks was to get some good shots of unspoiled rainforest canopy. We were advised to trek onwards, to an enormous flat-topped rock, some 27 kilometres through the jungle from the ranger's lodge where we had been invited to base ourselves. It would be tough going, the ranger warned, rugged steamy and steep, but we would be well rewarded. From the summit of that rock 'you could see forever'.

In 40-degree-centigrade heat and 99 per cent humidity, we trudged, clambered and sweltered through the thick rainforest, laden down with equipment. Every second step, it seemed, involved tripping over a fallen branch or exposed tree root. When we eventually reached the rock and scrambled perilously up it, we discovered that the forest had grown somewhat since the ranger's last visit. The canopy now towered above the rock, and you couldn't see a thing.

We made our way wearily out of the forest, but not all the way back to the lodge. Aching and barely able to stand, we staggered to a halt at a village some distance away. So rough had our hike been, that Salk lost both his big toenails. As night fell, we were bidden to make use of the ramshackle schoolhouse, where we clumsily rigged our hammocks between the desks. Deploying our mosquito nets properly was almost impossible, and in my case the net was too short anyway, so I was forced to sleep with the soles of my feet pressed against one end. In the morning my feet had been so badly bitten that they had swollen to the point where I couldn't get my boots on. I was later to contract cerebral malaria from those very bites.

169

This was despite having been meticulous in taking the recommended preventative medication before, during and after the shoot. Shortly afterwards and between series, Frances and I had taken Belinda to Disney World in Florida. It was swelteringly hot and I felt dreadful. The girls loved it, but I found the whole thing rather hard going – probably because I was overweight, said Frances. I was still sweating profusely on the plane home and the day I popped my last Paludrine, I came down with what my doctor said was probably a bad case of flu.

Years before, another doctor had voiced a similar opinion to a cameraman friend of mine called Laurie Rush, who had just returned from Mozambique. His high fever was unlikely to be malaria, the doctor had said, because Laurie had been taking the right anti-malarials. However, he'd arrange some tests just in case. By the time the results came back, indicating cerebral malaria, Laurie was dead.

Bearing that tragedy in mind, Frances and I weren't going to hang about for NHS tests. It took us all of ten seconds to decide I should go private. Blood analysis at the London School of Hygiene and Tropical Medicine revealed I'd been colonised by *falciparum* malaria parasites – and even the African location where they'd probably moved in. I spent ten days in hospital, some of the time in intensive care, and much of that either unconscious or bellowing delirious nonsense at the top of my voice. 'No change there, then,' my sympathetic colleagues had said.

Back at the schoolhouse, in the middle of the night, Salk had taken ill and slunk out into the yard. As he returned, just after midnight, we realised what day it was and greeted him with a muted chorus of 'Happy Birthday'.

"What did you get for your birthday, Pete?"

"Diarrhoea," came the grumpy reply.

After we had limped back to base camp at the ranger's lodge, we were welcomed with hot food. We were in for a real treat, we were told. The treat turned out to be a stew made from yams and other root vegetables, and the meat of a Mandrill, an ill-tempered baboon with a red face and a purple rear end. With a broad smile and an encouraging nod, the ranger offered us great wooden bowls of the rank-smelling stuff.

I had eaten some fairly ghastly meals in far-flung places in my time, but this one would be as difficult to top as it was to digest.

The worst part was the mandrill meat, cut into thin strips, which had curled up during cooking to resemble grisly, blue-grey Hula Hoops.

"What's this dish called?" I asked in mock appreciation, and was given the local name.

"And what's that mean?"

The dish was colloquially called – apparently after the Hula Hoops – 'Mandrill's arseholes'. I wished I'd never asked.

A few days later, we travelled further into the interior to meet a village chieftain whose traditional territory had been encroached upon by the loggers. He could tell us – reputedly in perfect English – of the untoward effects of large-scale logging on small native communities. We eventually arrived, after a two-day journey on foot and by canoe, and were greeted by the chief. He emerged from the shadow of the thatched portico of his mud brick house and extended a gnarled brown hand.

"Eaugh, good afternoon" he declaimed in an extraordinary, far-back accent.

Unfortunately, that seemed to be the limit of his 'perfect' English, and we had to resort to the services of our interpreter. In the subsequent interview, during which the old man became quite agitated, he was scathing about the logging companies. They took, and gave little or nothing in return, he claimed; they broke most of their promises and they viewed the locals as little more than an inconvenience.

Before we left, the chief presented us with a chicken, a rather scrawny rooster with its legs bound together and its wings clipped to prevent it from escaping. This was apparently a traditional departure gift, for which we were ostentatiously grateful. We thought we'd take the rooster back as an offering to our ranger, whose motley little flock looked as if it could do with some new blood.

The journey back was an eventful one. Heavy overnight rain meant that the river was now running its banks, and our canoes capsized several times. Our sound recordist for the trip, a ridiculously soft-hearted ex-actor called Del Fuke, repeatedly rescued the trussed chicken, sometimes at the expense of some of our valuable equipment. We finally struggled back to the lodge and ceremoniously handed over the precious bird.

"Oh thanks," said the ranger, and unceremoniously wrung its neck. It was tastier than the mandrill though.

Another interviewee, on the far side of Africa, had to be tracked like big game. He was a Tanzanian MP, with a constituency the size of Wales, and a reputation for his forthright views on conservation. He believed that no wildlife conservation policy could ever work unless it also benefited the local human population. This was a view we wanted to have reflected in the programme, even if only in translation. The MP didn't speak English, we'd been told.

To reach him, we had to cross the border between Kenya and Tanzania, a crossing for which we had no official permission. So we chose a remote border post, and smooth-talking Salk got us through with a quart-sized glass passport with a nice picture of Johnny Walker on it.

We finally came across Mr Parikapoon MP, quite by chance, out on his constituency rounds in his Land Rover. He was motoring fast in the opposite direction in a cloud of dust, but we managed to flag him down. We later filmed him, holding forth on 'conservation for the people' in the most erudite way – and in perfect English.

He offered to guide us back over the border through what he described as 'bandit country'. We set off, initially in convoy with a Jeep full of workers from IUCN (International Union for the Conservation of Nature). It was a dark and moonless night and our guide appeared to be navigating by radar. This was a feat that we found both impressive and rather worrying at the same time.

We parted company with the Jeep when the redoubtable Mr P. decided to take a short cut, which didn't look or feel like a road at all. He insisted it was safe, but which was the greater risk – being shot by an unseen assailant, or crashing into an unseen ravine?

However, having bucked and bounced through the bush for several more nerve-wracking hours, we finally pitched up at the border at sunrise. We were relatively unscathed, and we were some way ahead of the conservationists. Our rough ride had been worth it, but the IUCN conservationists had it even rougher. They arrived some hours later, exhausted and traumatised, in a Jeep full of bullet holes.

Back home, we came under fire ourselves. The WWF mounted an extraordinary and expensive campaign to have the programme scrapped. They hired a spin doctor and considerable pressure was applied to Central TV and to the then regulator, the IBA to pull the plug on the programme.

Prince Philip, the organisation's International President, wrongly accused us of stealing confidential documents (the leaked Phillipson Report). Despite all this, the broadcast went ahead and Prince Philip had to admit publicly that a number of the fund's strategies simply had not worked and that the rhino, elephant and panda campaigns had indeed all been failures. The panda, he concluded, 'was probably doomed'. WWF Director General Charles de Haes resigned shortly afterwards.

If I'd thought there would be some respite from the globe-trotting when the WWF film was finished, I was mistaken. They were crazy times. In one three-month period, Salk and I later worked out that we had flown 33 times.

We'd been to France and Libya on the trail of the missing National Union of Mineworkers' strike funds, back to Spain to check on the activities of the ever-industrious British criminal fraternity, back and forth to Africa to make the WWF film and, in the summer of 1990, embarked upon a veritable frenzy of air travel that culminated in what must be the ultimate in traveller-masochism – what amounted to a day trip to Australia.

The pressure was beginning to tell on the *Cook Report* staff. Divisions were appearing in the ranks. Some, who felt worn down by Mike Townson's 'heavy-hands-on' management style, gravitated towards my office to sound off about his latest demands. Others, who believed that Townson possessed some unique magic power to convert ideas into audience-pulling television, more readily accepted the immense workload placed upon us.

Townson himself appeared to thrive on the self-imposed pressure. As long as he had a cigarette to dangle from the corner of his mouth, his secretary to bellow at for coffee, and the power to direct members of the team at his whim, he seemed happy.

I was tired. But being away from home and a routine meant something worse was creeping up on me. For weeks on end, my body clock would be continuously wound forwards and backwards as I crossed from time-zone to time-zone. My metabolism seemed to change. I ate when an air-stewardess or night-duty waiter put a plate in front of me. I slept when the journey ended and the taxi dropped me at a hotel. Exercise was reduced to extended trudges through airport corridors or leg-stretching in the aisles of Jumbos on long-haul flights. Poor Frances grew used to the sound of my

173

dopey voice mumbling down the telephone line at unusual times of the night.

From my late teens, I had always been heavily-built, but now I was piling on the pounds because of my unhealthy lifestyle. What's the point of trying to diet when your body doesn't really know when the next meal will materialise? My body's philosophy became 'Grab it while it's there'.

Occasionally, I was able to spend a few days at home and attempt to restore my body to some semblance of normal routine under Frances and Belinda's loving care. Frances, quite rightly, does her best to keep me on the straight and narrow when I'm not away at work.

Fortunately, she's a very good cook and there's no hardship in eating salads and low-fat foods when she's responsible for the meal. I enjoy cooking myself, but with less culinary artistry and technique at my disposal, I tend to go for really good ingredients and flavours: fresh seafood, Scottish beef, Welsh lamb, local ham. I also love good cheese, but I know how fattening that can be – particularly for someone with my working lifestyle.

But wine – in moderation, of course – is one of my great indulgences. The New World wines – particularly the big Chardonnays of Australia and New Zealand – are close to my heart. They come from the countries of my earlier life, and that's as good an excuse as any for supporting them.

Bob Southgate, who brought me from the BBC to Central Television, was a soulmate for my enjoyment of the finer things in life. In an era when television executives were encouraged to adopt the leaner, hungrier style at work and play, Bob was a beacon shining in a fairly joyless world. His office in Birmingham was an oasis in an otherwise arid environment. A fan of Loire wines and the Sauvignon Blanc grape in particular, Bob could be relied upon to have something chilling in his office fridge. A corkscrew and glasses were always within easy reach, near the cabinet that held part of his collection of food, wine and hotel guides.

Such was his love for Sancerre – one of the Loire's finest white wines – that he would sometimes even sign his memos with the words: "Yours Sancerrely, Bob."

I would dream of such luxuries while recuperating under Frances' beady eye at home, but eventually the call from Townson

174

would come and off I would go again, my healthy diet and exercise regime abandoned once more.

Peter Salkeld was also finding the pressure hard to bear. I numbered loyalty and industriousness amongst his many qualities, but he was – and is – a stubborn bugger. And when Salk felt his principles were being compromised or unfair conditions were being constantly imposed upon him, he had to take a stand.

After a series of arguments with Townson over policy, working practices and the ethics of programme-making – none of which Townson was ever disposed to make concessions on – Salk decided to leave. It was a hard decision for him and one which I urged him not to take lightly. After much thought, he resigned.

Anyone who knew him appreciated that he had the drive and energy of someone 30 years younger, but he was in his early fifties and doing something regarded as a young man's job in our industry. The world of television was growing tougher and new job opportunities fewer and farther between. Salk struggled and was eventually forced to sell his beautiful, beamed medieval home on the Welsh borders. We kept in touch and at least he knew that, in his absence, life at *The Cook Report* wasn't getting any easier.

Series Four – broadcast in the summer of 1990 – was getting audiences of around twice the size of the second series. And it didn't take a rocket scientist to see that the audience we had built up had a predilection for exciting, confrontational subjects. When I challenged Arthur Scargill and asked him what had happened to his union's funds during and after the miners' strike of the early 1980s, we attracted an audience of 12.5 million. Costa del Crime villains, similarly, drew very good audiences. When we strayed over to subjects such as the National Health Service there was less interest.

However, just because important issues might not pull in record-breaking audiences doesn't mean that *The Cook Report* shouldn't cover them. In fact, I often argued that the programme ought to tackle difficult subjects precisely because of its proven ability to attract an audience.

British audiences usually found Northern Ireland and 'The Troubles' an instant turnoff, but we returned to the province whenever we felt that there was a story that needed telling in the public interest. This had yielded five complete programmes. One of them covered building-site racketeering by the paramilitaries, another, the financing of the IRA. Yet another was about clenbuterol, a drug that the IRA sold to unscrupulous farmers to enhance the size, and therefore the value, of their animals. This put at risk the health of anyone who bought and ate the meat in the process.

The other two broadcasts were about the criminal duplicity of Martin McGuinness, as told by the people who had suffered directly or indirectly as a result of his actions.

McGuinness is a man who despised being governed by the British, yet took unemployment and housing benefit from that same government; a man who had for years consistently denied ever having been a member of the IRA, yet was convicted of membership in the South – and had in his earlier days openly boasted about it in the North. More recently, having at last formally admitted to holding a top position in the illegal organisation that has killed hundreds of his fellow countrymen, he became part of the Northern Ireland administration, for God's sake!

Back in 1972, when McGuinness was second-in-command of the Derry Brigade of the IRA, 13 Republican demonstrators were shot dead by British troops in the Bogside area of the city. An official inquiry into this appalling incident, which quickly became known as 'Bloody Sunday', eventually opened under the chairmanship of Lord Saville in 1998. It came to an end almost six years later in 2004.

McGuinness was one of those called before the inquiry, where his testimony came into direct conflict with that of another senior IRA man, known only as 'PIRA 24'. On the final day of submissions, McGuinness was accused of 'lying to the inquiry', and his evidence was described as 'an elaborate deceit'. Such mendacity would certainly seem to be in character.

Though I had covered The Troubles from time to time since they began in 1968, I cannot recall ever having come across a more hypocritical figure than McGuinness. In 1993, when the first *Cook Report* programme about him was made, he had embarked on a campaign to be accepted as a purely political operator. Questions about his activities as the most important member of the IRA Army Council he brushed aside with surly counter-questions about the politicians who fronted the various Protestant paramilitary organisations. Any attempt to examine McGuinness's clandestine past and present was met with a wall of silence by those loyal to him. But away from the Sinn Fein hardliners, there were people whose lives he had torn apart and who could be encouraged to talk about it. Mind you, there were some in government who wanted the man left alone regardless, 'so as not to damage future peace negotiations'.

I had no compunction about examining McGuinness's past criminality. I found myself thinking of my early days at the BBC when Andrew Boyle and I realised how desperately the public wanted someone to address their problems head on. We had said then, 20 years before, that my remit would be to examine injustice, criminality and bureaucratic bungling. Two out of three of these elements would apply to any programme about Martin McGuinness.

By the late 1990s, several books had been written by repentant IRA members who firmly placed McGuinness at the heart of the killings and bombings both in Ulster and on the British mainland. In 1993, however, such exposure was unheard of.

In the Birmingham office, I sat with Townson and Clive Entwistle, who was to produce the first McGuinness programme, and talked the subject through. We were joined by Howard Foster, newly recruited from Sky Television. Howard was a substantial, square-rigged chap – amiable, well-read and well-versed in the good things of life. He was also a hard nosed crime reporter with a wealth of experience in Northern Ireland. Sylvia Jones, another old Ireland hand, was already on the ground there.

To be effective in our terms, the proposed programme would have to dig deep and be provably impartial. Fortunately, there would be no problems dismissing the allegations of partiality that would inevitably come from the Sinn Fein camp. The fate of Mr Sayers of the Protestant Ulster Defence Association and his companions after we had exposed their extortion racket was more than adequate proof of our unbiased stance. Digging deep would involve finding credible witnesses to McGuinness's criminality and persuading them to talk on camera. Those credible witnesses would also have to be very brave.

Some six weeks later, my colleagues on the ground in Ulster were ready for me. So, once again, I was off over the Irish Sea and into an RUC approved hotel. This time it was the Culloden, a fortress-like building on the slopes of the Holywood Hills overlooking Belfast Lough. Good though it was, the hotel still had pretensions above its station. As I presented myself for dinner on the first night, I was told that I couldn't enter the dining room without wearing a tie. I never wear a tie; they're too easy to grab hold of and I find them uncomfortable to boot.

I told the Maître D' so, and pointed out that my blazer came from Gieves & Hawkes, while the rest of my outfit was of a similar standard. Where had his shiny DJ come from, and was it any less likely to offend his sensitive clientèle? Eventually, I was led to an isolated table and my order taken. I had just begun my appetiser when two waiters arrived and ostentatiously erected a folding screen around me. They certainly know how to make a point in Belfast.

Painstaking research and gentle persuasion had by then produced several witnesses prepared to speak out against McGuinness and his cronies. They included one man in his early thirties who was living in fear of his life in England after escaping from his IRA torturers in Londonderry.

Paul McGavigan had been passing low-level information about the IRA in his native Bogside area of the town for months before he was found out by the Provos. Like McGuinness, McGavigan was a keen fly-fisherman. He would meet his army intelligence handler as he flicked his line out over the waters of the River Foyle, which flows through Londonderry to the sea. But he was being watched, and as he walked home to the Bogside one afternoon, he was kidnapped by a group of men who took him to an empty house on the other side of the estate.

For the next few days, McGavigan was held underwater in an overflowing bath, had gun barrels poked into his mouth and was forced to lie underneath a mattress on the floor while his captors took it in turns to jump up and down on his body. One man paid regular visits to the house during his ordeal – to ask about the progress of McGavigan's 'confession' – and occasionally to take part in the torture. That overseer was Martin McGuinness.

McGavigan eventually made a run for it when an army patrol, probably on the lookout for him, stopped outside the house. He then contacted his handler, who quickly arranged for him to be spirited away to the mainland.

Sylvia Jones and Howard Foster found McGavigan living in a rundown suburb of an English city. Like almost every fugitive from

The Troubles, the pressure had taken its toll on him. Frazzled nerves, family break-ups, and the taking of his children into care had worn him down. He had sought release in drink and now had a reputation in his street for causing trouble. But he was willing to talk about Martin McGuinness.

Another of those willing to testify for us against McGuinness was 82-year-old Rose Hegarty. Her son, Frank 'Franko' Hegarty, had been a Special Branch agent as well as the IRA quartermaster in Londonderry. After leaking the whereabouts of three massive ammunition and weapon dumps in the province, he was forced to leave Northern Ireland and to go into hiding. Lonely and homesick in his Kent safe house, he continued to ring home to talk to his mother and sisters. After the heat died down, he expressed an interest in coming back to Londonderry and Rose decided to test the water through McGuinness's offices.

McGuinness himself promised that Frank Hegarty would have immunity if he came back to Londonderry. Rose Hegarty told us the story of what happened next in one of the most moving, simple and transparently truthful interviews I have ever seen. Quietly, evenly, and only occasionally giving in to her emotions, Rose described how Martin McGuinness came to her neat terraced home in Rosemount; how he went down on his knees and took her hand in his, telling her that her favourite son would come to no harm if he came home. "I give you my word; Frank will be safe with me. Just tell him to come home and sort it out." Sadly, this cynical performance convinced her and she sent word to her son that all would be well.

Two weeks later, the local BBC television news carried a report that a body had been found lying by the side of a remote country road near Castle Derg in County Tyrone. It was Frank Hegarty. His hands had been tied behind his back and black insulating tape wound round his eyes before he was shot through the back of the head. He had also been tortured before being murdered.

We built the programme around these moving stories – helped by a variety of people whose identities we keep secret to this day. God help them should their names ever emerge.

Raymond Gilmour, a local man who infiltrated the IRA for the RUC and foiled many terrorist attacks, had also experienced the soft-soap treatment from McGuinness, who tried everything to coax Gilmour back to Londonderry.

"McGuinness was a two-faced bastard and I'd never trusted him," he wrote in his 1997 book, *Dead Ground*, about his time as a 'mole' inside the IRA. In it, he described how McGuinness tried to force him to withdraw his evidence against 35 IRA suspects.

Gilmour emerged from hiding to help Entwistle and Sylvia Jones expose McGuinness's past. He hadn't seen his wife and family for seven years and had lived in more houses in Britain and abroad in that period than most of us would see in a lifetime. For him, the reality of crossing the IRA was constant upheaval, and the fear that someone would betray him to the Provisionals' 'Internal Affairs' hit-men. So far, luckily, the death sentence he lives under has not been carried out.

Throughout the latter part of the production process, the *Cook Report* team had been trying to track down McGuinness so that I could confront him with these terrible testimonies. We knew it would be madness to show up at his home in Derry. Remember that Rule One of the 'doorstep' is never actually to arrive at someone's front door to demand an interview. All you are likely to be left with is a firmly shut door, and in this case, the near certainty of an angry and potentially violent mob to deal with afterwards.

At one stage, we thought we'd found McGuinness on a fly-fishing trip to the Republic of Ireland, but that had ended before we had all the allegations against him in the can. With just days to go before the programme's broadcast, we asked Sinn Fein to arrange an interview with him for us. They demanded to know what was going to be said in the programme, and who was going to say it.

Naturally, we didn't want to put the brave participants at risk, or have such pressure put on them that they withdrew their testimony and left us with nothing to broadcast. We could not therefore tell Sinn Fein what would be covered in the interview other than in the most general terms, and as a result we were told that no interview would be forthcoming.

We telephoned his home and Mrs McGuinness answered. She repeated my message, and as she did so, her husband's muffled voice could be heard in the background saying: "Tell him I'm not in." Somehow, I'd expected better than that. McGuinness then seemed to disappear from the scene for a while, and with him went the last chance of the team being able to turn up at some public gathering where I could catch up with him.

A memorable moment in Zambia, with white hunter and trumpeting bull elephant.

The elephant killing ground.

In a warehouse filled with illegal ivory in Tanzania.

In Hong Kong, illegal ivory trader Tat Hing Poon throws a missile at the camera.

The start of the heroin trail in Burma. Warlord Khun Sa exhibits an opium parcel.

With Khun Sa, inspecting his troops.

Salk gets to grip with African wildlife (and vice versa).

On location with the *Cook Report* editor, Mike Townson. Note the sign behind him.

Hot Dog Wars. Joe Persico (inset) leaps the counter to threaten mayhem.

My Ronnie Barker impression goes down a storm on Tottenham Court Road.

Being turned over - literally - by the opposition.

Ulster beef farmers, caught using illegal growth promoting drugs, turn to violence.

Replica Warrior armoured vehicles lined up for our 'friendly fire' experiment in the Mojave desert.

Our World War II Thunderbolt spotter plane taxis for take off.

In Indonesia: canoeing in search of Goffin's Cockatoos.

In another canoe, about to sink in Guyana.

We talked to the Central lawyers and decided that we would go ahead with the broadcast without McGuinness. This decision was reinforced by a government order of the time which would have compelled us to overdub McGuinness's voice with that of an actor. This order was a Thatcherite legacy which was intended to deprive terrorists of the 'oxygen of publicity'. For us it would have meant turning a potentially powerful interview into a complete parody.

I felt in my heart of hearts that we were on safe ground, but I must confess to a little trepidation as we watched the programme in the Central building that night.

Predictably, there was uproar in the Sinn Fein-controlled parts of Derry. The local newspaper decried the programme, digging furiously to discredit the participants. We waited to see if McGuinness felt he could risk taking legal action. Nothing happened – and hasn't to this day.

Two days after our first programme, we had an extraordinary phone call at our Birmingham offices from a man calling himself 'Jack', who said we didn't know the half of it regarding McGuinness and offered to tell us more. There was something about his manner and the clues he gave that told us he was genuine, so after taking all possible security precautions, we arranged a meeting in the car park of the Culloden Hotel. It was a calculated risk. For all his apparent authenticity, he could also have been a McGuinness supporter, bent on revenge.

Two team members were to meet him that wet August evening. Frank Thorne – an ex-*Daily Mirror* reporter who was spending a year or so with us as a senior researcher – sat in a car wired with concealed recording equipment, while Clive Entwistle initially kept a lookout in a nearby vehicle. At the same time, Sylvia Jones had organised a meeting with a Detective Chief Superintendent inside the hotel. She planned to pass on information for the investigation which had just been launched into the serious allegations made by *The Cook Report*. From a room overlooking the car park, she was also able to watch what was going on.

Bang on time, the thick-set, swarthy figure of Jack appeared and climbed into Frank's car. He explained that he had been a senior IRA member and close to McGuinness for twenty years. He confirmed McGuinness's position at the top of the IRA Northern Command, his role in initiating or approving major operations – including mainland bombings – his part in the execution of Franko

Hegarty and much, much more. Having later traced the number of the car in which Jack had arrived, the RUC officer was astounded. The man we had been talking to was Freddie Scappaticci, alias 'Stakeknife', perhaps the most important British mole in the IRA. We were also reminded that he was a very dangerous man, suspected of several murders.

Stakeknife left us with 50 minutes of tape containing an astonishing who-did-what exposé of the inner workings of the IRA. A subsequent meeting was much less productive, because by then his handlers had given him the third degree. Top brass in Army intelligence and Special Branch were furious that he had compromised his position in what they considered to be a very foolish way. They warned us that we should do everything possible to protect his identity, because even the slightest hint could put his life at risk and threaten a vital source of intelligence. However, they conceded that they couldn't stop us using what we now knew, some of which was included in the update programme which followed a week later, shorn of Scappaticci's distinctive phraseology and voiced by an actor. We also kept our promise to keep his identity secret for more than a decade, until his cover was eventually blown by British and Irish newspapers.

While we were filming in some of the IRA strongholds in Derry for our second programme, we happened to stop outside a pub in the Creggan, just as it disgorged a gang of tanked-up Republicans. I was instantly recognized and the gang surged towards us. I thought I was in for another beating at the very least, but they actually wanted to congratulate me on the first programme! We were all amazed and relieved, but the incident does go to show that what we said about the PIRA godfather was spot on.

The real satisfaction for me, the team and the brave contributors that had made these difficult – and at times, dangerous – programmes possible, came from knowing that the ten million people who had watched each of them would have seen Martin McGuinness in his true colours.

5

Heroin, Heritage and Hot Dogs

*On the heroin trail in Burma, on the trail of
stolen antiquities worldwide, and multi-million
pound hot-dog wars on Britain's streets*

Now well-established after more than 30 successful programmes,
The Cook Report was generously resourced. We had big budgets,
an investigative team that was second to none, and the whole pan-
oply of Central's resources behind us – reference library, editing
and graphics facilities, cameramen and sound recordists, a travel
department, press and publicity team and an accounts department
to keep track of our increasingly diverse financial needs.

We kept on getting letters from the public and we continued
reading them, grateful for the feedback. If, as was often the case,
we couldn't help someone, we rang the sender back, commiserated
and offered to pass on the details to a more appropriate outlet –
another television or radio programme or to friends in the national
or regional press.

If a government agency seemed to be the most appropriate
remedy to a problem, we suggested it. Surprisingly, we got less
mail and far fewer story leads from the public than we did in radio
days. Perhaps the audience thinks TV is omnipotent and that we'll
know about a given story anyway – or perhaps radio is more
personal and listeners feel it's easier to write in.

More and more, however, we looked to our extensive range of
contacts for new material. The team had a lot of top-level contacts
in the police, Customs, secret services, armed forces, political
parties, special interest groups and so on – and we had made
invaluable contacts abroad.

I was generally very happy with this state of affairs. The variety
of subjects suggested to us was immense. When I look at the range

183

of programmes we broadcast in the first few years – cult abductions, wildlife charity failures, fugitives abroad, cosmetic surgery scandals, the IRA, illegal drugs, credit card fraud to name but a few – I am reminded of the vast amount of ground we had covered.

Mind you, it is easy to forget, without any physical reminders. I used to keep, and occasionally replay, copies of past programmes. But I was usually disappointed for one reason or another. So now I keep nothing. No tapes, no files, no reviews. There isn't a programme I've done that couldn't have been done better.

But the viewers were obviously less critical and seemed to find the programme and its presenter memorable – as the ratings and still sizeable mailbag seemed to indicate. The fan mail was usually complimentary and always answered, but like the reviews – with one exception – never kept. That exception was a brief letter from a lady in Leamington Spa which came in shortly after I had joined Central. It goes as follows and it still makes me smile:

Dear Mr Cook,

I have been an admirer of your bravery and your probity for many years on BBC radio, and I am pleased to see that your investigative skills have been taken up by ITV.

Keep up the good work; it is much needed and much appreciated. However, I hope you will not mind if I make one further observation – and that is that you were much slimmer on the wireless.

Nevertheless, whatever shape I was in, I began to be recognised wherever I went. This, for me, was the downside of fame. It was one thing to be recognised in Britain, but when a Malaysian airport official asked me who I was after in his country – and much the same was happening in India, South Africa, Holland, Scandinavia, Spain, France and the USA – I was again reminded of the power and reach of television.

I try to remain as private a person as I can. It's one thing to promote yourself as an entertainer and willingly build up a following of fans. But that is not what I've sought to do. For me, public recognition is a by-product that spells hassle and can actually interfere with me doing my job properly.

A lot of people expect me to be a combative, confrontational type, but they couldn't be more wrong. In reality, I'm fairly retiring.

When, for a short time in 1997, it looked as if *The Cook Report* was coming to an end, one of the job opportunities my agent suggested to keep the wolf from the door was after-dinner speaking. I was petrified by the very thought. I'm happiest at home with my family, or out on a country walk, or messing about with motor cars, or just being with good friends and colleagues – where there is no need to explain myself, where I can relax and truly *be* myself.

By 1992 my face had become very well known – and part of the price of fame was potential danger. It didn't take me long to learn the ground rules. Ask for a discreet table at the back of quiet restaurants. Ask for the car to pick me up at the side-door of the hotel – one I had probably checked into using an alias anyway. And even that can go wrong.

At the start of one of our Spanish shoots, the crew and I turned up at the five-star Don Pepe Hotel in Marbella in the early hours of the morning to find that our accommodation arrangements seemed to have gone awry. The receptionist entered our names into her computer and stared at the screen, a look of puzzlement on her face.

"I am sorry señor, but we have no rooms reserved for you. There is no record, and the hotel is full. Very sorry."

It was dawn before the problem was sorted out. Someone back at base had apparently decided that for security reasons, we should all be booked in under aliases, but no one had told us that, or what our assumed identities were. Then we had to explain to a bemused duty manager why our names didn't match our passports. Unfortunately, that wasn't the last time we were landed in such an embarrassing situation either.

My recognisability did have its lighter side. I once turned up at the Intercontinental Hotel at Hyde Park Corner in London to meet a friend from Ireland who was staying there. I rang up to his room from the reception desk and he asked me to take a seat and wait for him in the foyer. As I crossed the marble floor, I noticed out of the corner of my eye a well-dressed man in his forties with an expensive-looking attaché case on the seat next to him. As I settled into my own seat, he looked straight at me.

There was a sharp intake of breath and an almost comical double-take. I had obviously been recognised. He sat bolt upright as if someone had electrocuted him. Then, with a half-choked cry of "Jesus Christ!" he clutched his attaché case to his chest, leapt to his feet and ran for all he was worth, down Hamilton Place and into Piccadilly. I hadn't the faintest idea who he was and I wish I knew what he had to hide, but there was definitely a story there somewhere.

In the world of professional programme-making, a high-profile could also help us get the stories. If there was a scent of danger, a whiff of adventure involved in a subject, journalists and film-makers in the freelance market often brought it to us first. And if that exciting subject happened to coincide with a breaking news story, so much the better.

In 1990, two teenage Birmingham girls, Patricia Cahill and Karen Smith, were stopped as they tried to fly back to Britain from a holiday in Thailand. The police at Bangkok Airport searched their baggage and found half a hundredweight of heroin. Protesting their innocence, the girls were thrown into Klong Prem women's prison – the infamous 'Bangkok Hilton' – to await trial. The press had a 'feeding frenzy' back in Birmingham, interviewing the outraged families of the girls as they prepared to fly out to Thailand to see them.

The *Cook Report* team, for once, had an investigation right on its doorstep. Townson called a council of war in his office. Who had put these seemingly naïve girls up to it? Researchers and producers made calls to the West Midlands police and to their underworld contacts alike. Progress was remarkably quick and we soon traced the girls' 'sugar daddy', who in recent months had paid for several long-haul trips for them. He lived less than a mile from the studios.

We put researcher Graeme Thomson on the case to find out everything possible about him. Thomson soon discovered that he was an intimidating and often violent man with underworld connec-tions and a conviction for fire-bombing a pub.

Meanwhile, Clive Entwistle, cameraman Grahame Wickings and I prepared to fly out to Thailand and, if possible, get an interview with Cahill and Smith. Our plan was to speak to the girls and put to them what we had uncovered about their case back in Birmingham.

Two things were worrying me, however. First, we still had some weeks to go before our programme would be aired. Any one of the dozens of newspapermen covering the story could discover our exclusive line of research and rush into print, thereby nullifying the lead we had on everyone else. Second, there was no guarantee that the girls would be allowed to see us – or, indeed, that they would want to. We needed something else to raise the story and make it run for 30 minutes.

As we were about to set out for Thailand, Entwistle took a phone call. It was a freelance producer called Patrick King. We knew his work – he was an ex-British Army soldier who had turned to film-making when he had left the services, and he had brought adventure-based ideas to us before. He asked if we would like to meet the man ultimately responsible for supplying the heroin Cahill and Smith were carrying?

Entwistle came into my office and explained the situation. King had recently been into the Burmese jungle to find Khun Sa, arguably the most powerful and elusive drug warlord in the Far East. Khun Sa, a former Chinese Nationalist *Kuomintang* fighter previously known as Chang Chi-Fu, ruled over a remote rebel enclave in the Burmese part of the so-called 'Golden Triangle' that produced more than 60 per cent of the world's heroin. He had raised an army resilient enough to repel everything the Burmese government troops could throw at it. King had found him, filmed him and had left him, he was pretty sure, on good terms. Now he was willing to repeat the process for us.

Naturally, I liked this idea very much. But I could tell Entwistle was holding something back from me. "Come on Clive. What's the catch?" I asked.

He licked his lips and paused before admitting that we would have to make the journey by mule. It would take three or four days and we would have to cross the border illegally from Thailand to Burma and spend much of the time before reaching Khun Sa's territory dodging Burmese Army patrols.

Entwistle could give me all the assurances in the world – he usually did – but the dangers from just about every quarter were obvious. Nevertheless, I thought, this is what I joined up for. This is what I do. The potential story was great. And there was still a chance that Patricia Cahill and Karen Smith might agree to talk to *The Cook Report* and give us what we needed to get to the bottom of their story.

"Let's take it in two stages," I said. "The prison first. If we aren't satisfied with what we get there, Patrick King can set up our border crossing with Khun Sa and his merry men."

King joined us for the flight out to Bangkok and worked with Entwistle to try to get into Bangkok women's prison to see the prisoners. After three days of applying to prison and government officials and traipsing back and forth from our hotel to Cahill and Smith's lawyers, it looked pretty bleak. The world and his dog had asked for the all-important exclusive interview and no one was prepared to let us in.

Graeme Thomson was finding more out about the men behind the heroin smuggling operation by the day, but it eventually became clear that we weren't going to get the chance to put our questions to the women who were, after all, on trial for their lives and for whom the smallest piece of evidence about how they were set up should have been vital.

I asked Patrick King to come into my room. We agreed that we should make the arrangements to leave Thailand for Burma as soon as possible. He switched into military mode and wheeled out of the room to make contact with Khun Sa's agents at the Thailand/ Burma border.

Twenty-four hours later, our small team found itself doing something even the hardiest members had never done before. Setting off from the northern Thai city of Chiang Mai in the late afternoon, we were bounced to the Burmese border in a couple of elderly ex-military trucks.

There we were met by a couple of Khun Sa's emissaries who guided us over the border at dead of night under the noses of both Thai and Burmese border guards. On the other side there was a prearranged rendezvous with some more guides and a team of mules, some of which were to carry our equipment while the others carried us. One unlucky mule was going to get me.

The leader of Khun Sa's Burmese muleteers called to his men. They walked towards us, carrying an assortment of dark green waterproof ponchos with hoods. Entwistle, Wickings, King and I distributed them amongst ourselves according to size. I was given the biggest poncho and the biggest mule.

We mounted the mules with the help of our guides, who, if they were amused by our clumsiness, didn't show it.

It started to rain. All around us were moss-covered trees and broad-leaved plants. The raindrops gathered up in the branches and periodically delivered a pint or so of warm water that hit the leaves below with a resounding 'plack!' Sometimes the payload landed on us and I thanked God we'd got our ponchos.

Every so often the riders in front would stop and turn to us, signalling everybody to keep quiet. I was concentrating so hard on just keeping in the saddle and avoiding low branches that I almost forgot we were actually making an illegal foray into a foreign and hostile country. Here, if the Burmese Army didn't shoot us as suspected heroin traffickers, we could, at the least, expect to be held in gaol and tried for just being where we were.

The terrain gradually became steeper and more dangerous with it. A mule carrying our water bottles and other supplies slipped over on a scree and had to be cajoled back onto its feet by its handler. Wickings checked his camera gear, which had been strapped, under his close supervision, to one of the pack mules which swayed from side to side under his anxious gaze just ahead of him.

"Still glad you came?" asked King, leaning over to me as I clung on to my mule.

In truth, I was almost enjoying myself. My backside was sore and my back, legs and arms were aching, but we were all together in adversity. Four white men in the hands of half a dozen members of a Far Eastern rebel army, in enemy territory and on our way to one of the biggest opium suppliers on the planet. I could have been doing the garden back at home, or sitting in my office reading interminable documents and listening to Mike Townson demanding that his secretary fetch him yet another packet of cigarettes. Still, as long as we steered clear of the border patrols and the official Burmese Army, we should be fine.

Patrick consulted his thermometer and disclosed that the temperature was around 44 degrees centigrade. We could tell that the relative humidity was close to 100 per cent, even between showers. We were sweating like fountains. And not just from the heat. The exertions required to traverse the mountainous terrain left us puffing like trains. Whenever there was a steep incline, we had to dismount and let the mules go up or down on their own. And going down was often safer on foot, because the tracks had turned into treacherous reddish-brown mudslides, some dropping as much as

60 feet. I remember unintentionally descending one such mudslide on my backside, closely followed by my mule on its haunches, braying its head off.

By nightfall, when we pitched camp, we could barely move and our conversation was punctuated by groans and curses. And it was so oppressively hot no one really felt like eating, which was just as well, seeing what was on offer. Trying to sleep under canvas was impossible. If you stayed in cover you gently simmered in your own perspiration, and if you stayed outside you were soaked by periodic bursts of monsoonal rain.

Our cameraman, Grahame Wickings noticed that although by his own reckoning, he'd drunk about ten litres of water in the past day and a half, he hadn't needed to pee, because according to him, it was all coming out through his skin.

We stopped for the second day at about five o'clock in the afternoon. Our guides had decided we'd had enough for the day. The Burmese put up their small, green bivouac tents and encouraged us to dry ourselves off as best we could before settling down to sleep. That night, hungry and exhausted, we actually ate our rather unappealing rations and, surprisingly, slept passably well.

I was awoken by the sound of our guides' high-pitched voices talking rapidly and excitedly just outside my tent. An intense 'Shhhhh!' went round our small camp. I lay back on my ground-sheet and held my breath. I could hear the blood pounding in my ears as I strained to pick up the sounds around me. This didn't look good. I couldn't make a run for it even if I wanted to. I began to rehearse my defence speech for the trial.

After about 20 minutes – which felt to me like five hours – our guides began to chatter animatedly again. Whatever the danger was, it had passed and we crawled out of our tents. After an approximation of breakfast, we remounted, instantly reminding ourselves of how painful our backsides were. Again we were into a seemingly endless cycle of crossing streams and rivers followed by steep ascents and descents, as we passed through a succession of lush, steaming valleys. The rain never eased and I began to wish the journey was over. Grahame Wickings helped pass the time counting the natural obstacles we had overcome on our journey.

"Thirty-four streams and rivers and six mountain peaks," he announced.

"And the same again when we go back," I rejoined, tentatively feeling my bruised rear.

After a third morning's trekking, we finally came within sight of the Shan settlement at Ho Mong – and it stopped raining. There were rows upon rows of neat, reed mat houses, a couple of recently built schools and a construction site for what we were told was to be a brand new hospital. There was no sign of opium poppies. They were apparently grown on the surrounding hills.

The settlement was ranged down either side of a broad dirt road which ran through two adjoining valleys, at the end of which was a parade ground and what I took to be barracks. Rows of large, tin sheds built around a clearing in the jungle. Small figures emerged to greet us. Our Burmese guides dismounted and we gratefully followed suit. We were led to one of the sheds and ushered inside.

Standing in front of a large yellow and white flag pinned to a wall below a map of the world, stood a figure dressed in smart, dark blue battle fatigues.

It was hard to guess Khun Sa's age, but he was probably in his late fifties. He had smooth, burnished skin, stood erect and tall at about five feet ten, with thick, black hair. He smiled at me and extended his hand. He had a grip of iron. He repeated the hand-mangling operation with Entwistle, Wickings and King, also giving Patrick a friendly pat on the elbow.

Through our interpreter we explained why we had come. Heroin was a massive trade in the West. Even as we spoke, two British girls were sitting in a Thai gaol and stood to lose their lives for possessing the deadly drug. We wanted to know the train of events that had led them there.

To my surprise, Khun Sa readily admitted that heroin was a 'dirty trade'. His story went that the Shan people, whose leader he was, had been under virtual siege by the Burmese for many years – well before their involvement with heroin. In order to support themselves, they first tried forestry, but couldn't ship their products through enemy territory. Then, in the interests of easy transportation, they tried emerald mining, but couldn't produce economically, even with negligible labour costs. So with great reluctance, he claimed, they turned to their only other option – growing opium poppies. It made the Shan people a living and bought them guns, and it made Khun Sa notorious.

During the course of our long conversations, it emerged that 20 years previously, Khun Sa had met 'representatives' of the US government, for whom he had offered to destroy his crop for its wholesale value. But the Americans hadn't wanted him to do that, he said – they actually wanted to buy the product of his poppy harvest for their own use.

It turned out that he had been dealing with CIA operatives, who, at that time, wanted to use the profits they could make from his heroin to fund their clandestine war in Laos and Cambodia – without letting a hostile Senate and House of Representatives know what was going on. Khun Sa suggested that the money had been laundered through the oddly named Nugen Hand Bank in Australia. I must say that I found all this difficult to believe.

"Now we go," said Khun Sa, in his only display of English. He rose from his wicker chair and beckoned us to follow. Then he showed us how he spent the heroin money he received – he certainly didn't seem to be spending it on himself and didn't really conform to my concept of a drug baron. There was the expected array of modern weapons, but that was by no means all. Over the past two years he had planned and begun to build a substantial hospital, to be fitted out with the latest equipment. He beamed broadly as he took us on a conducted tour of the foundations. The nearby new schools appeared to be well-attended and the market bustled with activity.

His people looked healthy and well-fed and clothed. As we rode with him on the back of a battered Japanese pickup truck, the response from passers-by was friendly and relaxed. He ran his fiefdom with the help of a small army, but no one displayed any fear.

Khun Sa himself slept on a camp bed inside one of the tin buildings. The floor was of earth. He told us that he ate the same food as his men and that they respected him. We were given identical food and facilities when we arrived, and even though it was primitive, I had the best and most welcome shower of my life – standing under a piece of perforated bamboo with clear, cool water piped straight from a nearby spring.

When he was outside the perimeter of the camp, Khun Sa was surrounded by armed guards. He told us that the Burmese government had been trying to capture him and annexe his people's land for decades, and that attacks could come at any time. When the British had relinquished control of Burma after the last war, they had promised independence for the Shan people. It had never come and so they had to fight and be prepared to die in defence of their homeland.

That afternoon, we did the filmed interview, during which Khun Sa reiterated his claim that he was 'trapped in a dirty trade'. We filmed the Shan people going about their daily business – and captured, inevitably, the vast hillside fields of long-stemmed, red and white poppies that enabled this isolated tribe to stay independent and alive.

That night I slept what I imagine to be the sleep of the just – on a rickety bamboo litter to which I'd not normally have given house room. It was lights out at ten, and the throb of the generator gave way to the eerie chorus of the surrounding jungle.

The next day – as we reluctantly prepared to mount our long-suffering mules and head back to Thailand – Khun Sa remonstrated with us. He said that most of his few Western visitors required several days rest before repeating their arduous jungle journey. We must be mad to leave after little more than 24 hours, but if we insisted, could we delay our departure for an hour or so? Apparently he had organised, for our benefit, a parade of troops from his *Mon Tai* Army.

Before he and I inspected his men, Khun Sa addressed them from a small green-painted dais. His chief aide, Kharnsai Jaiyen, whispered a translation into my ear. "We are honoured to have with us today a man who can tell the story of our struggle for independence to the outside world. His documentaries are watched by millions. He is the world famous television reporter . . ." Khun Sa paused, and Kharnsai Jaiyen suppressed a laugh. "What's the problem," I asked. "Well, Mr World-Famous Television Reporter," came the spluttered reply, "I'm afraid Khun Sa has forgotten your name."

This blip in Khun Sa's PR offensive was not noticed by his troops, who stood impassively under the early morning sun. They seemed to range in age from eight to 80, though there was a core of very fit-looking, well turned out fighting men. Khun Sa had said that anyone was free to join his 'People's Army'. The oldest leaned on their rifles rather than shouldering them and the youngest looked so proud to be wearing their uniforms, despite the fact that they were far too big for them. Several of the tiniest actually stepped right out of their oversize boots as they heard the order to march forward. It was a strangely touching scene and I almost felt sorry to leave. But leave we did.

The return journey was painful but uneventful. Back in Bangkok we tried, once more, to arrange an interview with Patricia Cahill and Karen Smith. But it was like bashing your head against the prison's brick wall. We had to make do with some telephoto footage shot through the prison bars. But we did have Khun Sa – a fascinating insight into a very topical subject.

From Thailand I flew on to Australia to investigate Khun Sa's scarcely believable tale of the Nugen Hand bank, through which the CIA had allegedly laundered the profits from heroin dealing in order to fund their unauthorised war in Cambodia. The bank had existed, after all. It had been founded by one Michael Hand, a former pilot for the CIA's dubious private airline, Air America. Hand's co-founder, Frank Nugen, had been assassinated in 1980, not long after an alleged plot – funded by the bank – to destabilise the Australian Government.

Nugen Hand had been based in Sydney, so I asked my old friend Barry to arrange an interview for me with the Attorney General of New South Wales, John Dowd. When I met him in his swish offices, not far from where the bank had operated, I fully expected him to deny any nefarious activities on his patch and to put me off with the usual politician's waffle.

Not so, for he was remarkably forthcoming in the circumstances. A large manila file lay open on his desk. The bank had been an embarrassment, he said, but after it collapsed in 1980 and the true extent of its activities had been revealed, he had made it his business to find out as much as he could about its modus operandi – even going as far as visiting Khun Sa himself:

"The Nugen Hand bank held funds on behalf of the CIA, funds raised by the CIA from covert arms dealing and drug smuggling. I went [to Burma] and saw the fields of poppies in an area controlled by Khun Sa, and I believe that the CIA supported the growing of them. I don't know how he [Khun Sa] would have met CIA officials, but obviously he was paid directly or indirectly by the CIA to keep this trade going."

Mr Dowd flicked the file shut. As far as he was concerned, Khun Sa's CIA story was true. "It is my information that the heroin

194

revenue so produced was used to fund large scale, unauthorised military action in the region."

He would not be drawn further, and would not go on record with his strong personal views about the 'criminal subversion' of the New South Wales banking system. Nevertheless, though pretty succinct, it was a surprising and illuminating interview on which I reflected often during the long flight home. It also made for a fascinating programme which drew the highest audience of the series. After transmission, we sent a copy of the programme to Khun Sa. A month or so later we received a letter from him. He thanked us for the film, which he thought was critical but fair.

He also added that the mule which I had ridden into Shan territory and back again had, sadly, died soon afterwards.

He made no direct comment as to why this had happened but mentioned that that particular mule had been the pride and joy of a close friend of his. While he understood the difficulty of despatching a mule to Burma from England, his friend had rather set his heart on a 50cc Honda moped. Could I kindly forward the cost of one? The letter caused much merriment in the office. Great guffaws emanated from Townson's office when the translation of Khun Sa's message was read out to him.

We kept in touch with his tiny, beleaguered Burmese enclave. Years later, Khun Sa gave us invaluable help when we were exposing the money-laundering activities of John 'Goldfinger' Palmer, providing us with a couple of totally believable 'drug barons' who claimed they needed vast sums of money laundered. By 1996, Khun Sa was a very ill man, and he surrendered to Burmese police, having negotiated a peace deal with the Burmese military junta that had hunted him for so long. Bearing in mind their treatment of opposition leader Aung San Suu Kyi, the worth of that peace deal is open to question.

The story of Patricia Cahill and Karen Smith ended the 1990 series on a high note for us. It ended pretty well for them, too, bearing in mind that convicted heroin smugglers in Thailand normally face the death penalty. After serving just a few months of their 25-year sentences, the Thai Government announced that it was prepared to show them mercy. Cahill and Smith flew home to freedom and family celebrations.

*

Drugs have featured in many of our programmes – directly or indirectly – an indication of the large part they have come to play in our society. Early in 1992 we were the first to warn that ecstasy was not the harmless recreational drug its promoters proclaimed. In graphic terms, the parents of one of the very first victims, Clare Layton, told us how their 16-year-old daughter had died in agony after taking her first and only 'E' tablet. "She had bloated up to three times her normal size and was bleeding from every orifice." Their story was truly shocking.

I can't think of another current affairs programme that has ever staged a rave, but *The Cook Report* did. At that carefully monitored event we told guests of the risks posed by E. We told them particularly of Clare's horrible demise, but the almost universal reaction amongst the youngsters was: 'There must have been something wrong with her – it wouldn't happen to me.'

Though it does seem to be true that some people are much more sensitive to ecstasy than others, finding out into which category you fall is the equivalent of playing Russian roulette. On top of that – as with other illicit drugs – you couldn't be sure how the E you bought was cut – what noxious substances were added to it during manufacture. You also couldn't be sure whether your newly acquired E (abbreviated chemical name, MDMA) wasn't the similar but even riskier MDA. Russian roulette, game two.

Our film was used by a number of educational authorities and police forces similarly interested in sounding a warning about E, but the youthful assumption of infallibility is difficult to counter and the death toll has continued to climb.

Other than recreational drugs taken to enhance experiences, we also came upon a story exposing the health risks taken by those using anabolic steroids to build their physiques for purely cosmetic purposes. Steroid use had moved out of the gyms and into the wider world, with tens of thousands of new users.

We met Zoe Warwick, a former female bodybuilding champion, who had virtually turned herself into a man through steroid use – and had irreparably damaged many of her vital organs. In constant pain, and unable to cope with the consequences of this chemical self-mutilation, she was later found dead of massive morphine overdose.

We also met the mother of Jimmy Kevill, another youngster who had used steroids to give him the muscles he thought girls admired

196

on shirtless men at raves. He started on steroids when he was 16 and soon began to display the classic symptoms of so-called 'roid rage' – fits of violent and uncontrollable temper.

Unable to cope with him at home, his mother finally had him committed to a psychiatric hospital. One visiting day, without reason or warning, 'roid rage' consumed him again. He circled the room, lowered his head and charged at the wall with colossal force, fracturing his skull and killing himself.

Other users made their friends and partners victims of 'roid rage'. There had been numerous serious assaults, several murders and also a number of deaths from liver cancer – all directly attributable to steroid abuse.

Steroids are not over-the-counter drugs, so where, *The Cook Report* asked, were they coming from? Paul Calverley organised the infiltration of a gang led by John Stiff, one of the major importers and distributors of steroids in Britain. We traced his supply route to a manufacturer called P&B Laboratories in India. There, the sales director, Humandra Patel, claimed that he had no idea what was happening to his products in the UK, and that he would cease dealing with Stiff forthwith. He was lying, but we didn't know that at the time.

Back in the UK, we secretly filmed dealers in action, offering to supply us wholesale. In one sequence, which had the editorial team in stitches – so much so that we inevitably included it in the programme – one dealer joked to our man on the inside: "I hope this isn't some stunt for that bloke on the telly – what's his name again? – yeah, Roger Cook."

He was not amused when I called on him later.

Another dealer – this time a glamorous woman – when confronted on camera insisted that she didn't want to talk to me, because, as she put it: "It would damage my reputation."

In the months after the first steroids programme was broadcast, John Stiff found himself the focus of police attention, and decided to hand his business over to someone else. So thorough had Calverley's infiltration been that Stiff – unknowingly – offered his business to *The Cook Report*!

We took him up on the offer in order to make another programme. From this advantageous position, we could now get inside the entire network, from manufacturer to supply chain, and on to local distributors. At this point we discovered that our Indian friend Mr Patel had been lying to us. He had in fact continued to supply the British black market with steroids, and had also provided phoney paperwork and bogus packaging in order to fool the authorities.

We confronted him again, after a secretly filmed meeting in a room in Mumbai's Holiday Inn. He came with a business plan designed to boost his production and maximise 'our' profits. Confronted by Roger Cook and a camera, he left in a hurry, threatening all kinds of mayhem.

But nothing happened to me, fortunately. Unfortunately, nothing happened to Patel either. The Indian authorities weren't interested, claiming that if Patel *was* committing an offence it wasn't on Indian soil.

I had been staying in a rather grand hotel near the city centre. We were well behind schedule and, as I lugged my luggage across the foyer in order to catch the late night flight home, the Duty Manager collared me. He claimed that I had vandalised a glass table in my room, and that if I didn't pay him a thousand rupees (then about £100) on the spot, he would call the police. The result of that would be that I would miss my plane and be forced to spend some time as a guest of the local constabulary in a rather less comfortable room than the one I'd just vacated.

The glass table top, I recalled, had already been cracked on my arrival. I was beginning to argue the toss when another hotel guest overheard the conversation and barrelled over. "Look here," he said, "this chap's just accused me of buggering up the taps in my bathroom. He wanted a hundred quid from me too. This is obviously a try on! Let *us* call the police."

The Duty Manager bolted, and I just made the plane.

In the meanwhile, back in the UK, the team had infiltrated part of the national steroids distribution network based, surprisingly, in genteel Torquay. There, the south coast distributor boasted that he even supplied the army – unofficially and illegally, of course, and without the army's knowledge. So confident was he of his position that at one of the meetings held in our camera-rigged house he even brought along his little daughter and sat her on his knee as he talked big drug deals. He wasn't only dealing in steroids.

Steroids have now been reclassified as controlled drugs, but, regrettably, it doesn't stop people getting their hands on them. The same is true, of course, of cocaine and heroin. That's why, during the filming of another programme – on the ever-decreasing age of drug abusers – we were readily able to find heroin addicts as young as nine years old. That's also why Keith Hellawell – then Chief Constable of West Yorkshire, but soon to become the government's new 'Drugs Czar' – told us: "My concern is that within the next decade, nine out of ten of our 16-year-olds will be drug users or drug dealers in one form or another."

I wished him luck in his new job – he was going to need all he could get. But it obviously wasn't enough. Eventually, his forthright views brought him into conflict with the politicians, and the politicians saw him off.

Politics rules television too. Central was proud enough of our steroids programme to enter it for a Royal Television Society award in 1997. They then decided they would prefer to enter in another category with a programme we had made about Colin Stagg, the man alleged to have brutally murdered Rachel Nickell on Wimbledon Common. The programme was based around a very revealing interview with Stagg. It made it to the last two in the interview of the year category, together with a very entertaining sparring match between Jeremy Paxman and the disgraced former MP, Neil Hamilton.

As the Awards dinner proceeded, and prior to the handing out of the gongs, our table was approached by an ITV Network Centre executive who was also the chairman of the judging panel. They had taken their final decisions that afternoon, he said. To the delight of Managing Director Andy Allan, Factual Controller Steve Clarke and me, he told us I'd won – and that perhaps I should have a few words ready. I sat, coyly toying with those few words, and waited for the call. It never came.

After the 'final decision', minds had somehow been changed. When the official announcement was eventually made, I'd apparently been relegated to the position of runner-up. I was slack-jawed with amazement, but Andy Allan said I shouldn't fret. It was just the result of TV politics. Jeremy's interview was excellent, as was mine. However, I'd got the more important recognition as far as he was concerned – a much bigger audience.

The first person I came across when I strolled into the office to start work on the fifth series was Salk.

"What are you doing here?" I asked. I was delighted to see him again but, the last I'd heard, he was struggling in the chilly world of freelance work after finally losing patience with Townson's incessant demands.

It appeared that he'd brought in a story that Townson wanted to turn into a programme. That was one of the things about Townson – he could be an absolute tyrant and make your life a complete misery without turning a hair. You'd think you had burnt your bridges with him because you had finally cracked and gone for him, then he was perfectly capable of welcoming you back into the fold as if nothing had ever happened. And he was as loyal to his team as he was irritating to them. When called upon to back the programme or its staff, Townson would back them to the hilt. But above all, he had a nose for a good story – where we usually differed was over how to bring it to the screen.

While working for the BBC, Salk had met a Turkish journalist who had told him of just such a story – about the organised plunder of his country's heritage in order to feed the West's hunger for Greco-Roman artefacts. The journalist claimed he could take him to villages where all the ancient statuary had vanished – taken by thieves in the pay of rich dealers who passed the artefacts through the world's most famous and, supposedly, most upstanding auction houses, in London and New York.

"It's got the scenery, grave-robbing, toothless bandits and smooth auctioneers in expensive suits," chuckled Salk. "Mike's already got a title for the programme – so I suppose he'll have to make it now."

Townson's choices of titles for *Cook Report* programmes were often as cringe-making as they were inappropriate. Several producers had totally failed to recognise their own programmes when Townson started referring to them by the titles he had decided to give them.

"What's he going to call it?" I asked, holding my head in mock weariness. "Raiders of the Lost Art," Salk replied, breaking into his infectious cackle. "My title, this time. What do you think?"

"I think it's good to have you back on board," I said as we settled down in my office to chew over the events of the past year and to laugh about some of the times we had spent together in far-flung parts of the world.

Salk's new Turkish friend, Melik Kaylan, seemed to know just about all there was to know about the billion dollar trade in stolen Turkish antiquities. It had been his journalistic specialty back home and he had a mass of evidence at his fingertips. He knew who was behind the trade as well as those trying to stop it, so we decided to fly him out ahead of us to set up interviews with Ministry of Culture officials, museum curators – and convicted looters. He had confirmed half a dozen key interviews and some location filming when Salk and I left for Istanbul. Unfortunately, the situation had changed completely by the time we arrived.

For a start, Melik was not at Ataturk Airport to meet us as arranged. We found him in his hotel room, looking very depressed. "I'm going home," he said, "the crooked dealers know we're coming and they'll kill me if I stay." And that wasn't all. For reasons we were never able to fathom, Melik had also fallen out with his museum contacts and all doors were now closed to us.

Disaster was averted by a Turkish archaeologist called Nezih Bazgelen, to whom Melik had previously introduced us. He believed the project would have a positive outcome and was able to persuade those who'd closed their doors to open them again. The fact that he had been to school with most of them was probably a help.

However, Melik still wanted to depart, leaving us without a researcher and translator. Frank words were had. "Listen, I've had a serious death threat," said Melik, "You obviously don't understand." I assured him that I did understand, because at that stage I'd had about ten such threats, and I was still here. Salk reminded him that for a young Turkish journalist, this could be the biggest story of his life, and that having a prime-time network television outlet for it was an opportunity not to be missed. Eventually, he seemed to be won round and grudgingly unpacked his suitcase.

The next day he sheepishly took us to the *Kapalicarsi* covered bazaar, where, as Salk filmed with a secret camera, we were offered a 2,000-year-old, carved stone sarcophagus for $2,000. For a little extra, the vendor could arrange to have it sawn up, so that we could smuggle it out of the country like a piece of flat-pack furniture.

Back at our hotel, Nezih turned up with a Sotheby's Auction Catalogue and thumbed through to lot 361. It was a magnificently carved Roman *steli* – or tombstone – that he believed had been stolen from a remote Anatolian village. "And what's more," he added enthusiastically, "I think its twin is still there."

We quizzed him further and agreed that making the two day journey to Gurcina on spec was a chance worth taking. Salk, Nezih and I duly set off, our four-wheel-drive loaded with supplies and equipment. Tarmac roads soon gave way to rutted tracks and the cream-coloured dust got into everything.

By day two we were beginning to doubt the wisdom of the trip, but Nezih would brook no argument. So convinced was he that he was right about the location of the *steli*, that he cajoled Salk into running his camera as we approached. Sure enough, there in the village square, was an identical *steli* to lot 361, now doing service as a fountain.

The villagers were amazed. Lot 361 had once formed the other side of a larger fountain situated on the edge of the village. But after the looters had been, they moved the remaining *steli* to the central square where they could keep an eye on it. The villagers excitedly pored over the auction catalogue photo and compared it feature by feature with their fountain. There was no doubting it; they were identical. The mayor decided they should appeal to Sotheby's better nature. He would write them a letter, explaining the circumstances of their loss and then surely the auction house would send back the other half of their fountain. The letter quickly became a petition, signed by every adult in the village.

Sotheby's ignored it. Their Chairman let it be known that we were 'beneath contempt' for daring to question the business ethics of such an august auction house. But the case of the stolen *steli* was not a one-off.

Former Sotheby's director Peter Nahum told us that many of the antiquities that went through the company's auctions were of doubtful provenance and that Sotheby's knew it. "They would certainly turn a blind eye if they knew something had come from where it shouldn't, and would sell it if they thought they could get away with it. Sotheby's knowingly deals in goods that have been stolen or smuggled." Is that company policy? "Yes." He added that the high prices achieved for stolen antiquities at auction had the effect of driving the looters and their masters even harder.

A confidential internal memo that came into our hands spoke

volumes about the company's cavalier attitude. It suggested ways of avoiding Customs and 'getting tracks comprehensively covered'.

Lot 361 was brought to Sotheby's by a Turkish born, Munich-based dealer called Edip Telli. We were to learn that he controlled most of this massive illegal trade, and had also handled the sale of the biggest ever treasure trove stolen from Turkey – the so-called Lydian Hoard, believed to have once been the property of King Croesus (as in 'as rich as'). Telli had a formidable reputation as a man you didn't cross, and a brother called Nevzat who added drug dealing to his looting portfolio. Nevzat was subsequently caught trying to smuggle 92 kilos of pure heroin into Britain and was gaoled as a result.

Telli would not have got his hands dirty digging the Lydian Hoard out of the ground, but with Nezih and Melik's help, we traced the man who did. Osman Unsal was a dirt-poor former blacksmith who took to selling the occasional artefact unearthed from the land surrounding his village in order to feed and clothe his family.

Over supper in his ramshackle house, he told us how he thought he'd struck it rich. In order to keep him talking, we actually had to eat the special meal his wife had prepared for us as honoured guests. It was couscous and grilled sheep's testicles. Picture the expression on our faces as we felt obliged to accept Osman's generous offer of seconds.

The area round the village of Gurek was once part of the kingdom of Croesus and was dotted with *tumuli* – small man-made hillocks – under which were concealed the tombs of the royal and the wealthy. Most of these tombs had been looted already, but Osman and his friends had come across one that appeared to be intact.

They broke in through the top of the *tumulus* and Osman was lowered in. As his eyes grew accustomed to the gloom, they caught the glint of gold. One by one, he passed more than a hundred priceless artefacts up through the access hole to his friends above. At this point, they seem to have ceased being friends. The story became one of greed, betrayal, a gunfight and finally a gaol sentence for Osman. His 'friends' got away with most of what became known as the Lydian Hoard.

At about this time, we almost lost Melik again. He said he'd received another threatening phone call which had really frightened him, and he now wanted to leave immediately. He told us that a year or so earlier, when he was covering the story for a Turkish magazine, the brake pipes on his car had been cut and he'd had a serious accident. He showed us the scars of the resulting injuries and reminded us that Edip Telli and his network were no strangers to violence. It took us half a day to talk him round again, and he finally settled for changing hotels rather than countries.

Once Osman's fellow looters had sold the Lydian Hoard to a local intermediary for a few hundred dollars, it had passed through the hands of several corrupt dealers and finally into those of the biggest dealer of them all, Edip Telli in Munich.

In 1966, Telli sold it to the Metropolitan Museum of Art in New York. Former Metropolitan director Tom Hoving was in no doubt that the museum authorities knew exactly what they were buying and where these exquisite artefacts had come from. As he memorably put it: "They knew they certainly didn't come from Boston or an archaeological excavation in Nevada; they didn't come from the ruins of a Greek village buried under the Los Angeles freeway. Everybody knew where they came from; they came from Turkey, because all of the great civilisations passed through Turkey."

Tom Hoving was firmly of the view that ancient artefacts should remain in their countries of origin – as several international treaties demanded – and pointed out that Turkey possessed more buried treasure than could be found in Greece and Italy combined. He added that wholesale looting in Turkey and elsewhere was commonplace and not only robbed these countries of their heritage, it also destroyed the archaeological record and therefore our main means of understanding ancient cultures.

After we'd finished filming the interview, Salk had a brainwave: "You know what we should do – we should bring old Osman over to New York to see if he recognises what the Met has on display and get his reaction." Even Townson thought it was a good idea, but in practice it wasn't easy to deliver. Osman had never left his village and didn't want to do so now. It took days to talk him into it, with tales of the wonders that awaited him in the land of the free.

Then, the US authorities wouldn't grant him a visa unless he was accompanied at all times by a responsible chaperone. We elected

Nezih, who flew back to Turkey to fetch him. Poor, jet-lagged Nezih had great difficulty getting him on the plane, because Osman didn't think anything that big could fly.

Once in the air, Osman loved it, and once in New York, he loved that even more.

When we told the Met's management what our film was about and who Osman was, they refused to put up an interviewee, or even to let our cameras in. So, as you might expect, we went in anyway with a small amateur video camera. Osman was obviously excited as we peered through the glass of the display cases. He could recognise every gleaming item. In fact, he could even remember in which order he found them. In the hushed atmosphere of the museum, he was now making quite a lot of noise, so we were forced to bundle him outside before he gave the game away.

Osman was very agitated as we barrelled down the museum steps. Nezih told us that this was for two reasons. First, having learnt that the Met had paid $1.7 million for the hoard, his bitterness at having been cheated all those years ago was reinforced, and second, in a bizarre leap of logic, he thought the museum was wrong to have bought the treasure and ought to return it to Turkey. Returning Osman to Turkey was another matter.

He'd plainly decided that America was the place for him. The following day, while we were all taking an early morning stroll in Central Park, Osman bolted. He was off like a greyhound and nearly ended his days under a Checker Cab. From then on, until we got him back on the plane home, Nezih kept him on a very short lead.

When I called on Edip Telli at his swish *Gryphos* gallery in Munich, he denied everything, including the evidence of his own eyes when confronted with the documents linking him with the theft and subsequent auction of lot 361. His fluent English conveniently evaporated. A balding, bespectacled and slightly schoolmasterish figure, Telli's looks belied his fearsome reputation. But eventually, perhaps to get rid of this persistent TV reporter, he did admit to handling the Lydian Hoard.

Following the programme and a successful legal action taken by the Turkish Government, the Lydian Hoard was returned by the Metropolitan Museum to its rightful home. Telli was arrested while on a trip to Switzerland, extradited to Turkey, and is now behind bars.

As each new series was planned, we would all sit together and throw ideas around. Sometimes the programmes would be self-selecting – stories which had already had some work done on them but hadn't been made last time around for pressure of time. Some hadn't yet been made but now their time had come – made relevant by current world events. And a few, like Raiders, almost came in on a plate and were so appealing they couldn't be turned down.

I really enjoyed these early get-togethers. There was a freshness that a month or so away from the grindstone had allowed into the faces and demeanours of my colleagues. A month or so hence, people would huddle anxiously over the telephone or sit, agonised, in hotels waiting for their contacts to deliver the goods. But now, refreshed from their time off, they sat, stretched out on their chairs, legs extended in a relaxed fashion. We also had some new blood in the team – Steve Warr, then a bright researcher who had cut his teeth on national newspapers and seemed eager to make his mark in television.

Over a couple of weeks, the 'goers' amongst the story ideas would emerge and stake their claims as future programmes. There were always about twice as many strong contenders as there were programmes to be made. Then, when everyone had had their say, and you thought you were about to enter into a democratic debate about the merits of what you'd heard, Townson would look over the top of his enormous spectacles and peer down at the back of one of his countless packets of cigarettes, cough and demand silence.

"So, I've decided we'll make the following," he would say, and he would read out six subjects which he'd jotted on the back of the packet – often including one or two that had never come up in discussion at all. Then he would assign producers and researchers to each of them.

When you got to know the system, you realised what had gone on. Clive Entwistle had long been Townson's close confidant and the two of them would hatch their plans in the absence of everyone else – including myself much of the time. And as my filming commitments mounted up, I didn't always have the time or the energy to argue.

In the early days, Entwistle would have been in conclave with the editor half a dozen times before the team get-together and, by then, the make-up of the series was sometimes almost cut and dried. The previously unheard of stories would often be ones Entwistle had got from his contacts, which he liked to keep very close to his chest.

I was always slightly at odds with myself when this happened. I felt that people in the team were being railroaded. "Ah, but it's for the good of the series," Townson would say, peering over the top of his big black-rimmed specs.

This time, I had to admit that on first hearing I remained to be convinced about the subject Entwistle had chosen. A half-hour programme on hamburger vans sounded distinctly unpromising – until Entwistle and his researcher, Steve Warr, explained.

Entwistle had heard an item on Central's regional news programme about the murder of Gary Thompson. Thompson had been killed by two unknown assailants who had stolen an estimated £200,000 – the proceeds from just one weekend's fast-food selling by his fleet of vans and stalls – from the boot of his Rolls-Royce. The news piece said that the dead man was the biggest hot-dog trader in the Midlands.

"I didn't know there was that much money in burgers," said Entwistle, who had then sent Steve Warr to the funeral for a quiet look.

Thompson's funeral had been reminiscent of an East End gangland burial. Large numbers of heavily-built male mourners throwing hate-filled glances – and, later, punches – at press photographers. The whole thing reeked of criminality. Entwistle persuaded Townson to give him the green light, not just on the murder of Gary Thompson, but to investigate the burger trade in general.

Warr unearthed a series of very frightened traders. They all wanted to remain anonymous and would only meet late at night in cars in country lanes. It appeared that everyone in the business was scared because they believed that there was bound to be a gang war for control of the lucrative burger stand empire that Thompson had controlled until his murder. People were going to get hurt in the process.

One reluctant interviewee even pulled a gun on Warr to reinforce his stated desire never to be identified.

The gun-toting interviewee named a Derby man who, using force, was the main contender to assume Gary Thompson's mantle. He painted a reassuring picture of him. "He is a very, very, very violent person. Like a mad dog." Everyone in the team sat up a little and listened as Warr continued. The man's name was Joe Persico. I hadn't heard it before but, in the coming months, it was to become very familiar.

Entwistle and Warr brought the meeting to a close by announcing that they had applied to Leicester Council for a permit to set up their own burger stand on a pitch habitually used – illegally – by one of the Persico-controlled vehicles.

Agreement came through the following day. Warr hired a large burger trailer and went off to find someone who knew how to work a hot plate without setting himself alight.

A few nights later, researcher Paul Calverley and a young gofer from the Central newsroom called Kester Demarr towed the white-painted stand out to the pitch in the middle of Leicester, stopping at Sainsbury's on the way to buy burgers, hot dogs and buns.

Warr and a camera crew followed in an unmarked surveillance van and parked down the road from the burger pitch. Calverley and Demarr manoeuvred the stand into position and unhooked it from their car. Half an hour or so later, their griddle was sizzling and they were in business.

It was an indication of the money to be made from this business that, wherever the team set up the stall, we always made good money – even though we were buying our raw materials at retail prices. If you were big enough and tough enough to control all the pitches at a major event – a pop festival or a motor race meeting – you could easily make several hundred thousand pounds over a weekend.

It was getting late when a truck pulled up about 50 yards away from our stand. Three men got out and walked purposefully towards Calverley and Demarr. Warr could see that one of the men in particular was extremely angry. He was clenching and unclenching his fists and seemed to be having difficulty controlling himself.

'Mr Angry' was a short, heavily built, scruffy figure with long, lank hair. He was wearing a bomber jacket and dirty jeans. He stood with the other customers and started to swear loudly at Paul, who feigned incomprehension. The cameraman focused on the agitated figure and waited for developments.

The man was demanding to know which firm Calverley and Demarr worked for and where it was based. He was clearly unimpressed with their replies. Suddenly, and with surprising agility, 'Mr Angry' vaulted the five-foot high counter and ripped our brand-new council licence off the wall behind Calverley's shoulder. He held it up to the flickering gas lamp at the back of the rig and pored over it.

He stabbed his finger at the type – almost poking right through it. "This is no good," he screamed into Calverley's face. He started pushing Calverley around the cramped cabin of the burger trailer. "This is Gary Thompson's pitch. If I ever see you here again ..." He left the threat unfinished, hanging in the smoky air.

He climbed out of the stand and beckoned his friends to walk with him back to their truck.

The truck moved slowly towards the Cook wagon. It reversed towards the tow hitch at one end of the stand. The trio climbed out of the truck and, without a word, started to rock and pull the stand off its blocks and to hitch it to their vehicle. Calverley and Demarr quickly leapt out the back door and stood at a safe distance as our stand was dragged down the road and dumped at an alarming angle a hundred yards away. The truck roared off into the night.

We had just met Joe Persico.

A week later, two men were arrested and charged with Gary Thompson's murder. The predicted burger war erupted as two equally nasty factions vied for control of the business. Persico was one of those vying to fill Thompson's shoes and he was not afraid to use violence in the process.

Our interviewees grew more frightened. I arrived at the home of one stall owner who claimed to be suffering from a bad bout of flu. The crew and I trooped upstairs to set up the interview at his sick bed. On the bedside table was a large club hammer.

"Things have got so bad, I've got to have protection 24 hours a day," croaked the interviewee, visibly shivering – but whether from flu or fear, I couldn't tell.

The programme also planned to focus on the problems faced by Westminster Council in central London where illegal street trading

– mainly from unlicensed hot-dog and burger handcarts – was rife. Warr's inquiries showed that the threatening atmosphere of the Midlands burger scene was replicated all over the country and in London particularly.

Westminster Council was engaged in a major operation against the illegal burger and hot-dog sellers, who in turn were fighting amongst themselves. Several of them had apparently been badly injured as a result. There had also been threats and actual instances of violence against the council's enforcement officers as they tried to clear scores of unhygienic, unlicensed handcarts off the streets.

In the Midlands, Joe Persico was determined to become the Mister Big of the burger business. In London, we were told that the man with the equivalent ambition was Ozdamir Mahmut, a Turkish Cypriot who surrounded himself with burly enforcers. His name was spoken of with awe by Council officials and burger vendors alike.

"If you try anything he doesn't like, there'll be serious violence and you'll come off worst," warned a Westminster Council officer. "It's bad enough for us when we set out to do his stands, but we can always take the police in there with us. If you go it alone, you'll be attacked for sure."

When you get information like this, and you do the sort of job I do, there's a thought process to go through. In the past I've been accused of seeking confrontation, of generating a showdown because it 'makes good telly' and the public expect it. I don't see it that way, and neither did our Audience Research Department. I know I've said this before, but it's worth repeating – according to them, you, the public, liked to sit on the edge of your seats to see how far I'd go, but didn't actually want to see me hit. If a programme turned out to be 'sensational', that's because the subject matter was, by its very nature, sensational – not because we tried to make it so.

The confrontations are, inevitably, a by-product of living the story. By placing me at the sharp end of the investigations – in this case, by playing the part of a burger seller in the street – *The Cook Report* got involved in a way that other factual programmes rarely did. I don't enjoy the confrontation, it's just that often it is the only satisfactory way of concluding a programme and making the point.

I'm frequently asked why – if things do turn violent in these circumstances – we don't just call the police and have the assailants arrested. This one is a real Catch 22. If we do call the police and charges are laid, then the film of the assault is part of the prosecution evidence and becomes *sub judice*. That means we can't broadcast the film until after any subsequent trial. With a programme approaching transmission and relying on the same evidence, we would be faced with an unacceptable delay, perhaps amounting to years. So we don't press charges, we just have to grin and bear it.

Mind you, it's not always the obvious ruffians who assault you. In an earlier *Cook Report*, my assailant was the chairman of Wyeth, an American based multi-national pharmaceutical company. Ativan, the tranquilliser they produced, had been promoted as being virtually free of side-effects when it was nothing of the kind. For many people, it was highly addictive and virtually impossible to come off.

We were alerted to the problem by a remarkable woman from Nottingham called Ada Niesyty. In fact, we called the programme 'Ada V Ativan'. Originally prescribed the drug for mild depression following the death of her first husband, Ada had quickly become addicted and had suffered such frightening and debilitating side-effects that she decided to wean herself off it. However, even her GP found it hard to believe how much more debilitating were the unsuccessful results of trying to do just that.

So, under his supervision this time, Ada volunteered to allow us to film her withdrawal from Ativan over a period of several weeks. It was almost too distressing to watch – a middle aged housewife, crouched in a corner, clawing at her face, arms and legs, sweating and shaking uncontrollably and occasionally screaming in panic. After just 72 hours, she was feeling suicidal and fell back into Ativan's chemical clutches. Hundreds of people wrote in to say they had endured similar suffering and a number of doctors, shocked by what they had seen, changed their prescribing habits. The manufacturers, however, took no notice. "They're bastards," said Ada. "They know exactly what their product does to people, but they keep on pushing it."

Wyeth had refused to take part in the programme. So I approached the company Chairman, Bernard Canavan, as he strolled down the fairway of the golf course at the exclusive

211

Philadelphia Country Club – the only place we could find him unaccompanied by the PR men who usually screened him from the press. I was shortly to find out why he needed them.

I introduced myself. "Get off my fucking golf course," was his charming response. "Do you realise," I ventured, "that the so-called safe product you marketed in Britain, long after you knew there were problems with it, has created thousands of Ativan addicts?" "Good!" came the singularly inappropriate reply. "Now bugger off while you've still got the chance." I don't know whether or not he realised that he'd just committed a PR blunder of epic proportions, but he then proceeded to make matters worse. With our cameras rolling, he belaboured me with a golf club.

As I nursed my many bruises on the drive back to our hotel, our PA got on the phone to report the events of the day to Townson back in Birmingham. Sympathetic as always, he had only two questions. "Did you get it on film?" Yes we did – and then, oddly. "What kind of club was it?" It was a number three wood, actually.

With our hot dog story, we had, as usual, thought very carefully through all the options on what was a potentially dangerous assignment. We could enlist the help of a genuine hot-dog seller – if we could find one brave enough to go against the bully boys. But what might happen? He could be seriously injured. We could have the police standing by to come in to rescue him but, from then on, he would be a marked man if he tried to ply his trade in London.

We could always film the hot-dog and burger traders at work and describe the intimidation and violence that went on behind the scenes – but would the public really be any the wiser? Would that really bring home the reality sufficiently to cause an outcry or create the sense of injustice that could be harnessed to stop what was happening?

Of course, there are times when it's just not possible to take on the role of active participant. The disguise doesn't always fit. But there are other times when there's no viable alternative. For example, in Northern Ireland, when I masqueraded as a London-based property developer in order to catch the paramilitaries at their extortion games, it wasn't something I did lightly. In Belfast, the RUC had told us it would be impossible for an Ulsterman to approach the UDA in the way we had planned. Our bait would have to be an outsider and the job was too dangerous to give to an actor.

We could have abandoned our sting and simply described for our audience what the men with guns were up to, but it wouldn't have had the same effect and, without the filmed evidence we obtained, it's highly unlikely that Eddie Sayers would have got ten years in gaol. As it is, the crime he and his friends committed remains in the mind of the viewer years later. The terrorists didn't forget either, to judge by the death threats I received whenever they found out that I was in the province. But our options, as with this hot dog story, had been limited.

So it was, then, that Steve Warr paid a visit to a catering outfitters to buy me a hygienic white coat and trilby, stopping off at a theatrical costumiers on the way to pick up a stick-on moustache and a large pair of spectacles with plain glass lenses. My disguise made me look rather like Ronnie Barker in *Open All Hours*, but at least I wasn't going to put the villains off by looking like Roger Cook working at his night job.

We were quite meticulous about hygiene and food quality. Our hamburgers were steak mince from a well-known hotel chain – far better than the congealed grey slurry usually sold from a burger van. However, I must confess that we did breach regulations – although unintentionally – on several occasions.

It turned out that the adhesive we used for my false moustache somehow lost its grip when exposed to the steam as I cooked. The result, more than once, was that customers got a little more than they bargained for with their burgers – but there were no complaints.

Westminster Council found us a previously confiscated hot-dog handcart and furnished us with a permit to occupy a sought-after pitch in the West End, opposite the Dominion Theatre on the corner of Oxford Street and Tottenham Court Road. The official who issued the licence restated his warning that we would be in for big trouble.

At eight o'clock every night, Ozdamir Mahmut's men would be turning up, expecting to set out their stall on the exact spot where the Cook handcart would already be open for business. Mahmut & Co would expect to take over the pitch, although they had no permit for it. They always worked without permits, instead preferring to pay a fine of £100 a day – another good indication of how much money there was in the trade.

A hundred yards or so from the pitch, Steve Warr stopped our big Transit van in Great Russell Street and deposited me and my heavily laden, four-wheeled handcart. With great difficulty, I manoeuvred it along the road towards the wide area of pavement where I would set up and start cooking. Far more wayward than any supermarket trolley, it clanked and clattered and fought me all the way. It certainly wasn't designed to mount kerb stones. Warr was within an inch of coming over to help me when the blasted thing finally conquered the kerb and I was able to push on to my destination.

Warr and cameraman Grahame Wickings had negotiated late-night access to a film-cutting office three floors above our street corner. Under cover of semi-darkness, Wickings felt bold enough to lean right out of the window with his camera. Getting good sound, however, was going to be a problem. As usual, I wore a radio microphone which transmitted from a little pack hidden in my pocket. Although generally an effective way of recording events, radio microphones are notoriously prone to electrical interference, particularly at long range.

We needed to get the receiver reasonably close without attracting attention to ourselves. The answer had come to us when we realised that our sound recordist was to be John Biddlecombe – a delightful chap blessed with a balding head and a bushy beard. "Don't wash or comb your hair," we'd told Biddlecombe on the phone the day before, "and bring an old blanket with you."

As I grunted and heaved my way down Tottenham Court Road, Biddlecombe was watching from a darkened shop doorway nearby. He sat on the pavement, leaning back on the roller shutter, his slightly-dishevelled head poking out from a voluminous tramp's blanket. The recording gear sat in his lap, safely hidden from view beneath it. Every so often, a passer-by would drop 50 pence or a pound in front of him. What with that and the profits from our hot dog and burger sales, we were coming dangerously close to becoming a self-financing programme.

Clive Entwistle hovered around the scene, disappearing periodically into Tottenham Court Road tube station and emerging to wander past me. Occasionally he would bring a message from the crew. "Grahame says do a bit more cooking, he wants some shots of you at work," Entwistle stage-whispered on one of his sorties past me. I kept my thoughts to myself but scraped industriously away at my sizzling griddle and rearranged my soft baps and soggy onions.

I'd been at work for about half an hour when two men walked up to me. I'd seen them conferring 20 yards away and guessed that I was the object of their interest. They looked like trouble – short, swarthy and thickset with mean expressions on their unshaven faces. One of them sidled up close and turned full on to me, his hands in the pockets of his bomber jacket and his face inches from mine.

"Unless you move, you'll be dead – know what I mean?" he said evenly. He sounded as if he was used to delivering such threats.

Both men turned and disappeared into the darkness. I almost had to pinch myself. Had that really happened or had I just imagined it? Perhaps I hadn't expected quite so direct an ultimatum in the middle of a busy London street.

Entwistle appeared again, for the last time. Whatever his other qualities, he did have a habit of absenting himself when things were about to get dangerous. "Hold tight – we're watching out for them," he hissed through gritted teeth. It clearly hadn't been my imagination.

Steve Warr came down from the office and stood a little way down the street, a tourist-style Hi-8 camcorder bag over his shoulder. If I was going to get my head beaten in, it was reassuring to know that the team was going to have the event captured on as many cameras as possible.

It's a strange feeling when you've been told something nasty will happen to you unless you go away – and you deliberately stay put. I knew damned well that there was no way I would move. We were there to show what happens when the bad boys move in. I had people around who would try and warn me when trouble approached, but in the interests of filming, nothing would be done to stop it unless I was in real peril.

Faced with danger, I was once again taken over by that feeling that it isn't me there at all, but someone else. What I found slightly harder to handle was standing out there like a piece of live bait waiting for the inevitable violent confrontation to take place.

I tried to keep my mind on the job. Customers came up to the stand. I sold them dogs and burgers, took their money and gave them change. I cooked some more food. Sometimes I glanced up and down the road, but found it impossible to gauge whether any premeditated attack was about to be launched against me.

Then I saw them. It was the same two, but this time they had brought real muscle with them. Now there were four of them. They all looked of Turkish extraction – dark, tough and purposeful. This time there were no words. The two I hadn't seen before crowded in on me, manhandling me away from the cart, holding their fists up to invite me to retaliate – which, of course, I didn't.

While I was being hustled out of the way, the other two set about wrecking my cart. I could see them rocking it violently. Then it toppled over with a tremendous crash as tins, metal fittings and glass shelves smashed into the ground. Hot dogs, burgers and onions plastered the pavement, decorated with shards of broken glass. The hot griddle plate melted its way into the tarmac.

A crowd of onlookers gathered as my assailants finished their demolition job, and kicked my uncooked food stocks into the gutter. I was pushed, shoved and elbowed. No punches, just a final "You've got no fucking right to be here, so don't come back" from the man in the bomber jacket before they all sauntered off down Tottenham Court Road as if nothing had happened. None of those watching offered to help.

The crowd melted away as I attempted to put out the still-sputtering burners and put the cart back together again. I understood why this sort of thing wasn't all that uncommon in the West End. I'd taken enough money to remind me again of the rich pickings possible in the hot-dog game. The attack must have looked pretty frightening, but I hadn't really been hurt and I just hoped that Wickings and Warr had got it all on tape.

We rendezvoused at Warr's Transit van half an hour later. Everything had been recorded perfectly. We would soon show the tapes to Westminster Council officers who would identify the men who had attacked me.

Steve Warr had made a tour of the other hot-dog stands around the immediate area to check if there was any more 'aggro' going on. There wasn't. But the man who had uttered the original threat to me was still hanging about. We didn't think he was Ozdamir, to judge from the physical description of him that we had been given by the Council officials. But he seemed to be important enough to be policing the hot-dog pitches and hadn't shown any inclination to evaporate into the night after his exertions with my handcart.

We decided to doorstep him there and then.

"You'll have to put that back on," said Warr, pointing to my left hand. I looked at it – I was holding my false moustache. It had been itching like crazy and I had been glad to rip it off once the earlier encounter was over.

I reluctantly pressed it back above my top lip. I wouldn't be wearing my white hat and coat when I went into action, but it had to be obvious to the man I was going to confront that he was being tackled by the same fellow whose business he had just trashed.

John Biddlecombe abandoned his shop doorway pitch, ditched the blanket and hooked his sound recording gear up to Wickings' camera. Warr went ahead of us to spot our target. He would stand nearby when he found him, giving us something to aim for.

Warr stopped about a hundred yards down Oxford Street. I strode towards him, scanning the crowds for my attacker. I wasn't angry enough for it to interfere with my journalistic task, but I felt it would be appropriate to challenge him with the same degree of indignation as would probably be felt by all his other victims.

There he was, talking to a group of men next to another hot-dog stand. He looked startled for a moment when he saw me and the camera. But then he threw his head back and laughed defiantly. I asked him who he thought he was to go around intimidating and attacking people who had every right to carry on their legitimate businesses.

He turned to me, his face alive with malice. Did he think he ran London? I asked.

"I run the fucking planet, mate. You don't like it, it's tough shit, innit?" he spat, turning back to his mates and ignoring us thereafter. His arrogance was amazing. He was obviously not going to answer any more questions, so I stopped asking.

It was only when Warr and Entwistle showed the tapes to the Council men that we discovered that Ozdamir Mahmut *had* actually been present that night. He'd been watching the destruction of my cart from the other side of the street, well out of the way, but Wickings' camera had captured his lurking image.

We had an address for Mahmut in North London, so we decided to go for him there. He operated from shabby premises on a small industrial estate. We couldn't do any prior surveillance on him because we would have been spotted by one of his gang, so we climbed into the back of our Transit van and drove straight into his yard at a time of morning the Council had told us he was usually arriving for work. And there he was, sitting in the passenger seat of a small, ex-Post Office delivery van outside his office.

The crew and I slid back the door of our van on Mahmut's blind side. Just as I got to his window, his driver saw us and drove off at high speed. Mahmut himself covered his face as soon as he realised what was happening. We jumped back into our vehicle and gave chase. We lost him, but picked him up again, and I tried the frontal approach once more. Again, he turned his face away from the camera and said nothing other than to deny any wrongdoing whatsoever. For a man so much enamoured of intimidation and public harassment, he seemed strangely shy. I wondered why.

Entwistle took our film to a friendly commander at the Metropolitan Police. He and his men identified several of my attackers as 'well known' to the law. When we showed him film of Mahmut and passed over his name, our friend took down the details and promised to get back to us.

Back in Derby, the battle for control of Thompson's empire had intensified and we were finding out more about Joe Persico. He had just been released from prison after serving a five-year sentence for kidnapping and torture.

Most recently, a small trader had obviously upset someone we knew. Although he only ran three hot-dog trailers, one of the big boys had decided he needed a warning. Three petrol bombs were hurled into one of the trailers and the fire completely gutted it – effectively cutting the man's income by a third. He agreed to give us an interview, in which he explained just how determined Persico was to take over the burger business.

But the war wasn't all going Persico's way.

Persico's cousin came out of his house one morning to find a dead piglet lying on the passenger seat of his van. It had the name 'Joe' daubed on its body in black paint. A scar had been cut into its face to match one on the real Joe Persico. A few days later, a rival gang attacked Persico's house, firing shotguns into the sitting room. Luckily for Persico, he wasn't at home at the time.

Then, the inevitable happened. We had been talking quite openly to the victims of this warfare – filming interviews where possible and sending crews down to the scene of the latest mayhem. Persico got to hear of our interest.

I had always assumed that Persico would be the last person to talk to me voluntarily, and I had resigned myself to attempting a potentially dangerous doorstep with a seriously violent criminal with convictions for torture. Instead, he telephoned me in the office to *ask* for an interview.

We were invited to his favourite hotel where, as we waited for Persico to arrive, we were able to film some of his henchmen. They tried to persuade us that they and their boss never intended anyone any real harm, but that people usually did what was best for them when an axe was waved in their faces.

Persico eventually appeared and tried to schmooze me with a performance that veered between soft-spoken contrition and barely-controlled hatred. He claimed that he couldn't recall leaping into our trailer and threatening Paul Calverley and insisted that he was just trying to earn a living in one of the toughest trades in the country.

When I pressed him on the violence we knew he had committed, he lost his veneer of charm. "It's all about an eye for an eye and a tooth for a tooth," he snarled. "If someone is good to me, I'm twice as good to them. If someone is bad to me, then I'm twice as bad back to them."

Persico later invited us to film him and his father at home – demonstrating a fearsome array of weapons which, they said they needed for their own protection. It was the last shot we needed for the programme.

Down in London, our police chum had run Mahmut through the records and – would you believe it? – he was on the run from gaol. He'd simply walked out of Ford Open Prison in West Sussex ten years before and he'd never gone back. No wonder he was so worried about his face being shown on television!

'Hot-dog Wars', as Townson had named it, was due to be transmitted on 8th April 1991. Mahmut had been free for ten years so we didn't have to do a lot of arm-twisting to persuade the police to leave him alone until the show had been broadcast.

The Mahmut case was typical of one of the greatest obstacles to producing *The Cook Report* in the way we preferred to do it. When we uncovered criminal activity and showed it on television, we inevitably attracted the interest of the forces of law, order and officialdom – be they the Police, Customs, Inland Revenue or Social Security.

If the law had been broken, then we had to allow the consequences to follow on. The reasons for this are obvious. If we let a criminal carry on, innocent people might be hurt. Justice – and this is my personal credo as much as the requirement of the law – must be done and be seen to be done.

So, if the authorities formally requested it, we gave them access to our tapes and our evidence on the people we all agreed should be prosecuted. We willingly gave statements and appeared as witnesses ourselves at trials. We also put the authorities in touch with our witnesses – but only if the latter agreed. However, all this could cause us problems – and I don't just mean retribution from the criminals, or their associates.

If we filmed criminals at work breaking the law, we often had to let the police – or other relevant parties – know. But, as has very occasionally happened, if we did that, arrests might follow before the programme could be transmitted. And as I've indicated before, that meant that we could not legally use the relevant film and might well be left with no programme to broadcast – with no time to make another in its place and certainly no budget to spend. It's something which gives factual programme executives sleepless nights. It worries the accountants too – but I don't particularly care if they don't always get their eight hours.

What we aim for is a mutual game plan between the law enforcers and ourselves.

That's what happened with Mahmut, who was picked up on the night *The Cook Report* went out. He went back inside and, a few nights later, we were out with our cameras on the streets of Central London with Westminster Council officials when 40 of his hot-dog stands were seized. It was a satisfying moment.

Townson was cock-a-hoop about our burger and hot-dog film. It appealed to his populist nature, and it had an element of surprise which sprang from an everyday, familiar source. The British public has grown up with the hot-dog and burger van. It is there after the pub shuts, at pop festivals, and at football grounds. The content of the burgers is the butt of many jokes, but they are what many people turn to when they're cold and hungry and away from home.

If you show the public a programme like ours and afterwards, in the office, or over a drink in the pub, people turn to each other and say: "Did you see Roger Cook last night? I never knew all that was going on with those burger vans. There are people who've been killed . . .," then you've shown them something they didn't know and encouraged them to take a different look at a small part of everyday life.

More than 12 million people tuned into 'Hot-dog Wars' when it kicked off our fifth series in April 1991. In the Midlands, 75 per cent of the people watching television that night were watching *The Cook Report*. I don't think people can view burger vans and hot-dog stalls in the same way again – even all these years on.

Joe Persico emerged from the programme as a violent and unpredictable man with a nasty streak slightly mitigated by short periods of charm. He seemed to love having been portrayed in this light and, for a while after the broadcast, he phoned me quite regularly to tell me what was happening in his sordid world.

Part of the film had involved my driving a huge trailer emblazoned with the name 'Happy Burger' around sporting venues to show how stall holders got ripped off by unscrupulous show organisers or how catering franchise holders were being consigned to remote parts of the venue unless sizeable backhanders were paid. Persico called me one day and asked if he could buy the trailer.

"Let's face it, Roger," he drawled, "you've made us hot-dog guys famous. Everyone will remember 'Happy Burgers', I just want to cash in and put 'As seen on Roger Cook' on the side of it in bloody big letters. How much do you want for it?"

Needless to say, we didn't sell him the trailer, which in any case had long since gone back to the company that we had hired it from. It wasn't long before Persico was back behind bars again either, so, mercifully, the telephone calls stopped.

Whenever we made programmes with a Midlands criminal connection after *Hot-dog Wars*, the Persico family almost always entered the equation somewhere, but our paths never really crossed again.

6

Dangerous Ground

*Media rivalries and over-zealous regulators,
avoidable air crashes, missing union funds,
quack doctors, dead parrots and bad beef*

Towards the end of the run of the fifth series – which was getting tremendous viewing figures of ten and 11 million – Mike Townson, rather uncharacteristically, took two weeks off. Looking back, it was then that the trouble really started.

You can never predict how long a half-hour investigative programme will take to make. The villains don't read the script and won't do what you'd like them to, or do it in the right timescale. But you can reckon on between three months for a relatively straightforward story and a year or more for a complicated 'slow burner'.

When Townson went away, he had commissioned only five of the six programmes. That meant we were going to be hard pushed to find a good story in time to fill the final slot, and unusually, it seemed we were going to have to do it without the editor's input. Steve Warr and Graeme Thomson had been working on something that I thought, in terms of time, would just about scrape underneath the wire as show number six. They had discovered a network of baby-smugglers operating in Romania.

Romania was in the death-throes of Communism and the rule of law and order had all but disappeared in some regions. The babies were 'liberated' from destitute families in remote parts of the country. Childless couples from all over Europe were flocking to Bucharest to buy children illegally, smuggling them out on forged papers provided by baby brokers and corrupt officials. The desperate purchasers included British would-be parents, so, all in all, it seemed like a very worthwhile programme.

223

Making *The Cook Report*, while being exciting, challenging and rewarding, was also an ongoing exercise in office politics. The team had, for some time now, been split, albeit in quite a loose and not particularly antagonistic fashion, into two camps. Mike Townson and Clive Entwistle largely kept their own counsel and tried to arrange every series in a way they thought best. One camp was centred on Townson and Entwistle, the other on me; the divisions usually marked by what we wanted to do and how we should go about doing it.

Salk, Paul Calverley, Tim Tate, Steve Warr, Graeme Thomson and John Cooke – as researchers or producers – moved, indeed, *had* to move, between camps. Such political pragmatism was sometimes the only way to get anything constructive done. Nevertheless, most of the time we worked extremely well together and most of us – the usual non-Townson camp – were genuinely good friends. We had been through a hell of a lot together.

What was particularly memorable about the Romanian proposal was that Entwistle appeared to have changed sides, leaving the editor, for once, on his own without a story of his choosing. As we were to find out later, this was an illusion.

Townson's attitude was that only he knew what was best for *The Cook Report*. In his view, no one could run the series like him. He kept the details, both in management and editorial terms, very much to himself. I doubt he could have told me what he had in mind for a particular programme until the production process was almost complete.

Everything remained in a state of flux until the very last moment, and I was often called upon to re-record parts of my script because they no longer fitted the pictures or because Townson had had 'a better idea'. Sometimes it was better and sometimes it wasn't, but it was never good for the nerves. Indeed, some of us suspected that Townson's fevered brain went on working on programmes *after* transmission.

Apart from Entwistle, the only team member who seemed to understand Townson's arcane approach was Graham Puntis, the videotape editor – and his knowledge had been won through long, arduous experience often running late into the night. Puntis, a jovial, bearded character, was blessed with a good sense of humour which seemed to sustain him through the wee, small hours in his edit suite, as he tried his best to make the images fit the labyrinthine structures Townson had hammered into his computer. Turning them into a coherent programme with a comprehensible script was never easy.

However, Townson acknowledged that I was 'the right man for my part of the job', despite our differences about what the job description should include. So from time to time, when he felt that he'd put my nose out of joint, I would be asked into his smoker's den to be buttered up. "I know you didn't have time to polish last week's script to you usual high standard," began a favourite line of flattery. "But not to worry, Roger. With a voice like yours, you could make the telephone directory sound good," Townson would tell me, his own gruff voice brimming with insincerity. And if that didn't appear to be softening me up, he'd launch into a eulogy about how brave I was.

It's hard to remain angry with someone who is, at least, trying to be pleasant, however poor a job he is making of it. He was clearly under a lot of pressure. He still ran *Central Weekend* – a regional live audience discussion show that went out every Friday night – as well as *The Cook Report*. Unbeknown to us all, Townson was burning himself out. And when his body – and mind – finally cracked several series later, it was devastating.

I should have known something was afoot. Towards the end of his tenure as editor, Townson began to share decisions with me and would call me in to his office to discuss the structure of the programme in hand. I thought this was perhaps because he had come to appreciate my talents more. With hindsight, it was probably only because the pressure – both external and self-generated – was beginning to tell.

He was smoking almost a hundred cigarettes a day. The office air extraction system couldn't cope any more. My office, next door to his, was a strictly no-smoking area. On the notice board behind my chair I had pinned a card that read: "You can smoke as much as you like around me – so long as you don't exhale." And I meant it. As a callow youth in Australia I had affected a pipe for a while – until I almost lost my voice. Since my voice was an indispensable tool of my trade, I packed in the affectation. I'd never really enjoyed it anyway.

Townson stuck exclusively to his office for his almost industrial tobacco consumption. He could sometimes be found with a newly-lit cigarette and a glowing butt between his stubby fingers at the same time. And I swear that on more than one occasion his shirt would part over his paunch as he leaned back in his chair to reveal a navel full of cigarette ash.

As time went by, the pervasive odour of tobacco smoke in my office was almost overwhelming. Then, one day, I found out the cause. Thick, grey smoke was snaking through the air-conditioning vent, swirling over the ceiling tiles and sinking slowly downwards to wreathe me in Townson's exhalations. The system was upgraded, but the relief was only temporary, and Townson didn't feel inclined to ease up on his deadly habit. He just lit up yet another B&H and smiled defiantly as he blew the smoke from the corner of his mouth.

The producers – Entwistle apart – were frustrated by Townson's need to control. Of course editors should edit, but investigations like ours were hard enough to do without the staff being subjected to constant badgering. Any member of the *Cook Report* team could expect to arrive at a hotel anywhere in the world to find a sheaf of faxes from Townson, each updating or sometimes countermanding the last. However jet-lagged a crew might be, Townson would override the protestations of programme manager Pat Harris and telephone them whenever he thought of a new order – even if it was three o'clock in the morning where the comatose recipients of his edicts were to be found.

It wasn't uncommon, either, for slumberers to be constantly interrupted by the sound of envelopes stuffed with new Townson missives being pushed under the hotel room door. This was bad enough when the ideas were good ones, but – with hindsight – as the stress began to take its toll, that was less and less likely. Sometimes his commands were simply unrealistic or even plain potty. So they were ignored.

The producers and researchers were largely excluded from the film editing process, which increased their frustrations still further. For sanity's sake, it became a matter of honour amongst the rest of us to do our jobs and, despite Townson, try to have a bit of fun in the process while out on the road.

This might take the form of staying on in a particularly pleasant location for an extra day or so – schedule permitting – or telling Townson that for some reason his hare-brained scheme for filming would not work, and continuing on the path that everyone on location knew was right.

On one occasion, Salk and Howard Foster had several nights of broken sleep as Townson bombarded them needlessly with telephone calls and faxes delivered to their hotel rooms in Seattle. They were there investigating problems with some of Boeing's aircraft designs, following the Kegworth air crash in 1989. Boeing routinely claimed that the cause of most crashes was 'pilot error', and they did it again here.

It was a convenient ploy, since few pilots survive a major crash to dispute the blame. Though in this case they had survived, they couldn't agree on what had actually happened. The co-pilot, David McClelland, was made to carry the can and sacked, but then successfully sued his airline for unfair dismissal.

Boeing clearly felt it was beneath them to talk to us and we were getting nowhere fast, but eventually, a promising interview with a lawyer who had mounted a class action against Boeing came into prospect. His clients were the relatives of passengers who had died in accidents also involving the company's B737 series aircraft – and they were alleging that this was due to a design fault of the kind which David McClelland claimed had brought his plane down. I still hadn't left England, so after a telephone briefing it was agreed that Salk and Foster would conduct this important interview on their own. They could do it in Seattle, said the lawyer's PA or, if they had to do it at the weekend, they would have to fly to Aspen, in the Rocky Mountains, where the lawyer and his wife kept a small skiing lodge.

Both keen but inexperienced skiers, Foster and Salk had no hesitation in deciding that the interview would have to wait until the Saturday morning.

On Friday night they boarded a flight to Denver from Seattle, then changed planes to a 12-seater to the winter playground of the rich and famous. The interviewee was keen to get his task completed by nine the following morning, so that he and his family could enjoy a full weekend's skiing. Salk and Foster wouldn't stand in his way. By ten o'clock, they, too, were on the slopes of the Buttermilk Mountain.

An odd pair they must have made as they slithered uncertainly on hired skis in thick snow – Foster in jeans and a Barbour jacket and Salk in his customary light grey suit, white shirt and tie.

"This snow's getting worse," Foster apparently observed to Salk after an hour or two on the piste.

"It certainly is," Salk had replied. "I don't expect we'll get out of here for a couple of days." "Shame," said Foster.

They phoned the office that night to explain that flights out of Aspen were on hold until the blizzards subsided. In two days' time they would be back in Seattle and the huge pile of Townson communications would resume. For the time being, a couple of days off would do no harm – either to the story or their own sanity.

Meanwhile, having just arrived from the UK, and during a connecting flight from Los Angeles up to Seattle, I'd had an amazing bit of luck. Seated next to me was a grey-suited, crew-cut American businessman who appeared to be a little the worse for wear. Fumbling with his attaché case, he somehow managed to dump its contents into my lap. As I helped him retrieve and reassemble his paperwork, I couldn't help noticing the logo on the engineering drawings and letterheads I was passing him. It said: The Boeing Company.

My travelling companion turned out to be Bert Williver, Boeing's Vice President, Engineering and Technology. I could barely believe my good fortune – and it wasn't long before I was his best friend. He made some interesting admissions about 'design problems' and 'avoidable accidents'. Without knowing it, he had given me a good deal of extra ammunition.

This I fired off later at Benjamin Cosgrove, Vice President of Boeing's Commercial Aircraft Division, as I joined him, uninvited, on his early morning constitutional in one of Seattle's swishest suburbs. He was shaken, but not stirred, repeatedly dismissing my perfectly proper questions as 'inappropriate' in time and place. He would not concede that Boeing ever got anything wrong. Neither he nor his employer came out of the interview well.

I had another airborne stroke of luck when we were pursuing a premier division rogue landlord called Ali Taefi. He had evaded us for weeks, but then we discovered he was due to fly to Gibraltar, en route to his luxury villa in southern Spain. Our information also allowed us to make a good guess as to which airline he would probably use and when. So I booked a ticket on GB Airways flight GT 102 – and ended up sitting right behind him, in seat 17c.

He was not best pleased, left without collecting his luggage on arrival and disappeared in his pale blue Rolls-Royce convertible before I could meet up with the crew. Then, that afternoon, as we filtered into stationary traffic on the road outside Marbella, there he was again, right in front of us, trapped. Naturally, he was filmed and questioned from every possible angle, his heavy gold bracelets rattling as he tried to hide his face behind his hands. I think that's what's called 'a result'.

After the programme, Taefi's previously charmed life got a lot more difficult and his empire went into decline. Another result.

Awful though the conditions endured by Taefi's tenants had been, they paled beside those endured by some of the Vietnamese Boat People intent on getting into Hong Kong before British rule ended. Most of the 17 detention camps in which they subsequently found themselves were relatively humane places, but as numbers rose towards 500,000 and the authorities began to run out of space, they turned elsewhere, to Tai A Chau Island. What we found there made a disturbing *Cook Report*.

Twenty miles away from the public gaze, out in the South China Sea, this near-barren island hid a shameful secret. Five thousand boat people had been herded into the less than basic facilities originally intended for a few hundred. It was very obviously overcrowded; there was no running water – none at all for washing – and food supplies were both inadequate and inappropriate. Detainees got a tin of baked beans or mackerel and a packet of custard cream biscuits once a day. To supplement these meagre supplies, inmates scraped shellfish off the rocks and cooked them in makeshift stoves made of empty bean tins. The results of this peculiar diet were made all the more obvious by the fact that there were no lavatories. There was little shelter and almost no bedding, and while there was no physical abuse, what remained conjured up images of Japanese POW camps during the Second World War.

After the programme and the row that followed it, the camp on Tai A Chau Island was closed down, though this could have been due in part to the fact that the number of forced repatriations went up. It was all rather depressing.

The only light relief for the crew was another of my unintentionally comic accidents. This had little to do with the filming and rather more to do with my unseemly haste to board one of Hong Kong's famous floating restaurants, The Jumbo, in Aberdeen Harbour. I missed my footing between the water taxi and the restaurant and ended up clinging to a rope with my legs dangling in the harbour. But after a couple of days sharing what little nourishment had been available on the island, getting access to something more palatable was well worth the wetting.

As I dried out over an average but welcome meal, I regaled my still-sniggering colleagues with the tale of a rather more impressive impromptu soaking in Monaco Harbour many years previously. I had been in the principality making a radio programme about tax exiles, when my tape recorder broke down during an interview with the late Prince Rainier. His Royal Highness happened to have a similar machine, which he kindly lent me. Several interviews later, down at the marina, I had been attempting to cross from boat to bobbing boat when two of them drifted apart, leaving me with one foot in each. Eventually, the inevitable happened and I fell overboard, taking with me the princely portable recorder, monogrammed case and all. I won't elaborate further on the embarrassing facts, but I believe the BBC sent HRH a nice new one.

When Townson took time off in May 1991, I felt it was important that the rest of the team presented a united front over the making of the Romanian babies story when he came back to work. There was no time to make anything else; we would tell him at the morning meeting upon his return. Warr and Thomson had already booked plane tickets. Interviews were in place and camera crews on stand-by. I had my trip to Bucharest pencilled in for a few days later. Even Entwistle seemed to agree that this was the best course to take.

On Townson's return, we all gathered in his office to have our say. Two minutes into the meeting and it was obvious that something had gone amiss with the united team approach. Townson seemed to know what was going on and, far from supporting the making of the Romanian programme, Entwistle was now arguing against it.

The penny dropped. Entwistle must have telephoned Townson the night before and they had devised their own plan for the last show of the series. Entwistle had seen a story in a national newspaper about parts of the Mosside area of Manchester being a 'no-go' area for the police, because of the growth of gangs armed with a fearsome arsenal of weapons. Townson took up the story.

Forget Romania, he said. Too expensive. We were going to make a programme on guns. He wanted *The Cook Report* to show how easily they could be procured in Britain today.

We were going to turn the shortage of time into an advantage. We had precisely one week in which to research, interview, film and edit a high-risk programme. We were about to break the law by trying to obtain a wide variety of pistols, rifles and even machine guns. We also had to find a villain who was already in the supply business in order to ensnare and expose him.

There was nothing we could do to dissuade them. Entwistle had already set the wheels in motion – arranging to send Warr to South Wales to meet one of Entwistle's criminal contacts. Warr would return several days later almost incapable of speech. Salk and Thomson were despatched to Newcastle to find more weapons.

The rest of the team moved up to Manchester to attempt to infiltrate the gun gangs. There we found a man who offered to sell one of our undercover informants several .38 calibre revolvers and a sawn-off shotgun, and said he could easily obtain almost anything else we wanted. He became our target for the 'doorstep'.

Entwistle's Welsh contact had taken Warr on an exhausting series of nocturnal pub crawls to meet the men who would procure the weapons. The contact – who had close associations with the old London criminal 'firms', the Richardsons and the Krays – kept himself going for the gun-hunt on strong lager and little bags of powder he called 'pink champagne' – a mixture of cocaine and amphetamine – constantly snorting pinches of it and blowing his eternally-streaming nose.

In three days, Warr had been offered and had filmed rifles, shotguns, handguns and a frightening World War II heavy machine gun with enough power to rip through the walls of a house. In Newcastle, Salk had similar offers.

Townson, having initially appeared to have lost his grip, now seemed to be more or less back on form – though it wasn't to last. He rubbed his hands with glee as the tapes arrived around the clock from his battle-fatigued staff. He set to work with Puntis in the edit suite behind his office. For once, researchers and producers were allowed into the room – a rare privilege, but only because on this occasion Townson hadn't had time to absorb all the material that was flooding into the Central studios. He needed input from other people so that he didn't get his facts wrong.

To this day, I don't know how we managed to make that programme. By the end of that week, everyone concerned with it had worked themselves to the point of clinical exhaustion – and that included Townson and Entwistle. I hardly remember the programme being transmitted – or if I was even in the office to watch it with the others – I was so tired. I do remember that I wasn't very happy with it.

By then it was the third week of May and already that year I had worked on programmes in Turkey, Germany, Brazil, Thailand, Burma and Ghana as well as all over Britain. Fortunately, there was a gap of two months before the 'update' programme in which we kept the audience abreast of any developments in any of the stories we had covered previously. Everyone needed a rest.

I make no secret of the fact that I enjoy the company of my fellow journalists and programme-makers when we can meet and talk over a good meal and a few shared bottles of good – not necessarily fine – wine. I also think that a lot of creative energy is generated when you are relaxing over a glass and a meal.

As the wine begins to flow, so do the ideas. After the second bottle, lateral thoughts tend to generate themselves. It is at this point in the liberating, creative process that my more convivial colleagues – such as Salk, Howard Foster or Steve Warr – made sure they had a pen and notebook to hand. It's sometimes hard to remember that brilliant idea you had when you wake up the following morning with a bit of a headache.

Mind you, I resist getting drunk and have only rendered myself totally incapable once. That was when I was in my early teens in Sydney, having consumed, with a school-friend, most of the contents of his father's cocktail cabinet. Enough to fell a small herd of oxen, apparently, so emergency medical intervention was a necessity. I never want to be that ill again, nor that far out of control.

As time went on, the biggest challenge for *The Cook Report* was to keep fresh ideas coming in. It was a constant challenge to avoid the tendency to feel you'd seen every investigative story before. It was sometimes tempting to concentrate on drugs. If you scratch the surface of almost any organised criminal activity, you'll likely find narcotics dealing underneath.

Money laundering, gun dealing, timeshare selling, credit card fraud, people smuggling, burglary and car crime at all levels – the worrying list of stories we investigated that turned out to have financial links to the drugs trade is a clear sign that the situation is getting worse.

However, just like compassion fatigue and charity donations – when the public reaches the point where it just can't care enough about the plight of its fellow creatures to keep responding to endless appeals – you can't keep making programmes about the same subject all the time. It loses the impact and almost reduces the unacceptable to the commonplace by endless repetition.

Five years into *The Cook Report*, we were by far the most watched current affairs television programme in Britain. It is a ranking we retained for 12 straight years. We also consistently scored well above the average for factual programmes on the scale which measures audience appreciation. Ten to 12 million people were watching us for half an hour a week, seven or eight times a year.

I am inclined to bang on a bit about audience size, but size *does* matter. A bigger audience means more resources and, more importantly, the bigger the audience the more people would have been made aware of the problems we sought to highlight. The greater the awareness, the more likely we were to 'get a result' – a criminal brought to book or a law changed for the better.

Good stories, well and accurately told, make compelling viewing and that's what attracts audiences. The challenge we faced was to attract and involve viewers without compromising the high standards of journalism that they – and our lawyers – had a right to expect. That we rose to that challenge far more often than not was a key reason for the programme's consistent success. However, it is possible to have too much of a good thing.

It was only a matter of time before commercial television realised that advertisers would pay heavily to have their adverts placed around *The Cook Report* for as many times a year as we could produce the shows. The pressure to make more was growing, but there comes a point when more is not necessarily better and I didn't want any dilution of the strength of what we did.

It was an argument I advanced successfully until 1993. By then, the demand for more had become universal within ITV. Central Television asked whether I would allow them to offer twice as many *Cook Report* programmes as part of their bid to renew their franchise. Loyally, and against my better judgement, I agreed. Sadly, there was no going back.

Even the blandishments of my cynically-minded agent, Jon Roseman, didn't help. He pointed out that as TV companies purchased programmes by the yard, I now finally had the chance to earn a decent salary. I relished the challenge, but dreaded the prospect of a doubled workload and worried that we might not be able to find enough good yarns to supply the yardage required.

A second series was scheduled for later in the year and the equivalent of three extra half-hours was squeezed into the current one. My schedule got even more hectic. Townson was positively manic. As well as the extra workload, he had to cope with an extremely complicated private life, which then involved three women, two businesses and a love-child. For the rest of us, the situation was made worse by the fact that the programmes we made were getting increasingly complicated. The amount of work that could go into 'bottoming out' just one individual part of a programme could be extraordinary. But it could also be rewarding as well as wearing.

At about this time, Central decided that their in-house lawyers needed help to cope with the *Cook Report*'s burgeoning legal workload. The man they chose for the job was a barrister called Peter Smith, formerly head of Legal Affairs at Thames Television and a freelance legal adviser to various newspapers and magazines for nearly 20 years.

He was the least lawyer-like lawyer you could imagine – and he certainly didn't look like one. Slight of build but sturdy of backbone – and an avid Wolverhampton Wanderers supporter, he was usually outfitted in one of the club's liveried black and gold bomber jackets, chinos and cowboy boots. He was also given to wearing a black armband when Wolves lost a match, so sadly for him, he wore it quite often.

Peter quickly made himself at home, working all the hours we did and seeking to strengthen every film we made. As a result, we found ourselves welcoming rather than resenting his advice. He was a breath of fresh air – and confessed that he soon felt the same way about us. The first programme he worked on was about cloned and stolen cars, particularly those welded together out of several wrecks.

We were able to tell him not only the history of every car we featured, but the provenance of every major part that had gone to make them up. "I was awestruck by the quality of the programme's research," he told me later. "I had rarely seen anything this thorough before." I explained that this was one reason why our programmes were so expensive to make. Another reason was the size and scope of the challenges we took on.

For a programme on the organised theft of art and antiques, series producer Philip Braund was commissioned to find a convincing but affordable piece of bait for the thieves we had targeted. He trawled through the auction catalogues and eventually settled on a painting being auctioned in Nottingham. The painting, titled 'The Millpond', looked like the work of L. S. Lowry, but the auctioneers had decided it wasn't. It had previously been withdrawn from auction after the Salford Museum had expressed doubts about it, and little had been discovered of its provenance.

The painting still looked something special to us and Braund was the successful bidder at £1,000. We decided it was worth digging deeper. Braund traced the Manchester art gallery which had originally sold the painting for £200 in 1961. He took it to Christie's who pronounced it a genuine Lowry and said it would fetch £25,000 at one of their auctions. From there, the painting went to Lowry's lifelong friend, gallery owner Andras Kalman.

Mr Kalman suggested that we had the painting cleaned by another Lowry expert so that they would both be in a better position to pass an opinion. The cleaning completed, they had no hesitation in declaring it genuine too. In fact, Mr Kalman offered us £28,000 there and then. However, the picture wasn't sold and the money didn't go to boost the *Cook Report*'s coffers. I'm told it now hangs in the office of a senior ITV executive.

Even more incredible was the story of the valuable miniature paintings that we recovered during the production of the same programme.

We had lured some professional thieves to a hotel room in Brighton, where they had laid out these precious objects for our inspection as possible buyers. Because they were late for the meeting, one of the team had been watching television to kill time.

When the thieves arrived, the set was still on, and as they set out their booty, the BBC's *Crimewatch* programme began. Nick Ross introduced one of their regular appeals for the return of stolen goods. To our amazement, the appeal was accompanied by pictures of a number of valuable miniatures – the very same miniatures that were spread across the bed in our hotel room. How my colleagues conducting the sting maintained their poker faces, I'll never know.

The thieves took their leave in a hurry when I came into the room, leaving their loot behind them. We rang *Crimewatch* and told them they'd got an instant result. When I later told Nick Ross our story, I'm sure he thought at first that I was pulling his leg. The paintings turned out to belong to Nigel Dempster, who thanked us fulsomely in his *Daily Mail* column, and at Norwich Crown Court in July 1997, Judge Geoffrey Barham praised 'the quality and thoroughness of our evidence', when the gang responsible for the Dempster theft and a raft of other offences was sent to prison.

One of the less desirable effects of doubling the number of programmes we made was that my already high profile was bound to get even higher. With increasing frequency, members of the public were not just acknowledging me in the street, but coming up and starting conversations at the most inopportune moments. This was happening despite the fact that I had always deliberately limited the amount of time I appeared on screen to deliver what are known as 'pieces to camera'.

Audience research confirmed our viewers agreed with me – that in the interests of objectivity, the subject matter should take clear precedence over the presenter. In my view, displays of ego like those indulged in by one or two latter-day *Cook Report* imitators, inevitably compromise credibility. Notwithstanding its eponymous title, the programme wasn't actually about me – and the first person singular was rarely used in the script. We once added up the in-vision links I did in a whole year, and they came to less than 15 minutes. Andy Warhol would have thought that was fair. But I was still readily recognised, not only because there were now more programmes, but probably also because of the unique nature of the series, the press attention it attracted – and its substantial regular audience.

By far the great majority of people handled a chance meeting with aplomb. Some, however, felt they had to act aggressively towards me – as though I was a self-proclaimed tough guy who needed to be taken down a peg or two. The culprits were usually young, male and irrationally belligerent.

On one occasion, I was accosted by four such young men as I was making my way through the maze of back alleys that lie between Oxford Street and what was then one of Central's London offices in Portman Square. They were coming out of a pub, probably after a boozy lunch, and recognised me at once.

"Hey, you're that nosey fat twat off the telly, aren't you?" shouted one, amid hoots of derision from the others. I ignored them and kept on walking. A beer bottle sailed past my ear and smashed on the ground ahead of me, so I quickened my pace. "Not so tough now, are you, you fucking coward?" they chorused. I wondered briefly why they were behaving in this unpleasant and unprovoked manner. It wasn't just the alcohol. Some of what was said made me think they knew someone who had appeared in a previous programme in a less than favourable light – but I couldn't fathom who.

Not too far to go now, I thought as I rounded the last corner – only to find my path blocked by a half-filled builder's skip. Taking a deep breath, I turned to face them and went into lion-tamer mode.

I planted my feet, folded my arms, and waited for the onslaught. "OK. Who's first in the skip?" I asked them. Truth to tell, if there had been an onslaught, the first person in the skip would probably have been me, but luckily their aggression drained away and they retreated, muttering darkly. I am happy to say that such incidents were rare.

There was also an assumption from some members of the public that if I'm out and about, I must be doing my job, so they followed me to watch. I was on surveillance amongst some shrubs once, waiting to confront a villain, when a group of Boy Scouts followed me in to the greenery to ask for my autograph. Other people buttonhole me as they might a doctor at a party, and expect a consultation about their problems. However, I have come to accept all this, albeit reluctantly – it goes with the territory.

National newspapers, of course, see anyone in the public eye as public property, and their fickleness is legendary – damaging or even destroying people far more famous than I shall ever be. One day I might be described in the tabloids as 'The Taped Crusader' or 'Fearless Telly-Sleuth Roger Cook'. The next, I was an over-weight has-been whose career was about to end. I particularly remember one tabloid centre-page spread which catalogued 'Twenty Things You Didn't Know About Roger Cook'. The funny thing was, I didn't know about them either!

One of the most bizarre examples of this came at the time when a contract killer had apparently been hired to shoot me at my home, following our programme about John Palmer.

For a couple of days there had been one or two telephone calls coming into my colleagues in Birmingham from *The Sun*. They were told that a freelance photographer had taken a picture of me as I left a patisserie in Bristol, where Frances and I had been having a coffee. Nothing else – I don't have a sweet tooth.

Based on this location snap and under the headline 'Cookie's Had His Hand In The Cookie Jar Once Too Often', *The Sun* proceeded to concoct a whole article about how my weight was seriously worrying my 'telly bosses'. They claimed that I had been warned to slow down or retire before I gave myself a coronary while confronting a villain. This was total nonsense, although I was having real health problems at the time as I recovered from a bout of malaria.

I steeled myself for the story, which was the kind of thing that always upsets Frances. I had come grudgingly to accept that if you are in the public eye, you are going to get turned over by the press from time to time, however unfair you might feel it is.

Then came the call from the police that a hired killer had been caught on his way to do what he claimed was Palmer's bidding. The story leaked out from the police in the South West and, the next day, the tale about my impending demise through my alleg-edly Olympian cake-eating prowess was a distant memory.

Instead, *The Sun* ran a huge story on pages one, two and three about the thwarted shooting of the courageous television investi-gator who had exposed so many bad people over the years. The story was dressed up with several photographs of professional confrontations which had ended with my being thumped by the reluctant interviewee.

At least that spread was loosely based on fact and largely positive. But even as a fairly hardened hack, I was still at times surprised by how keen the tabloids were to rush rumours into print. A few years back, a rather sheepish *Daily Mirror* reporter arrived, unannounced, on our doorstep. I answered the door and having introduced himself, he said that they had recently heard from an impeccable source that my marriage was effectively over and that Frances had left home and was filing for divorce. Perhaps I'd like to unburden myself to somebody sympathetic before the rest of the press pack got hold of the story? Their informant, he added conspiratorially, was a 'family friend' who naturally wished to remain anonymous.

I shut the front door behind me, and took him by the elbow round to the back of the house to where Frances was busy hanging out the washing. Eventually persuaded that the anonymous 'friend' was extremely ill-informed and clearly no friend of ours, the reporter beat a retreat accompanied by a very grumpy photographer who had obviously hoped for a really embarrassing shot. They'd been barking up the wrong tree. Needless to add, no story ever appeared.

A week or so later, however, they'd located the right tree and the story of a real collapsed marriage hit the front pages. The subject, another R. Cook – not me, but the late Robin Cook, then the Foreign Secretary.

The Cook Report, Checkpoint and I were often the targets of other radio and television programmes; 23 times in all – mostly as the butt of affectionate satire – in programmes like *Not the Nine O'clock News, The Benny Hill Show* and *Spitting Image*. It was also said that *Checkpoint* was the inspiration for the classic television series *Shoestring*, about a West Country radio reporter-cum-detective. I took all this as a sort of compliment. But an edition of Channel Four's *Dispatches* was pure vitriol. It was screened after our second programme on Arthur Scargill and what had really happened to money raised for the relief of hardship during the miner's strike of 1984.

Cudgels were taken up on Scargill's behalf by renowned film director Ken Loach, whose work I usually admire. This time he came up with a mixture of self-justifying balderdash, 'explanation' which relied on thousands of angels dancing on the head of a pin, and personal attack. This approach was echoed in *The Guardian*, which was also involved in the production of the film.

The producers had twice, in writing, been offered a formal

interview with me, subject only to an outline of the areas they wished to discuss. There was no reply. Their preferred approach seemed to be to doorstep the Great Doorstepper. This they did as I attempted to eat breakfast one morning in the Atrium restaurant of the Hyatt Hotel in Birmingham.

There were two cameramen and two interviewers shouting questions at me while Loach, at equivalent volume, urged me to 'Answer the questions, you fat bastard'.

I don't even treat murderers like that.

After their film ran out and they had reloaded, I was already running late for an appointment. So I left, still offering a proper interview if they cared to do one. On-screen, the episode came across very differently – a few seconds of a discomfited Cook with breakfast egg on his face, a couple of questions, an exchange in a revolving door and an image of my departing back – over which the commentary line implied that I was running away.

The accusations in our programme had been that Scargill had misappropriated National Union of Mineworkers funds and that money which should have gone to the striking miners had never reached them. Our witnesses said that, UK public donations aside, the funds had come from two sources – from Russian miners showing solidarity with their British brothers, and from the coffers of Colonel Gaddafi in Libya.

After the strike, and our programme, a new era of freedom in Russia was introduced by President Gorbachev. *Glasnost* allowed the release of many official documents previously classified as secret. Some of these were obtained by the BBC's former East European correspondent, Tim Sebastian. They confirmed that what had been said in our programme about donations from Russian miners was true.

Money intended for the NUM and the miners' hardship fund had been secretly diverted instead to another, totally separate outfit of which Arthur Scargill also happened to be President – the International Mineworkers Organisation in Paris.

Extracts from the Russian documents were forwarded to the *Dispatches* production company and to *The Guardian*. Once again, we got no reply.

As for the Libyan money, there was never any satisfactory explanation as to its final resting place. The NUM's former Chief Executive, Roger Windsor, had alleged that some of this money –

delivered in cash and passed through an offshore bank account in the name of a deceased relative – had been used by Scargill to pay off his mortgage. *Dispatches* was to argue that he didn't have a mortgage. What they didn't say was that he had an unsecured home loan, which in this context, amounted to exactly the same thing. This was the question Mr Scargill would not answer when I doorstepped him. All he would say – over and over again – was: "Put it in writing and I'll investigate." Why he needed notice to investigate his own actions was beyond me. Either he had used the money to pay for his house or he hadn't.

However, the NUM did eventually appoint Gavin Lightman QC to investigate the matter. His report did not substantiate Roger Windsor's home loan story, but was nevertheless sharply critical of Scargill's conduct during the strike. Following this, the NUM (President: A. Scargill) sued the IMO (President: A. Scargill) for the return of £1.4 million – finally settling out of court for around half that amount.

The whole messy business was best summed up by the *Mirror*, normally a staunchly left-wing newspaper, with which we had shared information on the story: 'Mr Scargill began the miner's strike with a very large union and a very small house – he ended the strike with a very small union and a very large house'.

But that's obviously not how Ken Loach saw it.

Andy Allan, then the managing director of Central Television, seemed to be almost as upset by the *Dispatches* programme as I was. He said that by the time I had returned from a between-series break, a writ for libel would have been issued following the positive advice of a leading QC.

When I got back, the writ had still not been issued. A visibly embarrassed Alan explained that it was now very close to franchise renewal time and Central Television's board didn't want to rock the boat by embarking on a legal action against another independent television contractor. Sorry, but I had broad shoulders, hadn't I? From then on, Central's policy seemed to be to rely on those shoulders rather than the laws of libel when the occasion arose.

Nevertheless, subsequent slings and arrows aside, the Scargill programme had made a real impact. It resulted in a large sum of publicly donated money being returned to the coffers of the NUM. It also gave us our largest ever audience and a taste for strategic cooperation with other sections of the media. Working with the

Mirror had been both pleasurable and profitable for both sides. *Cook Report* team members who watched the programme go out in the newspaper's offices remarked on the editor's enthusiastic exclamations as a story he already knew well unfolded on the screen. Such is the power of the moving image over the printed page.

Four years later, our only other co-operation in depth with a newspaper resulted in no programme at all. It was one of only two occasions on which we had to scrap a film which had already been partially made. The story was the notorious 'cash for questions' scandal and the newspaper was *The Guardian*.

We had heard allegations that an influential parliamentary lobbyist called Ian Greer was offering clients the opportunity to have questions which might help their particular cause raised in parliament. Greer boasted privately that he hired MPs like other people hired taxis. He'd apparently been doing this for years and had up to 20 MPs just waiting at the rank. During our researches, we discovered that *The Guardian* was on the same trail as we were. They had been approached by the controversial owner of Harrods, Mohamed Al-Fayed, who claimed that Greer had paid Neil Hamilton to ask parliamentary questions on his behalf at £2,000 a time. Remembering how well we'd done out of working with *The Mirror* – and putting previous disagreements behind us – we threw in our lot with *The Guardian*. Initially, we were pleased with the results. They found some more likely MPs and we secretly filmed Greer making the very boasts we'd heard about.

All this took rather a long time to achieve and we came to the end of a series before we'd been able to film the boasts being turned into reality. We had organised an elaborate sting to demonstrate how some MPs would sell their principles for cash. Members of the team posed as representatives of an American company with $40 million to invest. They made it clear that the money came from Russia – the proceeds of selling stolen national art treasures. The investors 'wanted to get close to the British government'. Several MPs looked as if they'd taken the bait. We regarded bringing off this sting as essential to our telling of the story and decided to hold off transmission, but continue work, until our second series of the year.

In the interim, however, *The Guardian* decided to go it alone.

Perhaps they'd decided to make the story exclusive or maybe they just ran out of patience. In any event they made a big splash, and our programme, unfinished, pre-empted and without a convenient transmission slot, simply sank. Just one of those media things, we thought, but then we had our noses rubbed in it.

It was put about that we'd pulled the programme out of journalistic cowardice – and later that we'd been nobbled by Michael Green (Chairman of Carlton, which by then had taken over Central), a man who was somehow beholden to Greer, having previously used his services as a PR adviser. Whatever the truth of the latter allegation – and we were assured at the time that it had no basis in fact – my belief remains that the programme was killed by circumstance, not by Mr Green. And the allegation of cowardice was laughable. In the whole history of *The Cook Report*, I never came across any attempt by management to influence us one way or the other in our choice of stories.

Libel actions subsequently brought against *The Guardian* by Greer and Hamilton both collapsed.

The tabloids, at least, maintain a simple approach to people like me – it's either love or hate. But the broadsheets can be worse. There, prejudice is compounded with the worst kind of middle-class snobbery masquerading as public concern. In some quarters – particularly where programmes like *The Cook Report* are perceived as not being 'proper documentaries' – you can find yourself an object of derision. We were an easy target to sneer at, primarily because we got a big audience. A big audience was wrongly presumed to equate with poor quality, which is not only an insult to the programme-makers, but an insult to the audience too. And some of the broadsheets have been guilty of the very same failings they impute to us.

Sadly, that brings us back to *The Guardian* again. It seemed to us that the newspaper was both blinkered and hypocritical in its coverage of a programme we made about dangerous 'quacks' who were peddling supposed cures for serious illnesses.

Amongst those we had exposed was a vet called John Carter, who, as well as claiming to cure animals of cancer, gave his liquid treatment to humans in the last throes of the disease. He promised that his 'cure for carcinomas' was '95 per cent successful'. We'd secretly filmed him giving it to our 'patient'. When we had a sample of it analysed, the treatment turned out to be orange juice.

He was later to claim that he'd given her orange juice instead of the treatment 'because he didn't trust her'. Mr Carter had also been economical with the truth when he claimed his treatment had been tested by University College London – implying that institution's approval.

In fact, he had not allowed the formula itself to be analysed and informal preliminary tests in which it was administered to mice had not shown enough promise to be pursued further. The results were, UCL told us, 'a million miles from justifying his claims'. Nevertheless, as was his right, the vet complained about his treatment by *The Cook Report* and we were summoned to a hearing before the Broadcasting Complaints Commission.

Along with a lot of people working in my area of television, bitter experience left me with little regard for the BCC. I had no objection to being held to account, but here was a body set up to ensure fair play which often didn't play fair itself. That the BCC and its successor, the Broadcasting Standards Commission (BSC), were biased against almost any contentious programme was well known, and as a result many complainants have used the organisation as a *de facto* libel court. In a real libel court, according to our legal advisers, most of our BCC/BSC complainants would have stood little or no chance of success.

A prominent member of the Commission once told our retained lawyer – Peter Smith – that the 'BCC was gunning for *The Cook Report*'. Another member, Tom Jackson – former General Secretary of the Union of Post Office Workers – told me that almost from his first day on the Commission it was obvious that his colleagues "felt it was their duty to put cowboys like us off the air." I had no idea why they took this stance, so I took the liberty of asking him when we bumped into each other in Grosvenor Gardens, not far from the Commission's London offices.

Behind his trademark handlebar moustache, Jackson was a bluff, likeable man who I had interviewed a number of times during my days at *The World At One*. As we strolled towards Victoria Station, he regaled me with several stories of my programme's alleged journalistic misdeeds – stories which had already gained currency amongst Commission members before he had joined.

The example he made most of was a programme about double-glazing which had apparently involved lying to, and invading the privacy of, customers and salesmen alike. I pointed out that the

244

BCC had never found against us on a double-glazing programme for the simple reason that we'd never made a programme on that subject.

The moustache twitched and Jackson fell silent. Eventually he cleared his throat. "All right, they may have got the wrong end of the stick on that one, but it is a fact that your record in front of the BCC isn't very good." I had to agree, but suggested on the evidence he'd offered, perhaps we'd acquired that record because we were already handicapped by a reputation not entirely of our own making.

Perhaps also his colleagues defined 'cowboy' as anyone who challenged the status quo? "Just as you tried to do at the Union of Post Office Workers in 1971," I added. A wry smile spread underneath the moustache as the disastrous strike he'd led back then was brought to mind. I explained that the only problem we had with watchdogs was when they bit us unfairly, as I believed the BCC usually did. I concluded by saying that I hoped he didn't think I was trying to nobble him – and the wry smile returned.

We parted on good terms and I think he must have taken the point I was trying to make, because he was notably more supportive in subsequent hearings. However, he was clearly outnumbered and soon to retire, so it made little difference. The Commission's standard response to the programme remained, in Peter Smith's words, 'an allergic reaction' – in stark contrast to the cosy treatment usually given to newspapers by the Press Complaints Commission.

The BCC and the BSC were typical examples of how the British Establishment seems to think things outside their immediate sphere of knowledge should be controlled. Instead of appointing people who are – or were recently – involved in journalism or television, the Establishment brought in a changing selection of 'The Great and the Good' – former headmasters, clerics and retired civil servants.

By and large, these undoubtedly upstanding people seemed to think that television journalists should leave matters of public concern to the Police or the Law Society or the General Medical Council, for example – all bodies which have, on occasion, conspicuously failed to protect the public. BCC members who'd ever had hands-on experience of television and its workings were very few indeed. Most of them seemed not to understand how television works. Some clearly expected all interviews to be transmitted completely unedited.

It was particularly ironic that the BCC should view us as they plainly did – by entertaining so many complaints against us – when it was we who had framed so many of the guidelines for how programmes like ours should operate when the genre was effectively created back in *Checkpoint* days.

And yet I suppose it was inevitable that this august body and I should fall out in a big way at some stage. The catalyst was the programme on quacks and dubious fringe medicine.

When Peter Smith explained to the BCC hearing that vets are not supposed to treat humans, Mr Carter claimed that he could do so because he was also a qualified acupuncturist. This came as something of a surprise, since acupuncture had not been mentioned in any of his lengthy prior submissions.

'Had any needles been used in his cancer treatment?' asked Smith. No – but acupuncturists sometimes used herbal remedies, so it was quite in order to give human patients a 'medicine'. It was preposterous, but the ploy worked. The BCC ruled in Mr Carter's favour. The Commission appeared to ignore the evidence about the true nature of his medicine – orange juice, remember – and the completely unsupportable claims made for it as a cure for cancer. In other words, they missed the whole point of the programme.

I suppose it is possible that John Carter may have been a well-intentioned but misguided eccentric. However, and this *was* the point, regardless of the guise under which he gave it, he had claimed that his treatment – 'my cure for carcinomas' as he called it – 'was 95 per cent successful'.

This claim was untested, palpably ridiculous, and gave false hope to desperate people. His irresponsible behaviour was not far removed from that of the charlatans in the rest of the programme. He also arguably contravened the Cancer Act of 1939 with his dangerous claims, and was certainly in contravention of the Medicines Act for treating patients with an untested, unlicensed product.

A woman who had gone to him in the last stages of cancer had been prescribed carrots. Her GP told us that she had quite needlessly been made to suffer in great pain towards the end of her life. She could have been getting relief from the conventional medicine that the vet had advised her to stop taking.

Mr Carter's BCC hearing took place in the morning. The afternoon was taken up with the hearing of a complaint by the parents of a 40-year-old woman who had died of cancer but had sought the vet's treatment in the last weeks of her life. The parents were upset because we had featured their deceased daughter in our programme, even though we had been to see them to explain why. They had not then raised any objections, nor had they wished to appear in the programme themselves.

Here, the BCC showed the true intellectual muddle it had got itself into.

Peter Smith had surmised that, to judge from the ruling in a couple of earlier cases involving Granada Television, the BCC wanted relatives notified if a loved one was to make a posthumous appearance on television. That seemed perfectly fair and reasonable.

Smith had therefore asked Howard Foster, who was now a producer, to tell the parents what we were planning to do. But that, it seemed, was no longer the issue for the BCC. They were angry, it eventually transpired, because *The Cook Report* had not reported the parents' positive views about the vet in the programme.

When Smith tried to explain that he was only trying to follow the BCC's previous rulings as expressed in the Granada cases, and that there was no obligation to include the parents' opinions, he was jumped on instantly. There was no precedent to follow, said the chairman, who added that every case was dealt with by the BCC on its individual merits. Quite how programme-makers were to proceed if no previous decision by the BCC could ever be relied upon was beyond me.

Eventually, the BCC was forced to change its rules on the notification issue to accord with what we had argued. The man who had made them see sense – Peter Smith – was given the job of overhauling that part of the system.

But on the day, we lost both tribunals. Our punishment, if you like, was that we should read out their findings at the end of the next available edition of the programme. There was much anger; we still profoundly disagreed with the ruling and yet there was then no right of appeal.

We decided to rebel. We would broadcast the BCC decision, but I would appear briefly beforehand and say why we felt the BCC was wrong – even perverse. It was a dangerous step, we knew, though there was nothing in the rules to prevent it. Bob Southgate wrote the words, Peter Smith 'legalled' them and I read them on air.

There was uproar. The BCC complained to the Independent Television Commission. They gave Central Television a rocket and, reluctantly, we were forced to broadcast the findings all over again, this time without comment.

When the Commission's findings became public, we were berated by a *Guardian* columnist who sided wholeheartedly with the vet, seemingly on the grounds that we had dared confront such a nice, well-meaning individual – and also that his 'cure' might well have been a major breakthrough.

The article was unfair and highly inaccurate, but as I've mentioned before, it was company policy never to sue. In most cases, I'd have agreed – given the choice – not because the stories were true, but because otherwise we'd have been in perpetual litigation. Unless the published allegations were seriously damaging, it was better to be pragmatic. 'Today's newspaper is tomorrow's fish and chip wrapper', was the MD's mantra on these occasions. Accordingly, the limit of Central's response was usually a letter to the editor of the paper concerned in the hope that they'd set the record straight.

Howard Foster and Peter Smith duly wrote to *The Guardian*'s editor. They pointed out the lack of any evidence that the vet had discovered anything remotely like a cure for cancer and that he had refused to allow it to be put through independent scientific trials on the grounds that the testers would steal his formula.

Smith and Foster explained he had boasted to us – on film – that his 'cure' for cancer was '95 per cent successful', which was arguably an offence under the Cancer Act, and that to give false hope to the terminally ill was morally questionable and certainly a point worth raising in a programme about the value of alternative medicine in general.

They also pointed out to *The Guardian* that the main 'witness' against us in the article, Professor Gordon McVie, had since told Foster that he'd been misrepresented and misquoted to suit their journalist's particular agenda. "She was obviously looking for a scalp," he had said.

The Guardian refused point-blank to print our letter as sent, or alternatively, to follow its stated policy 'to correct significant errors as soon as possible'. What eventually appeared on the letters page had been sub-edited to the point of meaninglessness.

When we asked why, the somewhat self-righteous response was that it would have been fundamentally unfair of them to print our original letter without giving their journalist the right to reply. The fact that that's exactly what they had done to us didn't seem to make one jot of difference.

Lest you think I have a general downer on *The Guardian*, let me say that I found this behaviour particularly disappointing because I'd always had a high regard for the newspaper – and as a regular reader, I had somehow expected something better than tabloid behaviour.

Mind you, I could go on at far greater length about the tabloids, but that would come as a surprise to no one. Let's hope that with *The Guardian*'s appointment of a Reader's Editor and the recent adoption of a clearer clarification and corrections policy, what happened to us on several occasions won't happen to anyone any more.

Our third hearing before the BCC that year came after another complaint from a quack we had uncovered in our fringe medicine programme. Elizabeth Marsh, a self-styled but completely unqualified 'professor' had a conviction for providing a potion closely related to creosote as a medicine for people dying of cancer. Our reference to creosote in this dubious context subsequently attracted a formal complaint from something called the Creosote Council. Peter Smith had to patiently point out that drinking the stuff was quite different from painting your fence with it – but that's another story.

Mrs Marsh's central claim at the hearing was not – as you might have expected – that we had rubbished her potentially dangerous treatment, but that we had stolen a bottle of it from her home. The hearing dragged on and on and we weren't believed until Bob Southgate found a piece of untransmitted secret filming in which Mrs Marsh was clearly pictured taking a bottle of her noxious concoction from her airing cupboard and openly giving it to *Cook Report* researchers. The Commission could not deny the evidence of their own eyes, and her complaint was rejected.

On another occasion, the BCC even gave a hearing to an extremely odious man who for years had systematically stalked a vulnerable woman – writing her several offensive letters a day and following her almost everywhere. He had reduced her to a frightened, nervous wreck. The only time she ever spoke to him was to tell him to leave her alone, and we had more than ample filmed evidence of what he was doing. Even the BCC eventually had to admit, albeit grudgingly, that we were right to unmask him – but not before allowing the time and expense of a full tribunal.

I took comfort from the fact that after our stalkers programme, regardless of the machinations of the BCC, measures were taken by government to have this appalling activity treated as a serious criminal offence.

Then, in the case of the lady mentioned above, the Criminal Injuries Compensation Board, in a landmark decision, awarded her £12,500 compensation. We reported this fact in our next update programme – and after yet another hearing, were again censured by the BCC.

Apparently, the mere mention of his victim's compensation award constituted an invasion of the stalker's privacy! No, I don't understand it either, but there was nothing we could do about it. A right of appeal against BCC/BSC findings was amongst the few changes we'd actually lobbied for over the years, but the BSC was eventually forced to introduce an appeal procedure only after the UK had formally adopted the European Convention on Human Rights.

Fortunately, the mounting of such time-consuming rearguard defences was rarely required. We just concentrated on making the programmes as good as we could make them, and were happy to let the public judge us on that. In 2003, the BSC was abolished. Its functions, in a simplified and far less heavy-handed form, were taken over by the Office of Communications. OFCOM says it aims to make its decisions 'evidence-based, proportionate, consistent, accountable and transparent' – all the things its predecessors failed to do. Let's hope they succeed.

The Guardian continued to misinform its readers about *The Cook Report* in a prominent article published in August 1999, under the headline 'DOCTORING THE EVIDENCE'. This libellous headline was unsupported by any facts, the programme to which it alluded was not transmitted until that evening, had not been previewed, and was only mentioned in passing. In fact, that programme – of which more later – focused on rogue doctors and the failings of the system charged with policing them. It was credited with causing a sea change in attitude at the General Medical Council, and several of the doctors featured were either struck off or successfully prosecuted or both. *The Sunday Times* used the programme as the basis of a major feature article. *The Guardian* however, simply took the billing for our latest programme as a cue to give a platform to someone whose prejudices they plainly shared. The result was a sweeping and, it is fair to say, vitriolic attack on *The Cook Report*. It's worth telling the story as an example of the way media politics and rivalries often drive people to behave very badly.

The article was authored by Steve Boulton – a former *World in Action* producer who was no stranger to controversy himself. I have never worked with Boulton, nor do I recall ever having met him or having expressed any opinion about him or his programmes. However, in his *Guardian* article, he well demonstrated the kind of professional jealousy that was often shown towards *The Cook Report* in those sections of the media that perceived themselves as our rivals.

Many *World in Action* staffers clearly regarded *The Cook Report* as an 'upstart' programme which was poaching on their long-held territory, and some said so publicly. The fact that we consistently outperformed their best efforts in the same territory was somehow held to be proof that we were practitioners of what they called 'junk journalism'. This crass thesis was proclaimed even more loudly when *World in Action* was subsequently taken off the air and *The Cook Report* remained as ITV's current affairs flagship.

The Guardian usually gave its unquestioning support to *World in Action*. That they shared political sympathies as well as a Manchester base might have had something to do with it. Boulton's article was largely hearsay, deliberate misinformation and unsubstantiated rumour, and was clearly unchecked and one-sided. The one section that had any connection with reality concerned our dealings with a young Scot called Neil Ryalls, who had offered to manufacture designer drugs to order.

The facts were that he had volunteered to provide this service – and showed samples of his wares – while being filmed in London by a freelance journalist called Brian Johnson-Thomas, whose credentials included working for *World in Action*.

251

Johnson-Thomas brought the filmed sequence to us and, having seen it, the editor decided to progress the story further for possible inclusion in a previously planned *Cook Report* programme on dangerous, but lesser-known so-called 'recreational' drugs. The 'tincture of khat' that Ryalls offered to produce was described to us as 'potentially very dangerous and in some circumstances lethal' by Professor John Henry of the National Poisons Information Unit in London.

Then, and only then, with incriminating evidence already on tape, we called on the services of a young female researcher who worked for Central regional programmes, but had not previously worked for *The Cook Report*. She was asked to spend some time 'on Ryalls' patch' in Edinburgh, in order to assist two experienced undercover operatives in garnering more information about his activities and if possible, to assist in filming them.

Unfortunately, and without any encouragement whatsoever, she fell for Ryalls, ended up in his bed, and then disclosed that she was working for us. We weren't aware of any of this until after I'd been north of the border to confront him on camera.

Shortly after my return, the rueful researcher confessed what she had done to Bob Southgate – then Central's Controller of News and Current Affairs – in the presence of Peter Smith, our legal adviser. Bob Southgate, who believed as Peter and I did, that her uncalled-for behaviour could have tainted the whole programme, ordered that section of the film to be scrapped forthwith. The erring researcher's services were also dispensed with, and there was no mention of her temporary bed-mate or his illicit business in the completed programme.

At around the time of the researcher's confession, and well before transmission, Granada wrote to Central to say they had information that we had acquired some secret filming of Neil Ryalls. They demanded that Central surrender the taped sequence to them on the grounds that Johnson-Thomas had made unauthorised use of their equipment to secure it.

As I recall it, Bob Southgate informed them that when the tape was brought to us, we were unaware that Johnson-Thomas had not used his own equipment, or of the circumstances in which the tape had been obtained. However, by then, and following the researcher's admissions, we'd had no intention of using the

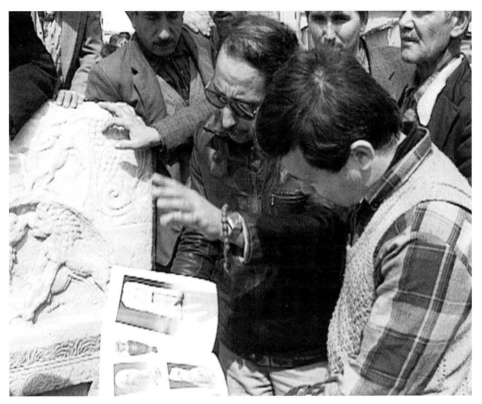

Turkish villagers find half of their ancient fountain in a Sotheby's catalogue.

A stolen Roman monument, flat-packed for smuggling out of Turkey.

Arkan strikes a pose with some of his brutal paramilitaries - The Tigers - and their tiger cub mascot.

Confronting Arkan with evidence of his war crimes in Bosnia and Croatia.

A Triad gang attacks undercover agent Joe Tan in Manchester.

Triad boss Georgie Pi loses face by making a run for it.

Caught red handed in Scotland stealing protected falcon eggs.

A fake sheik, ready to entrap the falcon thieves.

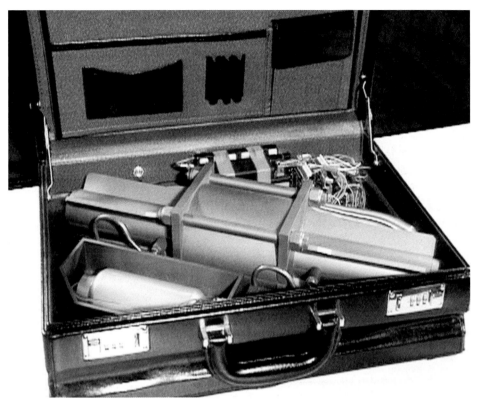

A replica nuclear device 'small enough to fit in a briefcase, but powerful enough to obliterate Manhattan'.

With our briefcase bomb in Red Square.

With Mafia plutonium dealers Gennady and Ilya in Moscow.

We blow up a commuter train in a simulated terrorist attack.

A Boeing 737, just loaded with our dummy bomb, prepares to leave Boston airport.

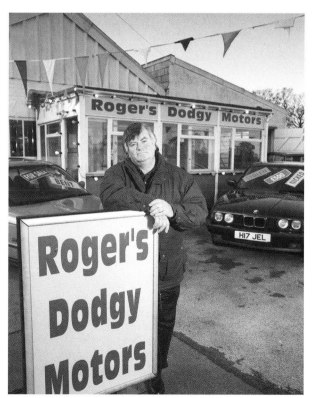

Filming 'The Dodgy Motor Show' with some of our collection of stolen, cloned and cobbled-together cars.

John Palmer and heroin baron Dr. Si celebrate a money laundering deal.

Palmer surprised at tea in the Ritz.

sequence in question in any case. There was no point in doing all the usual checking on a story that we had already dropped.

Nevertheless, Granada continued to make a fuss, in correspondence and in telephone calls. We found this very puzzling. I believe that there were also one or two meetings between Granada executives and Bob Southgate, during which he tried to determine their real agenda while at the same time defending our conduct, but to no avail. They insisted that Central give a (quite unnecessary) guarantee that the company would never in future use the sequence, and again demanded that the tape – and any copies – should be surrendered to them.

Even after the original tape was handed over – purely as a goodwill gesture – Granada management continued to make damaging allegations without apparent reason or factual backing. Basically, they claimed that we had cynically used a 'honey trap' in order to set up an innocent man and lure him into incriminating himself, and also that only prolonged pressure from Granada had prevented Central from broadcasting the results. The reason for this behaviour may well have been that Central – and later Carlton – were Granada's bitterest rivals. The truth was that Central had long since taken the decision not to broadcast – without any bullying from anyone.

Nevertheless, Granada's attempt at rewriting history was repeated some three years later in Steve Boulton's article. The allegations on which it was based were demonstrably false, and Peter Smith wrote to *The Guardian* accordingly. The paper refused to publish the letter, but the reason for Granada's agitation subsequently became clear. They had a substantial, but undeclared interest.

What we had never been told was that at the time we filmed him, Ryalls was due to be a key defence witness in a high profile libel action brought against *World in Action* by Marks & Spencer. He had worked undercover for Granada in a Moroccan clothing factory contracted by M&S, and alleged by *World in Action* to be a sweatshop which routinely exploited children.

Had he been included in our programme and been seen on film condemned out of his own mouth as a willing maker and supplier of potentially dangerous drugs, our target/their witness would have been thoroughly discredited. Hence the pre-emptive attack on us prior to our broadcast and the obsessive desire to obtain that secret film.

However, and even with Ryalls' vital testimony untainted by our evidence, in March 1998 Granada lost the action – at a reported cost to them in excess of £1 million. The guilty programme was edited by none other than Steve Boulton, but this fact, along with the truth behind the story (and the importance to Boulton and his former employers of being economical with the truth about Ryalls), was not reported in his article. Instead, he sought to portray us as seedy cowboys, when in fact, we had behaved entirely properly in the circumstances. You could argue that it was Steve Boulton who had been 'doctoring the evidence'. Shortly after the M&S court debacle, Boulton and Granada parted company.

In one of those odd coincidences, on the eve of the publication of Boulton's *Guardian* article, I was having dinner with Steve Hewlett, Carlton's ebullient Director of Programmes, when his mobile rang. After the call a rather bemused Hewlett told me that the caller was Boulton, who had wanted to forewarn him of the article, assure him that it was in no way critical of him – and ask for a job.

A surfeit of long distance international travel, exacerbated by some really rough conditions in the field, was now wearing my body down. Series Six is one I particularly remember because it brought me the closest I have ever come to being shot – at point-blank range – and because I sustained an accidental injury that put me in the consulting rooms of a brain specialist – and left me wishing I could lie down in a darkened room for a couple of years.

Townson's confidence in being able to choose the most disparate and unusual subjects and still keep our audience was undiminished, though physically, he was obviously slowing down. It was taking him longer to get things done, and with more programmes to do, less time to spend on each programme. He could now be found in the office at all hours, 24/7.

On the slate for the next run were programmes on a major building society's disastrously costly advice to many of its more vulnerable customers, the rise and rise in the use of the drug ecstasy, a collection of harrowing stories about bullying in the Army, a fascinating tale about the booming illegal trade in exotic and endangered birds and the unnecessary deaths of British soldiers by so-called 'friendly fire' in the first Gulf War.

Nine Royal Fusiliers had recently been killed when two US Air Force A-10 'Warthog' tank-busting aircraft had attacked a convoy of Warrior light armoured vehicles with Maverick missiles. The Warriors had apparently been mistaken for Russian-built Iraqi T-55 tanks. How could this have happened? No one in authority was saying, yet the vehicles in question were vastly different in shape and size, the British ones had all been carrying fluorescent identification patches, and it had been a bright, clear day.

We decided to seek answers in a very different and very ambitious *Cook Report*. We planned to recreate the battle scene in order to establish exactly what could and could not be seen by the A-10 pilot. Obviously, we couldn't do it in Iraq, so the search was on to find a location as close as possible in topography and climate. We eventually settled on the Mojave Desert in Southern California, where, as it turned out, the Americans had staged war games in preparation for the Gulf conflict.

In a logistical exercise that would have done credit to a Hollywood blockbuster, *The Cook Report* team and a squad of technical support staff built full-sized replica Warriors and deployed them in the desert in the same formation as that in which they had been mistakenly attacked. For comparative purposes, we also brought along a real T-55.

What we didn't have was an A-10. The normally cooperative US Air Force was anything but. "You wannna do *what* with it Buddy?" So we enlisted the services of the Confederate Air Force, a characterful group of Air Force veterans who restore and fly a magnificent collection of vintage warplanes. Amongst them, a TP-47G Thunderbolt, which, if required, could fly in pretty much the same way as did an A-10.

We flew in near identical weather conditions and at the same altitude, airspeed and time of day as the A-10 was reported to have done in Iraq. I was on board as an observer. Even at 10,000 feet, you could make out those fluorescent ID patches, and the difference in silhouette between the Warriors and the T-55 was very obvious – despite the heat haze. Aerial photographs reinforced the point. And if, as a rank amateur, I could readily spot the difference, surely a highly-trained pilot should not have made such a tragic blunder.

At the conclusion of the British inquest that followed the programme, the jury found the A-10 pilots guilty of 'reckless and unlawful behaviour', but no serious disciplinary action seems to have ensued on the other side of the pond. The pilots remained anonymous, their official statements appeared to be at odds with the known facts, and the on-board video recordings of the mistaken attack had somehow been erased. The bereaved families understandably cried foul and accused the US authorities of 'a shameful cover up of what amounted to murder'.

A system of infra-red tags and IFF (Identify Friend or Foe) beacons was subsequently introduced to reduce the incidence of friendly fire, but this didn't prevent further tragedies, including an almost carbon-copy A-10 attack on British armoured vehicles during the second Gulf war. Critics said that it was more of a cultural problem than a technical one: 'resulting from human error on the part of over-aggressive pilots determined to impress.'

After our Mojave filming, my craggy, perma-tanned pilot had decided it was time to play. "You ever done any aerobatics son?" he asked, with a glint in his steely-blue eyes. "Yes," I foolishly replied – having once been a slightly apprehensive passenger in a Pitts Special biplane that had looped the loop. "You OK with more?" He didn't wait for an answer – "then hold onto your lunch!"

With a guttural roar of her 2,000 horsepower radial engine, the old war-bird soared into a series of mind-boggling, stomach-churning manoeuvres that had me begging for mercy. The enthusiast at the controls took no notice. He seemed to be engaged in a private, one-man dogfight. Through my headset I swear I could hear him humming 'The Battle Hymn of The Republic'. Eventually, tired of his airborne antics, he returned to flying straight and level – upside down – 'so I could get a better look' at the desert below. I wondered if I'd done something to offend him.

After what felt like a hundred miles of total disorientation, my pilot calmly announced that he was 'getting low on avgas' and that we would not now be returning to our location. He would drop me off at a little airstrip on the margins of the desert and head off home. And that's exactly what he did, abandoning me at what amounted to little more than an empty bus shelter with a wind sock on it.

Then, having swung the aircraft round on the short runway, he bellowed over the spluttering din of the engine that he would radio my location to the crew – and with a snappy salute, slammed his canopy shut and was gone in a cloud of dust. Over the next few hours, as I slowly recovered my equilibrium, the temperature plummeted from sweltering to shivering level. The desert's a pretty chilly place at night and I wasn't picked up until the following morning.

Our next investigation – into in the illegal trafficking of rare and valuable birds – was prompted by a conversation between Steve Warr and an informant working for the Royal Society for the Protection of Birds. Steve had just been promoted to producer and this was a far-reaching programme whose storyline grew and grew from quite small beginnings.

The RSPB had some new intelligence on a Kent bird dealer called Phil Dobinson, who had 13 convictions for cruelty and forging import documents. Through his business, Safari Select, 'the UK's largest tropical bird specialist', he was moving rare and protected birds around the world and offering them for sale as 'bred in captivity'. Captive breeding doesn't threaten endangered species in the wild and is perfectly legal. However, the sheer volume of his business led the RSPB to believe that somehow, Dobinson was systematically cheating the system and passing off rare, wild-caught birds as captive-bred – a practice which is completely illegal.

As with our hot-dogs programme, it was surprising how much money there was in the exotic birds business. And money was all these hapless creatures meant to the heartless dealers. Birds worth thousands of pounds each were bought for pence from natives of Developing World countries, and shipped round the globe in the most appalling conditions – an estimated quarter of a million of them each year to Britain alone.

More than 80 per cent of such wild-caught birds die before reaching the market, yet such were the colossal profits to be made from the few that survived, that the trade continued to boom. And the more that died, the greater the market for replacements – rapidly propelling a number of already endangered species towards total extinction.

The RSPB informant, who was one of Dobinson's former employees, suspected his ex-boss was breaking the law and was outraged at the way Dobinson was mistreating his feathered merchandise. He told us all about it. All we had to do was prove what he was doing to get him stopped.

In England, Dobinson had recently received 130 rare birds from what he referred to as his 'new captive breeding project' in Zimbabwe. In other words, he was importing birds and claiming it was legal because he had supervised their breeding. The birds were Goffin's Cockatoos, which he was selling in Britain for £1,450 each. In fact, Goffin's only live in the wild in Indonesia. The experts told us that it would take many years to establish a breeding colony in captivity in Zimbabwe, or anywhere else. Our suspicions were confirmed, the programme got the green light, and we recruited the ideal director/cameraman for the job.

So it was that Salk and I resumed our globe-trotting partnership of a few years before, and caught the flight to Djakarta to find out what Dobinson was really up to. When we arrived, we spent the night in the splendidly neo-colonial Omni Batavia hotel, before picking up our internal onward flight which would island hop across the Arafura Sea to Tanimbar in the South Moluccas. There, we had been told, was most of what remained of the Goffin's cockatoo population.

We were in for another Developing World airline experience, courtesy of a subsidiary of the then notoriously unreliable national carrier, Garuda. With each island-to-island flight, the aircraft got older and smaller, but there were no significant problems. But the final leg of our journey was a classic. Several passengers joined us, bearing wicker baskets bulging with live chickens bound for market. The birds found this a very stressful procedure and made their feelings plain by clucking furiously as we took off.

We had just got used to the din when we hit a bad patch of turbulence. The crowded and ill-fastened baskets burst open as they crashed against each other and suddenly the cabin was filled with panic-stricken chickens, a snowstorm of feathers and a generous measure of manure.

Several passengers began to behave like the chickens. It took the rest of the flight to recapture and recage the birds and to calm the passengers down, by which time most of us looked as if we had been tarred and feathered.

There were no proper hotels in Tanimbar's largest settlement, Saumlaki. The single main street supported a collection of food shops, hardware stores and pool halls. Halfway down, on the harbour side, was our lodging house. Long, low and timber-built, it came highly-recommended as one of the few places on the island with a reliable electricity supply. It had its own generator but, sadly, that was not of much benefit to the guests because all the power it produced was almost entirely devoted to running the biggest karaoke machine I had ever seen – all flashing lights and a 60-inch screen.

My 'luxury' room had bathing facilities and a lavatory. The former was a brick-built pit half-filled with sea water. The latter, a trapdoor in the wall through which you were supposed to stick your rear end in order to relieve yourself into the stream below.

In the middle of the first night, I woke with a start. There was something, or someone in the room. I listened, hardly daring to breathe. I could hear the karaoke machine thumping in the distance. I tried to switch the bedside light on – nothing – thanks to that same all-consuming karaoke machine. I groped in my luggage by the camp bed for the torch I always carry with me and switched it on.

There, caught in the beam, was an enormous, mud-covered pig. I rose from the bed unsteadily, and a little nervously, wondering what to do. I kept the animal, whose tiny, rheumy eyes were trained on me unwaveringly, in the glare of the torch until I was upright. I shouted and waved my arms. That did the trick and, with a piercing squeal, the pig shot through the toilet flap from whence, presumably, it had come.

Bizarre incidents like that stick in my memory, and there have been a lot of them. But I tend to forget, or I minimise, the things that often go with a *Cook Report* investigation. The endless waiting for something to happen, the freezing cold or swelteringly hot stake-outs, the gut-wrenching worry felt by the whole team that something will go wrong, the hundred-hour working weeks . . . Still, I do recall that, apart from the porcine intruder, the remainder of our stay at Saumlaki all went more or less to plan and we were able to recuperate in comparative peace from the strenuous forays we were making from first light till dusk into the steaming, spice-scented jungle.

We were shown how the native people trapped the Goffin's cockatoos, sneaking up to them at night and firing glue-daubed arrows at the birds as they slept on branches high up in the trees.

259

It was extraordinary to see the birds plopping down to the ground around you, caught in the glare of the electric lanterns of the hunters, who then packed the stunned creatures into string bags.

While we were there, a top level conference of the Convention on Trade in Endangered Species was taking place in Kyoto, Japan. At the end of it, worried CITES members voted to categorise the Goffin's cockatoo as Appendix One – along with the elephant, rhino and panda – as a species seriously in danger of extinction.

We also discovered that it was from the Indonesian Islands that Dobinson was paying for the Goffin's to be shipped to Singapore and then Zimbabwe where they would be 'laundered' as captive-bred birds before being exported to European countries like the UK. Dobinson could expect to get at least £2,900 a pair for the birds he sold. The local trappers got around £1 for capturing those same two birds.

Before we left for Singapore and Zimbabwe to confirm at first hand what Dobinson was doing, we made it public that, to stop the birds falling into the wrong hands – literally – we would buy any Goffin's cockatoo trapped on Tanimbar. Our helpful landlady, Frany Melda-Go, who had taken the Goffin's plight to heart, offered to organise this. She also arranged to have the birds kept in a safe holding area until they could be released into the wild, away from danger, under the supervision of the World Parrot Trust.

All this was done with the best of intentions, but it had an unplanned and unwanted result. We created an even bigger local market for Goffin's cockatoos. Our landlady was paying better prices than the dealers and the parrot poachers didn't have the added hassle of smuggling the birds off the island. They worked even harder.

Eventually we were the owners of 500 of these rare creatures, which had almost eaten Frany out of house and home before the World Parrot Trust was able to move the majority of them safely back into their natural habitat.

Several weeks and many thousands of miles later, we had followed the parrot trail through Singapore to Zimbabwe and had gathered enough of the evidence we needed on Dobinson's cruel and illegal bird laundering activities to be able to confront him when we got back to England. So far, he had been able to shrug off his numerous convictions and the fines that went with them, because the profits far outweighed the penalties – and instead of going out of business, Dobinson had gone on expanding his markets at home and abroad.

Getting out of Saumlaki was a lot more difficult than getting in. At the local office of Merpati Airlines, the few flights always seemed to be fully booked, whether you had a reservation or not. The staff were giving priority – and free tickets – to their nearest and dearest. As a result, we fell further and further behind schedule.

Depressed and frustrated at having missed yet another flight, Salk and I sat gazing at the tatty advertising posters on the wall of the waiting room. Merpati Airlines. We burst into laughter and then into song simultaneously. Other would-be passengers looked at us uncomprehendingly as we chorused: "It's Merpati and I'll fly if I want to, fly if I want to . . ."

Shortly afterwards, we got our tickets. Perhaps it was the singing.

We were still giggling intermittently as we got out of our taxi at the airport. Just as we reached the head of the check-in queue, there was an ominous rumbling sound and the earth started to shake. The ticket clerk's eyes bulged, he flung our tickets down on his desk and executed a near-perfect barrel roll through the window behind him. The wall containing the window shook itself to pieces. We rocked and lurched, clinging to a buckled roof support. Then the earthquake stopped as quickly as it had started. Nothing really life-threatening, but enough to scare the ticket clerk out of his wits.

He reappeared, looking sheepish, 20 minutes later and told his dust-covered audience that although the terminal building was badly damaged, the airstrip was fine – so, to our enormous relief, the flight back to Djakarta would still run.

Our trip back was uneventful but, ten days later, that same aircraft crashed into a hill at the end of the runway, killing everyone on board, including nine of our island landlady's relatives.

Back in Blighty, we also targeted Brett Hammond – another major dealer in exotic birds – who worked regularly with Dobinson, and to similarly low welfare standards. Hammond had spent 18 months in prison for VAT fraud and was the subject of many complaints about how he operated his Essex-based business, Pegasus Birds.

The authorities indicated that they would close him down, but

261

did not do so. What they did instead is beyond comprehension. They later granted Hammond a licence to open a quarantine facility which was so badly run that cross-infections between batches of birds from different sources were not uncommon. The essence of quarantine is that such birds should be kept separate. But they weren't, and it was at this facility – ten years on – that the deadly H5N1 strain of avian flu first entered the UK. Fortunately it was contained, though more by good luck than good management.

The last part of the programme was to be filmed in Guyana, on the northern coast of South America. At the time, trapping birds in the wild was still legal there, despite CITES' best efforts. Steve Warr and Salk came with me to see some of the trappers in action in the dense Guyanese jungle. But first we had to get there – and on a pretty tight schedule too.

The flight from London to Trinidad went smoothly enough, though our equipment and personal possessions were then temporarily mislaid by our onward carrier and we nearly missed our connection to Georgetown. We were now flying with a small Caribbean airline called LIAT, which a local joker told us stood – appropriately enough – for 'Luggage in Any Terminal'.

As we descended into Timehri airport, the faded Dutch-Colonial splendour of the capital below looked rather inviting, but it was an invitation we had to decline. Instead, we transferred directly to a battered DeHavilland Twin Otter for the flight to the tiny town of Lethem on the Guyanese/Brazilian border. We didn't stay long – which was fine by me – for this was a one horse town minus the horse. A quick unauthorised trip over the Brazilian border to stock up on bottled water and we were on our way again, this time in an elderly four-wheel-drive, until the road north ran out by the banks of the Tukutu river. From then on it would be hard going.

The three of us set out with our jungle guide and a couple of local bird trappers, travelling for 36 hours up-river in dugout canoes and across land on foot, endlessly chopping away at the trees and chest-high undergrowth just to make modest headway. I did feel a bit guilty, hacking holes in pristine rainforest, but needs must, and it wasn't easy. Cutting your way through the jungle is hot, tiring work. Strangely, Salk, who was then about 53 years old, and I, at 49, seemed to find it easier going than Steve Warr, who was in his early thirties and claimed to be one of the fittest members of his hockey club. He certainly had the fitness, but we 'old boys' appeared to have the staying power.

Warr had hired three dugout canoes for the *Cook Report* personnel. He solemnly named them 'The Director's Canoe', 'The Cameraman's Canoe' and 'The Presenter's Canoe'. Mine was the biggest, for some inexplicable reason. As we reached a particularly spectacular part of the Tukutu, 'The Director' decided we should take some travelling shots.

Salk and Warr went ahead in their canoes and set up the camera on the river bank ahead of me. They filmed as I paddled past, trying to look reasonably proficient. On about the third 'take', I still hadn't given either of them the shot they wanted – and my backside was feeling rather damp. I had been concentrating so hard on steering and paddling against the current that I had failed to notice the fact that I was about to sink. I paddled like crazy for the shore, and just made it.

We dragged the canoe onto a mud bank and discovered a gaping hole in the bottom of it, part covered by a crude patch which was in the process of coming adrift. And there were crocodiles and innumerable other biting and stinging things in the waters we'd been travelling on. I shuddered to think what might have happened. Then our ever-helpful guide announced that the distinctive tracks in the mud all around us indicated that this was a favourite spot for crocodiles to sun themselves. We abandoned the idea of travelling further by canoe and pressed on over dry land.

If it wasn't for the fact that it was so cruel, and deprived the world of some of its rarest and most beautiful animals, one might admire the patience and ingenuity of the trappers who take the scarlet macaw. They would cut huge fronds of palm leaves and hoist them over their heads and shoulders, and make their way through the jungle looking like giant, shimmering, green beetles.

Then they would climb 80 feet or so to the top of a tree, holding a live macaw as a decoy on a rope. As soon as a free bird heard or saw the decoy, it would fly down and perch on a nearby branch, never suspecting it had landed right next to a human being with evil intent on his mind.

Salk filmed as an arm reached slowly out of the palm fronds and slipped a wire noose over the head of a newly-landed ruby macaw. In seconds, the bird's wing feathers had been clipped and it dropped out of the tree, flapping awkwardly earthwards, to be grabbed by the trapper's mate. A quid earned for the trapper. That ruby macaw would fetch at least £1,500 in the UK, with the rarer hyacinth macaws fetching up to £7,500. The native trappers had no qualms about showing us their side of the business – what they were doing wasn't against local law.

The following night, disaster struck – again. To avoid anything unpleasant that might enter the primitive hut where the three of us were to sleep, we had hooked up our hammocks to the rafters, six to eight feet above ground level. During the night, the rope holding the head end of my hammock worked loose. Fortunately, it unravelled slowly enough to prevent me suddenly crashing headfirst to the concrete floor below. But what did happen was arguably worse.

The hammock was still anchored at the foot end. So, barely awake and swaddled in the mesh of the hammock, my arms pinioned to my sides, I swung in an arc towards the ground. My head struck the floor a glancing blow and, still wrapped in my bedding, like a well-padded pendulum I was dragged back and forth a couple more times. The noise woke the others, who, with some difficulty, eased themselves out of their hammocks and ran over to see what had happened.

I was disentangled, swabbed down and at my insistence, eventually helped to my feet. Befuddled and bloodstained, I had difficulty walking and was in a fair amount of pain.

Luckily, we were almost at the end of what had actually been a pretty successful shoot, and after a couple of short interviews back in Georgetown and a welcome night in the soft beds of the Pegasus Hotel, we pulled out of Guyana the next day.

I floated around with double vision until, when I got home, Frances insisted I went to see a specialist. I had broken my neck once before and there was concern I might have refractured the bones. Fortunately, I hadn't, and further X-rays, together with a brain scan, didn't reveal any permanent damage there either, but I did suffer from chronic headaches for months afterwards.

I was still on strong painkillers when Howard Foster came to see me in my office to explain what he wanted me to do on his story about clenbuterol and the IRA.

This drug, although not technically a hormone, was capable of increasing the weight of beef cattle dramatically. However, it was and still is, banned for use with any animal in the food chain. Farmers north and south of the border in Ireland, who were corrupt enough to give it to their animals, could make £200 more per beast than they could usually expect.

Cattle were being slaughtered, sometimes at night, to avoid testing by the Ministry of Agriculture, and sold into the massive intervention market. This was the notorious 'beef mountain' dreamt up by the EU to take in surplus meat and keep up cattle prices for the farmers. Most of it would end up being fed to Eastern European families in times of famine.

But whoever ate the meat ran a serious health risk. In Spain, there had already been two thousand cases of clenbuterol poisoning. Farmers were overdosing their animals in the belief they could make them grow even more. In humans, high levels of the chemical caused permanent heart damage and huge increases in heart rate – threatening the lives of unborn babies and their mothers, and of anyone with a pre-existing heart condition.

As quick here to spot a potential easy profit as they had previously been with the building industry, the IRA moved in on the distribution of clenbuterol, ignoring the health risks. By 1991, they were making so much money selling it to farmers that they had virtually ceased robbing banks. Foster had gone to meet a disaffected Ulster farmer who had promised to spill the beans.

What he hadn't told Foster was that he'd also told 'the boys' that someone from *The Cook Report* was coming to see him about the clenbuterol they were supplying him. There was a welcoming party for Foster in the Dungannon pub where he had arranged his meeting. Threats were made – fortunately without violence at this stage – to the effect that the consequences of pressing on with the story would be terminal. Needless to say, we pressed on regardless.

The clenbuterol market was frighteningly similar to the more conventional, but equally illegal, narcotics trade. One of the main suppliers of clenbuterol to the Irish market was a man called Wynand de Bruyn, who ran an outwardly legitimate chemical business near Breda in Holland. Foster had already had de Bruyn watched when he went on a trip to Buenos Aires in Argentina, then the world centre for clenbuterol manufacture.

We knew that his supplies, which were smuggled from Argentina into Holland, were worth £80 million a year. He had even bought his own island near Curacao, off the South American coast. De

Bruyn had been arrested and charged by the Dutch authorities for smuggling clenbuterol a few months before, but he was released on bail and the police told us they believed he would shortly try to skip to his island retreat with his ill-gotten gains.

Foster, Grahame Wickings, sound recordist Keith Conlon, a Dutch researcher called Jos van Dongen and I tackled de Bruyn outside his home. We parked our minibus across his electrically-operated gates in case he tried to leave by car. Jos van Dongen pressed the button for the intercom to the house and asked to speak to Mr de Bruyn.

Nothing happened for 20 minutes, until the front door suddenly opened and two figures came striding towards us. I could never be described as insubstantial – and to a lesser extent, neither could Howard Foster – but de Bruyn dwarfed the pair of us. The man was at least six feet five inches tall and about half as wide. He didn't look pleased. We later found out from the police that the big blue Mercedes which we were blocking in had £300,000 stashed in its boot for deposit in his bank in Zurich.

The man with de Bruyn turned out to be his son. He wasn't as thickset as his father, but was also well over six feet tall, and just as angry.

I started to ask de Bruyn some pertinent questions, but he ignored me and made straight for the camera. De Bruyn Junior grabbed Grahame Wickings round the waist, locking his arms to his sides. The father seized the camera with his huge hands and wrenched it away from the pinioned Wickings' grasp.

He lifted £25,000 worth of brand new Sony Betacam above his head and smashed it to the ground. Then he picked up the crumpled camera and did it again, leaving Wickings' pride and joy in several mangled pieces. Next, they turned on the rest of us. I tried to put myself between Keith Conlon and the lumbering de Bruyn. I felt my shirt rip as he lashed out.

Foster and Conlon were struggling to keep hold of the sound equipment. Conlon's eye and forehead were dripping blood from where de Bruyn junior had dragged him along the road. Then the police arrived. Luckily, before the 'red mist' had descended over de Bruyn the elder, he had called the police in order to have us removed from the road outside his home.

While we were down at the station giving statements to the

police, de Bruyn's lawyer rang. De Bruyn was ever so sorry and was happy to buy us another new camera and pay all our expenses in cash – if he could just have the videotape we had shot of him. The battered *Cook Report* team answered the relayed request with one voice and a single word – 'Bollocks'.

Our inquiries plainly touched a nerve with the villains involved in making money from the cattle drug. Now Howard Foster wanted us to confront one of the Sawyers family – cattle farmers who had been illegally dosing their herds. It wasn't going to be easy. The Sawyers lived on a remote property situated right in the middle of pro-IRA 'bandit country'. Here, the police travelled in pairs and, from past experience, Roger Cook didn't advertise his whereabouts to the locals.

We arrived at the farm a couple of days later and came across John Sawyers, who had just been fined £2,500 for using and dealing in clenbuterol. He seemed quite resigned to talking to us. Then his father arrived and all hell broke loose. Derek Sawyers took a swing at Clive Entwistle, sending his glasses flying across the farmyard. I got between the furious farmer and the semi-prone Entwistle, still groping on the ground for his specs. If the farmer had a problem, I said, he should address it to me.

By way of reply, he launched a barrage of well-aimed punches. We were clearly not going to get an interview out of him, and I called Entwistle, the sound recordist, and cameramen Salk and Wickings back to the car. The farmers hadn't finished with us, however. As our driver fumbled with the car keys, the son steered the farm's forklift truck, its prongs a few inches above ground level, at the side of the vehicle. He obviously intended to tip the car over with us inside it, but his father called to him to stop.

This was clearly not because Derek Sawyers had thought better of it, but because he wanted a better shot at us. We'd just seen him load his twelve bore shotgun and we watched, mesmerised, as he lifted it to his shoulder. He was aiming to fire directly through the windscreen at my head, about five feet away. I was, literally, a sitting target. I ducked as low in the seat as I could go. The farmer squeezed the trigger. Mercifully, nothing happened. The gun had jammed.

He turned the gun round and held it by the barrels, smashing it hard across the windscreen. The glass crazed and buckled, leaving the clear outline of a shotgun butt right across it. He bellowed at us in rage as the engine burst into life and we sped off in a cloud of farmyard dust. Close call.

There was a twist in the tale. Although examples of meat tainted with clenbuterol had been found in Spain and the Low Countries, where armed gangs were distributing the stuff willy-nilly, no British beef had so far tested positive for the drug. Foster, stuck in Belfast at Townson's insistence for yet another weekend, did a sample buy from a dozen butchers and supermarket meat counters across Ulster. We had been told to buy ox liver because the liver retained clenbuterol in its greatest concentration. Foster duly bagged and labelled all his samples and took them to a laboratory for analysis.

Five days later, the results came back. One sample had proved positive. It was from Northern Ireland's leading supermarket chain and the measured clenbuterol level was several times the known safe limit.

When the programme was broadcast, there was uproar in Ulster. The Ministry of Agriculture tried to dismiss the laboratory findings, which annoyed the analysts there, who were put under pressure to retract what they had found. They stood firm. Next, the Ministry issued a statement saying that even though the clenbuterol levels were high, there wasn't enough to harm the consumer. This was hardly the point – what mattered was that farmers were routinely dosing their cattle with a banned and dangerous substance, and the enforcement agency charged with controlling and monitoring the industry clearly wasn't doing its job properly.

Ulster Unionist MP Ken Maginnis had given an interview in the programme about IRA involvement in clenbuterol dealing. In the public mind, the drug was now firmly associated with terrorism and health issues. After the fuss following the broadcast had subsided, the agriculture ministries both north and south of the border pledged to work together more closely.

Privately, we were told by friendly Customs officers and Ministry of Agriculture officials that there was little that could be done. Farmers would always be tempted to a use a substance they thought would help them turn a better profit. The IRA had already opened up new smuggling routes into Dublin Docks from South America, and were distributing the drug using time-honoured routes along the unguarded country lanes that criss-cross the Eire/ Ulster border.

More worryingly – particularly since the advent of BSE and all the grief that caused the British beef industry – there was a problem with the province's abattoirs. Northern Ireland boasted a unique, computerised monitoring system for its cattle. Records are kept of individual animals, the herd they belong to and where they go if they are sold on. Indeed, it is the probity of this system which led to the ban on beef exports being lifted first in Ulster after the terrible impact of BSE and CJD.

What we were told, unofficially, by people we trusted, as well as by senior Northern Irish politicians, was that the computer system was being sabotaged by a handful of slaughterhouses. By day, they processed the cattle according to the rules. Then, by night, the bad boys arrived with their truckloads of clenbuterol-dosed animals. The computer, of course, was switched off while this went on.

Agriculture officials who tried to intervene were attacked if they were discovered attempting to monitor the illegal operators. One farmer used his tractor to ram a ministry surveillance vehicle before speeding off with his trailer full of cattle to hide them over the border in Eire. Without increasing the resources to police the problem, it seemed unlikely that the situation would improve.

Institutions are always more difficult to influence or change than are individuals. After the Hillsborough Stadium disaster of 1989, the relatives of the 96 victims wanted the truth – and closure. We tried to help them to that end. However, though our programme, and the excellent Jimmy McGovern drama documentary which followed it, both drew massive audiences, they prompted little in the way of tangible results. To get what they wanted, the relatives had asked for a new inquest – since they felt the first had such narrow terms of reference as to be a farce – and judicial sanctions against the two senior police officers whose actions they claim triggered the disaster. A decade and a half on, they're still waiting.

Here's another example. I believe that ours was the first programme to expose the considerable shortcomings of the Child Support Agency. It had clearly not met its remit to recover maintenance payments due from absent fathers, and had displayed staggering levels of incompetence and insensitivity. There had just been the first of over 100 suicides involving desperate ex-partners of both sexes.

We showed how most claimants got either nothing at all or very little, very late; and how the Agency seemed only to pursue, often to the point of exploitation, soft targets – the fathers who would have paid up anyway. We highlighted how those determined not to pay usually got away with it, and how poor management meant that most of the substantial revenue they did actually manage to retrieve was swallowed up in administration and other costs. To that must be added £3.5 billon in uncollected arrears resulting from a backlog of some 330,000 cases at last count.

After the programme, the Chief Executive of the Agency resigned and there were calls for it to be wound up. However, that didn't happen, promised reforms couldn't be made to work, and the scandalous situation at the CSA remained pretty much the same for more than ten years – despite all the programmes and all the newspaper coverage that followed us. At the time of writing it had been announced that at last the CSA was to be scrapped and replaced – hopefully with something that works. Meantime, in a move that didn't bode well, government plans were mooted to write off around £1 billion in unpaid child support owed by absent parents. This caused understandable outrage amongst the carers they left behind, who pointed out that it wasn't the government's money to write off – it was owed to the abandoned children. Come the subsequent publication of the white paper on the CSA's replacement, the government denied it would be writing off anything, but had to admit that around the same sum – £1 billion – was probably 'unrecoverable'. Either way, the children in question would be no better off.

Of course it is naïve to expect much to change as a result of a single television programme, but a lot depends on the subject. It also helps if you are appealing to real people rather than faceless bureaucrats. Sometimes, the medium *can* make things happen – take Michael Buerk's memorable coverage of the Ethiopian famine, for example. That inspired a huge fundraising effort which saved many lives. People responded to the moving images of fellow human beings in terrible suffering. But there are few subjects that lend themselves so readily to this kind of visual treatment.

7

When Push Comes to Shove

A murderous Balkan warlord, the arms shipper who facilitated genocide in Rwanda, buying plutonium for a dirty bomb from the Russian Mafia, taking on the Triads, and foretelling 9/11

The Cook Report was subject-led, rather than taking issues and examining them. We brought those subjects to life by illustrating them with real case histories, secret filming of villains at work, and of course, the inevitable confrontation. A fair number of our programmes put an end to a criminal enterprise or were followed by official action against the perpetrators – though sometimes the latter took rather a long time.

In selecting a subject, I also tried to follow one of the principles advocated by Andrew Boyle on *The World At One* – that if a story had been spelt out in the newspapers, unless you had a completely different angle on it, rather than just follow the papers, you found something completely new. So there was always something you hadn't seen before in a *Cook Report*.

I believe that we also raised public awareness by focusing attention on examples of wrongdoing so that – even if there were no immediate arrests or no changes in the law – at least the audience was forewarned of a particular risk. And next time a topic like the leadership of the IRA, the conservation of endangered species or the hidden horrors of a new drug arose in conversation, someone might remember one of our programmes and be able to offer a better informed opinion.

From the short-list of subjects on offer, Townson had decided to start the next series with a particularly challenging one – an exposé of Triad gangs in Britain. It wasn't my idea, but I endorsed his choice. These violent Chinese secret societies had infiltrated and terrorised Chinese communities nationwide and were firmly entrenched in mainstream organised crime. Howard Foster was deputed to find the right location for us to demonstrate what generalised newspaper cuttings and his own nose for a story already told him was certainly out there somewhere.

Before that, there was more work to do, several thousand miles away – on an equally challenging, one-off special. Sometimes, a subject so compelling arises that we have to move heaven and earth to bring it to the screen. This happened soon after the end of the sixth series. That we should put ourselves in the way of an extremely arduous – not to say dangerous – undertaking so soon after working ourselves into the ground for eight or nine months, says something about how strongly we felt. Even more remarkably, we took on this hour-long special programme despite knowing that from then on our workload would double, to 14 programmes a year, split into two series.

In the summer of 1992, Paul Calverley had been contacted by a group of Muslims who told him about a route between Belgium and Britain used for smuggling in illegal immigrants. Long before the more recent rush of asylum seekers, we had followed that route on film – with one of our undercover team as part of the human contraband on the smuggler's lorry.

On arrival, many of the hapless hopefuls were pressed into virtual slavery as vegetable pickers in the fields of Lincolnshire and East Anglia until they eventually managed to pay the extortionate price they'd agreed for their 'trip to freedom'. We had also filmed their gangmasters at work – and both they and the smugglers had been gaoled as a result of the prosecutions that followed the programme.

During the research process, one of our original informants had also mentioned particularly brutal atrocities being committed against the Muslims by a Serbian paramilitary group in Bosnia. The man showed Calverley a gruesome amateur video of what appeared to be the genitals of the menfolk of one village, amputated and displayed on trays by the aggressor Serbs. We were all shocked and disturbed by what we saw. Calverley started to investigate to find out who this murderous group of Serbian irregular soldiers were.

To our intense relief, we discovered that the contents of the trays we had seen on that blurry video were actually a local sausage-meat delicacy, not what the Muslim propagandists had led us to believe. But by that time we had gathered enough independent information to know that we were on to a big story. One of the details might not have been quite as advertised, but we were sure that ethnic cleansing was underway on a large scale. We were to discover that, when given the opportunity, the Croats and Muslims had tried it too, but they were small-scale amateurs compared to the Serbs.

This round of Balkan ethnic cleansing had its origins in the gradual disintegration of the former Yugoslavia in the decade following the death of Marshall Tito in 1980. Serbia, Croatia and Bosnia each had ambitions for statehood along ethnic lines and Serbia had territorial ambitions as well. Historically, the Serbs and Croats detested each other and by 1991 it was all out war. The region's Muslim minority often got caught in the crossfire.

The concept of a Greater Serbia proved to be a great opportunity for freelance paramilitaries far more zealous in their operations than were the Serbian or Croatian armies. By 1992, the West had heard many stories about 'ethnic cleansing', an antiseptic-sounding phrase that masks the horror of wholesale genocide. But proof was hard to find. Naming and nailing the individuals responsible for it was unheard of.

For once though, the usually anonymous perpetrators of these mass murders could be identified. The sinister figure behind many of them was one Zeljko Raznatovic – nicknamed 'Arkan'.

Arkan was a man with a fearsome local reputation, but was not then well known outside of his home territory. Tough and cunning, he was born in Montenegro in 1953, the son of an army officer. He had begun to get into serious trouble with the police when he was recruited as a potentially useful secret agent. As a young man, he was sent all over the world to spy on the enemies of the Yugoslavian communist regime on behalf of the feared 'Second Section' of the Foreign Ministry. He was also believed to have assassinated half a dozen Yugoslav nationals living abroad in safety, or so they thought. This had clearly given him his taste for travel, high-living – and extreme violence.

Back in Belgrade, he started to amass the fortune he needed to indulge his material desires. As long ago as 1975, when he was just

22 years old, he was being described in the Yugoslav press as one of the most dangerous criminals in Europe. Bank robbery, murder, black marketeering – these became his specialties, and they soon made him seriously rich.

By the time the bloody civil war started in the former Yugo-slavia, Arkan was wanted in six countries – Holland, Italy, Finland, Belgium, Croatia and Sweden. He was captured in Sweden after a series of robberies and was arraigned before the courts. Just as the charges against him were being read out, Arkan apparently opened his attaché case and produced a sub-machine gun. He riddled the courtroom with bullets before escaping to a getaway car outside. He then made his way back to Serbia and had never been recaptured.

Apart from making money through crime, Arkan's other great passion in life was football, though not as an ordinary fan. He became the head of the quasi-fascist Red Star Belgrade football supporters club – which was army-run. He often used his position in the club as a cover for his spying and assassination activities, which were usually timed to take place when the team travelled abroad.

Red Star supporters were extreme, even by English soccer hooligan standards. Shaven-headed and seriously aggressive, they regularly hurled missiles and screamed racist taunts at the oppo-sition. Their xenophobia and love for all things Serbian was as vocal as it was frightening. Hardly surprising, then, that when Arkan decided to set up his own militia to attack Serbia's 'enemies', he chose his men from the ranks of the Red Star supporters club.

With the blessing of the authorities – Arkan was by then under the patronage of Serbian President Slobodan Milosevic – he formed the Serbian Volunteer Guard, nicknamed 'The Tigers'. He moved freely around Croatia and Eastern Bosnia, toting his Heckler and Koch sub-machine gun at the head of his 1,000-strong army. One report describes him as 'like a man possessed' as he laughed at the massacre of hundreds of innocent Muslim civilians. He clearly enjoyed his work.

Arkan and his men dressed in proper battle fatigues and were videoed for self-promotion on manoeuvres, crawling across scrub-land, firing at targets and spreading camouflage nets over their armoured vehicles. To complete the image – which would have been preposterous had it not been backed with such murderous intent – Arkan bought a tiger cub which was led on a rope at the head of his ugly band's impromptu parades.

Back in Belgrade, Arkan had robbed and looted from enough of his own people to be able to buy his own football club. His first ambition had been to buy his beloved Red Star Belgrade. This, apparently, was blocked by the President himself, who feared that such a takeover would give Arkan too big a popular power base, threatening Milosevic's own authority into the bargain.

Instead, Arkan bought bottom-of-the-table Obilic and became the object of hero-worship by the club's fans, who called him the 'Commandante'. The chants and songs that come from the terraces were often about ethnic cleansing and the purity of Serbia. Before long, through bribery and intimidation of referees and rival teams, Obilic began to rise through the league, backed by Arkan's huge personal wealth.

Meanwhile, in 1991, Arkan moved The Tigers into Croatia during Serbia's war with that newly-independent state. A year later, he led a murderous campaign to drive Croats and Muslims out of the eastern Bosnian town of Bijelina, where the Serbs greeted him as their saviour. He set up camp in a semi-derelict castle overlooking the town. Through this camp he would 'process' non-Serbs. One of his first acts was to seek out the biggest and strongest Muslim in town, a popular local wrestler. The man was publicly executed, dismembered, and his body parts put on display as a stark warning to those who might have considered opposing Arkan's objectives.

Calverley's Muslim contacts offered to find us survivors of Arkan's attacks. We were also told of a former friend of Arkan, a professional photographer, who had been invited to witness The Tigers at work. He had taken pictures of them butchering unarmed villagers in Bosnia. What he had witnessed had so disgusted him that he had fled to New York, where he maintained a frightened silence about the murders he had seen and the man who was orchestrating them. But at least his pictures of Arkan's bloody atrocities had come into our hands. Was there just a chance that this arrogant man, who invited a photographer along to a massacre, might consent to an interview for ITV's most-watched current affairs programme?

Calverley used a variety of intermediaries in an effort to get a message through. There was no response, so our man, heart in mouth, cold-called at Arkan's heavily guarded headquarters in Belgrade. After a nerve-wracking four-hour wait, he was finally ushered into Arkan's presence. Plainly flattered by interest from British television, he told Calverley that he would seriously consider our request and would give us an answer in a couple of weeks.

While we waited for the decision, the *Cook Report* team set off in search of more evidence with which to confront Arkan if we ever did get to meet and film him. One of Calverley's first and most important finds was the former Mayor of Vukovar, who had escaped what was, by all accounts, the bloodiest battle of the war. When the fighting had ended, and as the Red Cross and the UN observers left, The Tigers came to town. Surprisingly, cleansing did not seem to be at the top of their agenda, and initially Arkan was nowhere to be seen. From the relative safety of Zagreb, the exiled Mayor later explained why.

Before carrying out his 'public duty', Arkan's form in any new territory was to engage in a little private enterprise first. He would loot all the local banks. Eye-witnesses to Arkan's subsequent personal involvement in ethnic cleansing were difficult to come by, but the Mayor had taken statements from as many survivors as he could find. A number named Arkan as the perpetrator, and Calverley took copies.

As our team travelled through Bosnia, they were carrying several thousand US dollars in small denominations, with which to buy their way around the devastated countryside, and had also brought heavy, blue flak jackets and helmets purchased from a military supplier in London. They carried another, rather larger, set for me.

At my insistence, efforts were made to increase my personal insurance. In places like the former Yugoslavia they didn't play by the accepted rules, and if anything untoward happened to me in this lawless war zone, I wanted Frances and Belinda to be well provided for. Negotiations were still going on when I had to leave for another assignment across the Atlantic, before rejoining my colleagues in the Balkans – still uninsured.

In late August, Paul Calverley, cameraman Mike Garner, and producer Clive Entwistle arrived in the coastal city of Split. Their first scheduled filming was to take place in a refugee camp on the outskirts of the city of Zenica. Time was tight and there was only a narrow window of opportunity before the first snows rendered the local terrain almost impassable. A battered grey Mercedes diesel saloon was acquired as crew transport. In the circumstances, hiring a car was virtually impossible, and this one was expendable in case of attack.

By arrangement with the Muslims who had first put Calverley onto the Arkan story, the team was introduced to a student who spoke good English and was between terms at college in Zagreb. He was to be their guide around Zenica and then in Lechevo, a small town some 20 kilometres north of Sarajevo, where it was said there were survivors from a recent massacre who would name Arkan and his Tigers as the killers.

Initially, there were surprisingly few outward signs of conflict along the way. The crew were put up and fed by unfailingly generous and hospitable local families, despite an acute shortage of food. Eggs and bread were considered a feast. As the old Merc bounced and rattled along the pitted and rutted roads towards Lechevo, they came across an old man chopping wood in a clearing by the roadside. Paul stopped the car, and through our student interpreter, asked him what he knew of the massacre.

There was plainly no one else around, but he would only respond in a whisper. The fear in his eyes was obvious and he barely broke off his chopping action as he spoke. In the end, his instructions were simple: they needed to travel on a few hundred metres to the first house on the left. The young man there had apparently seen everything and might be brave enough to go on the record.

A few minutes later, this slight 17-year-old had committed his painful memories to videotape. He had hidden in a ditch while Arkan and his henchmen had mown down most of the locals with automatic weapons, and then callously picked off the survivors.

Later, an elderly woman, swathed in bloodied bandages, recalled how she had refused to leave her home, so The Tigers had made sport of her and set fire to it to drive her out. She was then shot three times and left for dead. Her slaughtered friends and relatives had been heaped on top of her, but she had managed to extricate herself and crawl to safety after The Tigers had gone. There were many more searing stories like theirs.

The crew picked me up a few days later in Zagreb, 'fresh' from a red-eye flight across the Atlantic. We headed back into the war zone. Picturesque stucco and terracotta-tiled houses soon gave way to shattered and smouldering ruins, once green trees were reduced to blackened abstract shapes silhouetted against the cold, slate-grey sky.

Nothing I had read or seen on television could have prepared me for this. Whole communities had been razed to the ground. Blackened holes had opened up in the earth where once there had been houses, shops and schools. The remnants of families wandered around, dazed and distraught, as if they expected more destruction to be rained upon them at any moment. Bodies lying by the roadside had not just been shot; they had often been mutilated as well.

We stopped in the small town of Voicin. In architecture and ambience it had once resembled an Austrian resort, but now most of it looked more like a moonscape. The Serb paramilitaries had almost blown it to bits. They had marched through murdering, burning, plundering and terrorising as they went. On the shell-shattered walls of the nave of the local church there were the remains of an ancient religious mural. Across it, someone had recently daubed a slogan in red paint. I asked our translator what it meant. "Isn't it obvious?" he asked, gesturing at the evidence of carnage all around us, "It says God has abandoned us."

Voicin apparently used to boast of its happy ethnic mix. Serbs, Croats and Muslims had lived side by side for years, but the Serb paramilitaries had forced neighbour to turn upon neighbour at the point of a gun. Many Muslim and Croat men were simply marched off to the woods and shot. Not content with that, the paramilitaries even victimised dissenting members of their own ethnic group.

One man, we were told, had been forced to attempt the rape of his Muslim next door neighbour's two teenage daughters. He was then made to douse the entire family with petrol, subsequently incinerating them inside their own house. When the paramilitaries left, he committed suicide. By heroic contrast, the local grocer, a Serb, had silently defied the invaders and risked his life by conceal-ing ten Muslims and Croats in the cellar of his shop for the duration.

What had happened in Voicin was a microcosm of what was still happening across the country. It was also beyond comprehension, and certainly beyond the scope of one small television programme to convey the scale of the atrocities anywhere near adequately.

And many of the images Mike Garner captured could never be shown anyway.

Garner, who now shared the camera work with Salk on tougher foreign assignments, had left his native Zimbabwe a few years before to try his luck as a freelance cameraman in Britain. He had found a natural home at *The Cook Report* and we had rapidly struck up a rapport – perhaps because of our shared colonial backgrounds. Garner was a no-nonsense character who quickly adapted to whichever situation he found himself in and never complained. When in mischievous mood, he would refer dismissively to reporters, producers and researchers as 'blowflies' – parasites of dubious worth when compared to the journeyman camera operator.

We had decided to base ourselves in the area's largest town, Podravska Slatina and arrived, pretty well exhausted, as dusk fell. The ever energetic Garner, however, set off to explore our rambling, shell-scarred hotel. He returned having made what he described as a great find. The hotel had an adjoining dance hall which he summoned us blowflies to see, drawing our attention to the far end of the room. There on a small, raised podium stood a splendid, dust-covered drum kit, with high-hat and all.

Garner sidled over and settled himself behind it. He found the sticks and started to beat out a rhythm, dropping in the odd bass beat with a push of his foot. He gained in confidence – this boy had obviously played before – and he let fly with a series of splendid drum rolls and cymbal crashes. We sat back and enjoyed the performance. Suddenly, he was silenced by the arrival of angry neighbours. Apparently, we were making too much noise! Quite how Garner's little performance could offend when, the town had recently come under rocket attack by Serbian Airforce jets, I couldn't fathom. We said goodnight and went up to bed.

We were reminded that this had probably been another example of ordinary people trying to get on with their lives in desperate circumstances when we went down for breakfast the following morning. A motley collection of rescued crockery and cutlery – some of it plastic – was neatly laid out for the hotel's few guests alongside crisply folded napkins on beautiful damask tablecloths.

Deeper into the hinterlands, over the next few days we filmed the most appalling scenes. Serb paramilitaries had surged across the countryside like a toxic tide. Locals who had survived, still grief-stricken by the recent carnage, took us around the houses of the dead. One man had been murdered by Arkan's thugs as he lay in his bed. They had cut his throat as he slept. All that remained was a pillow soaked in blood, now turned to the colour of the autumn leaves.

Just outside another village, there had been a horrifying discovery. The Tigers had recently swept through; looting property, randomly raping or shooting the womenfolk – and then marching all the males away to be gunned down in a nearby forest. Now, a shallow grave had been found. From the recently-turned soil protruded the hand of a small boy. One by one, they brought out the dead. Grieving began again with a howling and wailing that was truly distressing to witness.

Even in more rural areas where the landscape remained largely intact and the fighting appeared to be over, there was no room for complacency. Every spinney, tree-clad hillside or isolated farmstead could contain a group of Slivovitz-fuelled, armed men intent on destruction.

It wasn't long before we experienced this at first hand.

We were heading south for a place called Slavonski Brod on the Croatian border, en route – we hoped – to Belgrade. As we bumped and bounced through the potholed main street of one war-ravaged village, there was a sharp burst of automatic weapon fire from our right. We saw the bullets ripping lumps out of the concrete of the building in front of us.

When we looked behind, the same thing was happening to the walls of the block of flats on the opposite side of the street. Somehow, the strafing appeared to have passed in an arc right through the open windows of our car. We were all too shocked to speak for several minutes.

As we entered Slavonski Brod, columns of dejected, slowly moving refugees could be seen crossing over the border at the Sava river bridge. They had fled the cleansing in neighbouring Bosnia and several thousand of them were now huddled into the city's football stadium.

It was dark when we arrived at our hotel that night. We had telephoned ahead to make sure that our information was correct and that rooms would be available. The English-speaking manager had said there would be no problem – we could even get a decent meal. That was a bonus. For the past couple of days provisions had been extremely scarce. We had stopped whenever we saw anything for sale by the roadside and had subsisted largely on eggs or bread or the occasional piece of cured meat offered up by local people.

Something had happened between our phone call and our arrival, however. Where the hotel restaurant annexe had stood, there was now a smouldering hole in the ground. It had apparently taken a direct hit from a Serbian 155mm artillery shell. The manager was very apologetic. The Serbs had retreated and there had fortunately been no casualties, but there was now no food available. On the reception desk in front of us he placed three sets of keys, two cans of lager each and three black plastic bin liners.

"I can see what these are," I said, picking up the keys. "And these cans are probably our dinner. But what are these?" I enquired, indicating the bin liners.

"Your windows, sir."

In the morning, windows peeled back, came two more reminders of how people in the most wretched circumstances cling on to what remains of their previous, normal lives. In the shell of a block of flats opposite, there was one vaguely habitable unit. Over what remained of the balcony and across the twisted steel reinforcing rods jutting from the shattered concrete all around her, a middle-aged lady was hanging out her washing. In the street below, I could hear whistling. An old man in overalls was pushing a large, green municipal wheelbarrow. Along the pockmarked pavement, littered with rubble and strewn with the remains of burnt out cars, this man was carefully sweeping up autumn leaves.

Along with the bloodied corpses and shattered buildings, these are images I shall never forget.

We left the war zone with heavy hearts. The message had come through that Arkan would, after all, appear before our cameras, and with the prospect of confronting the man responsible for so much senseless barbarity, a little iron had entered my soul.

Two days later, our trusty Mercedes had taken us from the Bosnian and Croatian nightmare to the comparative civilisation and security of Serbian Belgrade. We were waiting in the incongruous surroundings of an ice-cream parlour – one of a chain owned by Arkan – just down the road from the Red Star stadium. We had been summoned there by his 'minders'. Behind the retail premises was Arkan's heavily fortified office. Outside, there were serried ranks of tables and benches leading down towards the football stadium, designed to catch the fans as they left after the game. Whatever else he was, Arkan definitely had an eye for business.

Before we had left our hotel, Mike Garner had put on his jacket camera, in case Arkan decided that he wanted to seize the tapes from his professional Beta camera. My radio mike was sending clean sound into the mini-recorder strapped under Garner's armpit as well as into the 'official' camera, so even if we lost the Beta tapes we would still have broadcast-quality audio to go with whatever secret filming Garner got with the jacket camera.

Just as we thought we were never going to get our interview, two black Mercedes drew up outside the ice-cream parlour. Four large men in charcoal-grey suits climbed out of each one. They were carrying Czech-made fully automatic weapons and looked warily around them in a way they can only have seen in bad gangster movies. The little gang waited on the pavement outside the shop until another black Merc drove up. The driver got out and opened the back door. A slim, dapper figure climbed out. Arkan had arrived.

He was about five feet nine inches tall, in dark glasses and wearing an elegant, grey Armani suit. A good-looking man with the cocky air of someone who expected to get whatever he wanted. We got up and walked out of the store to meet this ruthless murderer.

He seemed prepared to be affable – charming even. He took off his shades and we shook hands. He asked me, in fairly good English, where I should like him to sit for the interview. "Let's do it outside, just here at this table," I said, motioning Arkan to a bench facing out over the tables and the football ground.

Arkan lifted both hands in assent, and took the seat opposite me. Garner set up the camera beside me. Arkan looked towards the lens and squinted. Excellent. I'd got him staring at the sun. He was going to have to put on those villainous-looking shades again. Let no one be in any doubt here – appearances can sometimes be deceptive, but not in this bastard's case.

The man was immensely vain. Looking at his reflection in the lens, he smoothed back his hair. He spent what seemed like several minutes checking his collar and cuffs, the lie of his lapels and ensuring that our clip-on microphone did not wrinkle his tie. Then, with a self-satisfied smirk he indicated he was ready.

I started gently, asking him a bit about his past. He glossed over his criminal activity in Western Europe and started to portray himself as a good Serbian patriot fighting to preserve his nation and its culture. I nodded and listened. I thought to myself: Here I am, having a civilised conversation with a man I believe to be a genocidal psychopath. And what was more, we were sitting outside an ice-cream parlour conversing across a pink gingham tablecloth.

Whatever the consequences, I was going to have to break this cosy atmosphere and take a risk. The whole *Cook Report* team knew I had to do it. The reality – that we were surrounded by heavily-armed men in a country where law and order held little or no meaning if you disagreed with Serb supremacy – could not be allowed to affect what we had planned.

I handed Arkan some still photographs of The Tigers' bloody handiwork – of innocent villagers he and his men had massacred. He instantly knew the pictures were those taken by his former friend and were from areas that only The Tigers had passed through. The thin smile he had worn up until now disappeared. Keep up the pressure, make him lose some of his cool, I thought to myself. I pressed him on the pictures. "Don't they show that you are guilty of carrying out ethnic cleansing?" I asked.

Arkan's arrogance got the better of him and he began to boast. He was proud, he said, to be a war criminal if that meant that he was getting rid of the Muslims.

What an admission to make, I thought. You might come to regret it later. By now, Arkan had begun to get angry and I needed to pull the interview back from outright confrontation. This was a character who machine gunned defenceless men, women and children with a whoop of delight. I guessed that he didn't have much in the way of self-control once he'd been wound up sufficiently. I backed off and asked a few soft questions. He seemed to relax and, two minutes later, I ended the interview on an easy note, saying that we had another appointment and that we had enjoyed meeting and filming him.

Arkan and most of his henchmen retired to his offices behind the ice-cream parlour while we packed away the camera and sound gear. As they left, I could tell from the way they were looking at us that they hadn't yet made their minds up about the interview – or whether to let us go.

We sat and waited under the watchful gaze of one of Arkan's gun-toting cohorts. Perhaps the man himself was having second thoughts about what he had said in front of the camera. Whether he himself or one of his lieutenants was weighing up the consequences of his boasting, I couldn't be sure. If he did decide that the interview shouldn't ever be shown, there would be nothing we could do to prevent his men from taking the tapes from us. I prayed that Mike Garner had got some usable footage with his jacket camera and that the radio mike had worked properly.

We continued to sit tight and wait, feigning indifference to what was, really, quite a dangerous position. We had no allies, and we were at the mercy of a mass murderer.

Then, one of the two black Mercedes pulled away, a passenger wearing dark glasses in the back. Five minutes later, we were allowed to return to our hotel.

We then checked the tapes to discover something we thankfully hadn't noticed during filming. It might have been a disconcerting distraction. We had all been concentrating on playing a difficult interview just right. But as we listened back, and as the questions got more challenging – to the point where Arkan showed signs of losing his temper – we were pretty sure we could discern in the background the faint, but distinctive sound of his minders cocking their weapons.

The Arkan film went to air at the end of October 1992. We were told that after he had seen the programme he flew into a rage. He came across as exactly the man he was – a posturing, dangerous criminal who murdered innocent and defenceless people – however patriotic and macho he and his thugs tried to appear with their tiger cub mascot, their heroic marching songs, their banners and displays of weaponry.

Investigators at the International War Crimes Tribunal at The Hague agreed with us. A full transcript of our Arkan interview gave them, by his own admission, the first concrete evidence which put him in places and at times that linked him to known atrocities. And there was also his declared pride in being a war criminal.

A few months later, Tribunal officials told us that Arkan had been secretly indicted for atrocities in Croatia, Bosnia and Serbia. To make that public at the time, they said, would have been to close off completely any chance of having Arkan answer to international justice. If Milosevic had known he had a wanted war criminal in his camp, said our friends at The Hague, he'd make sure that the West never got its hands on him.

The Tigers continued with their murderous outrages – and now aware of the threat of indictment for war crimes, they took to wearing IRA-style black balaclavas with slits cut for eyes and mouth. In 1995 they appeared on the battlefields of Northern Bosnia, where they took to beating and humiliating their fellow countrymen for supposed cowardice in the face of the advancing Croatian forces.

Arkan also moved into politics, forming his own party – the Serbian Unity Party – and becoming an MP. He married a glamorous pop star, Svetlana Velickovic, Serbia's leading proponent of nationalist folk song – 'turbofolk', she called it. He became rich enough to build a huge, bunker-like house for himself and his family adjacent to Red Star Belgrade football stadium.

He controlled the lion's share of the local supplies of fuel oil and petrol, and the import of (stolen) luxury cars. He owned a major shopping mall and a bank in Belgrade. He still owned Obilic Football Club, a chain of bakeries, boutiques and ice-cream parlours, and a mobile phone company. He was courted by the press corps, who barely dared say a bad word against him, so powerful was he. The interviews he gave them turned out to be more promotional than confrontational.

Then, in 1999, when the Kosovo conflict blew up into full-scale war, there was Arkan again, offering to send his men into battle against the Kosovans and Albanians. They were to give support to the murderous Serb police as they moved into the province, supposedly to root out the Kosovan Liberation Army but, in truth, to evict the non-Serbian population at gunpoint – and to be rewarded for their presence with a licence to loot.

There is absolutely no doubt in my mind that it was the prospect of Arkan's Tigers rampaging mercilessly through the countryside that led to the mass exodus of the civilian Albanian population from Kosovo. At around that time, Arkan's war crime indictment was made public, but this only served to make him even more of a hero in Belgrade. Ironically, this may have caused him to be viewed anew by the Milosevic regime as a potential threat.

On his return from Kosovo, Arkan continued to hold court on a regular basis at Belgrade's Intercontinental Hotel, and it was there, in January 2000, that he was shot three times in the head by two masked men who burst in and sprayed the lobby with automatic gunfire. His bodyguards were killed outright, and the warlord himself was pronounced dead on arrival at hospital. Much as I would like to have seen him squirm in the dock at The Hague, this was unlikely to have happened, and I shed no tears at the alternative outcome.

There was a terrible sense of déjà vu when we subsequently made a programme about the civil war in Rwanda, and a man who made a fortune by supplying and/or ferrying arms to the combatants in defiance of a UN arms embargo. Willem Ouwendijk plainly didn't consider the consequences of his actions, which helped facilitate the genocide of between 800,000 and a million people in what became known as 'The Hundred Days of Slaughter'.

This was mass murder on an industrial scale, prompted by a mixture of deliberately inflamed ethnic tensions and naked political ambitions. Here, little or no effort was made to conceal the grisly evidence of genocide – whereas in Bosnia, for example, that evidence was buried as soon as possible. There were far fewer visible bodies, but the systematic destruction of buildings was clear to see.

In Rwanda, with some notable exceptions, there was by comparison relatively little architectural wreckage, but acres of corpses. The acrid smell of death was almost everywhere. And somehow, the atrocities stood out even more sharply against the backdrop of one of the most beautiful countries in Africa, its lush green mountains wreathed in mist. This tiny, landlocked state's main claim to international fame used to be the rare gorillas that made those mountains their home. Would it were still true.

The tragedy began in earnest in April 1994, when the majority Hutu tribe turned upon the Tutsi minority, following the assassination of President Juvenal Habyarimana, an ethnic Hutu. His Falcon 50 executive jet had been brought down by two ground-to-air missiles as it approached Kigali Airport. All on board, including the president of the neighbouring state of Burundi, died with him.

The mass killings that ensued appeared to have been planned in advance. Thousands of Tutsis and moderate Hutus were slaughtered. Pre-existing tensions meant that the United Nations already had a presence in the country under the banner of UNAMIR (United Nations Assistance Mission In Rwanda).

However, they were not allowed to intervene because that would be to break their 'monitoring only' mandate. When UNAMIR withdrew, the carnage escalated to the point where the International Red Cross estimated that more than half-a-million civilians were killed in the first few weeks.

A Hutu-controlled radio station – which soon became known as 'Hate Radio' – broadcast the names and addresses of Tutsi targets – *inyenzi*, or cockroaches, they called them. 'The grave is only half full – who will help us fill it?'

Hutu militiamen could be seen roaming the streets with a machete in one hand and a transistor radio in the other. The hastily-formed, Tutsi-led Rwandan Patriotic Front (RPF) fought back, making gradual inroads into the territory held by the Hutu Interahamwe militia. This was a perfect opportunity for the merchants of death, the arms dealers and shippers who were attracted to the conflict like moths to a flame.

One of them was a Dutch-born, Newmarket-based entrepreneur called Willem Ouwendijk. We traced his Africa-bound arms shipments from factories in Eastern Europe via Cairo, and another from Madrid via Malta to Goma on the Rwanda/Zaire border. We discovered to our horror and dismay that the shipments Ouwendijk had organised appeared to have been used to arm both sides. Certainly the weapons they used often proved to have come from the same initial source.

By now, the ground war was almost over, with the Tutsi RPF largely in control. UNAMIR had returned. The RPF leader, Paul Kagame, was later installed as President – and then accused of ordering the rocket attack that had brought down his predecessor's plane and triggered the massacre of his own people.

Our freelance specialist researcher for this programme was a well-padded chap called Brian Johnson-Thomas. He was subsequently rechristened BLT – in honour of what we soon discovered were his favourite sandwiches. BLT arranged for us to use the services of a battle-hardened cameraman who met us at Kanombe Airport. Looking like the cinematic equivalent of a hired gunslinger – which I suppose he was – Tom Sampson was dressed all in khaki, festooned with battery belts, and seriously fit. He knew Rwanda well, having just finished a long stint filming for German TV.

As the fighting petered out in the north of the country, the international press corps was billeted at the once-deluxe Hotel

Milles Collines, in the capital, Kigali. It had latterly served as a last refuge for nearly 1,200 Tutsis who had hidden inside for four months, as Hutus armed with machetes, guns and clubs raged through the streets outside.

The hotel's extraordinary manager, Paul Rusesabagina, had somehow induced the Hutu leaders to leave his temporary guests alone in exchange for regular access to the hotel's extensive wine cellar. That this risky arrangement had not backfired, with tragic results, amazed me. But Mr Rusesabagina was obviously as persuasive as he was courageous.

Now, the worst of the combat damage had been patched over and the staff managed to behave as if all was normal. Yet only weeks before, we were told, they'd been dodging bullets and swabbing blood off the walls. The newly refilled pool lay unused, because – so the story went – it had recently contained the bodies of ten Tutsis and a disembowelled cow. The one journalist unaware of this gruesome detail, shot from the water like a trained dolphin when told what had allegedly preceded him.

At 0530 the next morning we attended a UNAMIR briefing. The Canadian in charge was straight out of Joseph Heller's *Catch 22*. He strode into the room and said "OK guys, first let's have an attitude check." The war-weary press and military personnel present all chorused "I hate this fucking place," to which he responded "No guys, let's have a *positive* attitude check!" This was followed by the shouted reply: "I *positively* hate this fucking place!"

We were really there to try and blag the use of a helicopter in order to do some aerial filming, but finding out the flight schedules which would have enabled us to locate a helicopter 'going our way' was proving an impossible task for anyone not in the military. Eventually, after several days of hanging about, we spotted a Bangladeshi junior officer clutching the next day's schedule. He would not allow us to look at it and pointed to the words 'UN. Classified' printed across the top of every page. "No no," BLT said, trying it on. "It says *un*classified." The poor chap fell for it and we found our helicopter.

Its pilot was a very obliging chap. Ex-American Special Forces in Vietnam; he flew the chopper as if he was still there. Bizarrely, our take-off was delayed by the passing of a swarm of locusts, but once we got airborne, we were able to film all we wanted and get to some otherwise inaccessible places in relative safety. There was still the odd fire-fight going on in the lush green countryside below. Filming over, and as dusk fell, we had the ride of a lifetime on the way back to Kigali, skimming the lakes and hills with feet to spare – our bandana-wearing pilot whooping like a rodeo rider. In the circumstances, it was pretty surreal.

The genocide not only killed nearly a million people, it also created a similar number of orphans. Some of the tented displaced persons camps we saw had become *de facto* orphanages, because so few parents had survived. In the 'orphanage', situated near the airport at Kanombe, there were not enough adults left to care for the young ones, who were largely left to their own devices. They looked utterly lost. International aid had only just begun to trickle in.

In the south-western town of Cyangugu, there was no one to care for anyone. Even without the RPF/Interahamwe conflict, inflamed ethnic tensions had erupted. Doctor had killed doctor, nurse had slain nurse and members of the civil administration had murdered each other. Aid agencies thought the place was still unsafe, and stayed away. The town had been virtually razed to the ground and, we were told, 90 per cent of its inhabitants slaughtered. The waters of nearby Lake Kivu had run red with blood.

Japhet Nyilinkindi had a quiet dignity that made his testimony all the more impressive – and probably helped him cope with the horrors he had been through. He was the sole survivor of an extended family of 20. His brother and his brother's children were chopped to pieces before his eyes. His mother, father, grand-mother, aunts and cousins were all brutally murdered in a hail of gunfire.

"I do not know where their bodies are," he told us, pausing painfully between every sentence. "I do not know whether they were buried or eaten by dogs . . . I do not know how these things can happen . . . My family has almost been exterminated . . . I am the only one left."

Yet Japhet seemed less angry with the murderers than he was with those who armed them.

"I do understand that you have to make money as a businessman . . . but it should not be made out of a lot of dead bodies . . . It is bad business."

There were 8,000 dead bodies a day – the result of the biggest single act of genocide since the Holocaust. An estimated three million refugees – nearly half the remaining population – fled the country.

When the slaughter stopped, attempts were made to form a Tutsi-led government of national reconciliation, and we interviewed the new interior minister, a former dentist called Seth Sendashonga. He too blamed the arms trade for the scale of his country's woes – the governments that allowed the trade, and the dealers and shippers who made money from it.

"There were already tensions between the two major ethnic groups, but those tensions could have been contained if arms had not been readily available," he told us. "When a government allows the export of arms to a regime that is known to kill and intends to kill, this is wrong. It is also wrong to trade in those arms and knowingly ship those arms into a situation like that which we had in Rwanda."

Despite this, Mr Sendashonga was extraordinarily sanguine about the future of his country, but sadly, he too had been assassinated by the time our programme was broadcast. He had made the mistake of making public his intention to give evidence to the UN War Crimes Tribunal.

We took our evidence on the breaking of the UN arms embargo to UN Headquarters in New York. Under Secretary General Peter Hansen read our documentation and seemed resigned to what it revealed. Much to the obvious dismay of his press office minder, he admitted that the UN had "never had a totally effective arms embargo, anywhere in the world, ever." As his boss became ever more indiscreet, the minder paced up and down by the window, many storeys up, overlooking Manhattan. At one point he was so visibly agitated, we thought he might hurl himself through the glass.

A subsequent UN-sponsored independent report into the organisation's Rwandan 'peace keeping' activities was highly critical and concluded that not only the UN, but also the entire Western World had failed Rwanda badly. In effect, they had all stood by and done nothing as the genocide went on and on. Another report, from the UN High Commissioner for Refugees, on the revenge killings of at least 45,000 Hutus carried out by the RPF after the Tutsis had come to power has never seen the light of day. And twelve years after the fighting ended, the UN sponsored International Criminal Tribunal For Rwanda had made shockingly slow progress. It had promised to prosecute some 700 people regarded as the ringleaders of the genocide, yet after spending almost £550 million; it had secured only 25 convictions.

The UN failed again in Bosnia in 1995, when 8,000 Muslims in the 'UN protected enclave' of Srebrenica were slaughtered, 'protection' notwithstanding. As in Rwanda, UN officials had instructed their peacekeepers to stand back from the slaughter, despite having the means to stop it. Those heartless orders, difficult to comprehend in the circumstances, were apparently given in order to preserve the UN's impartiality – but in such crises, impartial inaction is surely at odds with the organisation's key founding principles: "to save succeeding generations from the scourge of war" and "reaffirm faith in fundamental human rights." Despite these noble-sounding words, at the time of writing the UN was failing yet again in the Darfur region of western Sudan, where in 2003 – according to a leaked interim report from the organisation's own human rights team – "the worst humanitarian disaster in the world" was looming.

Around the time that report surfaced, the emerging parallels with what I had previously seen in Rwanda had already alerted me to this shameful story, but I could raise no interest at ITV in making a programme about it. At that stage, there had been very little media coverage of events in Darfur and even less help from the international community. It was "Rwanda in slow motion", remarked one observer – and according to another: "When the massacring is over, we will all shake our heads as if we've learnt an unexpected lesson – and the sickening, unpardonable display of nation after nation falling over itself to say 'never again' will soon be repeated."

This appalling cycle began again in Darfur early in 2003, when Government-backed Arab *Janjaweed* guerrillas led what was described as 'a reign of terror' against non-Arab Sudanese. Despite the fact that both victims and oppressors were Muslim, the *Janjaweed* went on to ethnically cleanse the region of well over two million people and kill as many as 400,000, latterly aided by the Sudanese army. Rape and murder became systematic while aid organisations were effectively excluded. Independent observers feared that genocide was not far behind, if it hadn't begun already – and that on past form, the UN would do little or nothing to stop it. The only real official action, it seems – almost a year after the leaking of the report – had been to launch a witch hunt for the whistleblower, rather than solving the urgent humanitarian problem he had revealed.

Two wasted years further on, a watered-down version of the original report was eventually published. It stopped short of accusing anyone of genocide, but concluded: "The *Janjaweed* have operated with total impunity and in close co-ordination with the government of Sudan" and "the pattern of attacks on civilians includes killing, rape, pillage, including of livestock, and destruction of property, including water sources". Though the UN had adopted resolutions calling for international intervention, it had subsequently become mired in politics and failed to implement them. The Sudanese had described the proposed action as 'a hostile act.' A small force from the African Union, which had reluctantly been allowed into the country, was constrained by a chronic lack of resources and a time-limited, monitoring-only mandate – an externally brokered peace agreement had quickly collapsed – and the UN was still waiting for approval from the Sudanese government to send in a proper peace-keeping force.

It defies all logic that the UN should seriously expect those behind the ethnic cleansing to approve any action designed to end it. Meanwhile, the carnage continued unabated.

After our Rwanda broadcast, *we* were criticised yet again by the BCC. Ouwendijk, the arms shipper, had complained that we had treated him unfairly and invaded his privacy by confronting him outside his Newmarket office. He also claimed that all our evidence against him was 'forged', though it consisted of waybills and other verifiable official documents, statements from government officials, and from pilots and loadmasters, a critical UN Commission report to the Security Council, and a report from a Spanish Parliamentary select committee indicting Ouwendijk as an arms shipper. There was also documentation showing that Ouwendijk's companies had flown arms to Angola and the Yemen, both then the scenes of bloody internecine conflict.

Another Ouwendijk organised flight had been impounded in the Azores, when it was discovered that the 'hospital equipment' listed on its false manifest was in fact '104 tonnes of military equipment' bound for a UN embargoed destination. Nevertheless, the BCC accepted Ouwendijk's version of events at face value. They conceded that he was in the arms business, but decided that we had exaggerated his involvement in it – and held that we had invaded his privacy. That said, Ouwendijk no longer operates from Britain and no longer appears to be in the arms business.

We had more success on another story with a Dutch connection. Whereas Ouwendijk was a Dutchman based in England, Kevin Sweeney was an Englishman living in Holland. Claiming to be a millionaire publisher, he had spun an extraordinary web of deceit, forgery, death and insurance fraud. The police suspected Sweeney of insuring, and then murdering, three of his five wives – but there wasn't enough evidence to convict him, and he continued to live a life of luxury.

We took up the story on behalf of the bereaved parents of his fourth wife, Suzanne, who had met Sweeney after answering a lonely hearts advertisement in *Private Eye*. Following a whirlwind romance, Sweeney whisked her off to the Low Countries. He then insured her life for £700,000, and shortly afterwards, Suzanne was found dead at the scene of a suspicious house fire.

As a result, Sweeney had been tried for her murder, but was acquitted. The man clearly thought he was 'fireproof'. However, it looked to us that forensic evidence offered at his trial was inconclusive, some would say bungled, and with expert help, we thought we might be able to determine what had really happened.

Part of the interior of the Sweeneys' Dutch house was recreated inside a giant hangar at the Fire Research Station at Garston in Hertfordshire, and scientists simulated exactly what Sweeney claimed had happened. Forensic analysis of the results of 'our' fire proved conclusively that he had been lying, the fire was not accidental, and could only have been set by him.

Under the Dutch legal system, it is possible for the prosecution to take a previous verdict to appeal. Our new evidence was used to do just that, and Sweeney was sentenced to 13 years in prison, five long years after the murder.

Sweeney, Owendijk and Arkan had all profited by exploiting the misery of others. Indeed, it was that characteristic more than any other that most qualified someone to become a *Cook Report* target.

After we had finished filming in Bosnia, we had returned, tired and emotionally drained, not to enjoy a few days' respite, but to more of the same – the Triad story that had been 'on the back burner' for months, but was now developing fast.

Manchester had one of the worst Triad problems in the country. The extortion and violence practised by these violent secret societies were escalating out of control in the city's Chinatown district. The Greater Manchester Police had even established a special Chinese Unit to help the ethnic community which was increasingly in the grip of the gangs. The extent to which the Chinese, historically a reticent and self-dependent race, were prepared to take that offer of assistance remained to be seen.

We had tried for three months to persuade a member of the Chinese community in Britain to go undercover for us in Manchester. In an operation no one had ever tried before, we wanted to provide a new target for the Triads and film them in action. However, the very real likelihood of reprisals made volunteers for the job of undercover agent impossible to find. Howard Foster spent weeks trying to persuade just one Chinese individual to go undercover for us. Even men about to join the police force were too cautious to take the job on. "You don't understand," they would tell Foster. "These people don't forget. You can think you are safe for ten or 20 years. Then . . ."

The unspoken ending to the sentence was usually accompanied by a chopping movement made with the outside edge of the hand – directed either at the neck or back of the legs. If we wanted further proof that the Triads exerted an undue and illegal influence on the lives of the Chinese community in Britain, it was there in spades for the *Cook Report* team to see in the faces of the men we were trying to get to help us.

Finally, in desperation, we cast our net wider. Clive Entwistle, trusted by Townson to deliver this difficult but potentially explosive story, approached a small, unlisted company in London which specialised in providing close personal protection for wealthy international businessmen. Its boss listened carefully to Entwistle's request and opened his contacts book at the letter H for Hong Kong.

"Give me a week, I'll find you somebody good," he said. And we waited.

The operation had been set up in total secrecy. Howard Foster had been delegated to lose himself in Manchester's Chinatown for a few weeks to find out who the main targets and victims were.

Foster, who, like me, fancied himself as a bit of a *bon viveur*, managed to incorporate several visits to Chinatown's best restaurants in the course of his research. The story soon started to take shape, while Foster, dallying with the dim sum, started to lose his.

He made contact with the Chinese Unit's operational detective, Roy Tildsley, a thoughtful, bearded character in his late thirties, who spoke some Cantonese and knew most of the businessmen in Chinatown. He said it would be extremely difficult to reveal what was really happening in the Chinese community because of the fear the Triads instilled. In four years his unit had only had one successful prosecution – and that was because Tildsley had actually been the witness to an attack outside one of Chinatown's gang-run restaurants.

He told Foster that he would help *The Cook Report* if we could persuade his divisional commander to sanction it. Foster, Clive Entwistle and I arranged to meet the head of Manchester CID, David James, in his office at force HQ in Salford. James, an experienced officer with whom we had worked in the past, had asked Tildsley's immediate boss, Detective Chief Inspector Alan Boardman, to sit in on the meeting.

The policemen wanted to know what we planned to do and who our targets were. Tildsley, who was keen for the operation to go ahead, had confirmed what Foster was hearing about the identities of the principal Manchester Triad leaders and what crimes they were involved in. Foster repeated this to the senior officers and I added that *The Cook Report* wanted to expose these people doing what they habitually did by capturing it on film. Anything we got, the police were welcome to have after it had been broadcast. If it led to successful prosecutions, then so much the better.

There is always an inherent danger in situations like this, because any police officer worth his salt knows that the evidential requirements of a criminal court and those of an investigative television programme, no matter how thorough, can be poles apart. David James turned to Alan Boardman. "Are you happy to give this a go?" Boardman looked at Tildsley.

"If Roy thinks it stands a chance, yes," he replied.

Tildsley concealed his relief. "If we take this a stage at a time, plan it properly and keep the security in place, we could get somewhere, sir," he said.

Of the many police forces that *The Cook Report* has worked with, the Greater Manchester Police is one of the most helpful. The Obscene Publications Squad of the Metropolitan Police, with dedicated men in its ranks such as 'Moose' Donaldson, Michael Hames, Jim Reynolds and Bob MacLachlan, has also seen fit to work closely with us with mutually beneficial results.

I have no illusions about why policemen decide to help a television programme like ours. There are many hurdles to clear before a decent working relationship can begin. The first is to circumvent the force press office. That is something of a generalisation, as there are some excellent people working in police press offices, but the vast majority are civilians whose sole purpose in life seems to be to obstruct something which, by common consent, is probably going to do some good.

Next, you have to identify the detective 'on the ground' – the person who understands and controls what is going on – and reach an understanding with him. It might come as a surprise that some of the biggest investigations carried out in Britain are in the hands of Detective Sergeants or even Constables and – if it really is a major job – Detective Inspectors. By that, I mean, that they are the ranks most likely to be there, on the ground, dealing with the reality of any enquiry. That makes them the blokes to ask about what is really going on.

The more senior the police officer, the more likely it is that he or she has more than enough on his or her plate handling the day-to-day paperwork. Operations to catch criminals can often hinge on whether there is enough money in the kitty to pay for the necessary overtime.

Couple that with the common practice of moving people experienced in a particular specialisation into something totally unrelated to stop them getting stale – or possibly corrupt – and you narrow down even further the chances of finding someone with a mind to assist you. This time, however, we had been lucky and could build on the success of a previous venture.

It was with the help of David James, his uniformed opposite number Trevor Barton and Alan Boardman that as long ago as 1993, *The Cook Report* was able to identify paedophiles using internationally-based computer bulletin boards and the internet.

Paedophiles had been quick to exploit this new technology to distribute pornography and to 'groom' potential victims. The

Greater Manchester Police seconded one of their most precious assets – then the most experienced computer pornography investigator in England, Detective Sergeant John Ashley – to our Birmingham studios for six weeks.

The results of this unusual joint venture between the GMP, Scotland Yard's Obscene Publications Squad and *The Cook Report*, were four major prosecutions, a mine of useful intelligence for the police and key changes in the law covering electronic images. Not to mention a ground-breaking television programme that informed and forewarned its audience of the enormous potential risks posed to our children by the internet.

Researchers and producers on *The Cook Report* always knew when they had found a policeman worth talking to. They sounded like real people. They admitted that there were problems in the area of crime they deal with. Otherwise, they would be solving every case they investigate – and never have regrets that someone got away with something they shouldn't have.

I am no apologist for the police, and if they fail in their duty they deserve to be put under close scrutiny and censured where necessary. But the reality is that in the battle for supremacy between law and order and the criminal, the latter has so many more resources at his disposal. This is where *The Cook Report* and programmes like it can help.

No police force has all the resources it wants. With our big budget and our limited aims – to expose wrongdoing and to get a television programme out of our endeavours – there is often common ground between us. Ask any decent detective if there is an individual or gang he would like to target, but which he is too busy or understaffed to give his attention to, and he will probably answer yes.

Roy Tildsley was a policeman who recognised that we could achieve something with the resources at our disposal. Once he received the sanction from his bosses, he was free to help us – and more than happy to do so. They knew we would be able to expose the Triads in a way which they could not, so why not help rather than hinder?

An elaborate and secret operation began. Our target was the feared Wo Shing Wo Triad, which ruled supreme in Manchester and the North West. The head of the local Triad was a man called Yau Lap Yuen, known locally as Georgie Pi. The Cantonese word

Pi means 'cripple' – a reference to Georgie's limp, the result of a hip injury sustained in a gang fight in Hong Kong. His Number Two was Chan San Ping, otherwise known as Alan Chan. Under the command of these two, Wo Shing Wo was raking in a fortune in weekly protection payments made by hundreds of Chinese restaurants and takeaways within a 40-mile radius of Manchester's city centre.

It was a pattern being repeated all over Britain. The Triad gangs had largely carved up the country geographically between them. Another gang, 14K, ruled in London and the North East. The Wo On Lok Triad was, and is, the Wo Shing Wo's deadliest rival as it operates in much the same geographical areas.

Territorial conflicts between these two exploded from time to time, bringing the inevitable 'choppings' with beef knives. These substantial, broad-bladed knives were an ideal weapon for the Triads because they were so common in Chinese restaurants and were therefore easy to explain away if the police discovered one in a suspect's home or in his car.

Extortion from small businesses was carried out according to strictly-observed ritual. The amount each restaurateur or shop owner had to pay was often given in multiples of 36, based on some ancient rule that went back to the time when the Triads were highly-secret, Masonic-style societies in China. The money had to be placed inside a red envelope and handed, once a week, to the collector. Failure to pay would bring a visit from the much-feared *Hung Kwan* – or Triad enforcer.

Sometimes, the Triads would use Vietnamese 'foot soldiers' to do their dirty business, either to chop their enemies or to ruin their restaurant businesses by taking over several large tables and sitting there all night, every night, their feet all over the tablecloths, talking loudly and generally making it unpleasant for customers trying to enjoy a meal.

The legendary Chinese love of gambling also caused trouble, either because people got so heavily into debt that they couldn't afford to pay back Triad money lenders, or because rival gambling dens would use violence to try to put each other out of business. The Triads wanted complete control of all gaming. Even the New Year mah-jong marathon planned by a legitimate Chinese club in Manchester was called off following several threats and after superglue was poured into the locks on the front door and shutters.

Frustratingly for the British police, it was very rare for a Chinese Triad victim to complain. Arrests and convictions were few and far between. Even when someone had been 'chopped' and seriously injured enough to seek treatment in hospital, Roy Tildsley would be told by the agonised victim that he had 'slipped onto his own knife' or that a stack of blades had 'fallen onto him from a kitchen cupboard'. It was a difficult cultural adjustment for the British policeman to find that for many Chinese, after the taxman, he was the most loathed person to walk the earth.

As we started to make our programme, a gang of Triad sponsored Vietnamese from Liverpool had run amok in the 'I Don't No Club' and chopped two innocent English patrons who ended up in hospital minus several fingers.

Georgie Pi had also been suspected of involvement in heroin importation in the past. All in all, he was a formidable and completely corrupt character.

We knew that another of the illegal Triad operations was video piracy. Not the copying of mainstream Hollywood blockbusters, but of the dozens of Chinese-language soap operas to which many of the inhabitants of Hong Kong are addicted. Thousands of pounds a week were being made by the wholesale duplication of the latest episodes and their rental through Triad-run outlets in and around Manchester.

The Cook Report decided to go into the video business too. Roy Tildsley had noticed that a large, shabby 1930s office block on the edge of Chinatown was almost empty. A 'To Let' sign hung outside the window of a first-floor office. He jotted down the letting agent's telephone number and passed it on to Howard Foster. The landlord, an affable South Korean accountant operating from plush offices in Cheetham Hill, happily took three months' rent in advance and wished Foster luck in his new office furniture venture.

Meanwhile, we had found a company in London to supply tiny video cameras to fit into the walls of the office. Early one quiet Sunday morning, before the Chinese community awoke and began to fill its shops and restaurants, Entwistle and Foster unlocked their Chinatown office and led in a small team of camera technicians, carpenters and joiners.

The plan was to hide four cameras in the walls. The workmen were to build one false wall into the office, complete with a hidden door covered by a film poster. In this concealed void would sit a bank of video recorders. By breaking through the poster and leaning on the door, our Chinese manager – once we had found one – would be able to make a quick exit from danger into a long, narrow passageway that led to a fire door and a fire escape to the street below.

The final touch was to place a microwave transmitter on the ledge outside the office window, so that live coverage of what was happening inside could be transmitted to a television screen in a hotel room a few hundred yards away in Princess Street, where a member of the team could monitor events. After three days of sneaking in cables, video recorders and cameras, together with paint, ladders and plasterboard, the office was ready.

Twenty-four hours later, Entwistle's friend in the security company rang to tell him that our man was on his way from Hong Kong. Joe Tan – not his real name – was a 25-year-old security manager in a commercial bank. He was owed a couple of weeks' leave and was happy to come to the UK to do the job for us.

Entwistle and Foster met Joe at Manchester Airport and took him for a drink in the bar of the Portland Thistle hotel, 500 yards from the carefully-rigged video rental office. Joe, tall, thin and well-dressed, spoke good English. He knew what we wanted him to do and he was in total agreement – he'd run up against the Triads before and had a healthy respect for their power, but he also relished the opportunity to bring them to book if he could.

The following Sunday – the big day of the week for the Chinese community to meet, eat and mingle around the Dragon Arch of Manchester's Chinatown – Joe and his nephew Ralph, a student at London's Imperial College, distributed leaflets all over the area advertising his new company. We'd called it Flying Dragon Video, and the leaflets went through letterboxes, under windscreen-wipers and into the hands of Chinese passers-by. The telephone number and address of Flying Dragon Video were clearly printed on the bottom of the flyer.

Meanwhile, we had acquired 500 pirate Hong Kong video tapes from a distributor in London. They had been the principal exhibits in a recent court case and each one had an adhesive label marked 'Metropolitan Police Evidence – Do Not Remove' on its case. Over two days, with the aid of white spirit and fingernails, Howard Foster scraped every label off. Roy Tildsley's Chinese secretary checked up on the current soap titles sold on the black market in Britain and wrote the titles down in Chinese on 500 new sticky labels. Attention to detail was going to be crucial when the Triads came to check out Flying Dragon Video.

Howard Foster sat in his room in the Princess Hotel watching Joe and Ralph in their office on the microwave link. An extra camera hidden on the landing outside the door gave Foster a view of the staircase leading up to it. He hadn't long to wait before the action started.

For a full hour, Foster watched as a Chinese cleaner diligently swept the same piece of stair carpet outside the office door. Every few minutes, the cleaner would lean towards the door and peer through the keyhole. He was clearly checking out how many people were inside the office.

Suddenly, a group of men in jeans and bomber jackets appeared on one of Foster's TV screens. They had come into the hallway and were moving, single-file, up the stairs. Foster recognised two of them as Alan Chan's senior foot-soldiers. One, Patrick Keung, who was leading the group, ran the main Triad pirate video shop in Chinatown. At his shoulder was the athletic figure of Simon Chan, Alan's younger brother. Simon was suspected by the police of instigating a series of knife attacks by Vietnamese thugs in recent weeks.

Foster counted six men going into the Flying Dragon office. Two more stayed outside. Known as the Look See boys, they would keep an eye out for unexpected visitors or the police.

Patrick Keung walked through the office door. He sauntered up to Joe, who was sitting at his desk, demanding to know who he and his helper were, and how they dared to set up in business on his patch. Simon Chan advanced menacingly on Joe. He now stood between Joe and the secret escape door, which was hidden by a large movie poster taped to the wall. Ralph was cut off at the other end of the office.

Simon Chan dialled out on his mobile phone and spoke loudly in Hokkien, the dialect of choice for Triad members. The later translation told us that he was talking to his 'Big Brother Ping', Alan Chan. Simon Chan told his boss that the newcomers seemed to have a full stock of up-to-date tapes. Chan listened, nodded and handed the phone to Patrick Keung who listened briefly and then shouted an order to the others.

All hell broke loose. One of the gang aimed an accurate karate kick at the piles of videos, sending them cascading to the floor. Another lifted a heavy steel office chair and brought it down on Joe's head. Ralph was punched, kicked and had his glasses smashed and ground into his face. Simon Chan picked up Joe's own mobile telephone and rammed it into Joe's mouth. Foster, watching the horrific scene unfold in front of him, dialled the police and an ambulance.

At that moment one of the Look See boys rushed into the office and shouted urgently to Patrick Keung. Keung ran out of the room, gesturing urgently for the others to follow. Luckily for Joe and Ralph, something had spooked the lookouts and the beating was over – for the time being.

Foster also telephoned Clive Entwistle at his home in Rochdale, about 20 minutes drive from Chinatown. It had been Entwistle's 50th birthday the day before and he had hosted an elaborate fancy-dress party from which he and just about every other member of the Cook team were trying to recover. Entwistle shrugged off his half-century hangover, climbed into his car and headed for Manchester.

I travelled up to Manchester that Sunday night and went straight to the Royal Infirmary. Foster and Entwistle were standing by Joe Tan's bed in a private side-ward. Joe was being treated for concussion, deep head wounds and a crushed finger, hit as he tried to protect himself from the chair. Ralph was being treated for facial cuts and bruises.

Joe volunteered to be interviewed in his hospital bed about what had happened. His mobile phone had been taken by Simon Chan, an invitation, Joe knew, to call and talk turkey about protection payments from Flying Dragon Video.

We filmed as he dialled his own number on the hospital telephone. He spoke in Mandarin for about a minute. "They want me to meet them in the Kwok Man Restaurant tomorrow night," he said.

"Do you still feel like going on with this?" I asked him.

"Of course, I shall see this through," he answered firmly. We left him to get some sleep and went off to plan how we handled Monday night.

We decided to put Howard Foster and three of our occasional helpers – all burly lads – into the restaurant before Joe arrived.

They carried two cameras hidden in briefcases. Once Joe had walked in and sat down, the lenses would be aimed in his direction. He was under strict orders to stay put, whatever happened.

Monday evening came. The *Cook Report* contingent took up their places in the restaurant and ordered food. They saw Joe arrive and sit down – and waited for something to happen. Twenty minutes went by, and then one of the thugs who had attacked Joe the night before walked in. He had an urgent, whispered conversation with the manager who pointed towards the solitary figure of Joe Tan. The young gangster strolled over to Joe's table and leaned towards him.

Foster watched in alarm as Joe stood up and walked with his visitor to the door of the restaurant and out into the street. This was exactly what Joe had been told not to do.

Foster followed as soon as he could without alerting the restaurant staff. Outside, he looked up and down Princess Street. There was no sign of Joe. He called Entwistle and Tildsley. They were with the cameraman, Graeme Wickings, filming the scene outside the Kwok Man from the manager's office in the Princess Hotel. They had seen Joe leave with the gang member and were already on their way to see what was going on.

Five anxious minutes passed and then Foster saw something that made his pulse rate leap. There, weaving erratically through five lanes of traffic was Joe Tan. His arms and body were jerking and shaking like a drunken marionette. He was screaming with pain and trying to flag down passing motorists. Foster dodged through the traffic and reached Joe just as he passed out. He carried him to the pavement and, for the second time in two days, called an ambulance for him.

Joe came round. "My legs, my legs!" he wailed. He sat up and pulled off both his shoes. His feet were grotesquely twisted and swollen. He felt them gingerly and let out a low moan. "They're going to kill me – and you. We've got to get out of here now," he insisted, fearfully looking over his shoulder. Waiting for the ambulance was out of the question. At this point, Entwistle arrived and hailed a taxi, and the two men lifted poor Joe into the rear seat and took him back to the MRI, laying off the ambulance on the way.

Over the next few days, we got the full story out of Joe. When he had left the Kwok Man restaurant he had been taken to another

Chinatown restaurant, the Pearl City. The Pearl City was on the second floor of an old office building and was reached by a wide staircase that wound round a deep stairwell. Joe had been placed at a table well away from the other diners. The gang member who took him there assured him that there would be no trouble if he co-operated.

Then Alan Chan and several of Joe's attackers from the previous night walked over to Joe and formed a semi-circle around him, shielding him from the rest of the room. One of the men pulled a 14-inch beef knife, and motioned Joe into the toilets.

Joe realised he was probably about to be hacked to death and naturally took matters into his own hands. As he was being led to the toilets, he made a lunge for the main entrance of the restaurant and made it through to the top of the staircase. As the Triads came after him, he jumped over the banisters and dropped two floors down into the stairwell, landing awkwardly on his heels with pile-driver force. He told us he heard a sickening crunch as he landed.

How he managed to struggle out of that building and back down the street for help, we never knew. He was taken straight into an emergency ward and an orthopaedic surgeon was called. He told us that the 'jelly bones' under Joe's feet were both smashed. It would be a long time before he would be able to walk again. The awful irony was that even then, he was likely to have a permanent limp – just like Georgie Pi. For the next few months, he would be confined to a wheelchair.

This was shocking news. Back in the Birmingham office, Joe's plight cast a shadow over everyone as we ran up to the opening of the series.

Townson, quite rightly, decided to run the Triads programme first. Roy Tildsley and his colleagues had been busy for days identifying Joe's assailants from still photographs – known as 'grabs' – taken from the video footage we had obtained from the hidden cameras in the Flying Dragon office. We later found out that Patrick Keung, Simon Chan and a couple of others were already known to the police. The remainder were subsequently identified thanks to the help of the few Chinese brave enough to inform the police about Triad activity.

Part of Joe Tan's cover story had been that he was a member of a small Hong Kong Triad anxious to spread its influence to Britain. He had tried to get this across to the thugs who had marched into the offices of Flying Dragon Video before they attacked him. Evidence that he had succeeded came a day or so later.

Howard Foster and sound recordist Dennis Fitch had been told that Alan Chan and his men were using The Pleasure Restaurant for meetings and for lunch. Foster and Fitch had placed themselves as customers at a corner table to see if they could get some secretly-filmed footage of the Wo Shing Wo deputy.

Fitch saw Alan Chan walk in and immediately slid the attaché case with its tiny camera onto a chair, pointing the lens at the short, smartly dressed figure chatting to his men as he stood barely five yards from the *Cook Report* duo.

"He looks a bit nervous, don't you think?" murmured Foster.

"He does," replied Fitch. "And he keeps fidgeting with his coat sleeves."

Later, when they reviewed the tape, they saw what Chan was doing. Clearly visible in the palm of his hand was the handle of a beef knife. The 14-inch blade was tucked up the sleeve of his expensive, cashmere overcoat – probably in case reprisals were launched at him by Joe Tan's imaginary Triad colleagues.

We decided to confront Georgie Pi and Alan Chan with what we had on them. We knew that Georgie Pi had entered the country in breach of a previous deportation order. A helpful Immigration Department official had shown Foster a file on the man three inches thick. He had won his spurs as a Triad member in Hong Kong 30 years earlier – befriending, then seducing an under-age girl who he then forced into a life of prostitution; a common procedure amongst the lower level of Triad.

Years went by and Georgie married Sandy Wai, another Hong Kong national who had obtained the right to live in Britain after she had married – and divorced – a British passport holder. But Georgie's past criminal convictions, and his alleged involvement in hard drug dealing, had led to a refusal by the Home Office to allow him into Britain. Nevertheless, on at least two occasions he had been found here and kicked out. Now he was here under sufferance, allowed to stay while his case was under review. In the meantime, he had to report to Stockport police station every weekend. And that was where we confronted him.

As I walked up to him and asked him what he was doing in Britain and how he earned his living, he turned tail and limped rapidly back up the steps of the police station. We followed him inside, still asking questions. He rang the desk sergeant's bell angrily, shouting that he was being harassed and that we should all be arrested. But the desk staff knew what we were up to and had conveniently retired to a back room. Pi was on his own and rapidly losing face, not something many self-respecting Chinese people want to do.

"It's illegal, what you're doing, right," he shouted.

"No, you're the one that's breaking the law," I replied as Georgie Pi pushed through the door and stomped furiously off into the night.

For the next few days, as the programme was prepared for broadcast, we began to hear rumours that Georgie Pi was on the warpath. He had plainly lost an enormous amount of face through my confrontation with him. Almost overnight, he had gone from powerful ogre to virtual laughing stock in the eyes of the Chinese community. His anger was mounting as the prospect of his acute embarrassment being paraded before ten million television viewers drew near. A Triad boss seeking to have the police protect him from a television reporter wouldn't look good. My confrontation with tough guy Alan Chan would look even worse – he had bolted into a restaurant lavatory and hidden.

According to informants, a contract was to be taken out on the lives of Howard Foster and myself. By whom, exactly, wasn't yet clear. Then, a few weeks later, Howard Foster had a telephone call from a senior detective in one of the regional crime squads. A known Wo Shing Wo 'enforcer' had been arrested in London on suspicion of extortion. When he was searched, he had Foster's home and mobile telephone numbers written on a small piece of paper. I didn't tell Frances, trusting that the arrest of the man – and the neutralising of Georgie Pi – would deter the Triads from taking matters any further.

It was arranged that on the evening the Triad programme was transmitted, Roy Tildsley and a uniformed colleague, Mike Gallagher, would arrest the men who had been filmed attacking Joe Tan. Tildsley knew where four, possibly five, could be found amongst the restaurants, bars and clubs of Chinatown, and he positioned himself at an observation point overlooking the area. Walkie-talkie in hand, he was ready to move in a squad of uniformed officers to make the arrests.

The programme was due to be broadcast at 8.30 on the evening of 12th January 1993. Just after five o'clock, Central Television's legal department in Birmingham received an urgent phone call from Mishcon de Reya, then the company's solicitors. Lawyers representing Mr Yau Lap Yuen – Georgie Pi – were about to appear before a judge in the High Court in London seeking an injunction to prevent the broadcast of *The Cook Report* on Triad activity in Manchester because they believed it harmed the reputation of their client.

Facing the prospect of losing a programme at the hands of lawyers inevitably makes me angry, even more so when you know that the person bringing the action is a criminal who merely wants to hide what he has done from the public. Fortunately, High Court judges had taken a fairly consistent line on issues like this for some time. If a libel might be broadcast by a programme-maker, they reasoned, then let it go ahead and let the complainant sue afterwards. That's what I, Townson and Bob Southgate – who was always called in when trouble like this loomed – fervently hoped would happen in this case.

Townson had an even more pressing problem on his hands. If, by some ghastly mischance, the judge agreed with Georgie Pi's lawyers, what would be broadcast in the place of the Triad programme? Graham Puntis, the videotape editor, was hurriedly corralled in his room with 50 tapes, and was busily assembling the alternative – a programme on prescription drugs that killed people. Like the Triad programme, it was strong stuff, but needed quite a bit more work on it before it was ready. Townson worked away with Puntis. Southgate and I sat by the telephone in his office, awaiting the verdict. I crossed my fingers and trusted to British justice.

Six o'clock slipped by, then seven. The phone rang. It was Entwistle and Foster. They were in the bar of the Princess Hotel in Manchester, waiting to see how the evening's arrests went. Roy Tildsley was desperate to move in on the suspects but had orders to hold off until the court decision came through. At least one of the wanted men had moved out of the immediate area, making his apprehension difficult once the filmed evidence of what he had done was public knowledge.

We couldn't help. The matter was in the hands of the lawyers and the judge, and they were taking a hell of a time coming to the decision we were praying for.

It was almost 8.10 when Mishcons called us back. The judge had thrown out Georgie Pi's application for an injunction. We were clear to broadcast. Talk about cutting it fine. Over a glass of Sancerre, Bob Southgate and I both agreed we didn't want to go that close to the wire again.

Foster and Entwistle passed the good news on to the police, who promptly moved into action and managed to arrest three of Joe's attackers.

The programme was one of the most successful we had ever done, on a number of levels. Even today, more than a decade on, people still vividly remember its images – particularly that image of poor Joe Tan weaving painfully through the traffic. The violence of the Triads against him was truly shocking and brought home the reality that they were a criminal force to be reckoned with.

Joe remained in a wheelchair for almost two years. He had become a good friend to the team and often stayed with Clive Entwistle and Howard Foster and their families. When he was able, he flew home to see his parents in Hong Kong, but when he returned, he told us that he would be unable to live in his home country again. News of his role in the programme had quickly filtered through. Copies of *The Cook Report* were already in the hands of the Triads. He had been warned that he was a marked man and that he had better stay well away. The problem was, he reminded us, that retribution did not have to be swift where the Triads were concerned. They would wait decades for revenge if necessary.

Central Television paid for Joe's private treatment and for his relocation to another Far Eastern country where he has since made a full recovery and now works successfully in the computer industry. When last heard of, Joe, a good-looking, single fellow, was enjoying himself greatly and was much in demand by the young ladies of his adopted country.

In between operations and relocating himself, Joe made lengthy statements to the police to help make the prosecutions stick. One or two more gang members were arrested at their homes. Two fled to Hong Kong but were caught months later when they tried to re-enter Britain.

The effect of the programme on life in Chinatown was dramatic. For more than six months, the Triads stopped all illegal activity. Small businesses were left alone. No one came round asking for the red envelopes. Georgie Pi, no longer a power in the Wo Shing Wo, relocated to Cheltenham where he appeared to have reinvented himself up as an 'honest, hard-working restaurateur' in the hope that he would be allowed to stay in Britain. To that end, he instructed his lawyers to sue us for defamation, an action that eventually came to nothing. Much to my bafflement, he is now legally resident in the UK.

Alan Chan went back to running his restaurant, but was subsequently convicted of taking part in an affray in a Manchester casino. He was last heard of running the Wo Shing Wo Triad in the North West.

Patrick Keung and the rest of the gang appeared at Preston Crown Court to answer charges of violent disorder and attacking Joe Tan. The case came up about a year after the programme had been broadcast and, given how badly injured Joe had been, there was some concern amongst Roy Tildsley and his colleagues that he might not return from the Far East to give his vital evidence.

They needn't have worried. Joe Tan arrived at Heathrow and was driven to Preston Crown Court where his testimony helped to get Patrick Keung two years in gaol. Three others got between two-and-a-half years' and 18 months' imprisonment.

The Triad programme had been a violent one, but it hadn't directly affected my health – if you discount the death threats from the Chinese gangsters. I finished that series in remarkably good shape, having done relatively little international travel. But the respite was about to end. Two stories were surfacing that would push several of the *Cook Report* team right to the edge – physically and mentally. Myself included.

For some months in the early 1990s, there had been occasional newspaper reports, mainly tucked away in the foreign pages, of nuclear material being smuggled out of the former Soviet Union for sale illegally in the West. In just 12 months, the German police had made no fewer than 160 seizures of hazardous radioactive chemicals – many of them thought to be on their way to unidentified groups keen to obtain the wherewithal to manufacture nuclear weapons. But no journalist had yet sought to demonstrate how easily such material might be acquired. Could we?

By 1993, The World Trade Center in New York had been

attacked – for the first time – by what later turned out to be al-Qaeda backed Muslim extremists. Was it only a matter of time before some fanatical organisation upped the ante and got hold of enough plutonium to rig up a small bomb to be detonated in another Western city?

Almost before the dust had settled in New York, Clive Entwistle and Paul Calverley were on the case. Some of Mike Garner's friends worked for Greenpeace. They were in touch with a young Russian journalist who had contacts with one of the gangs now selling weapons-grade plutonium – and much more besides.

Entwistle went to Moscow to meet the reporter – Kyril – to see if he would help. Subject to certain conditions – that neither he nor his contacts would be filmed or identified in any way, he agreed. He reminded Entwistle that the people we would be dealing with were dangerous and that we had to be very careful.

"The Russian Mafia make the Italians look like amateurs," he told us. I flew out to Moscow to meet him. He was young and, understandably, nervous, but we persuaded him that we had the expertise and the resources to carry off a successful 'sting' on the plutonium purveyors.

The plan was that I would pose as the representative of a dubious Middle Eastern regime keen to buy enough Plutonium 239 to make several small nuclear bombs. Back in Britain, we hired an eminent consultant nuclear engineer, John Large, to see if it would be possible to build a hand-portable nuclear weapon. The simple answer was yes, and that the basic technology was actually available on the internet. There were several ways to go, but we opted to replicate a relatively simple bomb that would operate in one of two modes – in that even if it failed to produce a nuclear explosion, it would still act as a very effective Radiological Dispersal Device.

In fact, the prospect of a terrorist attack using an RDD had been worrying the experts for some time, though the concept had not yet entered the public consciousness. However, it soon acquired a colloquial name – a 'dirty bomb' – so called because triggering it would disperse countless millions of highly radioactive particles over the target area. This toxic, invisible cloud could condemn those beneath it to a slow and painful death and render a city uninhabitable for centuries. Plutonium decays very slowly, having a so-called half-life of 24,000 years.

John Large duly built us a non-functioning replica of a 'dirty bomb' small enough to fit into a briefcase. It was a genuinely unsettling experience clicking open such a commonplace piece of baggage to reveal a pre-assembled nuclear unit inside, packed with plastic explosive around a plutonium core and complete with battery-operated timing and detonation devices. It wasn't real, but it so easily could have been.

Another expert told us in interview that a small terrorist group would quite easily be able to find the necessary components if they were properly-funded. In Moscow, we were expecting to prove that he was right.

Mike Garner joined Entwistle and me in Moscow. He and secret filming equipment wizard Alan Harridan had hurriedly created two cameras that were built into clothing, which Garner was to use when filming secretly. In a series of cloak-and-dagger meetings at the *Slavjanskaya* Hotel, Kyril helped plan our meeting with the gang's representatives. He was beginning to have second thoughts about what was about to happen, and was only just holding his nerve. We were, after all, about to stage a sting on members of the Russian Mafia.

The following morning, Garner and I were joined by Kyril and two heavy-looking characters with suspicious bulges under their coats – Kyril's underworld 'contacts' – and we set off in an impressive-looking hire car for one of Moscow's outer suburbs. Eventually we stopped in front of a gloomy, low-rise, pre-war apartment block in a surprisingly leafy street. Kyril led us to the front door of a scruffy, ground-floor maisonette and rapped nervously on the frosted glass.

The door opened and a tall, dishevelled man in his late thirties waved us quickly inside. He invited us to sit down in a makeshift office, which was furnished with little more than a battered desk that was bare but for a telephone, a small half-open filing cabinet and several rickety swivel chairs. Garner, posing as my minder, sat down last, making sure he could get a good shot of our host with the miniature video camera concealed in the breast pocket of his denim jacket.

The man introduced himself simply as Gennady. He said we needed to know no more, apart from the fact that he could obtain most nuclear materials from a variety of sources. He pointed to the telephone. We just had to tell him what we needed and he would make a call to his 'business partner', who would arrange delivery. I told him that we wanted 25 kilograms of plutonium for our Middle Eastern clients. Gennady didn't bat an eyelid. He picked up the receiver and dialled his friend.

They spoke in Russian for a minute or so, then Gennady put the phone down and talked to Kyril, who translated for us. Weapons-grade plutonium would cost $1.5 million a kilo, but that for a large order such as we were placing, Gennady was prepared to close the deal for $20 million. Had we wanted a uranium/plutonium mixture, we could have had it straight away, and for rather less money. As it was, pure plutonium would take a little while to obtain.

He had uranium and plutonium straightaway? I asked.

Gennady smiled and told us to stay where we were. He opened the hall door and walked over to a cupboard under his staircase. He reached inside and, with a grimace, hauled something into the room – a lead-covered container about two feet high. Suddenly Garner dropped forward onto his knees. My God, I thought. He's been irradiated. In fact, he was just trying to focus his secret camera on the lettering and codes stamped on the outside of the container, while appearing to want to check out the details for his own professional satisfaction.

Before we left, Gennady gave us a small sample of nuclear material so that 'our people' could have it tested to prove he could deliver what we wanted. I hoped to God that the small canister he'd given us was leakproof. Everything seemed so ramshackle and amateurish – a scruffy man in a cardigan operating from a shabby flat with nuclear material stashed under his stairs. My blood ran cold. We left Gennady with a handshake and agreed that we would come back to him as soon as we had spoken to our clients in the Middle East.

After the meeting, it was clear that Kyril wasn't happy with what we were doing. It was just about the last time we saw him – and I can't say that I blamed him. We were all very nervous. We had also discovered that Kyril had a serious drink problem and usually spent his mornings sleeping off the previous night's heroic vodka consumption. In his absence, however, we were without an inter-preter for our covert meetings with Gennady. We could hardly approach one of the translation agencies and ask for someone to come and tell us when the Mafia man was planning to deliver our plutonium.

In the meantime, our sample had been taken to *Minatom* (Atomic Energy Ministry) approved laboratories in central Moscow. Screened by residential developments, the laboratories were housed in a series of low, characterless, cream-painted buildings which, on the inside, reminded me of Dr Who's Tardis.

A worried-looking scientist opened the sample with his hands encased in heavy metalised gloves built in to the side of a radiation-proof cabinet. He carefully emptied the silvery-grey contents of the canister into a glass dish, and we filmed him testing it.

Sure enough, it was exactly what Gennady had said it was. To our dismay, the scientist then confirmed my misgivings about the safety of the receptacle that had contained our sample by advising that both Mike Garner and I should be tested for radiation exposure immediately on our return to Britain.

We later interviewed a *Minatom* spokesman. It was obvious that he knew that his country was haemorrhaging nuclear material, usually courtesy of the Russian Mafia, but he put a brave face on things. It seemed our original sample had come from an obsolete nuclear submarine from the Northern Fleet, decommissioned at the Severodinsk base near Murmansk. Before *Perestroika*, Russian engineers and scientists working at nuclear related sites had been part of the country's elite, and as such were well regarded and well paid. After *Perestroika*, they were often not paid at all – and would apparently do almost anything to feed their families, including stealing nuclear material. While this might be understandable, said the man from *Minatom*, it was certainly not justifiable and he vowed to do everything he could to stop it.

Back in Birmingham, programme manager Pat Harris, who was trying to find us a replacement interpreter, had a brainwave. Central had just finished filming one of its most successful dramas – 'Sharpe', starring Sean Bean as the swashbuckling soldier hero of the Napoleonic Wars – in Eastern Europe. An English woman who spoke fluent Russian had been working on the production as an interpreter and she was coming back to the UK via Moscow. Would she help?

Surprisingly, given that I was honour-bound to tell her exactly what we were involved in, she agreed. Perhaps she thought she'd still be involved in filming fiction. At any rate, she didn't appear to be at all put off by what she'd heard and cheerfully set out with us on our second visit to Gennady. By now, we'd discovered his surname – Simonov – and also had it confirmed that he had some very serious connections with the Moscow underworld.

Gennady told us that our proposed deal was so big he thought he'd better involve his business partner, Ilya, in person. They'd been thinking, he added, and had a suggestion to make. If, as we said, we wanted the plutonium so that we could make a nuclear bomb, why did we not just buy one ready-made. They had an SS 20 ballistic missile warhead they could provide for us right now – what did we think?

As our interpreter translated, I felt a sense of unreality engulf me, as I had the first time I had met Gennady. Here we were in the back streets of Moscow doing a deal with a Mafia man who kept plutonium under the stairs and a nuclear warhead in his back yard. If we were finding it so easy to obtain these things, what the hell was there to stop a genuine terrorist organisation with real money behind it from doing exactly the same?

I obviously wasn't looking keen on their suggestion because Gennady and Ilya were now outlining to our interpreter how the original order of weapons-grade plutonium was to be smuggled out to us. It would be coming through Vilnius in Lithuania. When would we like delivery? And would I please take the details of how we should make the payment to their company?

Then, to our surprise and alarm, Kyril appeared. We had not told him of this visit, because we thought he wouldn't approve of it, and in any case would probably be nursing a sore head. Then it occurred to us that he might think we were tying to steal 'his' story and that he was now in a position to scupper us, at the very least.

Fortunately, a mixture of astonishment and alcohol left Kyril confused and virtually speechless. This gave us just enough time to beat a retreat. We bundled into our car and headed straight for the offices of the FSB (Federal Security Service), the latter day equivalent of the KGB.

We had all the evidence we needed that the fissile material for our 'dirty bomb' could be found here in Moscow. We flew back to Britain to prepare for the final stage of the programme. Mike Garner and I duly had our radiation tests which to our great relief, proved, that as Mike quaintly put it: "our balls didn't glow in the dark."

The evidence that we had passed to the FSB led to a spectacular armed raid in which Gennady and his dangerous cohorts were arrested. The FSB will provide no information about what has happened to them since.

We had decided to take our dummy 'dirty bomb' to the United States. The totally reasonable thinking was that the bomb so recently set off at the World Trade Center could easily have contained nuclear material. If not this time, maybe next time. We had arranged to get an expert assessment of what we had been able to achieve. We also wanted to ask the authorities if they had contemplated such a potential threat and, if so, what plans they had to deal with it.

It is worth reminding ourselves that the programme was made in 1993. Ten years later, MI5 made public its conviction that al-Qaeda now had the know-how to make a dirty bomb – provided they could get their hands on suitable nuclear material. Al-Qaeda's number two, Ayman al-Zawahiri, had boasted in 2001 that they already had it. For all of the previous decade, such material had been leaching out of Russia and other parts of the former Soviet Union. Indeed, in May 1997, General Alexander Lebed, then security adviser to President Yeltsin, admitted that complete nuclear bombs had gone missing. From a batch of 132 special 'suitcase bombs', 84 could not be accounted for. Between 1993 and 2005, the International Atomic Energy Agency had logged 827 confirmed incidents of theft, smuggling or the attempted sale of potentially dangerous radioactive substances – of which 224 cases involved nuclear material and 16 plutonium or highly enriched uranium. The agency also revealed that the number of illicit trafficking incidents had risen sharply over the last few years and warned that the real level may now be significantly higher than 827, citing 'several hundred' additional, but so far unconfirmed reports. These are very worrying statistics, highlighted by more recent events.

In November 2006, Dhiren Barot, an Indian-born, British Muslim convert arrested amid a massive U.S. security alert in 2004, was sentenced to life imprisonment by a London court. He had admitted conspiracy to murder on a scale to dwarf 9/11. His meticulous plans, encrypted and stored on computers, involved blowing up key financial institutions – such as the New York Stock Exchange, the International Monetary Fund, and the World Bank – and a series of co-ordinated attacks in Britain, including the detonation of a dirty bomb in London.

Barot emerged as a skilled, high-level terrorist, operating under seven aliases, who had selected and reconnoitred targets at the behest of the al-Qaeda leadership. Fortunately, the plot was discovered at an early stage. No radioactive materials had been acquired, but their continued availability on the black market meant that wouldn't have been an insurmountable problem. According to the prosecution, by means both conventional and radioactive, his plans were "designed to kill as many innocent people as possible", to cause "fear, terror and chaos" on both sides of the Atlantic and, in London, "to force the abandonment of very large areas of the capital." But was this plot a one-off – and is the age of nuclear terrorism closer than we think?

Back when we were filming the programme, we were aware of its potential to cause alarm, and so planned to carry out our American mission in a sensible, low-key manner. We informed both British and US Customs exactly what we were proposing to do. The briefcase was thoroughly inspected at Heathrow Airport and again when we arrived in New York.

Understandably, perhaps, the New York authorities – from the Mayor's office to the civil defence department – refused to meet us. Unfortunately, the story of what we had brought with us and our exploits in Moscow had been picked up and sensationalised by several New York radio stations.

We eluded the resulting posse of reporters and headed down to Washington DC to interview Bob Kupperman, a former US National Security Adviser, who examined the briefcase's extremely realistic contents and exclaimed: "My God. This could be my worst nightmare coming true!" A chilling comment, I thought, from the man who was once the chief scientist for the American side in the SALT Two disarmament talks. He went on to repeat the public warnings he had previously delivered – but which he felt had been ignored – that the ready availability of relatively small amounts of nuclear material on the black market would ultimately give the terrorists the power they had wanted for so long.

And there, on his desk, sat an accurate replica of a nuclear bomb – small enough to fit into a briefcase but, if deployed from the top of a skyscraper, still big enough to devastate much of Manhattan.

When news of our visit to New York surfaced in Britain, prior to the broadcast, we were lambasted by *The Sun*, which accused me of being 'irresponsible and naïve' for trying to 'sneak' the 'dirty bomb' into the US with me. This really annoyed me. We had moved heaven and earth to avoid scaring people. We informed all the authorities in Britain and the USA and, after all, we were making a very valid point, given our Russian findings. After its UK transmission, the programme was rebroadcast in a peak time slot on American network television.

I insisted that Central complained about the *Sun* article to the paper's then editor, Kelvin MacKenzie. Our press department advised against it. "If you cross *The Sun*, they'll never give you publicity again – not good publicity anyway," they warned.

I insisted, however, and, some weeks later, an apology appeared in the paper, printed as prominently as the original, condemnatory article. And, despite the fears of the Central Television press department, when we broadcast the first programme about the terrorist activities of Martin McGuinness a few weeks after that, *The Sun* described me as a 'national hero'. This was one 'national hero' who was ready to lie down and sleep for a year.

Frances was becoming increasingly unhappy with what I was doing. It was bad enough that team members had twice been beaten up on location recently, but to have been potentially exposed to deadly radiation led to a kind of nagging worry at the back of my mind which never quite went away again. But if I had been in the wars during that series, so too had Peter Salkeld. He was hoping to repeat the success of the programme Steve Warr had produced on illegal dealing in endangered species of birds. He had been told by friends at the RSPB about the systematic theft of wild falcon eggs in Scotland. The gang responsible apparently sold the chicks on to wealthy Arabs who trained them for hunting.

Peregrines are a rare, protected species and it is a criminal offence to take them or their eggs from the wild. Unfortunately there is a widely-held belief in the world of falconry that wild birds make the best hunters. Consequently, they are highly sought after. A single stolen egg can be worth in excess of £1,000.

The RSPB had pinpointed a nest site in the Scottish Highlands that was regularly robbed of its falcon's eggs every year. The society tried hard to keep an eye on the location but round-the-clock surveillance was beyond its means. However, it was certainly not beyond Salk's. He and a researcher pitched camp just inside the tree-line at around 1,500 feet above sea level. From a makeshift hide near their tiny, two-man tent, they could get a good view of the nest, perched high up on a rocky outcrop.

For 13 days, Salk watched the female falcon sitting on her clutch of eggs, undisturbed. He and the researcher spent the days together and took it in turns to slip quietly back to the local hotel for a much-needed shower and a comfortable bed for the night. The pair of them lived mostly on baked beans, tinned meat and malt whisky.

Just as he was starting to think that this falcon brood would actually hatch and survive in the wild, Salk saw something moving across the top of the escarpment. A human figure. Salk quickly turned to his camera, mounted permanently on its tripod for just such an occasion. He ran the tape as a man in his twenties with long hair tied back in a ponytail clambered carefully down to the nest.

He opened a flap at the front of his jacket and reached down into the nest. One by one, he carefully picked up the eggs and placed them in specially-made pockets inside his jacket – to keep them warm until he could get them somewhere safe.

A few days later, after the RSPB and local mountaineers arrived to check the eggs really had all been stolen, Salk tried to film the robbed nest. Disaster struck. One of his fellow climbers accidentally knocked a rock off the edge of the clifftop. It hit Salk, who wasn't wearing a safety helmet, on the top of his skull. He was hauled to safety, his head and clothing soaked in blood.

We eventually traced the stolen eggs to an unscrupulous Belgian dealer called Michel Martello. A specialist in rare bird eggs, he would carefully incubate them and then sell on the newly-hatched chicks to wealthy Arabs for as much as £15,000 each. We wanted to expose him, so we arranged a meeting between him and a potential Middle Eastern customer – a fake sheikh, aka Roger Cook.

For nearly four hours, a make-up artist and a wardrobe specialist worked to transform me from an overweight television presenter into an overweight member of the Saudi Arabian Royal Family. By the time they had finished, I hardly recognised myself. My skin looked realistically burnished; I sported a wonderful dark, drooping moustache, an exotic beard and I was attired in full headdress and djellaba. For the first time in the series, I was actually enjoying myself. I suppose it was probably relief that for once it was unlikely that my doorstep would result in a beating from an angry mob or expose me to dangerous radioactive material.

The meeting took place in the penthouse suite of one of London's more exclusive hotels. The mood was relaxed, expansive and obviously confidence-building. The scene was observed from every angle by miniature cameras concealed in lamps, picture frames and even in the keyhole of an antique bureau. In fact, we'd used this suite several times before and for the sake of convenience, the tiny cameras remained in situ in our absence – though de-activated, of course.

Leaning back in his ample armchair, the bird bandit was eventually led to boast: "I'm so good at what I do, that I'll never be caught, you know."

"Well, you just have been," came the inevitable response.

I was right. There was no violence, just an exquisite expression of shock and disbelief on Martello's face when I told him that I wasn't a sheikh, but a television reporter who had captured his every criminal move on film. Six months of painstaking work had come to a very satisfactory end. I felt so good that I was tempted to spend the rest of the day in my disguise and have a bit more fun. Martello later fled the country, but will be arrested if he ever tries to enter the UK again, the Scottish egg thief we had caught on camera went to prison and the programme presaged more vigorous enforcement of the law on the trafficking of endangered species.

While the team was scattered round the world, quite a lot was going on at Central's Birmingham headquarters in 1995. It wasn't long since the company had renewed its licence. By dint of skilled financial poker playing against other potential bidders, it had secured the licence for a payment to government of just £2,000. In other parts of the country, successful franchise bidders had paid tens of millions – more than their licences were worth, according to some.

Central was sitting on a pile of unspent money when the government relaxed the rules on the ownership of commercial television franchises and our employers were swiftly taken over. Most of the staff, including very senior figures, like Deputy Managing Director Bob Southgate, were taken by surprise. We had expected cash-rich

319

Central to be predator, rather than prey, and to have taken over Anglia, TVS and perhaps HTV. Instead, Central was sold to Carlton, the new London licence-holder – one of those said to have overpaid.

However, taking over Central, who'd paid only £2,000 for their licence, effectively halved the cost of Carlton's bid. Unfortunately, they were very different companies and there was bound to be a culture clash. Central had a proud record of producing programmes itself, whereas Carlton simply bought in its programmes from independent production companies. While this unexpected upheaval came as a bolt out of the blue for us, a cynic might say that it did no harm at all to the bank balances of the privileged few who orchestrated it.

One of the few new recruits at this troubled time was our new in-house lawyer, a small but tenacious and highly principled man called Simon Westrop. As an ex-BBC person, he must have found the contrast a stark one. As an ex-BBC person myself, I understood. Simon also understood *The Cook Report* better than most, having been a journalist before he turned his very capable hands to the law. He was to share legal supervision of the programme with Peter Smith.

Central in Birmingham was then a very sad place, with far more people leaving through the revolving doors onto Broad Street than were coming in, and many of the former were clutching their redundancy cheques. It was a signal that the days of good living at ITV were over. The future was certainly leaner, and some people would venture, quite a lot meaner. It seemed that no one would ever forgive Carlton for taking the London franchise from the much-loved Thames Television, and we were suddenly the least popular of the ITV companies.

It wasn't particularly popular with many of its remaining employees either. The Birmingham studios were to be drastically downsized, and most productions, including ours, were to be moved to the company's newer, but much less convenient premises in Nottingham. Our continued success did offer us some protection, though. Ours was one of the very few programmes not to have its budget cut, so we could continue to make programmes covering difficult subjects on an international scale.

*

Some of those programmes were extraordinarily prescient, and none more so than one we called 'Terror in the Skies', which was broadcast in October 1996, almost five years before the attacks of September 11 2001 which levelled the twin towers of the World Trade Center, badly damaged the Pentagon, destroyed three civil airliners, and took 2,973 lives. Our investigations had exposed colossal flaws in airport security, particularly in the United States, and specifically at Boston's Logan Airport, which was to become the initial departure point for the 9/11 terrorists.

We also revealed, for the first time to a British audience, the sinister activities of Ramzi Yousef, a terrorist mastermind with close connections to Osama bin Laden – a shadowy figure who was then almost unknown. Yousef had advanced plans to bring down twelve American airliners over a two day period – and plotted to follow that by using a hijacked civil airliner loaded with explosives as a huge guided bomb.

We were prompted to make the programme by Dr Jim Swire, whose 23-year-old daughter Flora was amongst 270 innocent victims when a terrorist bomb brought down Pan Am flight 103 over Lockerbie in December 1988. Dr Swire subsequently became a spokesman for all the bereaved British relatives. He had run a small-scale test, successfully putting a realistic dummy bomb through the security systems at a couple of European airports. "You could do it on a much larger scale," he suggested, "and showing the results on a national TV show might embarrass the powers that be into improving airport security."

We thought the Doctor's diagnosis had merit, and we recruited him to help make a programme on airborne terrorism which would include the testing of security at randomly selected targets in Europe and the US. Jim's 'bombs' had used a harmless organic substance rather like nougat which explosives experts had said produced an X-ray image which was virtually identical to that of Semtex. This powerful, Czech-made plastic explosive was the terrorist's prime choice – just 400 grammes of it had been enough to destroy flight 103. So we also borrowed the idea for 'Doctor Swire's Semtex Substitute', as we came to call it. And, as the Lockerbie bombers had done with the real thing, we hid a lump of the substitute inside a portable radio/cassette player.

Our first test was to send a suitcase containing a mock Semtex bomb from Ancona in Italy, via Rome, to Gatwick. We checked the suitcase in at Ancona without any problems and then got off the plane in Rome, leaving a theoretically lethal package to continue undetected and unaccompanied on its way to Gatwick. It was ludicrously easy, and we had followed the same modus operandi as had the Lockerbie bombers – getting off the plane at a stop-over point and letting the bomb go on. Four years after the disaster, security seemed to be as lax as ever.

At about that time, Manchester Airport was promoting itself as 'voted the best in Europe', and boasting that it also had the tightest security. Being *The Cook Report*, we took this as a challenge. The airport's CTX X-ray equipment was then probably the most sophisticated in the world, so we went looking for another security weakness. Ignoring the relatively well-protected terminal buildings, researcher Brian Johnson-Thomas soon found one, and our concealed cameras recorded how – with barely a cursory glance from security staff – our unmarked van was waved through the perimeter gates and onto the airport apron alongside a number of aircraft being prepared for service. We then filmed the loading of a dummy bomb concealed in cans of jet engine oil onto one of those unprotected planes. Our unauthorised presence in a supposedly secure airside area was obvious, but amazingly, nobody took any notice.

When we showed them what we'd done, an extremely embarrassed airport management publicly thanked us for highlighting the security lapse – and then privately shot the messenger. The aircraft loader who'd helped us expose the airport's potential vulnerability had his security pass revoked and lost his job as a result. Fortunately he was soon re-employed elsewhere.

By the time we had finished filming, we had got our dummy bomb through X-ray and security procedures – more or less at will – in passenger terminals at no fewer than nine different airports on both sides of the Atlantic. In the United States, where 50 per cent of the world's air traffic originates, the security situation was clearly worse than it was in Europe. One of our easiest targets turned out to be one of the busiest, Los Angeles International, the airport identifying code for which is – appropriately enough in the circumstances – LAX.

Worst of all was Logan Airport in Boston, where Salk couldn't believe his eyes. "Take a look at that," he said incredulously as our dummy went through the X-ray scanner. The operator was facing away from his screen, with his feet on the adjacent desk, reading a copy of *Sports Illustrated*. And there were no proper checks at the boarding gate either. Salk got through without presenting his boarding card. In the event, he didn't take the USAir flight to Buffalo, but the dummy bomb did – once again unaccompanied and undetected. One wonders whether it was this abysmally low level of security which caused Mohamed Atta, the leader of the September 11 terrorists, to choose Logan as his departure point.

We sat around the dinner table in Boston that evening, ruminating over the amount of flying our jobs required. David Alford, suave, suntanned and possessed of a wardrobe to put the rest of us to shame, rather put a dampener on things. In researching the North American leg of the story, he had already flown the Atlantic twice and criss-crossed the States several times. "Tell you what," he said, draining his glass, "totting up the air miles is all very well, but the more you earn, the greater your chances of being hijacked or blown out of the sky." That reminded us just how vulnerable we all were as regular air travellers. My own tally over the previous three weeks had included flights to Spain, France, Germany, Northern Ireland, the United States, and various parts of Eastern Europe.

Meanwhile, in the Philippines, researcher Paul Calverley was hard at work on the trail of Ramzi Yousef, the man who three years earlier had led the first assault on the World Trade Center – the 1993 bombing which killed six people and injured over 1,000 – and was suspected of planning other terrorist attacks. In the confusion that followed his evil efforts in Manhattan, Yousef had made good his escape, via Pakistan, to Manila. That much was more or less public knowledge, but after an unofficial briefing from the local police, Calverley was able to take the story a good deal further. The crew and I were greeted with a barrage of new information when we flew in.

In January 1995, Yousef was forced to flee Manila after a neighbour had called the police because of the suspicious chemical smoke billowing from his sixth-floor apartment in the nondescript Doña Josefa apartment block, not far from the international airport. He'd probably chosen the location for its easy access, and because it was the kind of place where 'professional ladies' rented rooms by the hour, so frequent comings and goings were not noticed. Having successfully eluded the police, Yousef sent his boyhood friend, Abdul Hakim Murad, to retrieve his Toshiba laptop, but Murad was arrested in the attempt.

Filming in apartment 603 was rather eerie. It was so very ordinary, yet such extraordinary plans for destruction had been hatched there. The flat had become a bomb factory, in which Yousef and Murad had made a large quantity of TATP liquid explosive – then a relatively new compound which was highly effective, difficult to detect and made of readily available chemicals like hydrogen peroxide. We now know it was also used by the London 7/7 suicide bombers.

Yousef had stockpiled more than enough TATP for his next project. He called it Project Bojinka – 'bojinka' apparently being the Serbo-Croat word for 'explosion'. From the records and documents he left behind, mostly on his laptop, it was clear that Yousef was planning to bring down a dozen American jumbo jets in a 48-hour period. The computer contained a carefully plotted schedule, based on the timetables of Continental, United and North West airlines, to blow up the selected aircraft over the Pacific – en route to Los Angeles, San Francisco, Honolulu and New York – and kill as many as 4,000 passengers.

Yousef and his accomplices were just days away from putting their plan into action. Only the fire in apartment 603 gave them away. In fact, they'd already staged a couple of rehearsals. Two incidents, for which the police initially had no suspects, now came into focus.

The first was the blowing up of a Manila cinema – using home-made TATP. The second was the bombing of Philippine Airlines flight 434, a Boeing 747 en route from Manila to Tokyo. Yousef had assembled a small explosive device in one of the lavatories before concealing it under seat 26K, and then leaving the plane at an intermediate stop. When this 'micro-bomb' was detonated by a digital timer several hours later, the unlucky passenger occupying the seat was literally blown in half, and a jagged hole was torn in the floor of the aircraft, damaging the control systems beneath. Fortunately, the pilot was able to keep the aircraft flying long enough to make a safe emergency landing at Okinawa. After this test run, as recorded on his computer, Yousef decided to increase the power of his micro-bombs by a factor of ten.

In the course of his researches, Calverley had met and befriended Manila's ebullient Police Chief, Hermogenes E. Ebdane

Jr. As filming progressed, Hermogenes invited us to chat over lunch at his Headquarters, a sprawling, blue and white painted low-rise building on a hill overlooking the city. He had told Calverley of the many excellent local restaurants that he was wont to patronise, and extolled the quality and variety of their cuisine. As a result, Calverley had us salivating in the belief that an exotic feast lay in store.

When we arrived, it was laid out on a circular table in the anteroom of his office, covered over in crisp, white linen. Beaming broadly, Hermogenes said he'd got it in specially, and whipped off the coverlet. The feast was Kentucky Fried Chicken. We made up for it the next evening though, dining in a rather good, but ridiculously cheap quayside fish restaurant as the blood-red sun sank spectacularly into Manila Bay.

By contrast with Hermogenes' culinary surprise, the levels of access and co-operation we were offered did not disappoint – despite the fact that the authorities declined to be interviewed. The Police Chief continued to help as much as his political masters would allow, on the basis that as America's staunchest ally, Britain was also likely to be in the terrorist's sights. He believed that the British public should be made aware of the tactics being developed by Yousef and his associates – all of which involved targeting or hijacking transport systems – because the same tactics might well be used against us. Indeed, ten years on, as this book went to press, British security forces believed they'd foiled what appeared to be a carbon copy of Yousef's original conspiracy – this time aimed at trans-Atlantic, rather than trans-Pacific flights.

Ten years back, the terrorist's personal computer records had been made available to us – and they'd had much more to reveal, including plans to assassinate Pope John Paul II and President Clinton, together with another audacious, aircraft-based plot. Unfortunately, something very like this last one was eventually implemented. Yousef's hard drive contained what could well have been the template for the previously unimaginable carnage of September 11.

Yousef had planned to hijack a civil airliner, load it with high explosives, and use a suicide pilot to crash it into the Central Intelligence Agency's Headquarters at Langley in Virginia. A number of other landmark targets were under consideration after that. Fortuitously, by then Yousef had been betrayed by an informer and arrested in Pakistan. He was subsequently extradited to the United States, where he was eventually convicted for his part in the 1993 World Trade Center bombing and gaoled for 240 years. His friend Abdul Hakim Murad, already in custody, later confessed to the FBI that he had taken his pilot's licence in order to be able to fly that plane into the CIA HQ. "Bloody hell," said Calverley, "I'm glad they've got the bastards now – that would have been horrific. Mind you, they'll not have been the only fanatics out there."

That was a sentiment echoed in the programme by terrorist expert Professor Paul Wilkinson of the University of St Andrews, who emphasised that there was no reason for complacency: "Despite the outrage of Lockerbie and all the rhetoric of governments promising to install proper airline security, the airlines are still vulnerable to the hijacker and the sabotage bomber." While events might have forced the authorities into recognising that airlines were now under threat, he was unconvinced that they were taking action commensurate with the gravity of that threat.

Leading American security consultant and futurologist Marvin Cetron agreed, and predicted that the situation would get a lot worse: "Terrorism is theatre," he said. "It's always got to be bigger than it was before. Taking down one airplane is no big deal any more. What's being done now [in terms of improving security] is too little, too late – it will not stop the determined terrorist of the future." Cetron was also worried that the widespread disruption and considerable costs involved in beefing up airline security might result in commercial and political pressures to cut corners.

The apparent lack of official action was also the likely reason that we got no official interview in the Philippines. All the information Hermogenes Ebdane and his colleagues had gleaned five years previously was promptly passed to the CIA, but they had been left with the clear impression that the Americans doubted their investigative abilities. Furthermore, senior officials stateside initially thought Yousef's plans were – quite literally – incredible, and that in any case his computer files were unlikely to be admissible as evidence in court. The net result seems to have been that they did not then take the threat Yousef and his kind posed seriously enough. The Filipinos certainly had. Security at Manila's Ninoy Aquino Airport was rather more thorough than anything we'd found in our travels around America.

However, by 1996, it was obviously felt that giving us an interview which, in the circumstances, would implicitly criticise the United States, might be taken amiss and spark a diplomatic incident with the Philippines' biggest benefactor. Yousef was still awaiting trial in New York, and it was taking an inordinate amount of time to marshal the evidence against him. For no apparent reason, the Justice Department and the FBI seemed to have restricted the flow of information to the security services.

This sad state of affairs was later to be confirmed by the US Attorney General, John Ashcroft, who in testimony to the National Commission on Terrorist attacks upon the United States (otherwise known as the 9/11 Commission) said that: "for nearly a decade, our government blinded itself to our enemies." He went on to suggest that legal and other constraints prevented key agencies from working together properly and taking effective action.

The FBI and the CIA responded by claiming that the Attorney General had starved them of resources and information. But at the time of Yousef's arrest, and without the benefit of hindsight, the authorities may simply have felt that his capture, along with 30 of his cohorts, had put an end to any imminent threat.

Our researches showed that too would have been a serious mistake. The al-Qaeda connections turned out to be astonishing. Yousef was apparently a graduate in chemical engineering from Swansea University, who also used the name of a recently deceased fellow student called Abdul Basit Karim, together with several other aliases. At one time he was thought to be an Iraqi agent, but he also had close ties with Muslim militants in Pakistan, where he had lived in a house then owned by Osama bin Laden. Although, of course, bin Laden had not achieved international notoriety by the time our programme was broadcast, he was already a wanted terrorist, and had declared a *jihad* against the United States two months previously.

Yousef had shared his Manila flat with Hakim Abdul Murad and bin Laden's brother-in-law, Mohammed Khalifa. Another disturbing connection, which came to light shortly after the programme, was that Yousef turned out to be the nephew of Khalid Shaikh Mohammed, who also lived in Manila at the time. Using money channelled from bin Laden, Mohammed financed and encouraged Yousef and friends – and later, as the head of al-Qaeda's military committee, became the alleged mastermind of the September 11 attacks*. If, five years before those attacks, we could collect and collate so much obviously significant information about Yousef's terrorist ambitions and connections, surely the security services could have done at least as well – and perhaps have been in a better position to avert the worst terrorist attack the world had ever seen.

Following our programme, but still well before 9/11, one of the American Federal Aviation Authority's most senior counter-terrorism officers, Bogdan Dzakovic, had his team run their own covert tests at a number of US airports. They used not only dummy bombs as we had done, but also potential gunmen and suicide pilots. He regularly reported the alarming results to his bosses, and having got no response, he blew the whistle: "We were extraordinarily successful in 'killing' large numbers of innocent people in these simulated attacks. We breached security with frightening ease – around 90 percent of the time, but the FAA suppressed our warnings. Instead, we were ordered not to write up our reports and not to retest particularly vulnerable airports to see if the problems had been fixed. Finally, the agency started providing advance notification of when we would be conducting our 'undercover' tests and what we would be checking. Surprise, surprise: the airports started passing the tests and the FAA praised their progress. In other words, the government was unwilling to go beyond maintaining appearances. It was unwilling to back up the test results with measures that would disrupt the politically powerful air carriers."

Mr Dzakovic was subsequently demoted to a junior clerical job in the organization that has absorbed the FAA, the Transportation Security Administration, and was threatened with criminal prosecution for having had the temerity to go public with his concerns. None of his recommendations were followed.

The 9/11 Commission, which finally reported in July 2004, concluded that the disaster 'could and should have been prevented' and laid the blame firmly on the failings of the FBI and the CIA. The necessary intelligence had been available to both organisations, but as one committee member put it: "They conspicuously

---

* Eighteen months after 9/11, Khalid Shaikh Mohammed was arrested in Pakistan – as Yousef had been before him – and extradited to the US, where he was said to have co-operated with the authorities. He was subsequently indicted on numerous terrorism-related charges, and when last heard of, he was held at Guantanamo Bay, pending some form of trial.

failed to join up all the dots." Despite this, as of September 2006, none of the Commission's recommendations had been implemented either.

"We have to make the most of our intelligence and stop the spread of terrorism – even if we have to fight dirty, like they do," concluded Marvin Cetron back in 1995, adding prophetically: "If we don't, it's going to be horrendous – because ever more devastating attacks are only a matter of time." Sadly, he was right a decade ago, and with al-Qaeda using the fifth anniversary of 9/11 to threaten more and larger attacks, he's probably still right today. He is also not alone in believing that those who govern us have let us down – and that by default, our politicians have contrived to hinder, rather than help, progress towards a safer world.

An interesting sidelight is that during the making of the programme we had negotiated to buy a retired Boeing 707, with which to demonstrate the effects of an airborne explosion, but none was available in our time scale. However, in another programme, we were able to show the horrific destructive power of a terrorist bomb on a suburban train – using crash dummies, redundant carriages, a professional armourer and a quantity of high explosives, the latter illegally acquired with worrying ease.

Looking back nearly ten years after the transmission of 'Terror in the Skies', Dr Jim Swire, the man who prompted us to make the programme, thought it was 'an extraordinary foretelling of an avoidable disaster'. It angered him that, had the authorities taken proper notice of the information contained in it, and also that passed on to the CIA from other sources, 9/11 could possibly have been prevented.

In April 2003, some 15 years after the downing of Pan Am Flight 103, the Libyan government finally admitted responsibility for the actions of its agents – and subsequently agreed a three-stage process to pay compensation to relatives which could amount to £6.3 million per victim.

Dr Jim Swire's reaction mirrored that of all the bereaved UK relatives: "Paying the money is all very well, but it doesn't bring back our loved ones. This is nothing more than a politically convenient deal which will allow sanctions against Libya to be lifted." The Libyan Prime Minister, Shukri Ghanhem later admitted as much, claiming that his country had no involvement in the Lockerbie disaster, but had paid compensation 'simply to buy peace'.

Dr Swire was disgusted. He believes that the politicians have let down the surviving families too. "This is a totally cynical arrangement in which the relatives have been left on the sidelines. The truth about what happened to Flight 103 has yet to come out, and until it does, those we have lost cannot rest in peace."

8

In the Can

*The cot death controversy, illegal commercial fishing,
illegal big game hunting and doctors from hell*

It is one of my life's ironies that, after having so many bones broken, so many blows to the head and other parts of my body – mostly in the line of duty – that my career almost came to a premature end courtesy of a little old lady in a blue rinse and a red Ford Fiesta.

After a long day's filming, not long before the programme decamped to Nottingham, Frank Thorne was driving us back to base as I dozed fitfully in the front passenger seat. We had just come to a halt at the rear of the semi-permanent traffic jam on the M6 at Birmingham, when there was a terrific grinding thump from behind us and the boot of the car ended up where the back seat ought to be. Waking up with a jolt, I knew straight away that once more something nasty had happened to my neck – and it was more than just whiplash.

I was in agony and phoned the office, where one of the team called an ambulance and the police. Meanwhile, from the stationary queue of cars, a lady in a smart blue uniform presented herself. On the grass by the hard shoulder, she proceeded to examine the shocked elderly lady driver whose demolished Fiesta now sat astride the central barrier. Fortunately, she was found to be unhurt and was asked if there was anyone she needed to speak to. She nodded that there was, and my mobile phone was snatched from my hand and given to the old dear, who then had a protracted conversation about how she didn't think she would make it to that weekend's bowls match.

By this time, the police had got the traffic moving again and an ambulance had arrived. One of the paramedics saw me leaning against a post, head tilted awkwardly to one side. Making a politically incorrect assumption, he said to the lady in blue: "Nurse, shouldn't you be looking at this chap now?"

"I'm not a bloody nurse, I'm a doctor," came the sharp reply, as she took umbrage and then her leave, stomping off down the hard shoulder.

My regular production driver, Declan Smythe, had overheard my call to the office, and had now turned up to see if he could help. I told the ambulance crew that as I was still upright and alive, if it was all right with them, I'd rather go with Declan. He drove me gently back to Central TV's headquarters, where the horrified duty sister had him take me straight on to Birmingham General Hospital.

They agreed with my amateur diagnosis that something dire had happened to my neck. In order to prevent further damage and until I could be seen by a specialist, I spent the night sandbagged and unable to move, on a steel plate in the casualty department. It was a long night, enlivened by the kind of strange behaviour you only find in hard-pressed, inner-city hospitals.

A man with a gaping wound in his arm kept coming in to have it stitched and dressed. He would then go out into the car park, undo all the good work and come back in again. A large West Indian lady chased a ginger-headed intern through my cubicle several times, accusing him – surreally, and at the top of her voice – of being a cannibal.

In the morning, the scanner I was supposed to have been examined under had broken down, so an ambulance was called to take me to a sister hospital some miles away in order to use their facilities. For some reason, no ambulance was available. Had I, perhaps, offended the crew from the previous evening? Eventually, strapped into a Meccano neck collar, I went by taxi, only to find that the second scanner was also inoperative due to lack of funds for routine maintenance.

I went private.

The specialist at The Priory Hospital got me an MRI scan almost immediately and, two days later, I was told that it was time to consider retirement – or suffer the consequences. A full examination of the Cook body had come up with a number of worrying malfunctions. My blood pressure was too high, I had a kidney

332

problem which they said probably resulted from having previously contracted dengue fever and malaria simultaneously – and the latest injury to my neck had aggravated all the previous damage it had suffered over the years. The specialist said my job was plainly wearing me out and recommended that I call it a day.

I didn't want to rush into any decisions, so, first things first; I let Townson and Bob Southgate know what the prognosis and advice were. Series Ten was due to start in production in a few weeks time, and they got it postponed for two months. I went home to Frances and Belinda to rest.

For the next few weeks, I agonised. Frances, I knew, deep down, would rather I did call it a day. As I swallowed the painkillers and lay down gingerly on my bed at night, I could see her point of view. Meanwhile, the rest of the team kept on working and the producers kept me up to date on how the stories were progressing.

As I recovered I was, for once, able to take a detached view of *The Cook Report*. I thought about what we had achieved, and what we still wanted to achieve. I thought about my fallings-out with Mike Townson and, yet, how together we still managed to bring out programmes of which we could all be proud. I wondered how long my battered frame would allow me to continue. I was still walking wounded, but I now felt I wasn't alone. I also worried about Townson's ebbing stamina and general poor state of health.

Then there was the team to consider, some of whom had stuck with me through thick and thin. They were an amazing bunch of journalists and film-makers. We had our disagreements too, but that was only natural given such a diverse collection of characters. They worked hard and played hard. There was no such thing as an eight-hour day or a five-day week. Everyone pulled together to get the job done, then they all laid down wherever they were to recover. But even then, the journalism carried on – contacts would ring in, the odd dossier would appear from mysterious sources, stories in newspapers sparked new ideas for another series.

If I stopped, so would *The Cook Report*. It was a simple fact. The team would find other jobs, of course, but there was nothing out there quite like what we did. We were all comfortable with the format. We knew instinctively what the right kind of story was for 'a Cook' – how the evidence should be marshalled, where the stings and the doorsteps fitted in, why some stories were important and others commonplace.

Six weeks later, the doctors gave me a partial clean bill of health. I had to have intensive physiotherapy, take courses of tablets and, above all, 'take it easy'. Not possible. I told Frances that we needed a plan. What I really meant was – let's try and work out how much longer I'm going to keep on doing this, and then you and I can look forward to riding off into the sunset together. Another three years – maybe four – we agreed. I went back to work – but carefully. Waiting for me there was the news that the elderly lady in the errant Fiesta had been convicted of driving without due care and attention – and had decided to hand in her licence.

We made national headlines with the first programme of the autumn series. In it, we had detailed scientific work carried out by a senior chemical analyst on a possible cause of Sudden Infant Death Syndrome (SIDS), otherwise known as cot death. We didn't claim to have found the definitive cause of cot death, but we did think that an investigation by the eminent consulting scientist, Dr Barry Richardson, was worth reporting.

In the course of trying to find out how to stop mildew appearing on marquees manufactured by a friend of his, Richardson had found that the fire retardant used in the material could produce noxious gases if it mixed with other elements.

Thinking laterally, he turned his attention to infant mattresses – which were routinely impregnated with the same rather worrying fire-retardant chemicals – such as antimony and phosphorus compounds. He carried out tests that seemed to show that if urine seeped from a baby's nappy into the fire retardant in the mattress, the chemical reaction that followed would cause a thin surface layer of poisonous gas to form over it. The theory was, if the infant was sleeping face down, he or she might well inhale something akin to nerve gas and simply stop breathing.

Our scientific advisers obtained tissue samples taken from babies who had died of SIDS. The levels of antimony in some were several thousand times the normal and acceptable reading. Similarly, they tested for levels of antimony in the hair of living infants who were using the suspect mattresses. Again, the readings were generally extremely high.

The public reaction to the first programme was amazing. Within hours, we had received 10,000 calls from worried parents. We hadn't scaremongered and we made no blanket claims to have solved the mystery of SIDS, but what parents everywhere wanted to know was where they could buy mattresses without these dubious fire retardants. Baby bedding manufacturers switched production to natural fibre mattresses at top speed. The big stores sold out of 'safe' stocks in hours. Interestingly, it emerged that Mothercare had reservations about these chemicals and had not used them for some time, despite government advice that they should.

A second programme was required to update the first. Townson and Salk, the producer, moved into top gear, giving themselves just a fortnight to put together the follow-up. Two days before broadcast, Graham Puntis sat in his video-edit suite waiting for Townson. The boss had been specific – he wanted Puntis to come in first thing, because there was a lot to do. By mid-morning, there was still no sign of Townson. This was unheard of. When the job needed doing, he was always there.

Then a telephone call came through to Pat Harris. Mike Townson had been found unconscious at home that morning. He had suffered a severe brain haemorrhage and was seriously ill. He would undergo a life-saving operation later in the day. The shock was terrific. None of us could imagine *The Cook Report* without Mike Townson. He'd been there from the start and, like him or loathe him, he had been instrumental in the programme's success. As we all waited for news from the hospital, the realisation dawned that we still had a programme to produce and broadcast in less than 48 hours' time.

The man who stepped into the breach was Mike Morley. A fast-track manager at Central, his star was in the ascendant. Still only in his mid-thirties, he was head of the Factual Programme Department and was technically Townson's boss. Although a department head, Morley's roots lay in hands-on programme making. He had made an award-winning film about the kidnap from hospital and eventual safe return of newborn baby Abbie Humphreys earlier in the year. Privately, he told colleagues that he would love to be editor of *The Cook Report*. Now, although it was none of his making, he had his chance.

Morley looked at the script notes and tapes Townson had been working on. As was always the case with Townson productions, they made little sense to anyone other than Townson himself. Even Puntis, who was well-versed in his way of working, could shed no light on how the editor had envisaged this second programme on cot death. Morley called in Salk and his researcher, David Alford. It now made sense to allow the men who knew the subject best to put the programme together.

The two men worked right through the night with Puntis, so that when Morley and I arrived in the morning we had a sensible structure available from which to script and fashion a finished programme. We then all worked through the following night and completed the programme, in traditional *Cook Report* style, barely half an hour before transmission.

Townson had survived his first operation but was still very ill. The surgeons were worried that he might suffer a second haemorrhage. All the years of heavy smoking hadn't helped. We all wished him well and waited to see how he progressed.

Morley stayed on as a temporary editor, working closely with me, until the end of the series. To his credit, he sought no recognition himself, leaving Townson's name as editor on the end of every programme.

Slowly, Townson started to improve and was considered well enough to take visitors. But even that was not without problems and there were some embarrassing scenes at his bedside. Bob Southgate had likened Townson's private life to a French farce in which everybody had to keep picking up their clothes and hiding in wardrobes until the coast was clear. Suffice it to say that a number of close friends and relatives – some unknown to each other – turned up to see Townson and the resulting encounters led the nursing staff to impose a strict visiting rota to avoid further trouble.

You had to take your hat off to the man; through all his travails, Townson maintained his unique sense of humour. On one of my visits, I found him surveying himself in a hand mirror. Indicating his partly shaven head, he enquired: "Do you like the haircut Roger?" I was about to come up with something diplomatically non-committal when Townson pre-empted me. "I think it's amazing," he said with a grin, "They did it from the inside, you know." The operation may have slowed his speech, but it certainly hadn't slowed his wit.

*

336

The two cot death programmes provoked a storm in the medical and scientific professions. Such are the politics of medical research that some of those who preferred different theories for the origins of SIDS decided to turn on *The Cook Report*. I suspect rival researchers may have thought their funding was at risk. Yet we had made no case for rejecting any of the other possible causes – parental smoking or babies sleeping face down, for example.

However, like Dr Richardson, we found it strange – and undesirable – that very high levels of the toxic chemicals contained in the fire retardants used in many baby mattresses were being found in post-mortem tissue samples taken from cot death victims. Similarly worrying levels could also be found in hair samples taken from living babies who had also used the suspect mattresses.

After all the fuss, the government invited Lady Limerick to hold an enquiry into the scientific findings we had aired. Two years later, she reported that her scientists had been unable to recreate the conditions under which Barry Richardson had first detected the presence of poisonous gases. But they had not tested post-mortem tissue of SIDS victims, where independent scientists – unconnected with Richardson, but working for us – *had* found alarming levels of potentially lethal poisons. So, even if Richardson's theory for the transfer of these substances from mattress to baby was wrong, such a transfer had definitely taken place.

A cynic might say that the government had shackled the enquiry. If the antimony theory was upheld, the government could have been faced with huge compensation claims, because it was on their advice that these chemicals had been used in mattress manufacture in the first place.

Dr Richardson's staunchest supporter through all this had been an eminent New Zealand scientist called Dr Jim Sprott. After the programme, he began a campaign back home to persuade parents to wrap their children's mattresses in polythene. This effectively blocked the process – whatever it was – that transferred toxic chemicals to sleeping babies. In New Zealand, his 'Cot Life' campaign was a great success.

At the time of writing, and in what would seem to be empirical proof that Richardson was largely right, in the last eight years there has not been one single cot death in New Zealand amongst babies – now the vast majority – sleeping on covered mattresses.

Britain can't claim such a good record. However, it remains an undeniable fact that since our programmes, mattresses using suspect fire retardants are no longer sold, and there has been a further significant drop in deaths from Sudden Infant Death Syndrome – over and above that achieved by the very worthwhile 'Back to Sleep' campaign.

From time to time, the younger members of the team lobbied for us to tackle more subjects of particular interest to their generation. Sometimes they urged us to 'lighten up' as well. Newly-promoted producer David Warren succeeded on both fronts, when he brought in a story about dodgy goings-on in the record industry. Over the years, tales of chart rigging had been so common as to appear apocryphal. But Warren insisted it was still going on – and what's more, he could do it.

However, it wasn't going to be easy. The charts were compiled from sales at a surprisingly small panel of 'chart return' record shops. Those who rigged the charts had obtained the list and bought back their own records from the shops on the panel. A relatively modest number of sales at the right outlets had a disproportionately positive effect on the chart position of the record concerned. With a little bit of luck we managed to acquire the chart return list too. That was the least difficult bit. We also needed a record of our own, good enough to gain acceptance but bad enough to make our point; that it could never have succeeded without a little help from its friends.

Finding a producer turned out not to be as troublesome as we had feared. Mike Stock, of Stock, Aitken and Waterman fame, was already on record (as it were) decrying the practice of chart-hyping, which he thought distorted the market and was often a barrier to real talent. Mike was highly regarded in the music industry and had more hits to his name than did the Beatles. He thought long and hard about our request and then agreed to help us and to choose a suitable song.

We then had to find ourselves a performer and a cooperative record company – and that took quite a time. We found the latter in the form of a respected independent label called Gotham Records, owned by Barry Tomes, the man who once managed Alvin Stardust and Lulu. The former we eventually found right under our noses in the person of trainee journalist Debbie Currie, daughter of the high-profile ex-government minister, Edwina. In fact, both women agreed to be part of our little scenario.

Mike Stock rang to say that he'd selected a song. Debbie would record a new version of a number three chart hit from 1973 called *You Can Do Magic*. We all trooped down to his London recording studios on what looked and felt rather like a successful school outing. Debbie gave the trial recording her all, but Mike's first assessment of her performance went something like this: 'Looks good, moves well, but can't sing. No problem.'

Using all his considerable talents, Mike proved he could do magic with less than top-notch material, eventually producing a respectable, if repetitive toe-tapper. Meantime, we had engaged the services of a professional promotion company – the same one used by the Manic Street Preachers – and a specialist sales operation, neither of which knew what we were really up to. We'd secretly filmed the sales boss explaining how to hype the charts, though he did have some unintentionally apt words of warning for us. "You've got to be careful," he said. "You don't want that Roger Cook on your back, do you?"

Nevertheless, he took the risk, sending out a team of 30 salesmen to help rig the sales of our record – and we filmed some of them doing it. In the right shops, they bought back the records our promotional team had just delivered, thereby artificially boosting the returns to the British Phonographic Industry (BPI), the umbrella body which arranges for the charts to be compiled. It certainly worked, and in less than 36 hours *You Can Do Magic* reached number 86 in the top 100, and appeared to be heading fast for the top 40.

All this had gone hand in hand with a big promotional push in the media, which lapped it up. Debbie and Edwina gave more than 70 press and radio interviews and appeared on *GMTV, Richard and Judy* and *The Big Breakfast*. They were absolutely brilliant as the proud mother and the ambitious daughter. I'll always remember Edwina hamming it up on the couch with a smile like a Cheshire cat. I imagine she adopted it in lieu of a straight face.

The tabloid newspapers in particular loved Debbie. Several of them got her to do photo shoots for them, and it was all too easy for her to get a little bit carried away. As a result, she appeared one morning spread across the centre pages of the *Daily Star* wearing nothing but a couple of fried eggs to preserve her dignity. Our editor hastily rang her with a diplomatic reminder that she was representing *The Cook Report* and should maintain a degree of decorum. Debbie was mortified. You may recall that eggs were also involved in some of Edwina's more embarrassing public moments.

We hired a choreographer to work out a dance routine for Debbie and a top director to shoot a video. Debbie threw herself into all this pop-star stuff with such enthusiasm that she almost convinced me she was the real deal. She mimed her way through a gruelling promotional tour of pubs and clubs – quite an achievement for someone who, by her own admission, still couldn't sing or dance. It was turning into such an enjoyable romp that we decided to run it over two programmes instead of one.

Those who were taken in by the whole thing shouldn't be criticised for it though, because they were faced with a slickly promoted record, produced by one of the best names in the business and featuring the glamorous daughter of a former high-profile government minister. It was meant to be an attractive proposition and it clearly was. More secret filming gave us the inside information on the huge discounts and free CDs demanded by the big retailers just to stock a record, and revealing footage of a tame retailer swiping singles into the electronic returns system without actually selling any.

Slap bang in the middle of our investigation came the General Election – the one in which Tony Blair and New Labour swept the board. Safe Tory seats tumbled all over the country, amongst them, South Derbyshire, long held by Edwina Currie. It must have been a huge personal blow for her, but seasoned pro that she is, even while conceding defeat on live television, she still managed to think of a way of promoting our programme: "At least I'll have more time now to concentrate on my daughter's pop career," she told her audience.

As our record continued to rise inexorably – and having shown how we'd made this happen – we decided that in order to distance ourselves from the real riggers, now was the time to pull the plug on our efforts and confess to what we'd done. By this stage, our dodgy sales team had bought back just 400 copies of our record out of a planned total of 2,000. If we had allowed things to run their normal course, we were told that we almost certainly would have ended up with a Top 40 hit on our hands. Chart manipulation was that simple.

When pushed in an interview, the Director General of the BPI, John Deacon, admitted: "We are aware that there are buying-in teams around and that it is seriously affecting the whole integrity of the charts." – a statement he later tried to downplay, post broadcast. He must have been more than a little disconcerted by what we'd been able to demonstrate on screen. Mind you, there was a lot of money at stake. The record industry in the UK alone turns over around £5 billion every year.

After the first programme was transmitted, the industry was in uproar. There were howls of indignation once we'd revealed the hoax. Nobody likes to be hoodwinked, but isn't that what manipulating the charts was doing to the record-buying public? Those caught out on camera protested their innocence so long and so hard we began to doubt their grip on reality. But there were a few notable voices raised in our support. There was Paul Gambaccini – pop's elder statesman, and Bruno Brookes – who for years presented the chart show on Radio One. But our most surprising backer was Noel Gallagher of Oasis, who managed to be both upfront and downbeat when he told us: "I don't see what anybody can do about chart rigging when the people who police the charts are also the people who run the record labels."

However, these voices of support were soon swamped by the unedifying sounds of an embarrassed industry closing ranks. Senior executives hoed into *You Can Do Magic*, declaring it a 'rubbish record', as if that proved their case. All it proved was our point; that it wasn't good enough to chart on its own merits. They said we clearly didn't know much about the record industry. Relatively speaking, this was true, but they certainly didn't like us telling the public what we did know. A pre-emptive attack was mounted on the second programme, in which it was obvious that more highly paid people would be seen making fools of themselves.

Then, as it so often does, it turned personal. I was dismissed as 'that self-important, over-lunched journalist', as if size meant I wasn't up to the job. The size was blindingly obvious, but had nothing to do with the quality of my journalism or that of *The Cook Report* team, most of whom were not overweight. In the midst of all this hoo-ha there were several diary pieces along similar lines, one of which was written by someone with whom I used to work.

341

It should be said that this chap had a good mind, but precious little body to go with it. He'd have had difficulty getting wet in the shower. So I seized the opportunity to make my point in person. I rang him up to ask what connection he thought there was between size and journalistic ability – his or mine. To illustrate, I asked him to recall Orson Welles, a man who considerably outweighed me, but who was also one of the greatest film directors of all time. I thought the point had been taken and we parted on good terms. However, in his next column, following some merry mockery about thick waists and thin skins, he asked: "What's up with old Cookie these days? He used to be satisfied just being the Taped Crusader, but now he thinks he's Orson Welles." You can't win, can you?

Times have changed rapidly for the record industry since those programmes. After years of price-fixing and chart-hyping, you could argue that the industry is now getting some of its own medicine from those who illegally and unfairly download music from the net – not that that's justifiable either. And with the advent of the first number one record generated entirely from legal internet downloads, chart rigging is probably a dying art.

All in all, this was one of our more enjoyable productions, but I don't play *You Can Do Magic* any more. It may not have been very good, but it was very catchy, and you can't get the damned thing out of your head.

As the months went by, it became obvious that Mike Townson would never be fit enough to come back to work – at least, not as editor of *The Cook Report*. We needed a new editor to hold things together. Speculation mounted amongst the team when it became known that someone had been chosen – but the identity was kept secret. Mike Morley and his boss, Steve Clark, held a rather melodramatic staff meeting to 'unveil' the new editor. And as the portly, silver-haired figure walked into the room, spontaneous applause erupted. It was none other than my old friend Bob Southgate.

On the face of it, Southgate was far too senior a management figure to take the job. He was the man who had written the franchise proposal that won Central Television the right to broadcast for ten years – at a cost of just £2,000 a year. He had retired as Deputy Managing Director a few months before.

Still, as he told me over a drink the first evening of his tenure, he was still a journalist at heart and had been involved with *The Cook Report* from the very beginning. He had brought me over to Central Television from the BBC nearly a decade earlier. He had hired Townson as editor and had viewed every single episode before broadcast to make sure that it complied with the ITC code. He relished the chance to 'play with the train set' for a year or so before finally embracing retirement for real.

Southgate brought an air of gentility and relaxation to the programme that had always been missing in Townson's day. Having come so close to leaving the job for good after my most recent car accident, I appreciated this change of approach. I no longer felt like a commodity to be freighted wherever I was needed.

The producers appreciated Southgate, too. At last, they were allowed to produce and edit their own programmes. Under Southgate's avuncular guidance they were motivated to bring in good programmes because they were fully in charge, and not because they were driven to fetch and carry material for Mike Townson. The programmes they produced differed from those he had made, but by and large they were none the worse for that.

By the end of 1996, about a year after their merger, Carlton's plans for Central were well underway. The company had been moved out of the original ATV Birmingham studios and in turn, *The Cook Report* was moved to Carlton's Nottingham outpost. We were no longer in the middle of a thriving city, but marooned on an industrial estate on the edge of town. I loathed the whole idea. We had previously been offered London as an alternative production site, and that had made much more sense to me.

The move coincided with the departure – for good this time – of Bob Southgate. Pat Harris had also decided not to make the move with us. She and her husband went off to retire to Cornwall. It was the end of an era. Peter Salkeld, too, was not coming with us. After all these years, the management had decided not to renew his contract. I felt very badly about this. He was my friend as well as a valued colleague and travelling companion, but there was nothing I could do to change the management's mind. Their view was that he had been there long enough and it was time to make way for new blood.

There was certainly going to be new blood at the top. Mike Morley, forbidden categorically by his boss Steve Clark to take over the programme, much though he was tempted, had found us a new editor for Series Fifteen. David Mannion was a familiar and respected figure in television. The former Head of News at ITN, he had diversified into running his own company, travelling the world to advise foreign television stations how to make themselves more successful.

Morley had persuaded Mannion to take on the job, but the new editor had stipulated that though he would be at the helm of the programme as much as possible, he did have other commitments to fulfil, and would at times be away from the Nottingham studios for prolonged periods.

One of the first things Mannion did was to try to plan the programmes more efficiently. While I applauded this intention, it remained an undeniable fact that the villains never read the script. However much you try to be economical by booking your camera crew and other staff members for specific times, it won't alter the fact that your target may not turn up and do what you want him to, and even criminals fall ill or go on holiday.

One story – tailor-made for us – stands out from the first series under David Mannion. It came to us in the form of a piece of amateur filming that revealed a distressing example of animal cruelty from what proved to be a huge and illegal industry. The film had been shown to producer Howard Foster by a senior director of a leading animal charity frustrated by the inability, or unwillingness, of conservation authorities all over Africa to stop a practice known as 'canned hunting'. This is where big game is captured from the wild and kept in small enclosures, often in a highly-tranquillised state, until a foreign hunter arrives to shoot the defenceless animal at close range for an exorbitant fee.

Foster brought the tape into my room and slipped it into the video player. "This isn't very pleasant, but I think you'll agree it's something we've got to take a look at," he said, and sat down next to me to watch the tape.

The opening shot showed a lioness standing uncertainly beside a high, wire mesh fence. As the camera pulled shakily away, we could see three small cubs on the other side of the fence mewling and looking longingly at her. Then a low, whispered commentary began as the cameraman, obviously afraid he might be discovered, described what we were seeing. The disembodied voice had a strong, South African accent. "These cubs have been separated from their mother so that she can be shot by an overseas hunter for a lot of money. She's still feeding them milk from her teats every day, but the hunters don't care."

We watched as the lioness wandered along the boundary of the small enclosure, unwilling to stray far from her young. Suddenly, the camera jerked as the soundtrack crackled and distorted with the sound of rifle fire. We saw the lioness leap at least ten feet into the air, her back arching in pain. She hit the ground, writhed for a few seconds and was still. Three men walked into shot and bent to examine their prize. One lifted her huge head and struck a macho pose. The camcorder's microphone picked up laughter and the sound of congratulations offered in German.

"This is going on all over Africa every day of every week of every year," the cameraman whispered, and switched off.

We showed the film to David Mannion who agreed that this was something that demanded investigation. Over the next two weeks, the research team headed off to every conservation group it could find with special interests in African big game. The key questions were: how widespread was 'canned hunting' and who were the men most closely involved in it?

A week later, Foster and his researcher, Peter McQuillan, had established that 'canned hunting' was very big business indeed, especially in South Africa, where the reorganisation of the new republic and the abolition of old state boundaries had left hunting laws in disarray. Two conservation groups had offered us lists of suspect game ranches and hunters, mostly in the old Transvaal area where the authority of the Mandela government held least sway amongst the independently-minded Afrikaners.

Several names appeared on both lists and we decided to concentrate on these, but in such a way that they would never suspect that they were under investigation. After several brainstorming sessions in the office and occasionally over the almost inevitable glass or two of New World Chardonnay or Sauvignon Blanc in the restaurant of my hotel, we built our cover.

Telephone calls and faxes to the suspect hunting outfits were never going to work. We had to get right up close to them with hidden cameras and tape recorders and get them to hang themselves conclusively, without believing for a single second that someone was trying to trap them. We needed to appeal to their greed by dangling a sufficiently succulent series of carrots in front of them.

We decided we had to get into the big game hunting business ourselves. Not at the 'sharp end' like the men we wanted to unmask, but as middlemen – 'fixers' – who could put wannabe hunters in touch with our suspects. And we needed to be based somewhere which had the smell of opulence and a big hunting tradition.

Three European nations are crazy about hunting – Italy, Germany and Spain. We decided to set up our stall on the Costa del Sol. Howard Foster and Peter McQuillan flew there and rented space in a small office block near the waterfront in Marbella. They installed a telephone and fax and arranged for an office servicing company to handle all incoming calls once the team had left. Calling itself Jackson & Co. – a cover name used successfully in a previous investigation – this front company was to approach every hunting outfit on the list with a business proposition that would be hard to resist.

Faxes from Jackson & Co. began to arrive in the offices of South African hunting companies, explaining that it had a portfolio of extremely wealthy clients for whom it provided every possible facility. A rich man in London demands tickets for La Scala in Milan, Jackson & Co. finds the best seats, books the flights, the hotel and arranges for the chauffeur to take him to his favourite restaurant and so on.

Some of these clients were now expressing an interest in big game hunting, an area hitherto unexplored by the sophisticated operators at Jackson & Co. So to please their valuable and cash-laden clients, the company was sending two of its senior representatives to South Africa in the next few weeks. By the way, most of these clients couldn't shoot for toffee but would pay handsomely for the chance to bag and boast about a lion, leopard or rhino. Was there enough interest to make it worth a meeting?

Within four days all the suspect outfits had replied to say they would be very pleased to see our representatives and were sure they could help us.

Foster needed a 'business colleague' he could trust. Someone who could manage a jacket camera, had the gift of the gab, could keep his nerve and – if at all possible – film with a professional

Betacam when the opportunity arose. He came to see me and made a suggestion which I wholeheartedly endorsed. Then he went in to see Mike Morley and made his case. He wanted Salk to work with us.

Although Salk had technically left *The Cook Report*, he was still in regular touch with his old colleagues. Morley realised that Foster was talking sense. Salk was the ideal man for the job, of course. Foster could hire him.

Both men had business cards and headed notepaper printed with their front company logo and motto: 'Jackson & Co. – The Complete Service'. It was decided they would use their real names because of the danger of being asked to produce a passport that was plainly at odds with an assumed identity.

They also took two Sony Digicams – small, unobtrusive cameras which would not attract the attention usually prompted by their bulky broadcast equivalents. The little Sonys would not look out of place in a tourist area. They were useful for secret filming at a distance, for future identification of targets and locations for colleagues and, crucially, as a legitimate tool for the open filming of animals, hunters and terrain to show the 'clients' back in Spain or London.

If you want to film professionally in South Africa, you need the written permission of the government and they want to know exactly what you plan to film. It was too early to tell the authorities what we were up to, so a professional Beta kit would be hired once we were in the country and we had something worth filming.

Salk, a cameraman by training but, now almost 60, doubling as a producer and director, also packed his miniaturised tie cameras. We often used them to obtain our secret close-up film. A tiny video camera was sewn into a tie with its lens seeing the outside world through a hole the size of a pinhead burnt through the fabric three or four inches below the knot. Microphone and camera wires were fed around the neck of the wearer, hidden by the material of the tie until they dropped through a hole cut into the back of the shirt collar. They could then be connected to a battery pack and a miniature video recorder worn round the waist.

Salk dismantled both cameras and hid the components in his clothes and packed the Digicams in his suitcase to lessen the chances of detection by the Customs at Johannesburg Airport. If the gear was found by British airport security people, there wasn't usually a problem. If I was flying with the cameraman, one glance at my face and all became clear to the puzzled baggage checker. "Who are you after this time, Mr Cook, or shouldn't I ask?" was the usual reaction. But we couldn't count on this on the other side of the world.

The night after their departure, I received a call from Foster and Salk. They had got into Jo'burg with no problems and were to make their first meeting, seven hours' drive east of the city, the following day. From then on they would be sleeping under canvas on a remote farm run by a friend of one of the conservation groups that had helped us identify our targets.

"Everyone in this camp's just had cerebral malaria," Salk cackled down the phone. "And crocodiles have eaten two of the three house-boys in the past fortnight. The third one was killed by poachers last month. Shall we book you into the penthouse?"

For the next week I had to put the progress of the investigation in South Africa to the back of my mind because we had just persuaded the fugitive businessman Asil Nadir to give an exclusive, no-holds barred interview. After the £2.5 billion collapse of his Polly Peck Empire in 1992, he had subsequently fled to Turkish Northern Cyprus, fearing he wouldn't get a fair trial on fraud charges involving £36 million.

The dubious behaviour of the Serious Fraud Office gave some credence to these fears – indeed the programme ended up being as much about them as it was about him – but if I was to put his claims to the test, I had to devote all my time to absorbing the exhaustive briefing put together for me by the research team.

One of the key allegations against Nadir was that he had treated the company's finances as his own, transferring nearly £200 million out of Polly Peck into secret accounts in Northern Cyprus.

However, what neither we, nor the SFO had access to were the company books. There were serious questions about their accuracy and authenticity, but the Northern Cyprus authorities would not allow the originals to be taken out of their jurisdiction to be examined by forensic accountants, and the British authorities wouldn't allow the accountants to examine the books in Northern Cyprus because they didn't recognise Northern Cyprus as a country.

Without this vital evidence and desperate for a conviction, there was some evidence that the SFO had resorted to a dirty tricks campaign, a tactic which was eventually the subject of an apology

With Irish Naval officers approaching a Spanish trawler loaded with illegal fish.

Discovering a secret hold, packed with tons of undersized hake.

With cameraman Mike Garner after an attack by Spanish pirate fishermen.

Asil Nadir attempts to explain his accounts.

With Debbie Currie while promoting *The Cook Report* pop record.

Debbie performs 'You can do Magic' live on TV.

In South Africa: a lioness meets a brutal end at close range during an illegal 'canned hunt'.

Out in the bush: confronting canned hunt organizer Sandy McDonald.

A long lost L.S. Lowry painting, rediscovered by *The Cook Report*.

Doctor Kolatur Unni: consultant psychiatrist and serial sexual predator.

Doctor Michael Schubert: consultant surgeon and international pimp.

NEWS OF THE WORLD

FEBRUARY 13, 2000   BOOKS FOR SCHOOLS, 4 TOKENS PAGE 22   Price 60p

FREE LOVERS GUIDE MAGAZINE

ROGER COOK SHOWS FAKED

EXCLUSIVE

TV CRIMEBUSTING series The Cook Report is today exposed as a cynical sham.

BY ROB KELLAWAY & PAUL LEWIS

Crew on the award-winning show, watched by up to 17 million viewers, conspired with crooks to set up crimes that sleuth Roger Cook could quickly solve.

■TOLD art thieves the easiest way to take a painting ■HELPED a man 'repossess' a motorbike, then called him a thief on screen. Researcher David Llewelyn, 40, admitted last night he

TELLY SLEUTH: Roger

---

38   NEWS OF THE WORLD, August 4, 2002

COOK REPORT

IN February and April 2000 the News of the World published three articles claiming that a number of Cook Report television programmes had been faked and that the series was a cynical sham.

The programme was accused of conspiring with crooks to set up crimes which Roger Cook could quickly solve.

Mr Cook and Carlton understood that the articles were accusing them of being a party to the dishonest deception of viewers.

The Independent Television Commission also looked into the published allegations.

However, in October 2001 it decided that there

was no evidence of fakery or breaches of the regulatory code.

Without the need for lengthy legal proceedings, the parties have now agreed to resolve their differences.

Mr Cook and Carlton accept that the News of the World believed that it had grounds to look into the matter.

For our part, we now accept that the three articles contained material inaccuracies which should not have been published.

We also accept that neither Mr Cook nor Carlton nor the editors, producers, legal advisers and television researchers were a party to any fakery or deception.

WHAT WOMAN MYS...

Valentine romance on the

Two and a half years on: the 'correction', buried on page 38.

One of 8 pages of libel over four weekends in *The News of the World*.

The Guardian Wednesday July 31, 2002

News

NoW admits Cook Report allegations were false

Ciar Byrne

The News of the World today admitted that a series of reports alleging that episodes of the investigative TV show The Cook Report were faked were inaccurate and should not have been published.

The newspaper's solicitor, Julian Pike, said the paper was "happy ... to make it clear that ... accept that neither Mr Cook nor Carlton ... editors, producers, advisers and rese ... were a party to any ... deception".

Roger Cook served a libel writ on the NoW in ... 2000 after the paper

The paper also wrongly accused members of the Cook Report production team of conspiring with criminals to set up crimes that Mr Cook could solve quickly.

Eight other members of the Cook Report team, including former editor Mike Morley, also sued the Now for libel.

Mr Cook's solicitor, Ian ... described ... alternative but to bring a libel action against the Now "Believing that if the accusation went unchal... ...

Now sent its dossier of evidence about The Cook Report to the independent television commission. In October 2001 the ITC decided there was no evidence that Mr Cook or his production team had faked programmes or breached its regulatory code.

"While it is accepted that the Now believed that it had grounds to ... should not have been published" Mr Bloom said today in a statement read out in open court.

were a party to any fakery or deception."

The paper has agreed not to repeat the allegations.

Mr Cook has presented around 125 editions of The Cook Report, first for Central Television and more recently for Carlton TV, since the show began in 1985.

The programmes have covered subject as ...

... in Bosnia and the Russian black market in plutonium.

In 1998 Bafta presented ...

The good news reported in *The Guardian*.

The 'Spitting Image' Cook doorsteps God for allegedly selling Israel as a timeshare to both Arabs and Jews.

Benny Hill, as 'Roger Crook', hilariously demonstrates how not to do a doorstep interview.

With Sir Trevor McDonald and a special award at the BAFTAs.

With Michael Aspel
and the big red book
on *This is Your Life*.

With Belinda,
Frances and oldest
friend Barry, taking
a bow.

With Professor Neil
Gorman, Vice-Chancellor
of Nottingham Trent
University, an Honorary
Doctorate - and an ill-
fitting hat.

in parliament. There was a mountain of sometimes conflicting paperwork to examine, much of which constituted a legal and financial minefield.

By the time we had completed the negotiations with Nadir's advisers and associates, kicked our heels for a while at the Jasmine Court Hotel in Kyrenia and then actually done the interview at his home, two weeks had slipped by. I now had to refocus my mind and update myself on every last detail of the next project in a matter of hours. A difficult feat to pull off – but as *The Cook Report* often had to juggle several major stories at once – at least I was used to trying.

Back in Nottingham, and after a night's sleep, I drove to the studios.

"Any news from South Africa?" I asked as I walked into the office.

"Your tickets are on your desk," replied Lynne Salkeld, Salk's daughter and our latest long-suffering secretary. "You leave this evening. Peter and Howard have arranged for you to kill a lion on Monday."

The pair of them had been busy over the past fortnight visiting a dozen suspect-hunting operators and covering several thousand miles in the process. In my hotel room a few miles from Jo'burg airport they filled me in on what had already been filmed and what had been set up for us to do in the next few days.

Four hunting outfits had promised Jackson & Co.'s mythical clients the chance to kill a lion in any circumstances they wanted. What had distinguished the company we had finally chosen from the others was the discovery that the lions it offered were actually being stolen from the Kruger National Park – the jewel in South Africa's conservation crown. The company was drugging the poor beasts and keeping them in small enclosures until wealthy clients arrived to shoot them.

Sandy McDonald and his wife Tracey ran their own hunting operation from a block of factory buildings next to the control tower of Pietersburg Airport, a four-hour drive from Johannesburg and a couple of hours from Kruger. They boasted to us that they had organised the killing of more animals each year than any other outfit in their part of the Republic of South Africa. Tracey Mc-Donald, an attractive and enthusiastic saleswoman, swiftly entered into the conspiracy hinted at by Foster and Salk.

When they told her how they overcharged their rich clients back in Europe her eyes sparkled. The prospect of a steady stream of gullible millionaires directed her way by these two middlemen excited her – she loved Foster's plummy Home Counties accent – and she happily told them the secrets of the canned hunting business. The fact that the clients were unable to shoot was not a problem.

As she counted out the $9,000 Foster had given her as a down payment for the hunting of one lion, she explained how their men dug beneath the electrified security fences that surround the Kruger National Park and lured their prey across by dragging bait under the fence to the accompaniment of loud tape recordings of lions and hyenas feeding.

"Before you know it, you've got yourself a Kruger lion. You dart it and keep it safe until your client arrives," she explained. Peter Salkeld leaned attentively towards her, the lens and the microphone in his tie relaying every part of her confession to the miniature video recorder nestling in the small of his back.

For the denouement, Jackson & Co. was to bring over one of its richest clients. His name was Mr James Rogers, he was worth in excess of £100 million, and he was used to getting his own way. He was unfit, couldn't possibly last more than half an hour in the fierce South African sun and he was a useless shot.

Tracey McDonald had the very lion for him. Husband Sandy had been out to the edge of the Kruger himself a couple of days before. It was a beautiful specimen, she gushed. He was about ten years old with a magnificent head and long, dark mane. "Don't worry, we'll make sure he gets his lion," she said, handing over a receipt for a deposit so large it had required the signature of Carlton Television's chief accountant to authorise it. Howard Foster slipped it into his breast pocket and hoped the budget-busting outlay would be worth it.

We had decided to keep well away from the Kruger area until the day of the hunt and had found ourselves an inn high up in the nearby mountain range. It had fabulous views over the Low Veldt and enjoyed complete privacy. Over some sumptuous Thelema Cape Chardonnay and some succulent steaks, the team discussed the best – and safest – way to handle what was to come.

We had been joined by Andy Rex, a white Zimbabwean camera-man under contract to ITN in Jo'burg. A big, bluff man who had operated in some of the world's toughest trouble spots and been under fire countless times in Bosnia and Rwanda, he saw no problem in what we were going to do. "I don't know why you boys are going to all this planning trouble," he said, lighting another Marlborough and settling his bulk comfortably down into his creaking chair. "If they don't like what you're going to do, we'll just tell them to piss off and we'll get on with it."

Somehow, I felt it wasn't going to be that simple.

So far we had maintained control. We had filmed our targets covertly and hidden the results in a safe back at the farm where Foster and Salk had been staying. Now we would have our own man openly capturing every cough and spit; an expensive camera filming an expensive vanity video for a very expensive man. But from the moment we were taken on to the killing ground, everything would change.

By midnight we had thrashed out a plan that seemed to afford optimum protection for humans, lion and equipment.

Mr Rogers and his cameraman would obviously be riding up front with the hunters. Foster and Salk would drive an air-conditioned back-up vehicle on the expedition. We added asthma to Mr Rogers' portfolio of ailments and insisted that the vehicle be in close attendance in case he needed to take a break in cool, dust-free comfort at any time.

Used tapes could then be smuggled across to the support vehicle from time to time, reducing the chances of the aggrieved hunters grabbing them during the confrontation that would inevitably follow. Salk and Foster would film on the tie camera and the Digicam from the van as we went along. All used tapes would be concealed under the springs of the rear seat of the back-up vehicle.

Crispian Barlow, an eccentric English baronet who ran the farm where the team had been staying, was to follow us discreetly. If we were gone too long he was to call the police. We had also met the local nature conservation rangers – a group of smiling and enthusiastic KwaZulu Africans – who promised to give us a powerful walkie-talkie on which we could either call them as they waited with Crispian, or use the emergency channel to call the police.

We telephoned David Mannion back in Nottingham and told him our plans. "Just take care of yourselves and I want a call the minute it's all over." It's an instruction Mannion had given to reporters and crews in tight spots abroad plenty of times before as

351

editor of ITV's news programmes. A kind and compassionate man, we knew he was genuinely concerned for our safety.

The morning of the hunt dawned bright and clear. I was up, showered and dressed by eight o'clock. Shortly, the others joined me, and we ran over the briefing once more.

Above all, I was to establish from the outset that I was in charge of the hunting expedition – to be dogmatic, bad-tempered, bullying if need be – and to try to maintain that atmosphere even after it became clear that James Rogers was Roger Cook. If I could keep the bad guys on the back foot, experience told me that we would probably improve our chances of making a getaway with ourselves and the tapes intact.

We left the hotel after breakfast and drove towards the Kruger. It was a glorious day, perfect for filming, but already heading for 40 degrees centigrade. I was glad of the cool interior of our minibus. We had been told to meet the hunters at a small safari camp a few miles from the western edge of the reserve.

But first, we parked, as arranged, outside the solitary row of shops in the village of Huidspruit and waited for the rangers and their walkie-talkie. After an hour there was still no sign of them. We checked the two sidestreets and the car park of the rough-looking hotel across the road. If we left it any longer, we would miss our rendezvous with Mr McDonald. With a last, anxious stare through the heat haze rising from the empty tarmac road, we pulled away towards the camp. We never did learn why the rangers couldn't make that vital rendezvous.

Salk switched the GSM mobile phone on and tried to call Crispian Barlow. He got a signal but couldn't get through. He tried again, and again. He tried ringing our hotel and then the UK without success. We discovered later that a £1,000 limit had been put on our use of the GSM by Carlton Television accountants. Our lifeline had been cut off.

Five minutes after we arrived at the rendezvous, a lumbering, long-wheelbase Land Cruiser turned into the track behind us, raising a thick cloud of dust. The hunters were an hour early. Crispian Barlow, who was supposed to follow us, wasn't due to arrive for another 30 minutes.

Now we really were on our own.

Five men descended from the vehicle and walked towards us. Leading the group was the bear-like figure of Sandy McDonald, already $9,000 richer and obviously looking forward to another $9,000 once the morning's business was completed. McDonald held out a paw and smiled. "Welcome to South Africa, Mr Rogers, you've picked a fine day to shoot a lion."

I went into grumpy old rich man mode: "It's too damned hot. I want to get out of this bloody heat and dust." I stomped back into the air-conditioned oasis of the minibus. The intention was to restrict my contact with McDonald and his hunters until Foster and Salk had established that this lion was to be shot in the controlled circumstances McDonald had promised.

Andy Rex sat with me, checking his camera gear and listening to the progress of the South African test batsmen against Australia on the car radio. Every few minutes he clambered outside to puff on another cigarette.

Foster and Salk took McDonald to the camp's bar and bought him an orange juice. Salk manoeuvred McDonald into the frame of his tie camera. "We want to be sure our client is kept safe," he said.

"Don't worry, make no mistake, this is a canned lion. I've drugged him too, so he won't be going anywhere. Your client can get as close as he likes."

"He won't think he's being conned?"

"We'll make it look good. We'll drive him round for a bit as if we're hunting, but we know where the lion is. Mr Rogers won't suspect a thing."

They were interrupted by a shout. The driver of the Land Cruiser waved them over. It was Mossie Mostert, a mean-looking man in his mid-twenties whose family had been near the top of the British conservationists' lists of suspects. The *Cook Report* team had been to his farm a few weeks before and been offered canned lion. Mostert had even shown them round the enclosures where his family kept 40 or more lions for hunting.

He had told us that he had been accused by the South African Professional Hunters' Association of running canned hunts. He had laughed it off, saying his accusers were the same men who came round begging for a spare lion for a foreign client when there was a shortage of big cats in the wild. If the McDonalds hadn't obliged, the Mosterts would have been next on our list. Now we had both in our sights.

McDonald confirmed to Foster that the hunt would be on

353

Mostert land and, pretending to visit the washroom, Foster left a note for Crispian Barlow with the camp owner, telling him where we'd been taken.

At the height of the South African summer the Low Veldt is covered in dense foliage. I wiped the sweat from my eyes and looked to my left and to my right in the hope of seeing some landmark I could use to guide us when the time came to make a run for it. Nothing – just the same unending pattern of tall grass and dark clumps of thorn tree. Unless you knew the territory, you could drive through the red dust of these dirt tracks for days and never find your way out.

I looked across at my unsuspecting companions. Perched next to me, high up on the observation bench at the back of the customised hunting wagon was one of the toughest looking men I had ever seen. Well over six feet tall with a grizzled, blond beard, Sandy McDonald must have weighed well in excess of 20 stones, not much of it fat. A Remington hunting rifle with telescopic sights rested across his enormous bronzed thighs.

In the canvas-covered driving seat, Mossie Mostert struggled with the wheel, the late-morning sun forcing him to pull his peaked hunting cap low over his eyes. As we bounced across the rough terrain, he steered us closer to our quarry. He stared fixedly past a pair of heavy-calibre rifles and a long, wooden gun rest which were clipped across the folded windshield in front of him. A small, wiry figure he had a notoriously short temper, and we were entrapping him on his own territory.

On the bonnet of the Land Cruiser sat the tracker, a fit, muscular Afrikaner in standard-issue hunting greens and the obligatory camouflage cap. He gripped the sides of his lookout seat perched over the front bumper. The butt of a Browning 9mm pistol protruded from a holster at his hip.

At my back stood two colossal Africans known in the big game world as 'skinners'. Their job was to use the fearsome array of knives which they carried strapped to their belts as soon as I had done what their bosses expected of me – to shoot and kill a North Transvaal male lion in the most inhumane and illegal way. Once they had removed the animal's skin and cut off its magnificent head and mane, it would be time for me to pay the white hunters their extortionate fee. Then I'd wait for my trophy to arrive a few months later, impressively mounted by a South African taxidermist.

But I wasn't about to do what was expected of me. In a few minutes' time the cosy atmosphere aboard this bouncing, dust-streaked wagon would be destroyed when I told them exactly who I was and that the cameraman who was filming them was not simply making a vanity video for me. I was there to blow apart a huge conspiracy within the worldwide big game hunting industry.

The *Cook Report* minibus followed the Land Cruiser along the red-dirt road towards the Mostert reserve. Then, without warning, Mostert swung his vehicle left down a narrow track and stopped in front of a 12-foot high electrified wire-mesh boundary fence. The two black hunters dropped from the back of their wagon. There was some movement of hands at chest level and we realised they were undoing a hefty padlock which kept two steel-framed gates closed.

"Crispian's going to have a hell of a job finding us here, we're miles from the main entrance," said Salk.

Foster tucked the first of the tie camera tapes under the back of the rear seat.

Up front on the Land Cruiser, I said nothing and concentrated on remembering my briefing. There's nothing you can do when things go wrong except make sure you do your job as well as you can.

Two or three minutes later our little convoy arrived at a small clearing. It was time for Andy Rex to start the vanity video filming. He stood back from us, the camera on his shoulder. McDonald and Mostert took me to the veranda of a thatched hut where a large, stuffed lion stared unseeingly across a man-made waterhole.

I have never been able to fathom what makes some men want to kill another living creature for 'sport'. McDonald pointed to the moth-eaten specimen before us and stressed the need to break one of the big cat's limbs with the first shot. I let his grisly tutorial run uninterrupted for the camera.

The next part of the charade was target practice for Mr Rogers. The muscular Afrikaner tracker turned to me and said quietly: "It doesn't matter whether you hit that lion or not. We'll be there to shoot it for you."

This wasn't what I wanted at all. I did not want that lion killed by anyone. In the light of what the tracker had just said, I now had to show them that I wouldn't need help – because I *was* a good shot after all.

They gave me three practice rounds with one of the Remington bolt-action magnum rifles clipped to the Land Cruiser windshield. A hand-drawn paper target was stuck to a tree trunk some 50 yards away. Andy Rex and Salk aimed their lenses at me and, forehead furrowed in concentration, I fired. Mostert went to collect the target: one bullseye, two inners, almost passing through the same hole. A look of puzzlement turned to a nod of approval. Now, with luck, they would leave the job solely to me.

Andy Rex and I joined the five-strong hunting party aboard their wagon while Foster and Salk followed in the minibus. Before we set off, McDonald gave them a walkie-talkie.

"Once we get near this lion you're going to have to hold back," he said. "Wait until I give the order and stay wherever you are. We'll come back and get you when it's all over."

The Land Cruiser dipped and bucked as the tracker at the front of the vehicle put on a bravura performance for the benefit of Mr Rogers – studying the ground, signalling urgently for Mostert to stop while he jumped down to examine the spoor of the lion and directing us once he'd found its tracks.

I had no idea how to find our way back to those gates, but I knew from looking at the sun that for the past 20 minutes we had been going round in circles. Then McDonald reached for the walkie-talkie that swung from a strap on the rear-view mirror. "Howard and Peter, you stay back now. We think we are near the lion now. See you later." Foster replied briefly in the affirmative and we moved slowly on in silence, leaving the dirt track and moving carefully across a swathe of thick bush grass towards a cluster of dense foliage. Mostert stopped and switched off the engine.

"There he is, under those trees." McDonald whispered hoarsely into my right ear and pointed. I looked across to the clump about 30 yards away. Under the low branches of a thorn tree I saw a massive, maned head swaying slightly in the shade. "I want you to shoot him underneath the mane," McDonald continued. "It's hot and he's in a cool place so he doesn't want to move."

He can't bloody well move, you've got him stoned out of his head, I thought. I told Andy to zoom slowly in on the lion and then pull out until McDonald and I filled his viewfinder. I could taste the tension. I took a deep breath and turned to look McDonald in the eye.

"I'll tell you why I'm not going to shoot that lion – because he doesn't stand a chance and you know it," I said. "And I'm not a businessman, I'm a television reporter making a programme about canned hunting and that's what this is, isn't it, an illegal canned hunt?"

I don't know what I expected to happen. People react in so many different ways. I had prepared myself for instant retaliation, physical violence, and rapid denial. McDonald registered nothing. "Just shoot it below the mane," he said, turning back in the direction of the lion. I found this rather worrying. The huge, heavily armed man sitting next to me was plainly not very bright.

I repeated what I had just said and the message gradually began to sink in. McDonald started to argue. Mostert began to get angry. The tracker, now kneeling a few inches behind my head told me to get out of the wagon and shoot the lion on foot.

"No, we're not going on foot," I said. "I'm paying for this. We're not shooting that lion. Let's get out of here."

Mostert restarted the engine and drove us back to an anxious back-up team. Salk switched on the Digicam. McDonald was still in shock but Mostert and the tracker were beginning to think more clearly. Mostert decided things had gone too far. He dropped the wagon into gear and headed back to the clearing.

Back at the camp the walkie-talkie crackled into life every 30 seconds or so and Mostert and McDonald launched into vehement streams of Afrikaans in reply. Mostert turned to me. "I should kill you for what you have done," he hissed. The tracker moved close to me and said in a lowered voice: "If you had come on foot I should have put a bullet in your head."

When we said we wished to leave they refused, saying that the police were on their way. This was bad news. We had been warned that we were in an area where farmers and even policemen met together on Sundays at the Dutch Reformed Church to remember communally the injustices heaped on their Boer forebears by the hated British.

I decided we should make a run for it. Andy Rex took his gear to the minibus. Howard Foster pushed every tape under the rear seat and we all climbed into the vehicle. Foster started the engine and we set off. Round the first bend the track forked. Andy Rex's experience of bush survival kicked in. "Go left here," he ordered. "Now right. See that tree there, I remember that. Left once more and we'll be on the right road."

He was wrong.

We spent a nerve-wracking few minutes looking over our shoulders and passing the same landmarks until, mercifully, Rex picked up the trail again. Another two minutes of bouncing and rocking over the potholes and hummocks and we saw the open gateway 300 yards ahead of us. "Howard," I said, "put your foot down."

We lurched forward, clinging on to straps, seatbacks and dashboard as we headed for freedom. Then two clouds of red dust appeared about 50 yards ahead of us. They converged just in front of the gates. As the dust settled we could see two hunting wagons blocking the exit and a swarm of angry-looking figures pulling the gates shut.

We slowed down and stopped ten feet from the wagons. Out on the public road a crowd of onlookers had gathered. Farmers with pickup trucks, three police cars, the tall, bearded figure of Crispian Barlow peering anxiously through the mesh – and a group of excited Africans in ranger uniforms. Too late, they had brought us the walkie-talkie they had promised us earlier that day.

Mossie Mostert, two of his brothers and his father, Albert, walked up to the minibus. "We want your tapes," said Mostert Senior. "You did not have permission to film on my land."

I pointed out to him that his son and McDonald had not objected to the video and, what was more, I had paid $9,000 to hunt on his reserve.

Howard Foster and Andy Rex got out and attempted to negotiate with the police through the wire. They came back ten minutes later: "It's looking bad," Foster said. "More farmers are arriving by the minute and they're pressurising the police to do what the Mosterts want."

At least with the police present, the likelihood of being summarily shot had diminished, but the prospect of having to hand over our precious tapes loomed large. Then I had an idea. Crispian Barlow was out on the road. Because he lived locally he didn't want to be associated with us once we had revealed who we really were. His pretext for being in this vicinity was that we had been renting accommodation from him and that we had left without paying. He was here to get what we owed him.

We retrieved every single tape from the back of the minibus and stuffed them into Salk's commodious jacket, leaving a decoy pile of unused tapes on the front seat. Salk and Foster walked to the gate and explained to one of the more reasonable police officers that we owed the man with the beard for several nights' stay on his farm. The banks closed in 20 minutes and would it be all right if one of us went with Mr Barlow to get his money?

Keen to remove any further source of conflict, the officer agreed and Salk slipped out of the gate, walked as nonchalantly as he could to Crispian's car and they sped off almost unnoticed, not stopping for nearly seven hours until they reached Johannesburg.

An hour or so later, the gates were finally pulled open for us. A burly Afrikaner cop walked up to the minibus and leaned into the front passenger window. He spoke to me quietly. "See, we have opened the gates for you, but take this advice. They will not kill you while we are here. If you were still here in a few hours, you could end up with a bullet between your eyes and there would be no witnesses. Go a long way from here, gentlemen, and take your tapes with you."

It sounded like good advice to me, even though the real tapes had long gone.

Twenty-four hours later, I shook hands with Andy Rex before leaving for Johannesburg airport with those vital tapes safely stowed in my luggage. He relaxed his crushing grip and smiled. "We should work together again sometime. I think I understand what you guys do it for now."

At that moment, I wasn't so sure that *I* did.

What surprised me more than anything was the viewing figure for the programme: just under seven million. To me, it was one of the most dramatic we had made for a couple of years, and it had been broadcast to a nation of animal lovers.

The truth of the matter was that the available audience now had more choice. The days of our pulling in ten or twelve million viewers were over. The BBC had got its act together, targeting popular ITV programmes and putting on strong shows to fight for viewer share. Now, satellite channels abound – and if there is Premier League football on, as there had been when the canned hunting programme was aired – a fair chunk of our audience was otherwise engaged. Add to that the arrival of Channel Five, and you began to see why the figures of a few years ago might not be achievable any more.

Nevertheless, the effect of the programme worldwide was incredible. It was bought immediately for showing on South African television. There was a huge outcry and Nelson Mandela declared that it was time to change wildlife laws and to enforce them properly. Ninety professional hunters had their licences suspended, including Sandy McDonald. Roy Plath, the man who allowed that lioness to be shot on his land – and had inadvertently led us to make our programme – suffered the wrath of the South African housewife.

He was a banana grower, supplying one of the biggest supermarket chains in the country. When it was realised that his bananas were on sale in their favourite foodstore, the housewives started petitions nationwide urging the supermarkets to boycott his fruit – and he lost his contract.

The programme was eventually broadcast three times in South Africa – where it spawned a couple of follow-up investigations by local television – as well as in Australia and Germany. We also won an award at the 'Animal Oscars' in Los Angeles, sponsored by the Hollywood celebrities of the Ark Trust. We were given The Brigitte Bardot International Award, for the best campaigning wildlife film, though we almost didn't get it at all.

We had not entered 'Making a Killing', but the South African network to which we'd sold it had cheekily put up the programme as one of its own. We didn't find out about our success until our cameraman was invited to the presentation ceremony in Los Angeles. That let the cat out of the bag and left the organisers with an embarrassing problem. Eventually they solved it by posting an award plaque to South Africa and inviting our producer, Howard Foster, out to LA to receive another one in person.

Unfortunately, much of what the programme helped achieve has now been reversed. President Thabo Mbeki has apparently not seen fit to carry on with the wildlife law reforms initiated by Nelson Mandela.

Mind you, the illegal pillaging of wildlife on an industrial scale takes place much closer to home – as we proved in an earlier investigation into the activities of the Spanish fishing fleet, much of which fishes in British waters.

I remember the programmes *The Cook Report* has made for lots of different reasons. We might have helped to get the law changed or perhaps I had been able to visit countries I had never seen before. But this particular programme will remain with me for ever because of the sheer force of the violence we experienced – both from the elements while out at sea, and from the angry people of one small Spanish fishing town who objected to us exposing how they flouted international law.

The story was one of those that grew out of another, unrelated enquiry, and illustrates perfectly how one can never tell where and when ideas will spring up. We were prompted to make the programme by a chance remark. Producer Steve Warr had been in Ireland, filming the Irish Rangers searching for an IRA arms cache, which they believed was hidden in woodland outside Dublin. The Provos had been busy in Britain in early 1993 blowing up trains and we were making a programme to show how easy it was to obtain explosives from all manner of sources.

In the regiment's mess one evening, Warr found himself chatting over a drink to the military attaché for the Irish Defence Forces. The day's filming had been eventful. The Irish soldiers had been using a new computer system, housed in a mobile caravan, to trace the arms cache. The power supply for the equipment was provided by a generator which, for some reason, had cut out at a crucial moment. Warr had been outside when the generator was restarted. A freak power surge overloaded the computer, and it went up in smoke.

The operator and his officers came out of the caravan spluttering and coughing, black-faced and embarrassed. After chuckling at the humour of the situation – and extracting a promise from Warr not to use the film of it – the attaché told Warr that IRA ammunition dumps and exploding computers apart, his biggest headache was controlling the 'Spanish Pirates'.

Warr asked him what he meant and was told that Ireland's naval patrol vessels were spending most of their time chasing Spanish trawlers, which were either fishing where they weren't supposed to be or catching undersized fish and hiding them in secret holds concealed below decks. Warr was intrigued.

Even more interestingly, the Spanish boats often flew 'flags of convenience', sailing with a token British member of crew to qualify as a British-registered vessel, thus allowing them to operate in British and Irish waters. The Irish clearly saw Spanish trawler activity as a threat to their own fishing industry.

The evening ended with an invitation to Warr to join an Irish naval ship on patrol to see the problem for himself. Townson sanctioned the trip and Warr spent several days at sea. The navy boat was equipped with the latest satellite and radar gear and it wasn't long before he witnessed the crew boarding one of the 'pirates'.

Once on board, the navy crew resorted to less sophisticated but equally effective methods of investigation. The leader of the boarding crew pulled out a tape measure and ordered his men to check the height of the exterior of the upper and lower decks. Two naval ratings then disappeared to measure the interior height of the two decks. There was a discrepancy of five feet. This begged the question of what was filling the five-foot space inside the boat. The Spaniards obviously knew they had been rumbled – they looked sullen and their captain began to argue.

The Irishmen dropped down to the bottom of the hold and began their search. One called out to his skipper five minutes later. He had found a trapdoor hidden under a carpet in the crew's quarters. The door was lifted. Down below, glinting in the torchlight was box upon box of undersized hake packed in ice. The tiny fish were all about three inches long and at that size are a popular Spanish delicacy, called appropriately enough, *Hake Ondaressa*.

We knew that they are openly sold in fish shops countrywide and even from the fish counters of posh department stores like *El Corte Inglés*. However, the illegal fishing that fulfilled the Spanish demand was a real threat to the survival of the fish stocks of those countries prepared to wait for the hake to grow to the legal length of about a foot.

When he reached dry land, Warr telephoned Townson to tell him what he'd seen. Townson responded in typically blunt fashion: "Steve, can you find a hidden hold and undersized fish being landed in Spain, and can we film all that?"

"Yes," Warr replied. He heard the heavy pounding of Townson's thick fingers on his desktop computer keys before the editor hung up. It looked as if 'Spanish Pirates' was going to go ahead.

For the next fortnight, on the advice of the Irish Defence

Attaché, Warr visited every Irish coastal town that boasted a courthouse. He took details of every recent conviction of a Spanish trawler for illegal fishing. He then spent a full week cross-referencing the details with those of the trawlers' owners. His research showed that the Spanish had chosen three British centres to register their boats – Cornwall, Wales and Scotland. There were no fewer than 250 Spanish trawlers operating in Irish and British waters, nearly all of them larger than their genuine British counterparts. Warr discovered that several of them had a dozen convictions or more.

The worst offender was a boat called the *Juan Mari*, which had been caught and convicted 17 times.

"Where's that one registered to?" asked Townson.

Warr checked his paperwork. "Cornwall."

"And where does this boat really land its catches?" demanded Townson.

A little port called Ondarroa on the northern coast of Spain near Bilbao, Warr's records told him.

"So find out what sort of place it is – and whether they're up to no good," was Townson's parting shot.

Warr telephoned Nigel Bowden, our 'man on the Costas'.

"It's ETA country," said Bowden. "You go in there and show what they are up to and you've got serious trouble."

ETA, the violent Basque separatist organisation, had a reputation even more fearsome than that of the IRA. Over the years it had murdered thousands of people from all walks of life who were perceived as the enemy. Presumably, television reporters who made trouble for their local supporters would fall into their definition of 'enemy'.

Bowden rang Warr back an hour later to tell him that Ondarroa was in that week's headlines. ETA had just blown up the local Customs post there. "Even the cops don't dare go in," he warned. "I suppose I can expect Roger tomorrow."

Bowden had performed the dual role of investigator and interpreter for *The Cook Report* in Spain a number of times. He knew what to expect, and always accepted the role with enthusiasm disguised as bad grace.

First, we needed to go out on the high seas to film the Spanish trawlermen at work. Warr, Mike Garner, sound recordist Dennis Fitch and I joined the Irish patrol vessel the *Eithne* in Dublin. She was a frigate equipped with sophisticated tracking gear and a reconnaissance helicopter. We were due to be on board her for a week.

Unfortunately – however well appointed a ship may be – it still has to go out to sea, which is something I have never been particularly comfortable with. I am almost capable of getting seasick in the bath. The cold Atlantic waters into which we were now venturing were the roughest I had ever seen. As we cruised slowly out of the relative calm of the harbour, they hit us, full on. "Storm force ten strengthening to force 12," the captain announced. "That's a hurricane boys," he added helpfully.

It wasn't long before the crests of the angry grey waves charging down on us approached the height of the bridge. We disappeared below, bouncing off the sides of the companion ways as the boat bucked beneath us.

Warr and Fitch had already started taking seasickness tablets. Garner and I held back on the grounds that they did no good anyway. Filming was impossible for the foreseeable future so I went to my cabin, already feeling distinctly unwell.

"You've gone green, Roger," remarked Warr as he clung unsteadily to a hand rail. "Are you sure you don't want some of these tablets?"

I stayed below for two full days, alternating between lying in my perpetually rocking bunk and throwing up – alongside Warr and Fitch – in the heads attached to our quarters. Everyday, some poor crew member had to hose them down, and even the crew was beginning to succumb to seasickness. Only Garner seemed able to tolerate the tempest and keep his food down. I had to admire the man for his constitution. He appeared to have a stomach of iron.

When the storm finally abated a little, Garner set up his camera on the bridge, ready to film my interview with the captain. Then, suddenly, as he framed his shot through the viewfinder, the sea finally got its revenge. "I've got to go," he blurted, before rushing to the side of the ship.

The winds had dropped, though the seas had not, and the *Eithne's* helicopter pilot suggested we went up. "You'll be glad you did," he said knowingly. I was pretty dubious, but accepted his 'trust me' invitation, and found he was right – it was actually a calming experience. I can't tell you how good it was to break free of that nauseating heeling and rolling and to feel the relative stability of flight, buffeting sidewinds notwithstanding.

While we were airborne, trying to keep the camera steady and my dinner down, the pilot spotted a Spanish trawler, the *Orlamar*, its nets spread out behind it. It had no licence to be fishing in those waters. The pilot radioed the bridge and the *Eithne*'s skipper decided to take a closer look himself and called us back.

By the time we landed back on the ship's pitching deck, Garner had staged a remarkable recovery and announced himself fit to join the Irish navy boys in the inflatable Zodiac boarding craft. Dennis Fitch fitted the boarding officer with a microphone and a mini DAT recorder, so that we could get an independent audio record of what had happened to go with whatever we captured on film. The prospect of my clambering aboard a heaving and hostile Spanish trawler was still too much for my sorely tested stomach to contemplate. I stayed behind.

The trawler turned out to have a hidden hold stuffed full of tiny hake, which Garner duly filmed, and the Irish prepared to escort the trawler to the nearest harbour at Castletown Bere. Thankfully, the arrest meant that we could, at last, get off the infernal boat.

As we stepped off the tender and on to the quayside, we all fell victim to that cruel trick the inner-ear plays upon people daft enough to take to the high seas. Terra firma became anything but, and we reeled around the quay like a group of friends returning from a long pub crawl – flinging our arms around each other for mutual support and giggling in relief at having made it to dry land at last.

The town's only taxi drew up at the end of the quay. The driver politely asked us if we would like to be taken to our accommodation. He seemed to know exactly who we were and what we were doing. There would be no charge for the service, he informed us.

This undeservedly generous treatment continued as we checked into a little quayside hotel to be told that we were expected at the town's sole wine bar for a meal and drinks. The owner greeted us at the door. "Mr Cook, you're a famous man. Welcome. You and your friends come in and enjoy yourselves. It's on the house."

We had the crew of the *Eithne* to thank. They had told the locals of the programme we were making about the 'Spanish Pirates' and, because the town relied upon fishing for its survival, the locals naturally concluded that we were doing something good.

In court, the Spanish skipper of the *Orlamar* decided to claim that he had been set up by the navy to get a film crew aboard his vessel. He asserted that Garner had forced his way on board illegally. Thanks to Fitch's mini-recorder, however, the court was able to hear the Irish officer telling the trawler that he had a film crew with him and asking if it was all right to bring the camera on board. The Spanish skipper could clearly be heard saying that it was perfectly okay.

The trawler crew was convicted of illegal fishing and was fined £60,000. The trawler was to remain anchored off Castletown Bere until the fine was paid.

Townson also wanted us to film on board a British trawler and interview the fishermen about the Spaniards and the 'flagging' that gave them the right to fish in British waters. So, from Ireland we headed for Newlyn in Cornwall, where the same members of the *Cook Report* team were greeted by exactly the same appalling weather.

Only this time, we weren't on a nice big frigate, but in a small trawler that bobbed and dipped around like a cork in a bucket of water. It stank of fish and diesel in equal, noxious measure. It didn't seem to bother the skipper one little bit but, ten minutes out of Newlyn harbour, as we headed for the Isles of Scilly, I felt yet again the irresistible need to throw up.

Garner couldn't keep the camera steady, and the waves were getting bigger. You couldn't see through the windscreen. Warr – and the captain – decided it was probably wise to turn back. I stood at the rear of the bridge, hanging on to a hand rail and heaving over the side of the boat. We were just about to reach the comparative safety and calm of the outer harbour when we were struck side-on by a massive wave that pushed the boat over almost onto its side. I disappeared completely under water. If I hadn't already been gripping the rail as tightly as I could with both hands, I would have been swept under the boat and God knows what would have happened.

As I surfaced, I heard Warr shout: "Where's Roger? Oh, shit!" Everyone looked at me. I was soaked from head to toe, deathly pallid, and still trying to be sick. I was told later that no self-respecting drowned rat would have let itself slip into such a state of dishevelment.

As we came alongside the fish dock, the radio crackled something indecipherable. The skipper told us that the weather was about to improve and suggested we might like to head out to sea again. I was pretty sure he was joking, but Warr told him in no uncertain terms that we were heading home and that that was it for the day. For life, I thought.

Over the next few weeks, we filmed a variety of ingenious illegal fishing ruses worked by the 'flagged' Spanish trawlers. Extra holds full either of undersized or illegal quota fish were found hidden in crew quarters, behind wardrobes and in secret compartments running the length of the boat. The extra storage room increased the catching capacity of these Spanish vessels by as much as 50 per cent. In Gibraltar, we found a boat builder who confessed to building most of his new trawlers with hidden holds already installed.

It was time to head for Ondarroa to get the evidence on the *Juan Mari* and her sister ships. We flew into Bilbao and drove along the coast. Cupped between two headlands on the Bay of Biscay, the picturesque little town of Ondarroa was to prove far less peaceful than it initially appeared. As in the tribal areas of Northern Ireland, walls were plastered with partisan slogans, in this case supporting ETA and its proscribed political wing, *Herri Batasuna*. There was even one wall declaring 'eternal brotherhood' between ETA and the IRA.

Garner, Warr and Bowden, who had been forewarned of the need for caution, arrived posing as an Australian film crew keen to do some filming about fishing in European waters. The British and Irish navies kept in touch with us and told us when the known 'pirates' like the *Juan Mari* were about to arrive back in their real home port.

Not surprisingly, these boats always landed their catches under cover of darkness. Coincidentally, the 'Australian crew' also favoured night-time working and, within two weeks, had filmed the *Juan Mari* landing six tonnes of minuscule, illegal hake and ten times its legal quota of cod.

Later, in a quayside bar, an unsuspecting dockers' union man told us that for every 500 boxes of fish his members landed from the trawlers, 200, at the very least, were illegal. The trouble with the British, he sneered, was that they were stupid enough to obey all the rules. "Here in Ondarroa, if the regulations don't suit us, we just ignore them, don't we?" A burly colleague nodded assent, his looming presence emphasising the union man's conclusion.

He warned that if ever our crew was caught filming or attempting to expose the nefarious practises he'd described, Warr, Garner and Fitch would, at the very least, undoubtedly end up injured and in the harbour, along with all their equipment.

The EU had recently tried to investigate the illegal fishing out of Ondarroa, but when the officials had arrived in the town, they had been told that they were not welcome and there was nowhere they could stay. They were kept virtual prisoners in their cars for several hours. This apparently delayed the investigation for long enough to allow all the undersized and over-quota fish to be moved out of the port and off to the wholesalers before any of the officials could see what the fishermen were up to. By then also, all the relevant paperwork would have been filled out to suit.

The time had come to break cover and confront the two-faced trawlermen of Ondarroa. Our team consisted of Warr, Garner, Fitch, Bowden, a former British fisheries inspector – who had brought along a measuring board to check the size of the fish being landed on the Ondarroa dockside – Derek Ive, a British photographer based in Madrid, and myself.

As we made our way down to the harbour that sweltering June night, we were quickly spotted. People streamed out of the fishing sheds, bars and store houses to see what we were doing.

I led our little group up to one of the trawlers from which box upon box of illegal three-inch hake was being unloaded under as little illumination as possible. We had previously discovered the owner's son spoke some English and I began to challenge him about his illegal fishing activities. His response was to lunge at the camera. He followed this by shouting – according to Bowden: "These bastards are trying to shop us. Come and help me stop them!"

Ondarroa then boasted a fleet of nearly a hundred fishing boats and about a thousand crewmen. A fair proportion of them soon appeared to be advancing on us down the steep harbourside streets with malice in mind. Suddenly, the fish quay was swarming with angry people. Some were brandishing bill hooks; others had long wooden poles used for dragging the boxes of fish around. The situation looked very ugly. I kept on trying to ask questions but was drowned out by the baying mob. Suddenly, they were on us. I remember Derek Ive trying to reason with them, but they just thrust him aside.

First of all, they wanted Garner's camera. He and I both grabbed hold of it and held on for dear life. There was no time to think of retreat. This wasn't about being brave, it was about pure survival. There wasn't even fear, just the sense that one had to get on with the job and the consequences would have to take care of themselves.

In the centre of the swirling crowd, half a dozen brawny Spaniards tried to wrest the camera from us. There was a brief seesaw tussle and I felt both my elbows click. I let go and they clicked back in again. Garner had been felled with a marlin spike and was bleeding profusely from an ugly, gaping head wound. Bowden was trying to crawl out of trouble while Warr was being held down and kicked.

The crowd now had the camera and the lighting gear. The Betacam disappeared into the melee while they worked out how to remove the tape – after which it was dumped, inoperative, on the dockside. The vengeful horde continued to rain blows down on all of us. Some of the attendant women hurled stinking fish – and everyone was hurling abuse. My back and legs were belaboured with bill hooks and I was punched in the face. Our fisheries inspector valiantly tried to defend himself with his plastic measuring board. Empty fish crates crashed down on our heads.

We had given Derek Ive a Hi-8 camera as a back-up in case things turned nasty. But the mob had taken that as well. Bar the broken Betacam, everything, including all our tapes, was thrown straight off the edge of the dock and into the murky waters of the harbour.

We were completely hemmed in and pretty nearly defenceless, but though all of us were being pushed, shoved and beaten, I was most concerned for Mike Garner. He was back on his feet again, but now appeared to be losing quite a lot of blood. Surely the police must have seen what was going on? There were several hundred people still after more blood – and the forces of law and order were nowhere to be seen. The police post was deserted.

And then a chant rose up.

369

"What are they saying now?" I asked a nervous-looking Bowden.

"String 'em up, I'm afraid."

Things weren't looking good.

Then, just as I thought we were about to be thrown into the sea or lynched from the nearest lamp post, the crowd seemed to lose interest and began to melt away. The whole brutal incident had taken maybe five minutes – though it felt much longer – and a few minutes later, our assailants had disappeared completely. We gathered together, breathing heavily and gingerly inspecting our injuries.

"Perhaps they finally twigged that we didn't have any evidence on them because they'd chucked all the gear into the drink," Nigel Bowden eventually suggested. "Good job they don't know what we've filmed here over the past few weeks."

"It's only a matter of time before they remember that you're that 'Australian crew' that was here for all those night-time shoots," I cautioned, "Then they'll come back and really do for us."

We were just getting into our vehicles to drive as fast and as far away from Ondarroa as possible, when a police car showed up. The two officers *had* seen what was going on, but had decided it was wiser to stay well away until the danger from the crowd had passed. The senior officer remonstrated angrily with Nigel Bowden for several minutes.

"Well?" I asked.

"He's saying that he could arrest us either for causing a riot or breach of the peace," said Bowden. "But he's not going to, because he'd be filling in forms forever. Besides that, I get the impression he thinks that though we asked for what we got, we've taken enough punishment already."

We left as quickly as we could, but we didn't give up on retrieving our tapes and camera gear. First, we tried to hire a team of Spanish divers to search the harbour waters for us. When we explained the circumstances, they refused to take the job.

Eventually Townson agreed that we could fly in a couple of ex-Special Boat Squadron divers from Britain. When the locals spotted the two-man team preparing to make their first dive, a delegation was sent over to them. The lead diver later told us that he had been told that whatever *The Cook Report* was paying to recover the tapes, the fishermen of Ondarroa would double it.

None of us on the quayside on the night of the attack could pinpoint exactly where the tapes and kit had been thrown and, after two or three days, the divers called the search off. The natives were getting restless again. Matters were made even more difficult because, before they'd destroyed our equipment, the fishermen had attempted to destroy the evidence we wanted to film by throwing a lot of their over-quota and undersized fish over the side of their boats. By then, this had left a putrefying carpet of rotting carcasses all over the harbour bottom.

As a result of our programme, the Spanish fisheries inspectorate made a face-saving visit to Ondarroa. Another near riot broke out immediately and the inspectors were forced to flee and take shelter inside a fish shed until the crowd were satisfied that none of their boats were going to be inspected. As far as I know, the situation is still the same.

The dockside assault left me sporting a black eye and an extensive array of contusions on my back and legs. Garner had to have his gaping head wound stitched together. Everyone had been badly bruised, battered and thoroughly shaken, but in the circumstances I suppose, that counted as a lucky escape.

The programme caused much indignation when it was broadcast. Questions were asked of the Spanish in the European Parliament and, for a while at least, our Fisheries Protection vessels increased their searches of the Spanish 'flagged' trawlers. But, at the end of the day, the right to fly a British flag also entitled them to fish where, perhaps, they morally should not – and unless a frigate was to sit by those trawlers day in, day out, the illegal fishing was bound to resume sooner or later.

Back in the Birmingham office, we looked at the still photographs Derek Ive had managed to take of us all on the Ondarroa quayside just after the attack. I stared at the pictures and felt shocked at what I saw. I looked exhausted, washed out. Mike Garner was battered and bleeding. We could all have been killed. Was it worth it?

The tabloid press seemed to think so. They carried the quayside pictures with bold headlines condemning the 'Spanish Pirates'. The intrepid 'telly supersleuth' had done it again, exposing wrongdoing on an international scale.

*

In 1997, we produced two series – covering stories as diverse as an exposé of organised credit card fraud industry, the rise of the neo-Fascist British National Party and its Machiavellian, Cambridge-educated leader, Nick Griffin, and the export to Britain of girls from the former Soviet Union who were subsequently forced into prostitution. The BNP programme was followed by Griffin's conviction for inciting racial hatred, and the programme on prostitution unmasked an extremely unlikely villain.

We had spotted a story in *The Daily Telegraph* which said that up to 500,000 women and girls – some as young as 14 – were being transported into the European Union to be sold 'like cattle' into sexual slavery and enforced prostitution. The culprits were East European pimps and organised crime bosses. Most victims were from the former Soviet Union, and concerned EU Home and Justice Ministers had recently met in The Hague to discuss the problem.

However, for our audience, the story needed the added interest of a British connection. Back in 1997, few of these girls ended up in the UK – though now it's an epidemic. Quite by chance, a week after the *Telegraph* article, a viewer contacted us to say that his girlfriend in Romania had received a suspicious unsolicited letter asking her to work as an 'escort' in London. The letter writer – a man called Mike – wanted the Romanian girl to bring herself and as many friends as possible to work as escorts – earning up to $2,500 a day. Mike claimed that one of his Russian girls was now actually earning $5,000 – and that when she arrived in Britain she had nothing.

Intrigued, we decided to find out who Mike was. Through contacts we found a Romanian journalist in Bucharest who was prepared to pretend she had received his original letter. Our girl, using the name Elena, started a fax correspondence with Mike. He was soon hooked – and invited Elena and her friends to London to work for him. Mike wanted to see photos of the girls – and gave a contact address.

We checked out the address and discovered to our amazement that Mike was in fact a doctor – a 34-year-old German called Dr Michael Schubert. Further checks in Germany revealed that he was a highly qualified surgeon, married with a new baby.

By an extraordinary coincidence, a secretary working on the Cook programme at the time also knew a Dr Michael Schubert.

She had previously worked for the humanitarian relief charity Merlin (Medical Emergency Relief International) – then busy in war-torn Chechnya – and Schubert had been on their books. We were appalled that a doctor working for such a charity could also be an international pimp. However, and quite without Merlin's knowledge, that's exactly what he was.

In the meantime our girl in Bucharest had changed her mind about flying over to meet Schubert and we had to arrange a hasty substitution. We recruited two very pretty East European girls to take part in our sting. They were both students living in Britain and did some part time acting for a respectable London agency. We briefed them thoroughly and assured them that we'd never let them out of our sight when they were with Schubert. Their safety was a prime concern.

We kept watch as Schubert met the girls at a hotel on the Bayswater Road in West London. A balding, bespectacled, but athletic man, he bounded up the front steps and into the foyer. At the meeting, he wasted little time in telling the girls that they would have to 'sell sex' to his clients. Dr Schubert said he would make all the necessary arrangements through his London company, Medical Services and Consultancy Limited. He would guarantee work permits, accommodation, newspaper adverts, phone box cards – he'd even supply his friends as customers 'if times were tough'.

The doctor set up our girls in a flat in Lexham Gardens, West London. He told them they'd have to earn enough money to repay the £400 a week rent, plus his 'expenses' in setting them up and promoting them. He already 'ran' some 20 girls in and around West London who charged about £80 for full sex, and was recruiting many more.

Before Schubert's first visit to the flat, Philip Braund went round to be on hand in case of trouble. Though he had a mop of curls that would not have disgraced Shirley Temple, he also had the physique of a Rugby forward. Being present without being seen was going to prove awkward since there was just one bedroom, a living room and kitchen. So, while Schubert explained to the girls what they'd have to do to make the money he required, Braund sat on the end of the bed in the room next door reading a newspaper.

He overheard Schubert say he wanted to check everything was

all right with the flat – and within seconds the bedroom door flew open. The startled doctor asked: "What are you doing here?" Thinking on his seat, Braund replied: "I've come for sex of course. What are *you* doing here?" Red-faced, Schubert retreated to the living room and could be heard praising the girls for finding a customer so quickly.

A few days later the girls were ready to open for business. The doctor had printed calling cards for them – 'sexy girl massage' – and included a phone number. The last part of the number – 377248 – in text form, actually spelt out the first part of his name: Dr Schu.

In order to lure Schubert back so that he could be confronted, the girls called the doctor to say the phone in the flat wasn't working and he needed to fix it straightaway. Within the hour the doctor arrived to find the girls in the lounge – while the Cook team were concealed in the bedroom. As he fiddled with the phone, the crew and I made our entrance. Schubert was stunned – and then having recovered some of his composure, denied everything.

Eventually he pushed past the cameraman and clattered down the spiral staircase to the street with the crew and me in hot pursuit. As he ran off down the road, I couldn't resist firing one last question at his fast receding back: 'Dr Schubert, why don't you come back and face the music?'

"Ouch! I'll buy you a drink on that one", said Braund as we helped pack the gear into the back of the camera car. Over that drink we discussed where the story might take us next. "Merlin first," I suggested, "and then let's trace the problem back down the supply line to its source in Eastern Europe." We all agreed, and phoned the editor, whose thoughts were running along similar lines.

Merlin's Chief Executive, Dr Chris Besse, was surprised and embarrassed. He confirmed Dr Schubert was once one of their leading field surgeons and had saved lives in some of the world's worst trouble spots. After the programme Schubert was in trouble himself, and quickly fled Britain with his wife and son. He was last heard of working in China.

In Hungary, we targeted a notorious 'woman-trafficker' called Gyula Gati. Our researches revealed that the front for his illegal activities was a company called Riel Ltd. in Budapest, which purported to be a school photography agency. Through our contacts in Copenhagen we also discovered that Gati had been thrown out of Denmark for smuggling women into the country to work as prostitutes.

He was now back in his seedy fourth-floor office in the Zresz Geza trying to find new markets for his endless supply of girls. The office walls were lined with box files and the phone rang ceaselessly. He was obviously a busy man. So how best to get to him? Fortunately, one of the Cook team's freelance regulars was a substantial, try-anything Hungarian called Zoltan – and he was more than happy to help out if it involved a trip home and the possibility of seeing his relatives.

Posing as a big-time London pimp, Zoltan contacted Gati, told him that he'd heard about his 'Danish difficulties' and said he could use any girls who were surplus to requirements as a result. Gati took the bait and two days later Zoltan and Braund were on a plane from Heathrow to Budapest. We were in the middle of a series at the time, so I followed them shortly afterwards, having finished the previous programme.

In the flesh, Gati was almost a caricature of an East European villain, though the police had assured us he was very much the real thing. He was short and rotund, with close-set eyes, slicked-back hair and a pencil-thin moustache. He was also obviously too big for his expensive suit and wore a flashy gold dress watch.

Gati got straight to the point in our secretly filmed meeting in room 467 at the Budapest Hilton. He could supply girls from five continents – he had hundreds available, and most would love to work in London. He would charge us £150 a month rent for each girl. "All my girls came with an AIDS free test certificate," he boasted, as if it were some sort of MoT. And he warned us not to miss the payments – he had friends in London who could make things very unpleasant for us if we did. It was also made clear that if we 'lost' any of his girls we would still be expected to keep up those payments.

"He's a nasty piece of work," muttered Zoltan as we drew breath after the meeting "and without a shred of humanity." Somehow, we felt it was particularly inappropriate that these negotiations should be taking place at the Hilton, which was built into the ruins of a beautiful mediaeval monastery overlooking the Danube.

At the time, Budapest was gripped by gang warfare, with arson attacks on nightclubs, car bombings and street shootings. Gati rarely travelled alone, and every time we met him, his 27-stone bodyguard stood close by. To emphasise his purpose in life, in the middle of the hotel foyer, the man-mountain slipped his silver-plated 9mm Beretta automatic from its shoulder holster and cocked it ostentatiously. In his guttural, broken English, accompanied by a slashing gesture across his throat, he boasted that he'd killed 'many men'. And enjoyed it, probably.

Gati agreed to sell us five girls from Kiev. He showed us their photographs and added that they had already been sold to work in a bar in Marbella – but we'd agreed a better price. The girls were never consulted – just sold and passed on like livestock. We would have to pay for them to be taken from Kiev to London, but Gati would arrange the paperwork. He said he didn't care what we did with them as long as he was paid, and suggested that confiscating their passports and beating them regularly would keep them compliant. Blackmail and threats against families back home had also proved to be useful constraints.

Later, in the Fortuna Bar, after finalising what he believed to be a good deal, Gati, together with his lawyer and bodyguard, toasted the Cook team with champagne. Of course, we had no intention of taking him up on his offer and handed our evidence to the Budapest police. I still wonder what happened to those five Russian girls.

We also came across another major pimp called Janos Petu. He boasted to us that he had 1500 girls on his books and could supply as many as we wished at $20 per girl per day. He invited us to see how these girls were lured into prostitution and took us to a downtown dive called the Caligula Club. The two front rows were packed with randy Russian Mafiosi ogling the scantily clad 'hostesses'. They brought to mind the classic Mae West line: 'Is that a gun in your pocket or are you just pleased to see me?' These evil-looking fellows could definitely answer 'both'.

After an hour – and a $400 bill for two bottles of rather poor mock champagne – we attempted to make our excuses and leave. We had learnt little and spent a lot – and Petu had disappeared into a back room with one of the girls. However, getting out was harder then getting in – with the hefty doormen demanding to know if we really wanted to leave so soon. Only after Zoltan had a quiet word with the 'madam' did the heavies step aside. It was all very depressing and degrading.

But the most depressing and degrading story of all had its origins in Britain. Nineteen-year-old Sarah Forsythe from Newcastle found herself trapped in a drug-ridden Amsterdam brothel – forced to have sex with up to 17 men a day – after she'd answered an advertisement for a nursery nurse.

She was interviewed and given the job by a man called John Reece and was soon on a plane to Holland. Almost as soon as they had landed, Reece held a stun gun to her head and took her passport. Before the day was out she'd been drugged and displayed under a red light in the brothel window. She was fed a daily diet of chocolate and cocaine and guarded by a pit bull terrier at the door.

She was treated like an animal. "Worse than the guard dog," she said – and felt "completely worthless" as a result. Pallid, trembling and still in the throes of cocaine withdrawal, she was virtually monosyllabic, and very difficult to interview. The camera had to be stopped several times as she burst into tears. "Sarah's a prostitute now!" she wailed. Over and over again.

We pieced together what had happened to her. After months of dreadful abuse, Sarah had finally escaped and run to the local police station. Unbeknown to Sarah, the desk sergeant was one of her customers, and she was taken straight back to the brothel. There, she was shown a so-called 'snuff' movie and told that she would be the subject of the next one if she ever tried running away again.

Eventually, without caring whether she lived or died, she did make another escape bid. This one was successful and she made her way back to Britain. She spent six months in counselling but no one believed her incredible story – except for us and one sympathetic policeman. Detective Sergeant Phill Adcock investigated Sarah's claims and later saw Reece gaoled for two years.

Not long after that programme, and for a number of different reasons, the retirement I had once contemplated but rejected, was almost thrust upon me.

As I've mentioned before, the programmes that are broadcast

on independent television are commissioned and scheduled by a central body called The Network Centre. The people who work there are vulnerable to removal at the drop of a hat – a reflection of the way commercial television is susceptible to market forces.

In autumn 1997, a new regime came to power. Part of its brief was to halt the slide in ITV viewing audiences. There was no question but that wholesale changes were going to be made.

Apart from a vow to move *News at Ten* to allow feature films and dramas to be shown uninterrupted, there was also an understanding that the new people would revamp factual programmes – of which *World in Action, The Big Story* and *The Cook Report* were the main examples.

A sudden paralysis overtook Carlton, which made my programme and *The Big Story*. Rumours of the imminent demise of Granada's venerable *World in Action* programme were rife. No one knew what was happening for sure, but it didn't look good. Carlton was already in the wars over a documentary called 'The Connection' which, it turned out, had been largely falsified by its freelance producer, who had roundly abused the trust of his employers. It was a shameful affair and the head of the London-based department that made the programme was heavily criticised. In my view, other senior executives also became sacrificial lambs.

The effect was to create a defensive atmosphere within Carlton, which was threatened with a heavy fine and, *in extremis*, the revocation of its licence to broadcast. The fine was duly levied – £2 million – but the company stayed in business. This was hardly a situation to encourage the recommissioning of contentious investigative programmes like ours.

By Christmas, it was obvious that *Cook Report* team members were not going to have their contracts renewed. I was told that nobody knew what the future of the series was. We knew the Network wanted a couple of hour-long investigative specials, but was that all?

I didn't know what to do, so I called my agent. Always a man with acute antennae, even Jon Roseman had to confess that nobody could tell what was happening at Network Centre.

I decided to take the bull by the horns and end the uncertainty. After 12 years and 125 high-profile programmes, I had long wanted to reduce my workload. I was very tired and some said the programme was getting tired too, despite its continuing success. So, after discussion with family and colleagues, I took the decision to announce that I was going to quit the series while I was ahead, as I had done in *Checkpoint* days. It is also possible that I jumped before I was pushed. Carlton issued a short press release, which included confirmation of the one-hour *Cook Report Specials.*

There were soon lots of stories circulating about me finally recognising that I could no longer cope with being battered and bruised. One paper, going one better, headlined its story: 'Cook Quits as Ratings Fall and Beatings Rise'. In fact the reverse was true. I hadn't been hit for a couple of years, and the average ratings, at around eight million, had actually risen over the previous series. But why let the facts get in the way of a catchy headline?

At the end of the day, the truth was that I, and just about every other programme-maker in commercial television, was still in the dark about the future.

Christmas and New Year came and went.

Then came news from the Network Centre. They wanted me to work with Yorkshire Television to present ITV's planned competitor for the BBC's *Watchdog.* I declined this offer. It just wasn't my kind of show, but I did accept the offer of two one-hour *Cook Report Specials* from Yorkshire to add to the pair already commissioned from Carlton. I was told that more 'Specials' would follow, but that they would be made by Yorkshire.

It was all very puzzling the way those at the top seemed to be blowing hot and cold. I learnt later that a senior Network Centre executive had been sitting in the back of a London taxi when the driver started to bemoan the loss of *The Cook Report.* I have the eloquence of the cabbie to thank for renewed interest in us because, apparently, it prompted the executive to review the programme's viewing figures. No doubt he was reminded that ours was still by far the most watched *and* most appreciated current affairs show in the country.

It certainly seems to have been appreciated by The British Academy of Film and Television Arts (BAFTA) which in 1997 was kind enough to make me a special award 'for 25 years of outstanding quality investigative reporting'. Those were the words intoned by Trevor McDonald as he handed me a surprisingly heavy trophy.

It was a televised event and making speeches in front of a live audience really isn't my thing, so a combination of my nerves and the trophy's unexpected weight nearly caused me to drop it. I regard the award as a great honour, and will certainly never use it to prop open the loo door, as some recipients claim to have done. I also took it a bit amiss, since it was the kind of award you usually only get when you're retired or dead. And I like to think I'm neither.

Back in harness with a new team at Yorkshire Television, we made a *Cook Report Special* on a subject I had examined several times before – the fugitives from justice who the authorities seemingly refuse to pursue. I enjoyed working at YTV, in particular with producer Andrew Sheldon. His programme was well-made and well-received.

TV Politics then intervened again.

It had been decided that most of ITV's current affairs output – *World In Action, The Big Story* and *3D* – was to be replaced by a new, weekly, big-budget programme which was initially put out to tender. The man in charge of commissioning factual programmes at the Network Centre at the time carefully considered all the proposals – and gave the job to his brother at Granada.

The result was *Tonight With Trevor McDonald*. Granada had just taken over Yorkshire Television, which was then employing me. That left Granada with all the current affairs programmes and the other major franchise holder, Carlton, with none – obviously an unacceptable situation. So my Yorkshire connection was terminated after just one programme and I was sent back to Nottingham. I was stunned, not least because I was only told of the reasons for this sudden change of direction well after the event.

At Carlton, Howard Foster had been kept on to make the two previously commissioned one-hour specials. He and his colleagues Philip Braund and Stephen Scott produced programmes on art theft and car crime – and we ended 1998 with an amazing audience of almost nine-and-a-half million viewers.

I was given a new two-year contract to make four one-hour specials a year, plus a possible further series of six half-hours. Those two years flew by – with further successful hour-long programmes, including one particularly memorable one in August 1999 on rogue doctors.

Our sources had told us that the General Medical Council, charged with policing the conduct and standards of Britain's doctors, was not doing an adequate job. Doctors were only struck off the register *in extremis*, and even then were able to reregister with relative ease, and relatively quickly.

This was not to say that you can't trust a doctor, the vast majority of whom are competent, humane and trustworthy. But how do you know who isn't, and are you being protected from them? They were good questions for which we decided to seek answers.

First, we commissioned a Mori poll which showed that two-thirds of us didn't know that struck off doctors could return to practice relatively quickly, three-quarters of us thought a seriously disgraced doctor should never be allowed near patients again, and nearly 100 per cent would rather not be treated by such a doctor. But as things stood, we didn't have the choice. This was the issue we had raised with the then Health Minister, Frank Dobson. Sadly, it was all too easy to find case histories which illustrated the failings of the system.

It is an unfortunate fact that most of the errant doctors we unearthed had qualified in other countries, usually in the Indian subcontinent. This raised further queries not only about the training standards in their countries of origin, but also about the system the GMC uses to vet applicants before allowing them onto the UK register.

In the case of Kolatur Unni, one wonders whether they made any checks at all. Dr Unni qualified in India, but subsequently took up practice in New Zealand, where he worked as a consultant psychiatrist. The kindest thing you could say about the man was that he was sexually incontinent. He abused his position of trust to prey on his patients, both male and female.

As a result, he was struck off in 1985, but a couple of years later, having apparently sought psychiatric help himself, he was allowed to practice again. He began to reoffend almost immediately and was struck off again. When I called on Dr Ian St. George of the New Zealand Medical Council, at his office overlooking Wellington Harbour, he explained that, as in the UK, the law didn't allow the Council to strike off a doctor for life. With Dr Unni, his preference would have been to do just that, but Unni had fled the country, leaving unpaid the $26,000 fine the NZMC had imposed on him.

Being New Zealanders, the Council had since found an original way of keeping dangerous or incompetent doctors away from the public. Now, before being readmitted to the register, an applicant has to resit all of his exams, and in the unlikely event that he should pass them all, the doctor must post a prominent notice in his surgery waiting room, warning patients that he has previously been struck off and giving the reasons why. Not surprisingly, there have so far been no takers.

The amount of research effort that went into this programme meant that by the time the last sequence – in New Zealand – was due to be filmed, we were tight on time and the producer couldn't leave the edit suite. The result for me was another solo day trip down under. It was a two-day trip actually, but I don't think I noticed the difference. I flew from London to Wellington, where I spent the night. Then, filming at several locations en route, I drove to Auckland.

New Zealand is a stunningly beautiful country, a country I hadn't seen for more than half a century and there I was, of necessity, exceeding the speed limit through most of it. I remember passing a sign that said 'Rotorua 2Km. Hot Springs and Geysers'. But I didn't have the time to stop and look at one of New Zealand's most famous attractions. Arriving at Auckland's spanking new airport with minutes to spare, I boarded what I believe was the same 747–400 that had brought me out, and flew the 14,000 miles straight back to London. Whew!

After his disgrace in New Zealand, Dr Unni turned up in London too. He was allowed onto the medical register at his third attempt, only to be struck off again when the GMC checked his history. Back in practice yet again by 1995, he headed straight for another *smorgasbord* of psychiatric patients, this time as a consultant at the Basildon Hospital in Essex.

We decided to lay a bait to see if he was the reformed character he professed to be. The bait was an attractive – and carefully briefed – researcher called Helen Keating, who sought and got an appointment with Dr Unni, ostensibly to discuss relationship problems. Her handbag concealed a video camera, and it wasn't long before we had clear evidence of his proclivities – enough evidence, in fact, to make it unsafe for Helen to see the doctor again.

When I confronted him with this, and with his sordid past outside his consulting rooms, Unni fled. He ran through the back doors of the pathology lab and bolted them behind him. He must have alerted the hospital administrators, because a phalanx of worried suits turned up shortly afterwards. They were dismayed to find *The Cook Report* on the premises, but were horrified when they were told why we were there. The GMC had told them nothing of Unni's provenance.

After the programme, they set up a local telephone helpline and received no fewer than 70 serious new complaints about Unni's behaviour. He was dismissed from the hospital, and the prosecution that followed resulted in an 18-month prison sentence.

During the trial, there was a clue as to why all these complaints had not surfaced earlier. As reported by one of his victims, Unni had a habit of saying: "There's no point in complaining, because you're a mental patient and nobody's going to believe you." Judge Leonard Gerber said that Unni's behaviour was genuinely shocking and that "having exploited vulnerability and weakness for his own bizarre sexual pleasure, Unni should never again be allowed to practice as a doctor in this country – or anywhere else." The GMC had no alternative but to follow that verdict – and Unni was struck off the register for the fourth time.

Jonathan Levy was a high profile doctor who courted publicity and appeared on a cable TV channel as 'The Doctor You Can Trust'. In reality, he was a liar, a cheat and a complete stranger to medical ethics. He first hit the headlines when he treated a 75-year-old man who fell ill on a flight from London to Jamaica. The grateful airline sent him a case of fine wine and champagne – and Levy sent them a bill for £1,350.

He was struck off the medical register in 1981 for carrying on an adulterous relationship with a patient. His mistress refused his demands to lie to the GMC and deny the affair. The GMC said that they 'took these offences very seriously' and in one of their tougher 'sentences' struck him off for four years.

Within a year of his reinstatement he was in serious trouble again. Andrew Fisher was a passenger in an MG Midget when Levy in his Volkswagen GTI took umbrage as the Midget took the place he'd been aiming for at a set of traffic lights. He pursued the Midget for some miles, eventually running it across the road and into the path of an oncoming vehicle.

Not only did Dr Levy speed away from the scene of the inevitable accident – a serious offence in itself – but then – as a doctor, remember – he also left young Andrew to die. He subsequently lied to the police, inventing a story about a dangerous mystery motorcyclist in order to cover his tracks. He was only caught when a witness was eventually found who could remember his number plate.

When the case came up at Norwich Crown Court in July 1987, Levy was found guilty of causing death by dangerous driving, but was gaoled for just nine months, that being the kind of penalty such an offence then attracted. Andrew's bereaved fiancé fully expected Levy to be struck off again. After all, at the hearing which had him struck off the first time, the chairman was moved to say: "You have demonstrated qualities of character which are the antithesis of those required by a member of the medical profession."

Yet, though he had betrayed his humanity and his Hippocratic Oath, he pleaded his case on prison notepaper and the GMC unaccountably allowed him to stay in practice. That he was a doctor who fled rather than trying to save his victim's life did not appear to have been taken into account.

As the film crew and I approached him from behind a wall as he was trying to park his car, he caught a glimpse of the camcraman and was off down the road in a pall of tyre smoke. Once again he demonstrated his penchant for avoiding responsibility, and he was out of the country by nightfall. This was one TV appearance he plainly didn't want to make.

Dr Mark Lister Patterson appears in *Who's Who*. He's a former Conservative councillor and would-be MP, and a Territorial Army major with an extensive estate on the Isle of Wight. What *Who's Who* doesn't tell you is that the doctor was also a dangerous criminal.

Over a period of four years he sold 12,000 litres of outdated blood processed in a less-than-sterile London lock-up garage. He had stolen the blood from his employers, The National Heart Hospital and it made him £158,000.

At the Old Bailey, Patterson was gaoled for three years, and the judge told him that his medical career was finished. But that's not the way the GMC saw it. Patterson was not struck off, just suspended for 18 months, and that meant he could go straight back to work as soon as he got out of prison. He was soon back in practice, this time as a consultant haematologist in Cheshire. Was this perhaps putting temptation in his way again?

My uninvited interview approach resulted in a display of self-righteous indignation. "This has nothing to do with you," he spluttered, pushing past me. This incident also resulted in a report to the Broadcasting Standards Commission, which somehow came to the conclusion that I had unjustifiably invaded his privacy. Another example of the Establishment protecting its own, perhaps?

We discovered doctors whose incompetence had resulted in death, a doctor who traded heroin substitutes for sex, doctors who stole and embezzled from the NHS, doctors who refused to treat NHS patients who were ill and charged to treat private patients who were not. We found a doctor who made his living by indiscriminately supplying prescription drugs, false medical certificates and phoney insurance reports. Most had only been admonished, or at worst, given a short suspension. Only the last, Dr George Udenquo, was struck off. This was as a direct result of our programme – but not until nearly three years after the broadcast.

At the London Headquarters of the GMC, Sir Donald Irvine was urbane, but not very helpful. He denied that his organisation put the interests of the profession above those of patients and said that he couldn't discuss individual cases, even those already in the public domain.

This meant I couldn't challenge what certainly looked like ill-advised decisions to reinstate some of the doctors we had featured. So I put it to him, as he leaned back in his comfortable leather chair, that though the vast majority of doctors were just as they should be, without knowing it, you might end up in the hands of, say, a serial sex offender. "You might indeed," came the less than reassuring reply. "In a population of 100,000 people (his figure for the number of doctors in the UK) you will get all the dimensions of behaviour which you find in the population as a whole."

Sir Donald wouldn't have it that the punishments meted out by the GMC often seemed not to fit the crime and reminded me that there was no mechanism for striking off doctors permanently. He suggested that the solution to the problem lay in the patients' hands. "Individual people themselves will determine how to solve this problem."

In other words, patients should ask their doctors if they had ever been struck off. Leaving aside the fact that the likes of an unprincipled crook such as Dr Jonathan Levy wouldn't give an honest answer, our MORI poll had discovered that this key ques-

385

tion was one that 92 per cent of you would never dream of asking. And in at least one of our cases the doctor's victims never saw him.

Dr Wayne Heaven worked as a locum in the Lake District. What nobody knew was that he was also a serial stalker, who selected his victims by trawling through the records in the practices in which he worked. He would begin by making obscene and menacing phone calls – a few at first, and then a veritable barrage.

One of his early victims was Beverley Dunn, a single parent with three young children who lived in an isolated Cumbrian cottage. After the phone calls had taken their terrifying effect, Beverley would be woken late at night by the sound of her windows and door locks being tested. She took to sleeping with a knife under her pillow.

Eventually she cracked under the strain and took an overdose of sleeping pills. Fortunately, she survived, and her pleas for help were then taken seriously. A trace was put on her line and the police arrested the perpetrator. To their surprise and dismay, he was a doctor – the inappropriately named Dr Heaven.

It turned out that Beverley was not his only victim. Others, as young as 17, had been subjected to a similar barrage of obscene calls, describing in detail the perverted sexual acts Heaven planned to carry out on them.

Dr Heaven was subsequently convicted of making obscene and threatening phone calls – but escaped imprisonment. The judge apparently felt that what the GMC had in store for him would be punishment enough. He would surely be struck off for a very long time. However, when his GMC disciplinary hearing came up, the panel seems to have decided that the lenient court sentence imposed on him was an indication that his offences were not particularly serious. They therefore only 'admonished' him and he was allowed to continue in practice.

The cruel irony here is that Beverley Dunn was a nurse, and because her professional body took her Heaven-driven suicide attempt as an indication of instability, she was not allowed to continue in her chosen profession.

Heaven, who'd created hell for patients he'd never met, would not take responsibility for his actions and when confronted, showed no remorse and offered no real answers:

"Dr Heaven, I'm Roger Cook from Central Television."

"I know."

"I trust you can currently resist the temptation to victimise vulnerable women, can you?"

"I've sought legal advice and that advice is that I don't say anything about all this, so that's what I'm going to do."

"You've nothing to say about Beverley Dunn, whose life you effectively ruined?"

But the one well-rehearsed reply was all I got.

The broadcast caused something of a stir – no one had quite so publicly challenged the status quo before. Doctors had been treated as being above suspicion, and the system for policing them had never been effectively questioned – though it appeared fundamentally flawed, tending to protect the minority of rogues in the medical profession rather than rooting them out.

According to one commentator, the programme 'seemed to open a Pandora's Box'. More scandals came to light, notable amongst them, the cases of the gynaecological butcher, Rodney Ledward, and the serial killer Dr Harold Shipman – who was able to murder at least 215 of his patients before being discovered, almost by accident, after a clumsy attempt to forge the will of one of his victims. Shipman later hanged himself in his cell at Wakefield Prison.

The various official enquiries into some of the cases we had raised and into those of Shipman and Ledward left the General Medical Council reeling from a range of well-deserved criticisms about their potentially dangerous shortcomings – many of which we had previously highlighted.

In one report, they were accused of being 'self-serving, biased in favour of doctors, failing to protect patients, being overly secretive and of acting through expediency rather than principle'. Obviously chastened, the Council then embarked on what they called 'the most wide-ranging reforms in the 150 year history of medical regulation'.

Already, as a direct result of our programme, though it is still not possible to strike off a doctor for life, those doctors who are erased from the register can no longer apply for reinstatement just ten months later. They must now wait for a minimum of five years. And all doctors are to be subjected to a five-yearly performance check, a sort of MoT for medics. At some stage there will also be a new body to oversee such regulators as the GMC.

Pandora's Box clearly needed opening.

It was a worthwhile conclusion to a very successful season, and the programme attracted an audience of around nine million viewers.

Five years on, the impetus for much-needed reform was kept up by the findings of one of a series of judicial reports on the Shipman affair, the fifth of which focused on the general workings of the GMC. High Court judge Dame Janet Smith found that the culture and procedures of the GMC were fundamentally flawed. "Having examined the evidence I have been driven to the conclusion that the GMC has not, in the past, succeeded in its primary task of protecting patients," Dame Janet said. "Instead, it has, to a very significant degree, acted in the interests of doctors."

She stopped short of calling for the abolition of the GMC altogether, but listed more than 50 recommendations for substantial change, over and above those proposed by the Council itself. "I have concluded there has not yet been the shift in culture within the GMC which will ensure that patient protection is given the priority it deserves. The current perception is that the GMC is representing doctors – it is not, it is regulating them."

However, the GMC continued, in the words of one critic, "to tinker round the edges of the problem", making some improvements in the system for detecting rogue doctors and tightening up on discipline – in that the percentage of doctors struck off went up slightly – but the fundamental changes called for by Dame Janet never came.

Now at last, it seems they have. The GMC is no longer to act as judge and jury. In July 2006, Sir Liam Donaldson, the Chief Medical Officer, recommended that the Council should lose its disciplinary role, though it would still be responsible for registering doctors and for gathering evidence needed to take unfit practitioners to court. That evidence would be presented to a new and independent tribunal, which would judge each case on the balance of probabilities, the civil standard of proof, rather than beyond a reasonable doubt, the criminal standard, which the GMC has previously used.

This shoud mean that that many more doctors who have transgressed and subsequently appear before the independent tribunal are likely to be struck off. The GMC would still be responsible for ensuring the basic competence of doctors, though it would lose some of its role in medical education, and it would become directly accountable to parliament.

Concluding his announcement, Sir Liam had this to say: "Every day, thousands of patients place their trust in a doctor, and, in my view, they are right to do so because standards of medical care in this country are very high, but that trust must be underpinned by robust systems based on standards and delivery."

In other words – as was said of the GMC at the time of our programme, seven years earlier – "The public needs to know that doctors are overseen by a watchdog, not a lapdog."

9

The Hunter as Hunted

Defeating the tabloids – and calling time

I was in the process of negotiating a new contract when the sky fell in. I should say here that I believe that if you're in the business of turning over stones, you must expect to be turned over yourself from time to time. No one is infallible or invulnerable.

I have been a target myself several times over the years, but I and the *Cook Report* team survived because, to the best of our knowledge and abilities, each programme was ethically made and truthful. Libel actions against us have failed, faded away or in a couple of instances have been settled commercially without admission – and those critics who from time to time derided the programme were plainly ignored by our substantial audience.

But this was different. In a concerted attack on us by two News Group newspapers, the 'truth' – or what was claimed to be the truth – was bought and sold like a commodity. The vast majority of witnesses against us had been paid to say what suited our attackers, or had criminal records, or were the deserving targets of previous *Cook Report* programmes – sometimes all three.

Saturday, the 23rd of January 2000, was just another busy day – until the phone rang. I was away on location, so Frances took the call. It was from Stephen Scott, one of the newer *Cook Report* producers, who had apparently fallen out with the then editor Mike Morley. He told Frances that an article critical of the programme was about to appear in *The Sunday Times*, but that he wanted me to know that he was not critical of me and had no wish to damage my reputation. In fact, he said he held me in high regard.

Frances then phoned me and we discussed Scott's call. I thought the article concerned might be about a part of the programme on organised car crime that he had produced. The relevant part was a

391

sting we had mounted to illustrate the activities of the son of a notorious Liverpool family called the Charlesworths.

Caught on film, Ian Charlesworth had offered to supply to order a range of expensive stolen cars and had boasted of having served two prison sentences. He then organised, and we filmed, the theft of a valuable Ducati motorbike. We'd been working on the programme for nearly two months and because Charlesworth was unable to supply a van on the day, we let him use ours.

None of us, including Scott, was particularly happy with this arrangement, but Charlesworth had made it plain he was prepared to steal a van for the job, and we couldn't allow that to happen. Having consulted Carlton's in-house lawyer, Simon Westrop, we had made this clear in the broadcast programme. The company's senior press officer, Peter Rushton, apprised *The Sunday Times* of the facts, and was convinced the story would be spiked.

Not so. The next day, a blazing headline across the top of page three proclaimed: 'Cook Report Crime Scenes Faked'. Interestingly, in later editions, the word 'faked' appeared in inverted commas, indicating a degree of legal uncertainty in the editorial offices. The article no longer made much of Charlesworth's men using our van, though it claimed – wrongly – that *Cook Report* personnel had driven it to and from the scene of the 'crime'.

Instead, the paper sought to give the impression that Charlesworth was an innocent abroad who'd been conned into stealing the bike on the pretext that it was a legal repossession. There was no evidence whatever for this claim, apart from the assertions of a self-confessed career criminal. In fact, Terry Fox, a former police chief inspector who had worked as a *Cook Report* consultant for several years and who had also worked undercover on the sting, had made it abundantly clear to Charlesworth that what he'd agreed to do was illegal.

Naturally, I pressed Carlton management to take action, but little was done. There was a warning letter from the legal department putting the paper on notice that the article had been grossly libellous and that a dim view would be taken of any repetitions or future libels. When that letter was ignored, no further action was taken.

At that time, the man to whom everyone deferred in the day to day running of Carlton was Waheed Alli, co-creator of 'The Big Breakfast' and 'Survivor' and also a new Labour peer. Although not the most senior executive by title, he acted as if he had been given *carte blanche* by the board to run the company as he thought fit. It seemed that no one cared to challenge him – and on this issue, he was adamant that we should not react to the article in any way and that the problem would simply 'go away'.

Another phone call, on the afternoon of Saturday, the 12th of February 2000, proved he was wrong. This time it was from a man called James Hadfield-Hyde, who had just been visited by a reporter from *The Sunday Times'* sister paper, the *News of the World*. Mr Hadfield-Hyde had previously lent us his mini-stately home in Cheshire in which to mount yet another sting – as part of a programme about works of art being stolen to order. The target was a valuable painting – or in this case, a very good copy of one.

However, because we had engineered this 'crime', the *News of the World* denounced it as a fake, despite the fact that it was just the kind of sting in which that newspaper now appears to specialise. The crucial difference was that in our case, using seven hidden cameras, we were filming professional criminals at work, not just any likely lads with no previous relevant record who could be persuaded to oblige.

As a result, we successfully exposed Paul Bowler – a legal executive falsely claiming to be a qualified solicitor – whose profitable sideline was in recruiting gangs of career criminals to steal expensive art and antiques as he directed. Bowler was subsequently struck off by the Institute of Legal Executives.

Mr Hadfield-Hyde told us that he was sure from the *News of the World* man's attitude and the questions he asked that we were in for trouble. He was also concerned – rightly, as it turned out – that the sting would be misrepresented and that he would be misquoted.

That call was followed by a visit to my home by another *News of the World* reporter called Rob Kellaway. I was out, so he left his card with Belinda, then just 14. When I returned, I called Peter Rushton in the Carlton press office. He cautioned me not to ring Kellaway back 'to be ambushed' as he put it, with no time to prepare a defence. He told me he'd been given less than an hour to respond to more than eight pages of allegations, of which the Bowler story was only one. I can only assume that the newspaper didn't wish to be burdened with the answers.

In part of another programme – about juvenile crime – we had been accused of introducing an 'innocent and bewildered' 15-year-old boy to illicit drugs and a criminal career. The newspaper's reporters had plainly not watched the programme, because during the course of it, in an interview given with his mother's approval, the lad admitted having committed more than 50 burglaries since the age of ten. The money often went to feed a pre-existing drug habit.

We were also wrongly accused of involvement in a burglary for which the young man had already long been convicted. In court, he made no mention of having been aided and abetted by *The Cook Report*, an unsupportable claim only made six years later by the *News of the World*.

The false allegations made in *The Sunday Times* a fortnight before were repeated, as was an earlier *News of the World* story on a programme we'd made about professional hit-men. Two years previously, the newspaper had claimed that the hit-man featured in our programme had made fools of us because he was only a nightclub bouncer. This wasn't even true then, but in their second publication, they went much further, claiming that we had cynically foisted a phoney hit-man onto our viewing audience.

In fact, far from being the flimsy fudge suggested by the *News of the World*, that programme led to two major convictions. As a demonstration of how easily a hit-man might obtain a suitable firearm, we had secretly filmed two Derbyshire dealers who claimed to specialise in perfectly legal, de-activated 'collectors' guns'. Where William and Mitchell Greenwood differed from legitimate dealers was that they would sell these weapons to anyone, no questions asked, complete with a do-it-yourself kit of parts to make them into lethal weapons again.

When the Greenwoods eventually appeared in court (where *The Cook Report* was shown in evidence) it transpired that they had sold over 4,000 illegal firearms, including Uzi sub-machine guns and AK-47 rifles, to criminals and terrorists. Police had linked some of the guns to at least eight murders, a string of robberies and numerous gangland shootings. Both men were gaoled for seven years.

Some of the programmes referred to in the *News of the World* article were ten years old, the staff responsible had moved on and the records had been archived. So just one hour on a Saturday night was nowhere near long enough for the considered response these serious allegations deserved. I knew it was going to look bad.

I didn't sleep that night, and got up at the crack of dawn to go out for an early edition of the *News of the World*. I could see the headline on the paper in the service station rack from 50 yards away. 'ROGER COOK SHOWS FAKED', it screamed. I felt sick, but I forced myself to read the article. It covered all of the front page and three more following. I skimmed it first, and then went through it line by line.

Strangely, after I'd read it, I felt a little better, because what they'd published was little more than the uncorroborated evidence of a disgruntled former employee called David Llewellyn. As indicated earlier, this 'evidence' was supplemented with what looked like the paid testimony of a series of people with criminal records, or of the deserving targets of the programmes in which they'd featured. The stories were provably false and I was advised that we would clearly win at law. But the reading public wouldn't have known that and the *News of the World* was Britain's biggest selling newspaper.

At two o'clock that afternoon there was another, fairly bizarre, phone call – reminiscent of the one we'd had from Stephen Scott a couple of weeks earlier. It was from the aforementioned David Llewellyn, a pint-sized junior technician, whose job it had been to install and maintain our secret cameras.

He confirmed that he was the source of the story and said that he was very sorry that the resulting article was so damaging to me. He said he had nothing against me and that I was a decent, honest bloke, but that he didn't like the way he'd been treated by the editor and the series producer. He must have been very naïve to think that a tabloid newspaper would be interested in the back room boys.

I later learnt that his main complaint seems to have been the regular pruning of his inflated expenses, and that when Carlton didn't react to the *Sunday Times* article he felt that the way was clear for him to 'recoup his losses' by selling more nasty tittle-tattle to the *News of the World*. He claimed he was paid £4,000 for his efforts. In the phone call – which was recorded – he also said that he'd told Rob Kellaway only what he thought the paper would want to hear.

Frances was extremely upset when she read the article. She has been very supportive over the years, but now wanted me to give up my particular brand of investigative journalism forthwith. This was not because she gave any credence to the flimsily supported allegations against me, but because although she reluctantly accepted that I would face up to and do battle with wrongdoers, she felt that being stabbed in the back by fellow journalists as a consequence was the last straw.

I sat her down, dried her tears, and eventually we agreed that giving up would be taken as an admission of either guilt or of defeat. With her support, I would fight.

The article had an immediate effect on the public too. That evening, I was filling my car at a petrol station when another customer on the forecourt remarked: "I always felt your shows were too good to be true, you fucking hypocrite." On the following day in the street, I was asked: "Haven't you been thrown off the telly yet?"

Someone else suggested: "You got what was coming to you, you lying shit." And I'll always remember, a few weeks later at an ITV gathering, when one of my fellow guests tried to introduce me to Linford Christie. Turning on his heel, Christie snapped: "He's a lying bastard, and I don't want anything to do with him." There was some irony in that, bearing in mind the fact that Christie was later found guilty of using the illegal performance-enhancing drugs he'd always claimed to have shunned.

Such remarks as those, previously rare except from the mouths of yobbos, were fairly typical of the adverse public reaction I then faced, though our local taxi driver was kind enough to say that he 'didn't take that comic seriously'.

And to be fair, it wasn't *all* bad. There were the occasional bright patches in the gathering storm. I remember one afternoon, driving along the nearside lane of a busy dual carriageway looking for house numbers, when a car pulled alongside. In it was a group of rowdy youths clearly on their way to a football match. Their pimped-up BMW was swathed in scarves, a club banner fluttered from atop a six-foot aerial and they were swigging lager to the accompaniment of loud, thumping music.

Then, and obviously as readers of the aforesaid comic, they recognised me. A barrage of foul-mouthed abuse began. I ignored it and tried to drop back out of the firing line, but to no avail. I was pelted with empty lager cans, but still refused to give them the pleasure of a response.

Eventually, up ahead on the outside lane, I saw something that could be turned to my advantage with a little luck and a bit of prompting. Perhaps I shouldn't have done it, but I couldn't resist. At the next salvo of obscenities I *did* respond, with a vigorous 'V' sign. Overcome with road rage, they were now more focused on me than they were on where they were going. The driver hammered his horn and veered towards me. One of his passengers pounded his fist down the side of my car. Another dropped his trousers and mooned out of the BMW's nearside window.

As he did, I accelerated gently away – and they ran slap bang into some unmanned, cordoned-off roadworks – where they were immediately pounced upon by the occupants of a stationary police car waiting to turn right, just ahead of the big hole they were now in. Poetic justice, I thought. Let them talk their way out of that!

Then it was back to everyday reality – and something approaching a siege mentality. I was already feeling like a pariah and began to spend much of my time indoors. I even grew a beard to hide behind. Friends and business contacts, though supportive, occasionally and very tentatively asked me if there might not have been some fire to produce so much smoke in the *News of the World*. I assured them there wasn't even any kindling.

Then I began to get phone calls from colleagues with whom I had worked as long ago as 20 years, telling me that the *News of the World* had been in touch, 'looking for more dirt' on me. I was assured that no one had obliged them, not least because there wasn't any dirt to dish, but knowing what was still going on behind the scenes only served to increase the pressure on me and my family.

Frances recalls me sitting by my desk in my old mahogany captain's chair, with my head in my hands, muttering 'What are they trying to do?' But I already knew the probable answer. As with so many tilts taken at the programme in the past, I believe their actions were largely prompted by professional jealousy. *The Cook Report* was thought to be just too damned successful, and in keeping with the British press tradition of 'build them up and knock them down', it was bound to be targeted. It shouldn't be forgotten either, that sensational allegations about a high profile programme like *The Cook Report* would also sell more newspapers.

I called a council of war with my agent, Jon Roseman, and my personal solicitor, Ian Bloom. Having considered all the available evidence, Ian's opinion was that I had clearly been libelled, unjustifiably and in the most damaging possible way. Jon agreed, but pointed out that win or lose, taking solo action against the likes of the *News of the World*, could, and probably would, cost me everything I'd worked for over the last 30 years.

Then Ian leaned forward over the conference room table, fixing me with his owl-like gaze. A former publisher turned lawyer, he'd caught up and passed most of his contemporaries – and though his serious intent was often masked by a mordant wit, he planned his actions like a championship chess match.

I should understand, he said, that our eventual victory – presuming my finances would last the course – might well be a pyrrhic one. It was an unfortunate fact that libel actions often ended that way. But they both concurred that for someone in my position, doing nothing wasn't an option either. So it was agreed that as a first step Jon would write formally to Carlton, suggesting that they had a duty to take immediate action in defence of the company, the programme, and me.

At about this time, the rest of the production team involved in the programmes savaged by the *News of the World* – producers, researchers and legal adviser – all signed a letter written by the latter – Peter Smith. It was dispatched to Lord Alli, then the Director of Productions at Carlton. In it, they pointed out that they too had been grossly libelled, set out the reasons why the allegations made were provably false and asked for Carlton to take prompt legal action. Though Peter Smith had actually helped Waheed Alli set up *The Big Breakfast*, they never had the courtesy of a reply.

I had no response either until after the second article, when once again I pressed for action. This produced a telephone call from Waheed Alli, who had previously written to my agent to say he accepted that I was 'wholly blameless' and that the allegations made by the *News of the World* were false. However, as His Lordship was at pains to point out on the phone: "You obviously don't understand how to deal with these situations Roger, but as a master tactician who's often beaten the tabloids at their own game, I do. There's been no real damage done to you personally, and making a fight of it will only make matters worse." And on what was probably intended as a reassuring note, he concluded: "I'll call in the *News of the World* editor, give him a good lunch, and I'll persuade him to see the error of his ways."

He'll laugh at you, more like, I thought as I paced round the garden. By then, the *News of the World* had made a formal complaint to the ITV regulator, the Independent Television Commission, and I was off the air and on much reduced pay for the duration, pending the results of the investigation that the newspaper had demanded.

In the first article, I was portrayed as a buffoon who didn't know or didn't care what his allegedly corrupt production team was up to. In the second, I was the author of all the 'fakery' from the very first programme – an exposé of British fugitives on 'The Costa del Crime'. To reinforce their 'fakery' allegation, they made much of our use of a six-second clip of Ronnie Knight on library film, which had been openly purchased by the producer from ITN.

Knight, now out of prison and one of their key witnesses, was quoted as saying that: "a leopard doesn't change its spots," thereby suggesting that I had always been a liar, and also claiming that in that original *Cook Report* I hadn't flown in a helicopter over his Marbella barbecue at all. 'Cook's Copter Showdown With Ronnie Was All Pie In The Sky', declaimed the headline. This was extremely odd, since we'd filmed and transmitted the event and Knight had previously described it, in some detail, in his autobiography.

Then Waheed Alli summoned me to a meeting at the House of Lords. To my great relief, he said he had instructed a leading firm of libel specialists to commence an action for libel against the *News of the World* and its proprietors. The firm would also act on my behalf – though not for long as it turned out.

A few days later, in a brief two paragraph note, Lord Alli's chosen solicitors said they could no longer represent me because to do so might lead to a conflict of interests. The long-promised writ had still not been issued by the time the *News of the World* went into the attack again, on 3rd April 2000, more than two months since the first libel.

This time they made perhaps the most serious allegation of all – that we'd set up 'an innocent man' as a cocaine dealer. The relevant programme wasn't about drugs, but about organised burglary and the subsequent disposal of the stolen goods.

The 'innocent man' was actually a notorious Cambridge fence called Peter Warwick, who boasted on film of having eluded the law for 30 years, and who was later filmed melting down an ingot of stolen gold. During the course of our dealings with him, as an aside, he twice supplied us with us a small quantity of cocaine – which he subsequently claimed was jeweller's chalk, despite police forensic evidence to the contrary.

The *News of the World*'s distorted version of all this was prepared with the help of another former *Cook Report* technician called Nigel Fielden. I had come to regard him as a 'potentially unstable time-bomb' – a phrase I used in a cautionary memo to management, but my warning had fallen on deaf ears. Fielden was an ex-police informer whose services we mainly used as an undercover cameraman. He was actually very good at it, and the film he took of the alleged cocaine incidents conclusively proved the *News of the World*'s claims to be false. But he hadn't given the newspaper the film.

Instead, he took £27,000 from them, apparently for making up stories he thought would suit them. After all, if David Llewellyn could make money from the newspaper without any comeback from Carlton, why shouldn't he? And under the heading "Seven More Lies" he went on to assist the paper in telling just that – seven more lies – about insubstantial parts of several other programmes, two of which were unfinished and hadn't been broadcast. On the strength of this the newspaper condemned whole programmes, indeed, *all* our programmes, 125 in total. And this time they didn't bother to seek our side of the story at all.

Talk about double standards. Given half a chance and rather more courage, the *News of the World* might have themselves targeted the very people whose part they had now taken, and upon whose evidence they heavily relied. In fact, they and their sister newspaper, *The Sun*, had previously picked up and rerun several of the stories about which they were now complaining.

Shell shocked, I went again to see my lawyer, Ian Bloom. I'd had the house valued and Frances and I were prepared to put it on the line. My reputation was, and is, the most valuable thing I have. Having taken counsel's advice and having discussed the case with his partners, Ian was prepared to issue a writ on my behalf and to progress the action on a *pro bono* basis. My Queen's Counsel, Desmond Brown, was prepared to help too.

I was stunned – and then almost grovellingly grateful. I don't know whether Ian was gambling on this or not – and he's never admitted it – but the day after my writ was issued, Carlton also decided to sue. And then, thank God, they told Ian that they would underwrite our action as well.

Unfortunately, that was only the beginning.

Even if I was free to set it out, the detailed evidence I now have on the case would daunt even the most dedicated reader. I have two filing cabinets full, so you can imagine how much effort went into it. For months on end, I became a full-time legal researcher, producing so much paper that the long-suffering Ian Bloom confessed he sometimes had difficulty keeping up with it. But it was a useful, and to some extent cathartic process.

I was often appalled by what I discovered about the *News of the World*'s professional conduct. For example, a damaging quote from an RSPB investigator they used in an attack on our programme about the illegal trade in protected peregrine falcons bore no relation to the transcript of his original interview. In fact, it gave exactly the reverse impression to that which the RSPB man had sought to convey. Mind you, we were lucky to get that transcript. The newspaper later claimed that a number of key tapes and reporters' notebooks 'had gone missing' or 'had been destroyed'.

The *News of the World* was defended by Farrer & Co, the Queen's solicitors. I have never met any of the *News of the World* defence team, but from what I've been able to gather, they somehow seem to have concluded that I was amongst the worst of villains.

They certainly pushed their luck in pursuit of my scalp, by disregarding court approved dates for disclosure of documents – and as you'll see later – even putting themselves at risk of contempt proceedings by breaching the confidentiality of the court approved settlement they were eventually obliged to reach.

Then, in a demonstration of solidarity and loyalty, the eight members of the production team involved in the programmes attacked by the *News of the World*, entered the fray. Mike Morley, Phil Braund, Howard Foster, Peter McQuillan, Tina Dalgleish, David Warren and Steve Warr all sued for libel too, supported on a no win, no fee basis by their lawyer, David Price. I no longer felt quite so isolated, but Carlton's lawyers, having initially encouraged their action, later came to feel that it complicated things unnecessarily. The one lawyer who didn't feel that way was the *Cook*

401

Report's own legal adviser, Peter Smith, who thought that showing a united front was vitally important. I think he was right.

I have never worked with a better or more able programme lawyer, but for sticking his head over the parapet, Peter was subjected to an astonishing and undeserved personal attack by a senior member of the defence team – somebody he had previously worked with closely for many years. I wonder what her motivation was.

There were several interlocutory hearings at which a significant part of the *News of the World*'s evidence in defence was struck out. They had actually tried to invoke the European Convention on Human Rights, claiming that if they were not allowed to include this 'evidence', the paper's right to free speech would be infringed! The material struck out included a fourth libellous attack on *The Cook Report*, via a subsequently published article on a programme that had nothing to do with anything they had previously printed.

This particular programme had featured an incompetent, dishonest and disbarred IVF doctor who had managed to kill one of his own patients, but who the newspaper now portrayed as some kind of Good Samaritan. The paper then took the opportunity to repeat the original libels – after the writs had been issued – something that is not supposed to happen. I was not impressed and I'm pretty sure the judge wasn't either.

Mind you, there were times when I wasn't impressed by members of the judiciary. At one appeal hearing, the three venerable judges seemed to need having some of the finer points of libel law explained to them by counsel for both sides. One of the judges gave every impression of having nodded off. It certainly appeared so to a bluff Northern chap in the visitors' gallery who rose to his feet, pointing at the bench as he bellowed: "That booger's asleep!" He was promptly ejected from the court, but the judge did seem to pay more attention thereafter.

As our case was being carefully constructed, I found it somewhat disconcerting to have sections of our programmes nit-picked over by our own lawyers, and to have news of possible oversights or omissions delivered in a rather reproachful manner.

Hindsight is a wonderful thing. These were programmes that had been thoroughly researched, scripted in good faith and legally scrutinised before broadcast. But ultimately, I suppose, no programme made in weeks or months – let alone a newspaper article written in hours – could stand up to years of legal analysis and interpretation. Our legal team was only doing what the other side would try to do later.

On occasion, I also had difficulty in getting some of them to understand the grammar of television; that documentary programmes were not transmitted uncut and in real time, and that whereas a newspaper could easily alter a quote, we were limited to the quotes we had recorded on film. Nevertheless, we came through this scrutiny pretty well and were looking forward to our day in court.

Time dragged by – in my view, slowed down by Farrers' tactics. Perhaps they thought that if they spun it out long enough, I might eventually be worn down and give up. I'm pretty sure that's what their clients hoped for. I also formed the impression that in our legal system, winning has less to do with fairness or justice than with playing a protracted and profitable game at someone else's expense.

It was a game that involved exploiting or circumventing the rules, and if that also involved skewing or skating over the facts, so be it. Of course, the *News of the World* lawyers didn't invent the system. Nevertheless, it seemed to me from the inside that incredibly complex rules of procedure do more to inflate legal bills than they do to uncover the truth.

It was not a good time to be Roger Cook – nor indeed, a member of his family. I was perpetually frustrated, often grumpy, and after years of being on the road, rather too much under Frances' size-three feet. I was desperate to get working again. I came to know, all too well, that the process of going through a libel action actually magnifies the hurt and the injustice – and to believe that the Woolf 'reforms' designed to simplify and speed up libel proceedings have done nothing of the kind.

Frances and I were being worn down by all this, so when the opportunity presented itself to spend ten days with good friends in Spain, we jumped at it. We flew out on a charter plane, something I was dreading in case any of our fellow passengers believed the *News of the World*'s scurrilous stories. Fortunately, if any of them did, they didn't say so. Many came by to ask when I'd be back on the air, and the flight turned into something of an autograph signing session.

The break built on that good beginning, with lots of sun, sangria and sympathy. We met up with some other old friends and Frances indulged in a little retail therapy in Puerto Banus. Those few days did us a power of good – it was a great relief to be distanced from our ongoing legal trauma, even for so short a time. Unfortunately, the feelgood factor faded almost as soon as we arrived in the departure lounge on our way home.

While we sat over coffee waiting for our flight to be called, we were approached by a man with a vaguely familiar face. As you are inclined to do in these circumstances, I greeted him cordially. He asked for an autograph, which I gave him on the back of a napkin. He inspected it and nodded in satisfaction. "You *are* Roger Cook, then, hiding behind a beard now," he said. "I'm Chris Bray." He waved the signed napkin. "I'll have some fun with this on the internet." And as he turned on his heel to leave, he added: "I'm going to make your life a misery."

It then dawned on me that Bray was the proprietor of a strange shop called The Sorcerer's Apprentice, which had featured in a programme on Satanism which we had made in 1989. Apart from selling artefacts and regalia for Satanist rituals, the shop and the publications it also sold acted as contact and recruiting points for at least two fringe organisations advocating child abuse and violence. Following the programme, he had complained to the BCC about our treatment of him and the allegations we had made. In the event, his complaint turned out to be one of the relatively rare ones that the Commission had actually rejected outright.

Not long after our return from Spain, we learned that Bray's website had published several pages of unfounded inventions based on the *News of the World*'s falsehoods and on his rejected BCC complaint, which he now mendaciously claimed had been upheld. Worse, he had revealed where we lived, together with what amounted to an invitation to his readers to take whatever action against me they thought fit.

In the circumstances, this was pretty nearly the last straw. It took several worrying weeks to get the website removed by the hosting company. Meanwhile the *Daily Star* had somehow been persuaded to take Bray's side. They went into print suggesting that he was an innocent 'victim' of *The Cook Report*, repeating some of his false, decade-old allegations and directing readers to his website

404

with its clear clues about how to find our home. This was grossly irresponsible.

Carlton wrote to the newspaper accordingly, also pointing out that they had never sought my account of events and enclosing a copy of the BCC judgement. They reluctantly agreed not to pursue the story further, but would not retract or apologise. I didn't have the energy to take the matter further, and in any case, I had more important things on my mind.

When the *News of the World* defence team eventually got round to disclosing documents, most importantly, the available tape transcripts and notebooks of their 'witness' interviews, Series Producer Phil Braund went through them all with a fine-tooth comb.

Years as a Fleet Street news editor had made him both healthily sceptical and extremely thorough. He could find none of the quotes attributed to any of the witnesses in the published articles. Perhaps they were all in the missing or destroyed documents? In any event, the *News of the World*'s rota of key witnesses looked pretty poor. Many of them had criminal records and/or axes to grind and one of them was actually in prison.

There followed what some of my legal friends said should have been a double-edged *coup de grâce*. After an 18-month investigation into the *News of the World*'s published allegations, the Independent Television Commission delivered its considered conclusions.

The Commission found that *The Cook Report* had not broken their regulatory code, and that 'there was no evidence that Mr Cook or Carlton or the editors, producers, legal advisers and researchers were party to any fakery or deception'. Having asked for an ITC investigation, but not having got the result they wanted, the newspaper promptly dismissed its findings as a whitewash.

However, the ITC could hardly be portrayed as Carlton's poodle. It wasn't long, remember, since the broadcast of *The Connection* – an independently produced documentary which turned out to be largely faked – over which the Commission had fined the company a record £2 million. Some poodle.

Then, Nigel Fielden changed sides. Possibly feeling guilty for what he'd done to his former workmates, and certainly without any financial inducement, in some 40 pages of detailed statement he retracted everything he'd told the *News of the World*. The cocaine story wasn't true – as his filmed evidence proved in any case. Kevin Duigan, an alcoholic ne'er-do-well described as Fielden's 'co-investigator' in a number of stories, didn't work for us and wasn't actually present at the events described. He too had been paid by the *News of the World* and he too had given us a voluntary sworn statement in retraction.

Fielden's statement was also revealing about how the *News of the World* is inclined to behave in pursuit of a big story when they think they can smell blood. Fielden claimed he was in the editor's office when the newspaper's legal manager, Tom Crone, told the then editor, Phil Hall, that so serious was the cocaine allegation that further checking was advisable. After all, the only testimony they had was paid for, uncorroborated and from a disaffected former employee. Hall was reported as saying that I was a crook who deserved all I'd got, and that he'd be publishing that weekend anyway.

By then, Waheed Alli had left Carlton, and with the new ammunition described above, the company began to press harder. The *News of the World* defence team, however, ploughed on regardless. It wasn't until nearly three years had passed that they saw sense, and then only when costs were astronomic for both sides. At that time, it would have cost the best part of another million pounds to get into court and our legal advice was that we would certainly emerge victorious – though possibly damaged, because mud sticks. It made no sense for either side to continue.

A confidential settlement was hammered out and an agreed statement read in open court. The one thing the newspaper would not do was use the word 'apology' – presumably so they could say they hadn't – but the statement was otherwise an unequivocal capitulation.

In essence it said the *News of the World* now accepted the Independent Television Commission's verdict that we had not done any of the things of which the newspaper had accused us. None of the team, myself included, had faked anything or deceived anyone. In other words, the newspaper now had to admit that there was no basis in fact for what looked and felt to all of us like a systematic and malicious attempt to destroy *The Cook Report* and the careers of those who worked on it. Unsurprisingly, the *News of the World* itself buried the court-ordered report of their climb-down in a small piece on page 38.

I thought, briefly, of complaining to the Press Complaints Commission, since the newspaper had clearly not given their admission the 'due prominence' the PCC demands in these circumstances – bearing in mind the amount of front page coverage the *News of the World* had given the original story over three weekends. But the Commission's record is one of bias in favour of newspapers and I quickly concluded that involving them would only prolong the agony for little or no result. And I wanted my life back.

Our vindication did make headlines elsewhere though. I most liked the one in *The Guardian*, which as you will have gathered, was not normally a purveyor of good news about the programme: '*News of the World* Admits Cook Report Allegations Were False and Should Not Have Been Published'. It is difficult to describe my feelings about the outcome. I was angry at the *News of the World*'s unprincipled hypocrisy and about what they'd put us all through, but I wasn't unduly bitter; after all, the newspaper's journalists and lawyers had behaved just as badly as I would have expected them to. To them, we're all cannon fodder.

However, exculpation was not followed by the expected elation. Frances, Belinda and I were relieved, but it was all a bit of an anticlimax. One day I had been working full-time – living and breathing the defence case in minute detail – the next, it was all over. We had not had our day in court and suddenly I had no job at all. I felt as if I'd been parachuted into a vacuum.

But that wasn't the end of it either. Our feelings of relief were short-lived. Farrers apparently did not like the taste of defeat. I can see no other reason for their subsequent dog-in-the-manger actions. The next edition of their regular media bulletin broke the court approved confidential settlement agreement. It included an article which clearly implied that we were guilty as charged by their clients and that we hadn't really won after all.

After a further legal tussle, Farrers withdrew the publication, which had gone out to around 500 newspaper, radio and television editors. Without admitting liability, they eventually agreed another settlement in favour of Carlton, me and all the other claimants.

Time is a great healer and I must admit that for me, the process accelerated when the *News of the World* came under judicial attack for doing exactly the kind of things they had falsely accused *The*

Cook Report of doing. Ironically, had this happened just before instead of just after the newspaper had settled in our case, the settlement might have been a rather better one for me and my colleagues. But it didn't – and it wasn't – and life's like that sometimes.

In June 2003, the *News of the World* and its 'investigations editor', Mazher Mahmood, were in serious trouble. In November 2002 they trumpeted a world exclusive, claiming to have stopped 'the crime of the century', a supposed kidnap attempt on Victoria Beckham. The subsequent trial of those arrested quickly collapsed when the prosecution came to the conclusion that the evidence of the key witness provided by the *News of the World* simply could not be trusted.

The five suspects had not been potential kidnappers at all and had been set up by the newspaper with the help of a convicted criminal to whom they paid £10,000. Martin Hicks, QC for one of the defendants, said of his client: "He has been the victim of a set-up by Mr. Mahmood and his associates, on the face of it, designed to further Mr. Mahmood's notorious career and improve the circulation of a tabloid newspaper by offering financial gain to others."

You'll forgive my feelings of *schadenfreude*, but during the *News of the World*'s libellous attack on *The Cook Report*, the paper's Legal Manager, Tom Crone, had taken the very unusual step of going into print himself. He had suggested that the Cook team consisted of corrupt and incompetent amateurs who should leave investigating to his expert colleagues, led by the incomparable Mazher Mahmood.

At that time, their witnesses against us – nearly all of them with criminal records – were paid not £10,000 as in the Beckham case, but well over £30,000 between them. And as you'll recall, two of their three key witnesses voluntarily retracted their statements. The third had decamped to Spain and was unwilling to return.

I should re-emphasise here that *The Cook Report* neither paid witnesses anything other than legitimate expenses, nor induced people to commit crimes they were not already familiar with. It is also worth pointing out that our targets were not the minor celebrities (with a drink or drugs problem) and small-time criminals (encouraged to operate out of their league) who were the usual quarry of the *News of the World*.

Some of the paper's few larger targets – like the Countess of Wessex or Sven Goran Eriksson – were not guilty of any criminal offence. Even when prompted by avarice, being boastful or indiscreet is hardly a crime – though presenting the public with heads on pikestaffs plainly sells newspapers. We certainly wouldn't have operated like that.

Hence my interest in the Beckham kidnap story, but lest you should think I'm grinding an axe, let the story continue in the words of the Professor of Journalism at City University and ex-*Daily Mirror* editor, Roy Greenslade:

"The five alleged kidnappers were the victims of a disgraceful sting operation," said Greenslade, having read through the voluminous transcripts of the audio and video recordings made by the *News of the World*.

"The transcripts suggest to any reasonable, objective observer that this so-called terror gang were largely a group of not very bright people living on the margins of society who were being manipulated. At every turn, the key speaker is the sinister figure who is sitting down with them while secretly recording what they say and filming them with a tiny buttonhole camera ... It is he who first suggests the kidnapping, he who provokes the discussions about it, he who produces a gun for one of them to hold, he who leads them to the gates of the house where the Beckhams live.

"The sad truth is that the *News of the World* and Mahmood have been operating for too long in a journalistic and legal grey area. There have been too many cases – including those involving the actor John Alford, the Earl of Hardwicke and the Newcastle United directors – in which there have been doubts about the paper's methods. Several judges have raised questions about the thin line between exposing crime and stimulating it ... The fact that the judge stopped the case because the central witness had been paid by the *News of the World* shows how cavalier the paper has become."

A fortnight later, judges again strongly criticised the *News of the World* following the collapse of a drugs trial involving the pop singer Brian Harvey, and the gaoling of a fantasist who falsely claimed to have been sexually assaulted by Neil and Christine

Hamilton. Both judges clearly felt that the newspaper's witnesses had been paid for false or unreliable testimony and that the courts had been left to clear up the mess.

Perhaps as a result of judicial criticisms like those, the Commons Select Committee on Culture and the Media shortly afterwards recommended that the newspaper industry's system of self-regulation should be completely overhauled. It plainly wasn't working, but then that is no surprise, since the Press Complaints Commission has amongst its most influential members, the editors of the tabloid newspapers most likely to offend. To date, the recommended overhaul has not taken place.

If the system can't be made to operate smoothly and fairly then the ending of self-regulation is probably inevitable in the circumstances, but I take no joy from it. It does the cause of investigative journalism no good at all, and plays into the hands of those who would like to see the genre shackled or eliminated altogether. Mind you, the swingeing budgetary cuts imposed by ITV management in recent years might achieve the same end.

As for me, in a fashion business like television, when you've been dismissed by at least one senior executive as 'an expensive dinosaur', you're clearly out of fashion. While I was off the air, times changed. It is also possible that after our bruising battle with the *News of the World*, management thought that giving a home to a high profile, high risk programme like ours was too much like hard work. So whatever I do next, it's unlikely to be another series of *Cook Reports*.

Meanwhile, I occupied myself rebuilding my MG and a Morris Minor Traveller for Belinda, having the worst of my knackered knees replaced with an artificial one, working for my favourite charities, and being a visiting professor at the Centre for Broadcast Journalism at Nottingham Trent University.

I've been doing this for some years now, and I can tell you, there's no better way of keeping your feet on the ground and your brain cells working than being challenged by a group of bright, post-graduate students. It wasn't work as I've known it, but it was a damned sight better than vegetating. The University was recently kind enough to make me an honorary Doctor of Letters, in recognition of work done in both broadcasting and education.

*

In the autumn of 2002, and unbeknown to me, Frances had agreed to have me ambushed by *This Is Your Life*. She tells me she'd been approached twice before over the years and – knowing I'd rather walk on hot coals than take part – she had declined. This time, however, she and my agent colluded. They had decided that appearing would remind the public and television executives alike that I was still around – and more importantly the programme would give me the opportunity to tell more people about our libel victory than those who had seen it reported on page 38 of the guilty paper.

I hadn't the faintest idea what Frances was up to. Because I had previously pleaded with her never to get me involved with *This Is Your Life*, it didn't enter my head. There was the odd clumsily discontinued phone call when I came into the room, and if I didn't trust her totally, I might have suspected a toy boy – but that was it.

In September, I planned to visit the Motor Show – as is my habit – and had been invited to the Jaguar stand for lunch. My very tall friend Martin Broomer from Jaguar's Public Affairs Department was in attendance, and I didn't notice a conspiratorial air to him either. I did wonder what he was up to when there was no lunch and he gave me a very protracted guided tour of Jaguar's brand new XJ8 instead.

I was luxuriating in the front seat, being told about the cruise control for the nth time, when my attention wandered and I looked out of the window. There, approaching fast in the rear vision mirror I saw him – Michael Aspel, Big Red Book in hand. There was no escape, just a terrible sinking feeling and a fleeting desire to strangle Martin Broomer, now revealed as a conspirator. I hastily collected my thoughts and got out of the car to face my fate.

My manufactured meeting with Michael over, I was limousined down to London and the BBC Television Centre, to be welcomed by members of the production team, and deposited in a dressing room. The programme was due to be recorded three hours hence. Frances had brought up some smarter clothes, and had arranged for some sustenance.

But even on this celebratory occasion, I remained as accident-prone as ever. Frances had suggested to the production team that having been denied the promised lunch, I would probably appreciate something to eat when I arrived at the studios. She was asked

411

what I might like and recommended smoked salmon sandwiches, with the clear proviso that they didn't contain any cucumber, to which I am very allergic.

This was duly noted, and a cling-film wrapped tray of splendid looking sandwiches was waiting for me in my dressing room. I fell upon them, and had wolfed one down before realising that they were not as described on the post-it note stuck to the wrapping. They were not 'Smoked salmon. *No cucumber*', but tinned salmon, *with* cucumber. Almost immediately I felt a tingling in the throat. My face and throat began to swell until I looked like an angry chipmunk. I found it difficult to breathe and my heart raced.

I go prepared for such occasions, rare though they fortunately are, and took a whacking dose of the anti-histamines I always carry with me. I didn't need the adrenalin shot because, in the circumstances, there was more than enough flowing already. After about half an hour, the swelling subsided – and then I was spectacularly sick – all over the dressing room and all over the shirt I was to wear. Shamefaced, I got down on my hands and knees and cleaned the place up.

By the time I was ready to face the world it was about an hour to go to the recording. Jack Crawshaw, the usually amiable producer, was furious about what had happened, and not just because it had put his programme at risk. I was given profuse apologies, a new dressing room with somewhere to lie down, and a freshly laundered shirt. Unfortunately, when the recording began, I still felt like death warmed up. Fortunately, with a thick layer of television make up on, no one could tell.

As I stepped through the doors of the set, friends and family were arrayed before me. I was, of course, pleased to see them, but very embarrassed too. Contrary to what you might think, I do not like being on public display. Having watched the programme on transmission, I could see myself wincing on several occasions. I was even more embarrassed by some of the family anecdotes on the one hand, and touched too, by the kind and over-generous things friends and colleagues had to say about me on the other.

Sir Stirling Moss was the most down to earth. He said that if I was a motor vehicle, I'd be a tank – otherwise I could never have attempted half the things I've done. Floella Benjamin described me as a real live superman, exposing evil and wrongdoing all over the world. Michael Hames from Scotland Yard said the programme had twice been responsible for changes in the law on child pornography and that I was therefore a hero to children everywhere.

Will Travers of the Born Free Foundation praised our campaigns against the illegal exploitation of endangered species and said I was a hero to the animals of the world – and Sir Trevor McDonald said that whereas most journalists reported the news, I was one of those who had made the news, and that I had changed the face of investigative journalism. As a surprise finale, my old friend Barry Eaton appeared, having been flown in especially from Australia. Eying my waistline after a brotherly embrace, he said that he'd always known I'd make it big, but was amazed at just how big. (I chose to take this as a compliment.)

Despite my embarrassment, I couldn't help feeling proud of what I and my colleagues had managed to achieve over the years. I was also proud of Frances and Belinda 'my support team at home'. They looked gorgeous.

There was much, much more. I was overwhelmed and mightily relieved when the praising stopped and Michael Aspel handed me the Big Red Book – intoning, in time-honoured fashion: "Roger Cook, this is your life."

Well thanks, Michael – it's been challenging, rewarding and mostly enjoyable, but it's not over yet.

10

Second Thoughts

Second thoughts are always useful in establishing a true perspective on characters and events. The following thoughts come verbatim from an article written by our last in-house solicitor after the demise of the programme, and are reproduced with his blessing. Simon Westrop's personal perspective is unique, since he has seen factual programming from both sides of the professional divide.

I had been a journalist before becoming a lawyer and, amongst other things, I had produced *Face the Facts* on BBC Radio 4, the softer successor to Roger's legendary *Checkpoint* programme. The fact is, however enormous the BBC might be, it was always too small to contain Roger's heroic style of journalism. But moving over to ITV enabled him to develop a style of confrontational investigative documentaries that were hugely popular, though expensive to make.

Legal time and expense was inevitably high too, and the lawyer's job was not made any easier by the programme's habit of recording the finished show just hours (sometimes minutes it seemed to me) before broadcast. It's the only television programme I have ever known, before or since, in which the lawyer was given an on-screen credit – I always suspected out of pity more than anything else. To keep on top of what was happening, the lawyer had to be nosey, to keep himself informed by talking directly to the researchers as well as the editor, and to make himself part of their world.

And what a bizarre world it was. More or less from the first day, I found myself dealing with two major legal actions, both claiming defamation of character. One claim was from a man who had been identified as an international bandit and gangster, the alleged UK leader of the notorious international Chinese Triad gang called the

415

Wo Shing Wo. We were paying London solicitors thousands to travel out to Hong Kong to gather evidence. It was never needed in the end because the claimant got cold feet and we never heard from him again. So I spent more time seeing to it that Joe Tan, one of the special researchers on that particular programme, got his hospital bills paid. Of Chinese extraction himself, Joe had been hired to infiltrate the Triads and had paid for it with serious leg injuries when he had jumped down a stairwell to escape a certain beating and possible death.

The other claimant, equally extraordinary, was a man called John 'Goldfinger' Palmer, Britain's wealthiest criminal, according to the *Sunday Times* Rich List. He had a property empire in Tenerife and money laundering connections worldwide. Famously acquitted of any criminal blame after being charged with melting down the bullion from the £26 million Brinks Mat gold robbery, he was now the man Scotland Yard most wanted to nail. Though he hadn't complained when Cook revealed him as a big-time drugs money launderer, he did issue a writ complaining about a later programme which revealed that we had been tipped off by a senior police officer about a contract on Roger's life. Palmer's defamation claim withered away after he was arrested and eventually gaoled for defrauding 17,000 customers of his timeshare business. In court, Palmer blamed *The Cook Report* for putting him there.

For the next five years, this was pretty much par for the course. No libel claims actually came to trial. In one or two cases we came to terms of course, but it was a remarkable record for a programme that was exceptional in the history of current affairs in having the courage to name names with a boldness never attempted previously and since only rarely. The fact is that the Cook team got it right most of the time, and most of it right the rest of the time. The research was always impressively thorough. And I should add that some of the undercover and openly filmed evidence could not have been gathered without team members exhibiting great stamina and, on occasion, physical courage.

Sometimes I was dazzled by the sheer chutzpah of complainants to the Broadcasting Standards Commission – successor to the Broadcasting Complaints Commission – the public body charged with enforcing regulations on fairness and privacy in television. Like the particular 'Doctor from Hell' who, in the eponymous Cook programme, was identified as the National Health Service's

416

very own vampire. He had been convicted of stealing the blood from thousands of donors to use in his own profitable private pharmaceutical business. He always maintained that taking the blood wasn't a crime because it didn't belong to anybody. Now he was upset because we exposed him as still working in the NHS in a hospital in the North West. Not only that, they had put him in charge of the blood bank.

After that programme, the General Medical Council vowed to – and did – clean up its act. It was one of many programmes that had a positive influence, not just on ITV's audience figures, but on the way our world is run. During my five years with the Cook team, I appeared in the witness box, saw men convicted and worked with the police to help them bring prosecutions against wrongdoers identified and confronted by Roger in his much-copied style.

For more than a decade, *The Cook Report* was one of ITV's principal prime-time scheduling weapons, guaranteed to return a big audience share of up to ten million viewers. It had won over from the outset because of its bold approach to investigatory documentaries – no hesitation, no regrets, Cook caught them red-handed doing what they did for a living and hung them out to dry. Just to the same extent that this was popular with the viewers, it was diametrically unpopular with the rather more squeamish regulators at the Broadcasting Standards Commission (now superseded by Ofcom). It wasn't that they could often find a Cook programme to be in the wrong, though if they could possibly do it they would. It was more than that: this assembly of worthy establishment hirelings, public authority careerists and one or two old-school factual television programme-makers, simply found *The Cook Report* – well, how can I put it? Far too popular and therefore – vulgar, that's the word.

It was a relationship of cordial disdain, at least on their part. And Roger always felt it keenly. It was unwarranted because *The Cook Report* had created and maintained high standards of balance and fairness in its programmes. Right from the beginning, ethics were a prime concern and internal regulations were drafted on the circumstances in which 'doorstep' confrontations were justifiable and how they might be fairly carried out, in addition to and, in fact, preceding the BSC's own attention to the subject.

The relationship with the police was not always easy either. At

417

first, Roger was seen as an asset by some officers because *The Cook Report* had the resources to carry out investigations unencumbered by the numerous constraints of police procedure. Of course, we were making television programmes, not gathering evidence for a criminal prosecution, but frequently the show ended with Roger saying that we would be voluntarily handing over the tapes and the files to the police.

As time went on, and Cook spawned imitators, the courts became more wary of prosecutions based on television investigations, not necessarily because they were beneath the dignity of the courts, but because of an increasing (and entirely proper) emphasis on evidential completeness and continuity. More and more, I found myself asking producers to ensure that useful materials were deposited in police-style evidence bags and, with increasing frequency, programme-makers were asked to make witness statements after filming. Some members of the judiciary praised *The Cook Report*, others did not. On one occasion, a very disapproving judge dismissed charges against a car thief resulting from offences committed long after the transmission of the programme which exposed him – on the grounds that his previous exposure in the commission of entirely different crimes would make it impossible for the man to get a fair trial on the later offences. Where was the logic in that?

The Cook Report had, of course, pioneered the use of 'sting' operations on television, and the sophisticated secret filming techniques that went with them. The programme had been highly successful as a result. Time and again, from illegal lion hunters to world-class criminals like John Palmer, the chosen target was lured into a trap by his own greed and was then caught on camera plotting with Cook undercover men to break the law. But again, after a time, the courts found themselves harangued by defence lawyers who argued that televisual finesse of this kind was no more than a mischievous incitement to crime, albeit under carefully controlled conditions.

Frequently I had to remind everybody involved that though we only ever sought to show what our targets did as a matter of course, this was, in the end, only television – we didn't bring the prosecutions, nor were criminal convictions ever the programme's prime objective. That wasn't our job and we didn't pretend it was.

Some very senior police officers didn't seem able to see the wood for the trees either.

The Cook team once ventured undercover onto a Coventry housing estate to investigate and expose large-scale drug dealing to children for a major hour-long documentary on the plight of underprivileged young people in modern Britain. For years, the police had failed to solve the problems on the estate, but all that the West Midlands Chief Constable could think of was to condemn us for engaging a teenage lad to help make contact with the dealers, even though he was fully chaperoned and protected. Ironically, the lad's father was a police officer and had approved his son's role in the film. Furthermore, in policing terms, Coventry was not part of the West Midlands, and the Chief Constable of Warwickshire, whose patch *did* cover Coventry, had approved our film.

The fact was the success of *The Cook Report* had begun to annoy people. It annoyed some senior policemen because it showed up their failings, and also because the programme-makers had a freedom to pick and choose what they did that was in practice denied to the police, to their intense and perhaps understandable frustration. Sometimes we found ourselves stepping on the toes of active police investigators who wrongly regarded us as self-appointed vigilantes who kept getting in their way.

There was another bout of correspondence when the programme went undercover into the notorious Black and White Café in Bristol, said to be the centre of local drug dealing. The Chief Constable was furious because he claimed, erroneously, that we had disrupted his force's own surveillance operation. In fact, the café had not been under police surveillance for months and *Cook Report* undercover researchers were then working closely with the Avon and Somerset drugs squad, giving them free access to all our evidence. Drugs squad officers were actually viewing our secret filming at our Nottingham studios when the Chief Constable's first missive arrived. The Black and White Café has now closed down.

One of the *Cook Report*'s problems was that its makers were so good at what they did, and so comfortable with their way of doing it, that they made it all seem too easy. Of course, there were the occasions when thugs lost their temper on camera, and that could never be predicted. But no one saw behind the scenes and so they never realised that it might have taken surveillance teams many days shivering in the back of a van to get a crucial 30 second shot, and only then after months of work to set up the opportunity in the first place.

No one heard about the time a *Cook Report* crew was chased by suspect villains along a leafy suburban pavement and then through North London to the M25 before they were shaken off. And on another assignment it was only because cameraman Peter Salkeld had spent two long weeks camped out on a freezing Scottish mountain that he was able to get pictures of a falcon egg thief that were later to astonish audiences around the world. The team consistently delivered the result that people wanted and expected. The drawback was that, gradually over time with each outing, the show lost some of its impact. Like the housewife working hard to put the supper on the table each night, the family just took it for granted.

The show's forthright and sometimes almost theatrical approach made for good entertainment, though again it meant that it sometimes wasn't taken as seriously as it might have been, and on many occasions certainly should have been. Remember, it wasn't *World in Action* or *Panorama* that was bringing proof to our television screens of the ruthless IRA career of Martin McGuinness and the corrupt criminal double-dealings of Loyalist paramilitaries in Northern Ireland – it was *The Cook Report*.

Nevertheless, Roger rapidly became one of the most recognisable people in Britain, and being out on the public streets with him in the heyday of *The Cook Report* was an extraordinary experience. I remembered having been warned about the 'Cook effect' and, having witnessed it myself, I can vouch for the truth of it. Following a meeting with legal counsel at the Inns of Court in London, Roger, I and one of the producers headed for a small Italian restaurant for a quick lunch. As we went into the restaurant heads turned in our direction (or at least in Roger's direction) and voices hushed. The owner welcomed us with operatic hospitality. Others seemed not quite so pleased to see us. Close to the door, two guests immediately got up after we had passed, hurriedly paid their bill with far too big a tip and left, grabbing their coats in a hurry, not even pausing to look back. The fact was that this kind of thing happened nearly all the time when Roger was about. Such was Roger's power to inspire guilt and fear amongst the wrongdoers in the general populace, and such was the vanity of the criminal mind in thinking that Roger had come in person to get them rather than just a plate of spaghetti.

So why then did *The Cook Report* ever come to an end? Leaving aside Roger's desire to take things a little easier after 30 years, the answer is probably because television changed direction. We are now in the new era of increased competition, lower margins and lower budgets. Cook was high-impact programming – but it was potential trouble and, as I've said, expensive. And that was the last thing the bosses in the new age wanted.

With hindsight, it seems the show probably lost some of the momentum generated by the workaholic genius of Mike Townson after his catastrophic illness forced him to retire to the Lake District. Three succeeding editors, patrician Bob Southgate, hyperactive Mike Morley and focused professional David Mannion (now Editor-in-Chief, ITV News) found themselves driving a big steam train through a changing landscape with no obvious way of redirecting it.

In the end, the series came apart because of the build up of internal tensions, the mistaken hiring of some unsuitable undercover operators and the pressures generated by more than a decade of amazing success – finally yielding to the enervating effects of a legal action prompted by the rabid attacks of a national newspaper. The action taken in defence of the programme came rather late in the day and had allowed libel after libel to go unchallenged over a period of more than two months. Eventually, the newspaper had to admit in open court that its allegations were false and without foundation, but by then, immense damage had been done. It was a loud and messy ending. Well, at least it didn't go quietly. But then, could it ever?

POSTSCRIPT

In the summer of 2003, I returned to New Zealand with Frances and Belinda to meet members of the family down under I never knew I had. They were an eclectic collection – sheep farmers, an engineer, a printer and a disc-jockey – amongst others. The Gibbs, McGechies and the Somervells treated us royally during our visit and made us feel very much like, well, family.

They had been discovered during some genealogical research undertaken by my sister Jane after Mum's death – and the Cook connection was as a result of her 'dark secret'. In her youth, my mother had been a star golfer and at the age of 17, had fallen for – and fallen pregnant by – a member of the Miramar Golf Club. These days it would hardly be remarked upon, but in the New Zealand of 1927, the disgrace of having a child out of wedlock was absolute.

My grandfather apparently went into shock. His convent-educated daughter was going to have an illegitimate child by a married man! I can't imagine how my mother must have felt. Abortion was out of the question, so she was despatched to another town for her confinement, and when Patricia was born, the little girl was placed in an orphanage and put up for adoption.

Eventually, my grandmother persuaded grandfather that they should adopt Pat themselves. My mother's firstborn was then brought up by her grandparents as my mother's sister. To avoid further disgrace, the family moved from Wellington to Auckland. Mum was not allowed to mother her own child, or even to tell her the truth. It seems she couldn't bear it, so she moved away and eventually lost contact altogether. Grandfather never forgave her for bringing such shame on his family.

My mother always claimed they'd disowned her and rarely spoke of them. Hence her reticence to discuss her past – and her

423

willingness to indulge my father's wish to leave their homeland for good back in 1945.

So, much of my newly extended family stems from Pat, the half-sister I never knew I had. Sadly, she had died before I had a chance to meet her. Isn't it ironic that having spent my life unearthing other people's secrets, I've gone all these years unaware of a secret so close to me?

INDEX

426

Mosside, Manchester 230–1
Mostert, Mossie 353–8
motor racing 42
Mumbai, India 198
Murad, Abdul Hakim 324, 326, 327
Murmansk, Russia 313
music industry
  chart rigging 338–42
  managers 82–3

Nabarro, Sir Gerald 48
Nadir, Asil 348–9
Nahum, Peter 202
Nairobi, Kenya 159–60
Namatjira, Albert 43
National Art School, Sydney 4
National Commission on Terrorist
    Attacks upon the United States
    (9/11 Commission) 327–9
The National Heart Hospital 384
National Housebuilders Registration
    Council (NHBC) 56–7
National Poisons Information Unit 252
National Union of Mineworkers (NUM)
    173, 175, 239–42
Nationwide (BBC TV) 67, 87–8
Netherlands
  child pornography 110, 113–14, 135
  clenbuterol trade 265–7
  Kevin Sweeney 293
  sex trafficking 377
The Network Centre 91–2, 378–9, 380
Neville, Richard 34
New Musical Express 82
New Zealand
  leaving 1–4
  return to 423–4
  rogue doctors 381–2
  Sudden Infant Death Syndrome 337
Newcastle United Football Club 409
Newlyn, Cornwall 366–7
News at Ten (ITN) 378
News Review (ABC) 30
News of the World 393–6, 393–410
Newsnight (BBC TV) 88
NHBC *see* National Housebuilders
    Registration Council
Nickell, Rachel 199
Niesyty, Ada 211–12
Ninoy Aquino Airport, Manila 326
Nolan, Sydney 43
Norfolk Hotel, Nairobi 159–60

Northern Cyprus 348–9
Northern Ireland
  IRA and clenbuterol 264–9
  Martin McGuinness 175–82
  paramilitaries and protection money
    110, 115–21, 125–7, 212–13, 420
Not the Nine O'clock News (BBC TV)
    239
Nottingham 320, 343
Nottingham Trent University 410
nuclear trafficking 309–16
Nugen, Frank 194
Nugen Hand Bank, Australia 192, 194–5
NUM *see* National Union of
    Mineworkers
Nyilinkindi, Japhet 289

Obilic Football Club, Belgrade 275, 285
Obscene Publications Squad,
    Metropolitan Police 296, 297
O'Donnell, Lord Justice Turlough 125,
    126–7
OFCOM *see* Office of Communications
Office of Communications (OFCOM)
    250
Omni Batavia Hotel, Djakarta 258
Ondarroa, Spain 363, 367–71
opium 186–95
opticians 54
Orlamar 365–6
Ostrich Farming Corporation 76
Ouwendijk, Willem 286–7, 292–3
Oxberry Aerial Image Animation
    Camera 27–8
Oz (magazine) 34

P&B Laboratories, India 197–8
paedophiles 110, 113–14, 124, 296–7, 404
Palmer, John 130–4, 195, 238, 416
Pan Am Flight 103 321–2, 326, 329
pandas 162, 173
Panorama (BBC TV) 40
Paraguay 99, 102–4
paramilitaries
  former Yugoslavia 273–86
  Northern Ireland 110, 115–21, 125–7,
    420
Parikapoon, Mr, MP 172
'Pat' (half-sister) 424
Patel, Humandra 197–8
Paxman, Jeremy 199
PCC *see* Press Complaints Commission

434

437

Index prepared by Indexing Specialists (UK) Ltd